Faith, Science, & Reason
Theology on the Cutting Edge

By CHRISTOPHER T. BAGLOW, Ph.D.

Second Edition

Faith, Science, & Reason
Theology on the Cutting Edge

By CHRISTOPHER T. BAGLOW, Ph.D.

Science & Religion Initiative
McGrath Institute for Church Life
University of Notre Dame

Funded by a Grant from the John Templeton Foundation

MIDWEST THEOLOGICAL FORUM
Downers Grove, IL

Published in the United States of America by

Midwest Theological Forum
4340 Cross Street, Suite 1
Downers Grove, IL 60515

Tel: 630-541-8519
Fax: 331-777-5819
mail@mwtf.org
www.theologicalforum.org

Second Edition
ISBN 978-1-939231-99-4

Author: Christopher T. Baglow, Ph.D.

Publisher: Rev. James Socias

Content Editors and Contributors: Cory J. Hayes, Ph.D., and Jordan A. Haddad, Ph.D. (cand.)

Cover Design: Jesus Cardenas

Design and Production: Marlene Burrell, Jane Heineman of April Graphics, Highland Park, Illinois

Acknowledgements

English translation of the *Catechism of the Catholic Church* for the United States of America, copyright ©1994, United States Catholic Conference, Inc. —Libreria Editrice Vaticana. English translation of the *Catechism of the Catholic Church: Modifications from the Editio Typica* copyright ©1997, United States Catholic Conference, Inc. —Libreria Editrice Vaticana.

Scripture quotations are from the Catholic Edition of the *Revised Standard Version of the Bible*, copyright ©1965, 1966, National Council of the Churches of Christ in the United States of America. Used by permission. All rights reserved.

Excerpts from Vatican II documents from Vatican website, "Resources: Documents of the Second Vatican Council": *www.vatican.va/archive/hist_councils/ii_vatican_council/index.htm*

Nihil Obstat
Reverend John Balluff, S.T.D.
Censor Deputatus
September 20, 2019

Permission to Publish
Most Reverend R. Daniel Conlon
Bishop
Diocese of Joliet
September 20, 2019

The *Nihil Obstat* and *Permission to Publish* are official declarations that a book is free of doctrinal and moral error. No implication is contained therein that those who have granted the *Nihil Obstat* and *Permission to Publish* agree with the content, opinions, or statements expressed. Nor do they assume any legal responsibility associated with publication.

Printed in Canada

TABLE OF CONTENTS

TABLE OF CONTENTS

TABLE OF CONTENTS

TABLE OF CONTENTS

TABLE OF CONTENTS

ABBREVIATIONS for BOOKS OF THE BIBLE

Old Testament

Genesis	Gn	Tobit	Tb	Ezekiel	Ez
Exodus	Ex	Judith	Jdt	Daniel	Dn
Leviticus	Lv	Esther	Est	Hosea	Hos
Numbers	Nm	1 Maccabees	1 Mc	Joel	Jl
Deuteronomy	Dt	2 Maccabees	2 Mc	Amos	Am
Joshua	Jos	Job	Jb	Obadiah	Ob
Judges	Jgs	Psalms	Ps	Jonah	Jon
Ruth	Ru	Proverbs	Prv	Micah	Mi
1 Samuel	1 Sm	Ecclesiastes	Eccl	Nahum	Na
2 Samuel	2 Sm	Song of Songs	Sg	Habakkuk	Hb
1 Kings	1 Kgs	Wisdom	Wis	Zephaniah	Zep
2 Kings	2 Kgs	Sirach	Sir	Haggai	Hg
1 Chronicles	1 Chr	Isaiah	Is	Zechariah	Zec
2 Chronicles	2 Chr	Jeremiah	Jer	Malachi	Mal
Ezra	Ezr	Lamentations	Lam		
Nehemiah	Neh	Baruch	Bar		

New Testament

Matthew	Mt	Ephesians	Eph	Hebrews	Heb
Mark	Mk	Philippians	Phil	James	Jas
Luke	Lk	Colossians	Col	1 Peter	1 Pt
John	Jn	1 Thessalonians	1 Thes	2 Peter	2 Pt
Acts of the Apostles	Acts	2 Thessalonians	2 Thes	1 John	1 Jn
Romans	Rom	1 Timothy	1 Tm	2 John	2 Jn
1 Corinthians	1 Cor	2 Timothy	2 Tm	3 John	3 Jn
2 Corinthians	2 Cor	Titus	Ti	Jude	Jude
Galatians	Gal	Philemon	Phlm	Revelation	Rev

FOREWORD

By Stephen M. Barr, Ph.D.
Professor, Department of Physics and Astronomy, University of Delaware

A central goal of education is to give students a framework for understanding reality. For Catholics, of course, the overarching framework is the Catholic faith and the revealed truths it teaches about God, humanity, and the world. There is another order of truths, however, that we know, not by divine revelation, but by reason and experience. Of this kind are the truths discovered by science. How do these fit within the wider framework? A truly educated Catholic is one who is able to integrate the different kinds of knowledge he or she possesses and keep them in proper balance and perspective. In other words, he or she does not "compartmentalize" life but has a coherent view of it. This is an important reason for a textbook such as this. But there is another reason, which makes the need for Dr. Baglow's book especially urgent.

A Catholic student going out into the world will face challenges to his or her faith. Some of these will be in the form of sharp questions about Christian beliefs. These questions may come from those who wish to mock or from those who sincerely wish to learn. In either case, the questions will not always be easy to answer for someone who has never thought much about them. Or maybe the Catholic student has thought about them but has been left in a state of confusion. For example, he or she may be asked, "How does the biblical account of Creation relate to the Big Bang theory? How do Adam and Eve relate to what we have learned about the evolution of modern humans from *Australopithecus afarensis* and *Homo habilis*? How do spiritual realities, such as the soul, fit into the world of matter described by physics, chemistry, and biology? Is it possible to believe in miracles and also the integrity of nature? Is scientific reason compatible with religious faith? Do the discoveries of modern science really imply that we are just material beings without free will, as some scientists have claimed? Does the case of Galileo show that the Catholic Church is hostile to science?"

Some people avoid these questions because they do not know the answers and are afraid that the answers may be unsettling. But avoidance only means that students will grow up nursing secret doubts and fears and be easy prey for the first scientific atheist they meet in college or in later life. Nor is avoiding questions compatible with our nature as rational beings made in the image of God. For, as such beings, we hunger for truth, and the quest for truth always brings us closer to God if we follow it to the end.

What we have to fear is not truth, but rather half-truths and untruths. And, sadly, these abound when it comes to the relationship of the Catholic faith and modern

FOREWORD

science. There is hardly any subject about which there is more widespread ignorance, misinformation, and misunderstanding. Much of this concerns the historical role of the Catholic Church and Catholic believers in the development of science, the true story of which has been left almost completely untold even in Catholic schools.

Even more unfortunate is that few Catholic students (or adults for that matter) have been given adequate theological tools to deal with faith-science questions. In particular, they need to know the answers to such questions as these: What does it mean to say that God "creates"? How does God govern the universe, and what is "divine Providence"? In what sense is God the "First Cause," and what are "secondary causes"? What has the Church historically taught about evolution and about human origins? What does it mean to say that we have "spiritual souls"? What is "faith," and what is its relation to reason? In what way are human beings the image of God, and what makes us different than any of the other animals? And what hope might we have for eternal life when we live in a universe that will definitely come to an end?

In this remarkable book, Dr. Baglow does a masterful job of explaining the relevant Catholic doctrines and the insights of Catholic theological and philosophical tradition. He does so in a way that captures their richness and depth while being accessible, engaging, and highly readable.

There are many ways in which books on science and faith go wrong. Some are weak on science, others on theology. Some authors think it is necessary to jettison or radically revise doctrines of faith to be consistent with what science says, while others think it is necessary to dismiss well-established truths of science to be faithful to Sacred Scripture and Catholic doctrine. Some put Catholic theology and science into a blender and end up with a pseudo-mystical mush that is *neither* genuinely Catholic nor genuinely scientific.

Not this book! Dr. Baglow takes authentic and unadulterated Catholic teaching and authentic and unadulterated science and shows them to be in wonderful harmony. His sound analysis and lucid exposition make one apparent difficulty after another melt away. His careful accounts of history show that the record of the Church in relation to science (despite the Galileo affair) is one to be proud of, and indeed quite glorious. The student will come away with a deeper understanding of the Catholic faith, of science, and a greater appreciation of their harmony. He or she will be able to bring them into the "relational unity" described by St. John Paul II when he said, "Science and religion can draw each other into a wider world, where *both* may flourish."

The first edition of this book appeared in 2009 and remained unexcelled in the breadth of topics discussed and the soundness and beauty of its exposition—until now. For this second edition, much revised and expanded, has managed to set an

FOREWORD

even higher standard. Without losing any of its clarity and readability, it goes into greater depth on many issues, especially creation, the "problem of evil," prayer, miracles, the origin of the human race, the fall of man, and eschatology. It engages a wide range of scientific literature and brings new scientific discoveries into dialogue with the great thinkers of the Catholic intellectual tradition, especially St. Thomas Aquinas. Dr. Baglow has woven together much new material, including history and biography, wonderfully apt quotations, illuminating analogies, scientific accounts, and theological explanations into an even more beautiful work.

The Catholic world is deeply in Dr. Baglow's debt. There has been a terrible drought of classroom instruction in this area for many decades. This book is not just a few drops of water on the parched earth—which itself would have been welcome—but a drenching, reviving rain.

St. Thomas Aquinas explained God's relationship to the universe.
How does God govern the universe, and what is "divine Providence"?
In what sense is God the "First Cause," and what are "secondary causes"?

"May God, whose infinite love and wisdom fashioned the heavens and established the moon and stars, ever guide you into his grace and peace."

—St. John Paul II

PREFACE

On this great feast day, ten years ago, when I wrote the preface to the first edition, I observed that—had it not been for Hurricane Katrina—I would never have written a textbook on faith and science. What I didn't know in those desperate months after the storm was that a cultural storm was brewing, a monsoon of ideas that would challenge the faith of many young Catholics, marked by the rising floodwaters of atheist propaganda in the broader culture, of ideology masquerading as science.

I began writing the first edition in October 2005, and completed the draft in May 2007. At exactly the same time, the writings of the so-called "New Atheists" were popping up on bestseller lists. Sam Harris produced *The End of Faith* in 2005 and *Letter to a Christian Nation* in 2006; also in 2006, Richard Dawkins produced *The God Delusion*. Finally, in 2007 Christopher Hitchens would produce *God Is Not Great: How Religion Poisons Everything*. All four are among the top-selling books promoting atheism in publishing history, and all were produced within that two-year window.

Hurricane Katrina left behind a landscape of devastation that stretched across New Orleans, Louisiana, my beloved native city, and many other places that I have loved since childhood, such as the Mississippi Gulf Coast. But the devastation wreaked by the cultural storm on my beloved spiritual home, the one, holy, catholic, and apostolic Church, has been just as bleak and even more wide-ranging. My daughter Margaret, who was in kindergarten and first grade while I was writing the first edition, is now nineteen, a new member of the current young adult population. According to recent data, 70% of her Catholic peers see science and religion as locked in conflict, and say that the discoveries of modern science have not strengthened their faith. Young Catholics have in large part unknowingly accepted the sinister memes that faith and reason cannot be reconciled, and that science has shown the Christian faith to be false, even ridiculous. This should not be surprising, because the New Atheists are marshalling scientific ideas and seriously (although perversely) interpreting the world as understood through science. Most Catholic priests, religious educators, and parents are not.

Lest anyone misunderstand, this is not a crisis that affects only young Catholics who love science. The more that scientific literacy and discoveries become part of our common worldview, the more a sense of their relation to our belief in a Creator who is Love and who created us out of love becomes essential for us to be compelled by the beauty, goodness, and truth of the Catholic faith. The late, great Pope St. John Paul II knew this, as he once said in a letter to Fr. George Coyne, S.J., the then Director of the Vatican Observatory. As you read his words, imagine a young Catholic studying genetics or biology or physics, whose religious education never engaged science in any thoroughgoing way, or worse, who was subjected to attempts to use science to prove (or disprove) the existence of God, or even worse, who was taught

PREFACE

pseudo-science in support of biblical creationism and fundamentalism: "*Christians will inevitably assimilate the prevailing ideas about the world, and today these are deeply shaped by science. The only question is whether they will do this critically or unreflectively, with depth and nuance or with a shallowness that debases the Gospel and leaves us ashamed before history.*" In our scientifically literate culture, ignoring science, or offering only shallow reflections upon it, leads to the impoverishment of evangelization and catechesis and to the scorn of a world that needs the Gospel. With this in mind, it is no wonder that in a culture where science is the cutting edge of human knowledge, young people who do not hear the truth of the Catholic faith in relation to it all too often question their religious instruction.

This Second Edition is my attempt to answer this need, one that I would have overlooked but for the instigation of a friend. In August 2015, Dr. John Cavadini, Professor of Theology and the McGrath-Cavadini Director of the McGrath Institute for Church Life at the University of Notre Dame, contacted me with the invitation to write a Second Edition as part of the Institute's new Science & Religion Initiative. I discouraged the idea at first, and encouraged him to focus on educating teachers. But he was insistent, and when he showed me the data about young Catholics mentioned above (and discussed in Chapter Two), I recognized that this invitation was a moment of divine Providence. There were many issues I had not covered the first time around, such as the problem of evil, science and spirituality, and the historical roots of the warfare model of science and faith. Plus, I had come to a deeper understanding of the Galileo Affair, of the biblical creation accounts, and numerous other topics essential to understanding the Church's approach to science. Above all, I wanted to give more attention to the incredible advances in the sciences of human origins, having learned a great deal about this field thanks to a program of research and teaching funded by a grant from John Carroll University's "Science and Faith in Seminary Formation" program.

Cavadini's prophetic idea turned into a year-long research and writing sabbatical (July 2017–June 2018) sponsored and funded by the John Templeton Foundation, the McGrath Institute for Church Life, and Notre Dame Seminary as part of a larger program, "Training Catholic Educators to Engage the Dialogue Between Science and Religion." This incredible outreach, which has trained hundreds of science and religion teachers from Catholic high schools since 2016, received an Expanded Reason Award in Teaching from the Vatican Joseph Ratzinger/Benedict XVI Foundation and the University of Francisco de Vitoria, awarded at the Pontifical Academy of Sciences at the Vatican in September of 2018. As the award was bestowed and I listened to Dr. Cavadini's heartfelt and moving acceptance speech, I knew I had made the right choice to accept his invitation.

As in 2009, many thanks are in order. But first and foremost, all praise and thanksgiving is due to the Sacred Heart of Jesus and the Immaculate Heart of Mary. *Thanks be to you, Lord Jesus Christ, for the grace to begin this project and to see*

PREFACE

Christine and Chris Baglow

it to completion. It is dedicated to you, Savior of Humanity and Savior of its science. Thanks be to you, Our Lady, New Eve and Mother of the Church, for your intercession and tender care.

Among all those who supported me and endured my efforts, all of my love and devotion go again to Christine Kelly Baglow, Margaret Jane Baglow, John Trevor Baglow, Peter George Trevor Baglow, and William Edmund Baglow. *I could not have done it without you, and I did it all for you.* Thanks also to my parents, Melanie and Richard Baglow, my in-laws, Mimi Kelly and John Kelly, and my brothers and sisters: Julie and David Goodman, Jennifer and Mike Brady, Regina and Brett Grau, Richard and Suzanne Kelly, and Patrick and Stacey Kelly.

A book about the dialogue between faith and science would not truly be a dialogue if it were written alone, and for this I am grateful to numerous colleagues and collaborators. To John Cavadini, whose visionary leadership inspired me to write. To Jay Martin, whose sincere encouragement, ingenious academic advice, and tireless support kept this project moving forward. To Patricia Bellm, whose efforts in program management and budgeting made the writing sabbatical possible. To theologians Cory Hayes, Jordan Haddad, and Jean Paul Juge, who lent their incredible minds to content editing, suggestions, and revisions, but most importantly, to conversation about ideas, analogies, and sources. To the many scientists who offered me guidance on the scientific content, especially Stephen Barr, whose masterful editing and brilliant ideas made the first edition possible, and also Randy Ford, Don Frohlich, Dan Kuebler, Matt Rossano, and Stacy Trasancos—thank you! And last but not least, many thanks to the Catholic educators who offered crucial feedback, especially Robert Simpson, Tim Burgess, Chris Culver, Matt Foss, Heather Foucault-Camm, Mark Gonnella, Clare Kilbane, Madelyn Maldonado, Tom McDonald, and Katherine Schilling.

My work would not have been possible without the support of the administration, faculty, staff, students, and seminarians of Notre Dame Seminary. Special thanks to Archbishop Alfred Hughes, who lent spiritual direction, guidance, and fatherly encouragement; to Fr. Jim Wehner, Rector, who approved my sabbatical and gave support to my efforts; to Fr. Deogratias Ekisa, Nathan Eubank, Jim Jacobs, Fr. David Kelly, David Liberto, Becky Maloney, Tom Neal, Brant Pitre, Fr. Philip Neri Powell, O.P., Mario Sacasa, Bobby Thomas, and Pat and Susie Veters for their encouragement and helpful feedback. Last but not least, to those who first heard many of the

PREFACE

concepts in this text as students in my courses, especially those whose feedback was particularly helpful in shaping my reflections: Nick Adam, Trey Ange, Kim and Jamie Anson, Austin Ashcraft, Suzanne Bercier, Donald Bernard, Doug Busch, Caroline Butterworth, Jill Cabes, Dina Dow, Brad Doyle, Blake Dubroc, Olivia Gulino, Andrew Gutierrez, Ryan Hallford, Felix Hinambona, Tim Kettenring, Francis Matiru, Andre Metrejean, Timmy McCaffery, Augustine Odhiambo, Jeremy Reuther, Luke Robicheaux, Andrew Rudmann, and the inimitable Heidi Radabaugh, Administrative Assistant Extraordinaire.

Special thanks goes to the faculty, staff, and seminarians of St. Joseph Seminary College in Covington, Louisiana, and, above all, to Dr. Daniel Burns, Academic Dean, and Fr. Gregory Boquet, O.S.B., Rector, who offered me their generous hospitality as a scholar-in-residence for the term of my sabbatical. Also to librarians Bonnie Bess Wood, JoAnn Montalbano, and the staff of Rouquette Library, who made resources and space available for me. Nearly all of the text was composed at that wonderful place.

Midwest Theological Forum has been amazing in their support, patience, and careful attention to this project. Special thanks goes to all who contributed their time and creativity to the production of the text, especially Fr. Jim Socias, Jim Coughlin (who composed the Glossary and the Student Workbook), Randy Powers, and Stephen Chojnicki. But it is to digital artist Marlene Burrell that not only thanks, but accolades and awards, should be given for the amazing job she has done of selecting and captioning images, text layout, and choice of colors, font, etc. Because of her, it is the most beautiful textbook I have ever seen.

"Beautiful is what we see; more beautiful is what we understand; most beautiful of all is what we can never understand." May these words of Blessed Nicholas Steno, saint and scientist, as well as his heavenly intercession, guide us all to rejoice in the unity between what we see with our eyes, contemplate with our minds, and grasp with hope and love through faith, so that we may ever adore the Father, Son, and Holy Spirit, Beauty ever Ancient and ever New.

Chris Baglow
Director, Science & Religion Initiative
McGrath Institute for Church Life
University of Notre Dame

Feast of the Assumption of the Blessed Virgin Mary
15 August 2019

"Beautiful is what we see; more beautiful is what we understand; most beautiful of all is what we can never understand." —Bl. Nicholas Steno

Part I

Seeing the Whole: Natural Science and Supernatural Faith

Chapter One

Faith and Science at the Crossroads of the Human Spirit

Why do we need both faith and science to understand the world?
How are science and faith related to each other?
How do faith and science come together in the human spirit?

Faith and reason are like two wings on which the human spirit rises to the contemplation of truth; and God has placed in the human heart a desire to know the truth—in a word, to know himself—so that, by knowing and loving God, men and women may also come to the fullness of truth about themselves.

—St. John Paul II, *Fides et Ratio*, Prologue

With this beautiful image of the human spirit soaring in flight upon two wings, **St. John Paul II** (1920-2005) began his famous 1997 letter on faith and reason. This course is about applying his Catholic vision of faith and reason in general to the scientific investigation of the universe—which is one important example of human reason in action—in order to bring faith and reason together in a coordinated vision of reality. Since the concepts of faith and reason will reappear many times throughout this textbook, let us define these terms.

Reason is not merely the ability to think clearly and come to correct answers about certain kinds of problems. Rather, it is the capacity for wisdom. In the words of **Fr. James Brent, O.P.**, "Wisdom is an all-embracing understanding of reality as a whole in light of ultimate causes, especially in light of the end or goal of all things."[1]

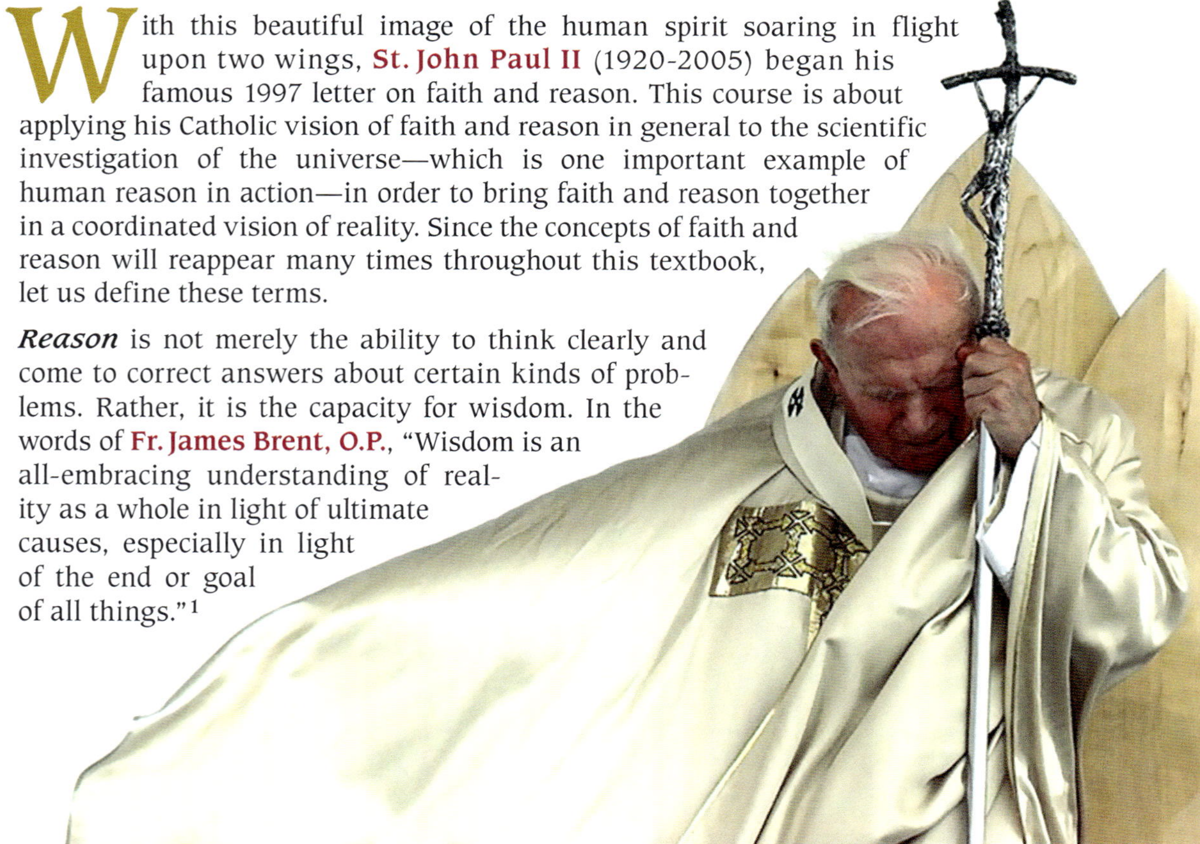

St. John Paul II extolled faith and reason as both necessary and harmonious.

An act of reason may involve specific problems, but reason understood as wisdom is never limited to this or that intellectual activity or inquiry. Physics, psychology, mathematics, etc., are all examples of reason in action. But wisdom is more than physics, more than psychology, more than mathematics. It is any authentic pursuit of truth and the openness to all things true. Modern science in all its forms counts as an authentic and often difficult application of human reason to the material world, and a true way of wisdom, but by no means the only one.

If reason is open to all things true but above all to the causes and goal of all things, then of course the question of the greatest truth, the Truth behind all truths, questions about God and the meaning of reality, can never be neglected by it. But because our capacity for reason is limited, we know that "the meaning of it all" is not accessible to our minds alone. ***Reason leads us to pose questions we could never use reason to answer.*** And it is here that a whole new kind of knowledge, the knowledge brought about by entrusting one's whole self to God, can give us answers beyond the capacity of the human mind left merely to its own natural abilities. This entrusting of one's whole self to God, and the new path of knowing it makes possible, is called ***faith***. In the words of **Cardinal Joseph Ratzinger**, the greatest Catholic theologian of our day who later became **Pope Benedict XVI** (1927-), faith "is not an act of [reason] alone, not simply an act of the will, not just an act of feeling, but an act in which all the spiritual powers . . . are at work together. It is only because the depth of the soul—the heart—has been touched by God's Word that the whole structure of spiritual powers is set in motion and unites in the 'Yes' of believing."[2] The practice of faith in prayer, worship, and daily life is called *religion*. Faith is an act and disposition of the mind and will; religion is the practice of life and worship in the light of faith. The two terms are often used interchangeably, as they will be in this course.

The Apotheosis of St. Thomas Aquinas

St. John Paul II not only extolled faith and reason in general as both necessary and harmonious, but he also applied this vision to the scientific investigation of the universe. He declared, "Science can purify religion from error and superstition; religion can purify science from idolatry and false absolutes. Each can bring the other into a wider world, a world where both may flourish."[3] Since scientific discovery is such a powerful work of reason, the specific relationship between faith and science will be our focus in this book. Many struggle with believing in God because of what they think science says, and many others struggle with accepting the discoveries of modern science because they fear that it leads away from God. Perhaps looking at them together, as St. John Paul II recommended, can help us embrace both.

To investigate this, let us begin by considering the two perspectives—science and faith—and what they show us about reality. Seeing these perspectives side by side goes a long way toward understanding how science and faith are different, what they have in common, and how they can complete each other.

A. Science and Faith, How and Why: Different Perspectives on the One Universe

BOTH SCIENCE AND FAITH involve encountering and understanding the same universe, but they do so in unique ways. The word *universe* is derived from the Latin phrase *unum in diversis*, or "a diverse unity," a complex collection of very different things that are all connected in some real way, the sum total of all beings that are changeable and material.[4] It includes things as different from each other as subatomic particles and animals. No catalog of everything in the universe can be made, as the universe is far too vast to ever be accounted for in its entirety. But we can come to understand it, and science and faith are two very different ways of doing so; so different that despite all of the claims to the contrary, they can never be in any real conflict. In the words of **Rabbi Jonathan Sacks** (1948-), "Science takes things apart to see how they work; religion brings things together to see what they mean."[5]

The universe, "a diverse unity": From subatomic particles to human beings, no catalog of everything in the universe can be made. The universe is far too vast to ever be accounted for in its entirety. But we can come to understand the universe from the perspective of both science *and* faith, which are two very different, though complementary, ways of doing so.

To make the difference between the two even clearer, Sacks provides a helpful thought experiment, which I have reimagined as the appearance of aliens at a music festival. Imagine enjoying the finale of an incredible set from a favorite band on a sunny afternoon. Afterward an alien spacecraft lands, and an alien (who strangely can understand and speak English) approaches you and asks about the noise that had been coming from the stage. You begin by explaining what the music being played is called (blues, folk, rock n' roll), and you go through the type of music it is, the instruments it involves, a little music theory about harmony, keys, and octaves, etc. Once you have said enough for the alien to understand, he responds: "Now I understand *how* the music is played. But I don't understand *why* everyone here is so excited about it." At that moment you realize that the alien still has no idea about *why* music is composed and performed and what *meaning* it has to you and the other fans.

Thinking about the *how* questions and the *why* questions about the universe makes a deeper understanding of reality possible.

Now you have an entirely different task of explanation. Ultimately, you might say that people love music because it moves them by putting the experience of being human into beautiful sounds—music is about experiencing your ordinary life from a new perspective. Or you might say that it unites the music fans into a common experience—music is about relationships. Or you might say that, through the poetry and musical artistry, you are drawn out of ordinary life and your own experience for a moment—music is about transcendence.

Notice that, in order to explain the music festival, you have two choices. You can explain the internal logic of the music, describing *how* it is composed and played. But in order to explain the *meaning* of music to those who play it or enjoy it, you have to go beyond how it is played and answer *why* questions about it. This fanciful story offers a helpful way of thinking about science and faith. Science approaches the physical universe according to its internal rules and patterns, telling us *how* it all works, like your first explanation of music. Faith and philosophy approach the universe according to what the whole system of the universe means: *why* it exists, its role in human happiness, and questions about its Creator and his intentions for it, like your second explanation of music. Just as they are in understanding music, why questions and how questions about the universe are very different, but taken together they can provide a fuller picture, a deeper understanding of reality.

With this important distinction in mind, let us consider two individuals who embody each perspective. As we learn the details of their lives and achievements, we will see the differences between science and faith more clearly. Then we can begin to appreciate the harmony that exists between them, and some surprising characteristics that they share in common.

B. Two Lives: Awe and Wonder in Science and Faith

1. Dirty Bandages and DNA: A Scientist in Search of Answers to "How" Questions

SCIENCE CAN BE, AND INDEED OFTEN IS, VERY HARD WORK, and some scientists have given whole lifetimes to the difficult, frustrating pursuit of scientific discovery, often suffering great hardship. The life of Friedrich Miescher is a telling example.

Friedrich Miescher (1844-1895) was a nineteenth-century pioneer in the field of cell biology. The center of his scientific curiosity was the center of the cell—the nucleus. In his day, no one knew what was in the cell nucleus, nor what purpose it served. In 1869 his lab assigned him to the study of white blood cells, and he focused on the nuclei of these cells. White blood cells are very common in pus, so much of his time was spent collecting bandages from a nearby hospital and going through the difficult process of collecting the cells and then extracting their nuclei, using painstaking and tedious applications of chemicals that took weeks. Ultimately he extracted a gray chemical compound "not comparable" to any other known at that time. It wasn't a protein, the most common kind of compound found within cells, so Miescher named it "nuclein." For this discovery he received the honor of publishing perhaps the most unattractively titled article one can imagine: "On the chemical composition of pus."

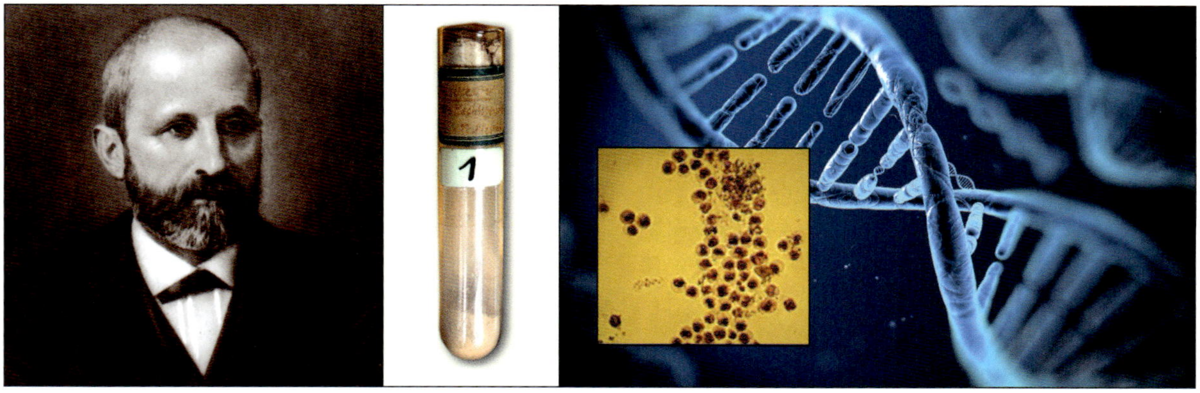

Friedrich Miescher's tireless dedication and sacrifice highlights the *awe and wonder* that characterizes the scientific endeavor for so many scientists.

Later in his career, Miescher discovered that nuclein could be found in high quantities in animal sperm. At last he had found a clue about the function of nuclein, at one point suggesting that it might have something to do with heredity: "If...a specific substance is the cause of fertilization, one would without doubt have to think of the nuclein." Yet he was never able to obtain conclusive evidence of the function of nuclein, despite spending almost all of his time in his lab. After stressing himself through overwork in extremely cold lab conditions, he developed tuberculosis and died of pneumonia at the age of fifty-one. Only after his death would "nuclein" be renamed deoxyribonucleic acid, or "DNA" for short, and only a half-century later would Miescher's discovery become the chemical foundation of all modern genetics. What we now understand about heredity, we owe to DNA studies, of which Miescher's was the first and perhaps most difficult to accomplish.[6]

Miescher's tireless dedication and sacrifice highlights the awe and wonder that characterizes the scientific endeavor for so many scientists. Astronomers peer deep into the sky, paleontologists dig deep into the earth, and microbiologists probe deep inside living cells. Miescher spent the large part of his scientific career discovering and studying a substance that brought him no acclaim and without ever having the satisfaction of discovering its function, and yet his wonder drove him to continue. Without knowing it, he was serving to provide answers to the questions, "How does the cell function?" and, "How does animal reproduction work?" He ultimately was able to contribute to the progress of science, but only because of the work of others who took his discovery further than he was able. However, the lack of reward did not stop him—the pursuit of the truth about the nucleus and its function was sufficient. Somewhat like the music theorist who tells us how, but not why, music is composed, Miescher had to go to the parts of the cell and break them down to gain insight, and from this he achieved a valuable scientific breakthrough.

2. For the Greater Glory of God: A Spiritual Seeker in Search of Answers to "Why" Questions

UNLIKE FRIEDRICH MIESCHER, who from an early age knew he would be a scientist, the young **St. Ignatius of Loyola** (1491-1556) certainly never dreamed he would be a man of faith, the founder of a religious order, and one of the most renowned Catholic saints in history. His passion for military fame led him to the life of a warrior, fighting many duels and becoming a successful soldier. At the age of thirty, during the Battle of Pamplona in 1521, a cannonball wounded his legs, fracturing his left leg in multiple places. Ignatius underwent several operations, all without anesthesia, leaving his left leg shorter than the other and ending his military career for good. His pursuit of personal glory on the battlefield, in the hearts of beautiful women, and in the eyes of his peers was over.

This began a complete change of heart for Ignatius and a long process of spiritual searching that brought him to the small town of Manresa in Spain. Wounded in body but still having the stubborn perseverance of a soldier, he put himself through tireless efforts to find peace of heart and union with God, attending daily Mass, praying seven hours a day, and living as a beggar. One day while he was walking to a nearby church to pray, he stopped to gaze at the river Cardoner that ran near the path, and had the following experience:

While he was seated there, the eyes of his understanding began to be opened; though he did not see any vision, he understood and knew many things, both spiritual things and matters of faith and learning, and this was with so great an enlightenment that everything seemed new to him. It was as if he were a new man with a new intellect.[7]

Later he would name this experience as the greatest gift he was ever given by God—the ability to see the world in a new way, with a new understanding. Notice that it was not this or that thing that he came to understand. In this moment of encounter with God he was given a new perspective on *everything*—truths of faith and of reason. He became such an inspiring religious leader that his order, the Society of Jesus (the Jesuits), went from a few friends to 1000 priests in his own lifetime, spread out across four continents, and continues to this day. The path of Christian prayer and spiritual growth that he mapped out, the *Spiritual Exercises*, has inspired millions.

The *Spiritual Exercises* would take far too long to summarize here, but when we consider its beginning, which Ignatius called "the First Principle and Foundation," we can see that his Cardoner experience was all about answering the question "Why?" about his life: "The human being is created to praise, reverence, and serve God our Lord, and by this means to save his soul. . . . And the other things on the face of the earth are created for the human being that they may help him in achieving the goal for which he is created." These are not the words of a theorist, who sees a part of a whole and tells us how it works. These are the words of a prophet, whose perspective on the whole is different from, *and not in competition with*, the "How?" perspective of the scientist.

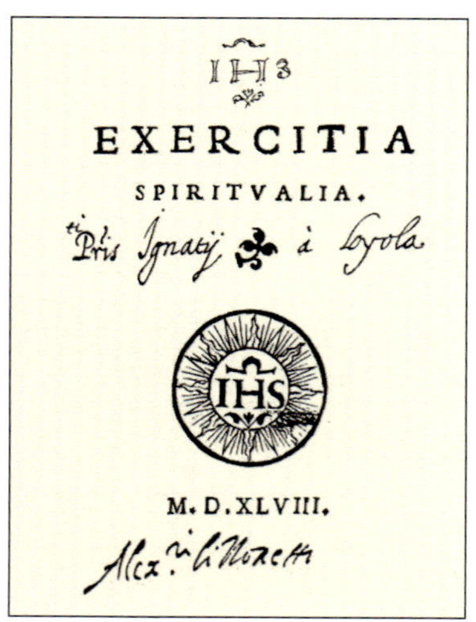
IHS

EXERCITIA

SPIRITVALIA.

IHS

M.D.XLVIII.

Spiritual Exercises of Ignatius of Loyola, First Edition, 1548. The words of a saint addressing *why* questions.

"Science takes things apart to see how they work; religion brings things together to see what they mean"—the lives of Friedrich Miescher and Ignatius of Loyola show us the truth of this "First Principle and Foundation" for relating faith and science. Interestingly, Ignatius' Jesuits would produce an impressive number of priest-scientists in the centuries to come, men who would make fundamental contributions to astronomy, physics, and numerous other sciences, while at the same time living the *Spiritual Exercises* as men of faith. These Jesuits show that "how" questions and "why" questions can go together as long as we unite them correctly.

But different though they may be, science and religion are both perspectives on the same universe; therefore, there should be some commonalities between them. Let us consider, then, what science shows us about the universe and what faith shows us about the universe. The perspectives are very different, but in some important ways we can see how they can be united without damage to their unique characteristics. We begin with science.

C. Order and Openness: The Physical Universe from the Scientific Point of View

SCIENCE, APPLYING ITS METHOD through disciplined and thorough processes of investigation, has made characteristics of the universe accessible to us in ways unimaginable in the ancient past. Common-sense notions that things are exactly as they seem to us have often been modified, even corrected, by the closer look that the scientific method makes possible. Our sense experience tells us that the sun moves around the earth and suggests that the kinds of animals we see are the only kind possible and have always been the same. But both of these positions have been shown to be false by modern science. Science has shown us that the universe, life, and even human nature are more surprising than an initial, simple view allows.

The power of the *scientific method* to reveal the way the universe works comes from its exclusive focus on material things and their interactions, the way the action of material thing A causes material effect B. It begins with material things and it ends with material things. It formulates questions, carries out investigations, analyzes and interprets data collected, and constructs explanations on this basis.[8] An explanation to be tested and possibly disproved is called a *hypothesis*; when it survives many challenges and becomes well-tested and well-developed as an explanation of material realities, it begins to be called a *theory*.

The hallmarks of scientific investigation include observing patterns; thinking about material causes and effects; measuring size, proportions, and quantities; modeling systems of interactions; tracking energy and matter as they change within systems; detecting the functions of material structures; and observing rates of stability and change.[9] Through the various applications of these methods over centuries, a picture of the universe has emerged, one of order and openness. In almost any area of scientific inquiry, both can be seen.

1. Order: A Universe of Patterns

"THE ETERNAL MYSTERY OF THE WORLD is its comprehensibility. . . . The fact that it is comprehensible is a miracle."[10] These famous words of **Albert Einstein** (1879-1955) lead us to the first characteristic of the universe: that within it we find orderliness—predictable patterns that can be understood and described with laws, laws that can be formulated in mathematical terms. The great moments of scientific discovery in history have usually been the discovery of these regular patterns, such as the discovery of the laws of genetics by the Augustinian monk **Gregor Mendel** and the law of gravity by **Sir Isaac Newton**. The assumption that the universe is orderly and patterned is foundational to science, and again and again that assumption has been confirmed. The words of the German physicist **Carsten Bresch** capture this hallmark of the universe:

> **If we were to describe the fundamental property of the matter of the universe in a single sentence, we would have to say that matter is formed—or created—so as to show continuously accelerating growth of patterns. . . . Everything around us consists of patterns. Matter is patterned, atomically and molecularly. Organisms are enormous patterns of cells, each of which in turn consists of a wealth of biological patterns. . . . We are so used to being surrounded by patterns that we do not give a thought to this fundamental property of our world. But it is matter *and* pattern (structure, form) that determine the properties of an object.**[11]

The assumption of order by science has been essential to its success in understanding the physical universe; at times it has even helped scientists predict certain discoveries in advance of experimentation. In the 1960's, when great advances were being made in understanding the tiniest known units of matter, called *subatomic particles*, the physicist **Murray Gell-Mann** (1929-2019) accurately predicted the existence of a subatomic particle based simply upon a sense of order and beauty. In 1961 he created a chart of every subatomic particle that had already been discovered, plotting them in relation to each other based on shared characteristics. The particles formed a pyramid without a point, an incomplete pattern. Gell-Mann hypothesized that a

Murray Gell-Mann predicted the existence of the Omega-minus particle, which would complete a subatomic particle pattern he had charted.

particle would be discovered that would complete the pyramid, and included a prediction of its exact properties. In 1964 the "Omega-minus particle" was discovered, and it fit his prediction exactly. Science again and again confirms our suspicion that the universe has a profound and beautiful order to it.

The presence of order throughout the universe has been so impressive to scientists that some have gone as far as to assume that the universe is so orderly, so thoroughly law-governed, that the laws of the universe absolutely predetermine everything that happens within it. This belief is called *physical determinism*. According to this idea, if someone knew all of the laws of the universe, as well as everything going on in the universe at a given time, he or she could predict exactly all the events that would later happen in the universe. (Of course, such a person would have to have a mind of infinite power to do the calculations.) This is often called the "billiard ball" hypothesis because it makes the whole universe like an enormous pool table—as long as you know the data about the balls (size, mass, position, relative distance, etc.), you know exactly what will happen when this one hits that one, and when that one hits the next one, etc.

However, the progress of science has demonstrated a picture that is not so rigid. The intrinsic order that we see is real, but the universe is also characterized by a significant amount of intrinsic unpredictability. This brings us to the second hallmark of the universe.

2. Openness: A Universe of Emergence

WHEN THE GREAT DISCOVERIES OF MODERN SCIENCE were being made, it brought many to conclude that physical determinism best described the way the universe works. Over time, however, it became clear that many things in the universe are not the simple result of all that went before. The universe is full of examples of order that are not fully explained by prior events, and full of systems that are not reducible to the sum of their parts. For example, the water molecule profoundly affects the properties of the hydrogen and oxygen of which it consists—water has physical properties that are entirely unlike the physical properties of hydrogen gas and oxygen gas. This kind of newness is especially true of living organisms, which exhibit a control over their individual parts, ordering those parts in new ways not seen in the nonliving universe. When new entities occur that cannot be explained simply as the sum of their parts, and that must be understood by beginning with the whole and working down to the parts, scientists call this phenomenon *emergence*. Water is emergent from hydrogen and oxygen; life is emergent from nonliving chemicals, and so on.

Thanks to gravity, "lumpy" regions throughout the universe *emerged* as galaxies, including our own Milky Way.

In the fields of science that study emergence, the words *random* and *chance* are very often used to describe emergent processes. These words are easily misunderstood by people who are not scientists, and many find them troubling because they seem to deny any order whatsoever. In a later chapter we will investigate the relationship between order and chance, especially in regard to the science of evolution. But for now, let us simply note that, in this context, these words indicate that emergent realities are not the strict outcome of rigidly uniform processes. They are surprising and not able to be predicted simply by knowing the laws of the universe and the initial conditions of a physical system.

The universe is a balance of order and openness, law and flexibility, symmetry and surprise.

For the purpose of characterizing the universe revealed by science, what such emergent realities do show us is a universe of *openness*. Science reveals a universe full of novel possibilities that become realities through surprising events in which causes merge to bring about unexpected results, things that exhibit new levels of order.[12] For example, about 380,000 years after the Big Bang, matter was spread smoothly throughout the universe, but with some "lumpy" regions randomly distributed throughout. Thanks to gravity, these lumps became the galaxies, including our own.[13] The *placenta*, the key to the protection and nourishment of embryos in the wombs of most mammals, has features that indicate that it evolved through the insertion of strands of DNA by a virus into the genome of the ancestors of mammals millions of years ago.[14] Viruses bring disorder and death, and yet in this case and others, viral DNA became a key source of order and a new way of producing life, a way through which even new human beings are brought into the world. *Emergent systems*, arising from things much simpler and displaying new levels of complexity, distinguish our universe as one that is not closed and clocklike but open and surprising.

In short, the universe is a balance of order and openness, law and flexibility, symmetry and surprises. A fundamental order exists, but that order is flexible in ways that are open to the emergence of new levels of order that are not simply reducible to simpler levels.

D. Traces of the Divine: Human History and the Universe from the Point of View of Faith

AS WE HAVE SEEN, SCIENCE IS A PROCESS OF INVESTIGATING the physical universe in which various proposals (hypotheses) are made and then become subject to rigorous processes of testing. In science, thinking about things with calm objectivity comes first, and only when a discovery is made and solidly confirmed does the scientific community assent to this or that scientific claim as true, and then build upon that truth (theory). Consider Miescher's musing over nuclein. He speculated that it might have to do with heredity, but he stopped short of affirming this because he had no way to test his hypothesis.

But as the story of St. Ignatius reveals, faith is about our response to God, the source of all reality who is Truth. This means that faith involves assenting to what God has revealed even prior to our understanding of it. Faith follows its own "method" that is different than science because it is not about answering science's "how" questions. God's self-Revelation in the history of salvation as contained in Sacred Scripture and in Sacred Tradition requires the *obedience of faith*, which is "a personal adherence of the whole man to God... an assent of intellect and will to the self-

The Eternal Father
We are encouraged as Christians to question and engage our faith both critically and rationally, but always in humility and reverence before the mystery of God made known through Christ.

revelation God has made through his deeds and words."[15] God approaches us not as a problem to be solved, but personally, as a loving Father, and we respond with personal trust. Of course, we do not do so without any thinking at all; there are many indications in life and experience that there must be some cause that is the source of all things, and that Jesus Christ is truly the divine Savior of all mankind who established a Church to speak and act in his name.

Although we assent to God's personal invitation prior to understanding, faith is not blind; our assent to God's Truth still leaves us with questions, especially when there seems to be a disagreement between what we experience and what God has revealed. According to **Cardinal Joseph Ratzinger**, in faith "struggling and questioning thought remains present, which ever and again has to seek its light from that essential light which shines into the heart from the Word of God."[16] In addition, the infinite richness of the knowledge of God made available through faith summons our reason to explore those riches. As St. John Paul II made clear with his image of two wings, trying to believe in God and the Christian faith as if reason had nothing to contribute is misguided and futile. Faith is not on the side of the irrational. We are obligated as Christians to question and engage faith critically and rationally, but always with the humility to recognize that many truths of faith, though not contrary to reason, are *super-rational*, beyond the mind's capacity to comprehend.

Faith, like science, must embrace reason in order to gain insight into the mysteries of faith. According to the great bishop and theologian **St. Anselm of Canterbury** (ca. 1033-1109), *theology* is "faith seeking understanding," the study of God and his Revelation using human reason in order to understand it more deeply and live in accord with it more fully. Theology is what faith looks like when it turns to thinking about what is believed. This use of reason never rejects God or his truth, but takes God and his revealed truth as its basis, its first principles, the fundamental "data" and "theories" that make all theological thinking possible. Much as a chemist relies upon the periodic table of elements without going back to reinvestigate it, theology relies on what God has revealed in the quest for theological understanding.

While taking God's Revelation as certain, theology can and must inquire into the relationship between the knowledge given through faith and the knowledge acquired through reason and experience, including scientific knowledge. Do the "how" insights of science and the "why" insights of faith share any common characteristics? To answer, let us consider order and openness, the hallmarks of the universe discovered by modern science, but this time from the point of view of faith, which sees both order and openness in what God has revealed about human history and the universe.

1. Divine Order: The Son "Through Whom All Things Were Made"

THE CENTRAL DOCTRINE OF THE CHRISTIAN FAITH is the doctrine of the Trinity, that there is only one eternal God in three divine Persons—Father, Son and Holy Spirit—each of whom is fully God. In their perfect, divine life, the Son is eternally begotten of the Father; "consubstantial with the Father and the Son, the Spirit is inseparable from them, in both the inner life of the Trinity and his gift of love for the world" (the *Catechism*, no. 689). These three divine Persons exist as the one God in the eternity of their divine life and love, independently of the universe that they have created. This is not something that could be known by the human mind unless revealed by God, whose inner life is not accessible to us. Furthermore, the three Persons act as one in bringing the universe into existence, and so ours is a universe willed by God that reflects something of his inner life, of the divine Persons who created it.

The second Person of the Trinity, the Son, is given a special name in Scripture—he is called the *Logos*, a Greek word which literally means "Mind" or "Reason." From this we see that the Christian faith begins with placing faith in the Reason of God—no wonder **St. John Paul II** calls upon believers to use their minds! Of the Divine *Logos*, we are told that "all things were made through him," (Jn 1:3) and "in him all things hold together" (Col 1:17). Like the scientific perspective, then, the perspective of faith turned toward the universe begins with a vision of orderliness. Faith reveals that from all eternity the Son is God's perfect wisdom, and so the universe is lawful, full of patterns that are intelligible. Scientists like **Murray Gell-Mann** marvel at the effectiveness of mathematics for describing the universe; but why should mathematical order be the foundational characteristic of reality? The Christian might respond, "because God is Truth, and so the universe reflects his wisdom"; in the words of Psalm 104: "O LORD, how manifold are thy works! In wisdom hast thou made them all..." (v. 24).

The Holy Trinity
There is only one eternal God in three divine Persons: Father, Son and Holy Spirit. This is the greatest of the Christian mysteries and could only be known by the human mind once it had been divinely revealed.

The primary concern of faith is the coming of the Son-*Logos* into the universe and human history as a human being like us in every way but sin for the sake of our salvation, which is the mystery we call the Incarnation. Fully coming in the flesh about 2000 years ago, Jesus Christ, the Son-*Logos*, began his work of salvation long before, beginning with the creation of the universe and later in the history of the Israelite and Jewish people. God was always speaking through his Son-*Logos*, and so we see God establishing an order for his people in the Law he gave through Moses and in the moral teachings of the prophets he sent over the centuries. After much reflection, this people came to realize that the order God had given to their lives had a perfection about it that reflected the order that they saw in the sky and on the earth. They recognized with God's guidance that he was not simply one god among the many pagan gods, or even the greatest of the gods, but the Lord who made all things, the one Creator, the only God. The ancient Israelites were not a scientific people, but neither were they blind to the order that science

The more science understands the universe and its laws, the more the certainty of faith in the Son-*Logos* as the very source of reality is reconfirmed.

investigates. When the time of the Incarnation had come, the final and greatest of the Jewish prophets, **St. John the Baptist**, called the people to repent and return to the law that had been given to them, the order that the Lord had established for them. The Son-*Logos*, the Lawgiver, had come into the world, and to return to life according to God's order was required in order to prepare oneself to receive him.

Faith, then, reflects upon the orderliness of the universe just as science does. The more science understands the universe and its laws, the more the certainty of faith in the Son-*Logos* as the very source of reality is reconfirmed. The universe begins in divine thought and so can be understood, feebly and incompletely but nonetheless really, by human thought. In this way faith cherishes as a gift from God the same assumption of order that fuels scientific investigation.

But this picture of order that animates faith is an incomplete picture. When the Son-*Logos* became man, he announced new things, even while fulfilling the Law and the prophets. He corrected those who were not open to new things, including his own divine identity and mission as the long-awaited Messiah, commanding and announcing things that transcended the Law. We call the announcement of these new things the *Gospel*, the announcement of salvation through Jesus' life, Death, and Resurrection, which included mercy for those who had rejected and broken the Law, and salvation for those outside of the Jewish people, the Gentiles. While pointing back to what had been given and what God had done in the past, Jesus went beyond it in ways unanticipated by anything before. In other words, faith sees not only order but also openness to an unheard-of future; faith is filled with *hope* and spiritual and divine *emergence* from beyond the horizon of the natural world.

The Lord is *Logos*, Mind, and so the universe's order is affirmed. But how does faith affirm the amazing and unexpected openness that science also sees? To answer this we must remember and reflect more deeply upon the Trinity, where with the eyes of faith we see the Third divine Person at work in the world.

2. Divine Openness: The Holy Spirit, "the Giver of Life"

A FEW VERSES AFTER PSALM 104 celebrate the universe being made in wisdom, the same psalm makes a prayerful plea: "When thou sendest forth thy Spirit, they are created; and thou renewest the face of the ground" (v. 30). This idea of the renewal of the earth is a vision of openness and newness that is associated with the Third divine Person of the Trinity, the Holy Spirit. Here we can see that faith has its own vision of "emergence" that corresponds to the universe's openness discovered in science.

This Third Person of the Trinity is often referred to in Sacred Scripture as the gift given by the Son through his Death and Resurrection. In the words of **St. John Paul II**, "Through the Holy Spirit God exists in the mode of gift."[17] Gifts are unmerited and involve the unexpected and unpredictable. The Spirit is also associated with love; as **St. Paul the Apostle** wrote: "God's love has been poured into our hearts through the Holy Spirit which has been given to us" (Rom 5:5). Love, which is something freely given, is surprising when it is directed toward us by another and has the capacity to change our lives in new and unpredictable ways. The Holy Spirit, the divine Person who is Gift-Love, is always associated with what is new and surprising in God's work in history, when old patterns are taken up and brought to new levels not reducible to what went before. At the beginning of the universe, the Spirit is depicted as "moving over the face of the waters" as new things are to be brought forth (Gn 1:2); and so the very order of creation comes into existence whereas before there was none. The Incarnation of the divine Son is a new event, expected by no one, not even by his own mother, who received the Holy Spirit in order to conceive him in her womb: "The Holy Spirit will come upon you, and the power of the Most High will overshadow you; therefore the child to be born will be called holy, the Son of God" (Lk 1:35). And so, through Mary's "yes" to God and the overshadowing of the Holy Spirit, what it means to be human, the true way God intends, is revealed in the life, Death and, Resurrection of her Son. Not only is human nature taken up into the very life of the Trinity for all of eternity, but Mary herself becomes the "*Theotokos*," the Mother of God according to his human nature.

The descent of the Holy Spirit upon the Apostles and Mary at Pentecost marks the birth of the early Christian church.

Wherever faith sees order, it also sees that this order is open to an even more marvelous and surprising order. The Law given by Moses is not thrown out when Jesus, the new Lawgiver, comes. Rather, the Holy Spirit is offered by him to take that Law to a whole new level, correcting its imperfections and plumbing the depths of its possibilities. "You shall not kill" becomes deeper: "You shall not hate." "You shall not commit adultery" becomes "You shall not look at another person lustfully in your heart." The Gift-Love, the Holy Spirit, takes what is old and makes new patterns. He even takes what is broken and transforms it, as he does when the tragedy of the Crucifixion of Jesus becomes the source of new life, in fact eternal life, for all who believe. Here we see that the Son-*Logos* and the Gift-Love always work together. Faith sees all reality as coming from God in a way that the Son and Spirit can be distinguished in their work, but never separated. In faith, as in science, there is no order without openness, and no openness that leaves behind order.

Through the Son and the Holy Spirit, God the Father both creates and redeems the universe. The Trinity, the Three-in-One, is a mystery, which does not mean that nothing can be known about it but that it is beyond full human comprehension, ultimately unfathomable to us. It is a *paradox*, a truth made up of two truths (God is One, God is three) that seem irreconcilable to the human mind. There are many who claim that this is why the Christian faith ought to be rejected by reasonable people; science, they would claim, is about removing mystery and resolving paradox. Perhaps this is where science and religion part ways and become irreconcilable perspectives—science clarifies, faith mystifies. Let us explore this dilemma.

E. Paradox and Mystery: Uniting the Perspectives of Science and Faith

"RIDICULE IS THE ONLY WEAPON which can be used against unintelligible propositions. Ideas must be distinct before reason can act upon them; and no man ever had a distinct idea of the Trinity. It is the mere Abracadabra of the [tricksters] calling themselves the priests of Jesus."[18] With these words **Thomas Jefferson** (1743-1826) derided and rejected the central doctrine of the Christian faith. His logic was that, since we cannot comprehend how God is both one and three, it simply cannot be true. In other words, he rejected this article of faith because of its paradoxical nature. If something cannot be resolved into distinct ideas in the human mind, then it must be a trick, an "Abracadabra."

If you think about the teachings of Christianity, you will see that paradoxes abound. Jesus Christ, we believe, is both fully God and fully man; the Eucharist is really the Body, Blood, Soul, and Divinity of Christ although it has all the chemical properties of bread and wine; salvation is a pure gift of grace, but we must work it out "with fear and trembling" (Phil 2:12). None of these can be easily resolved into distinct ideas; in each case, two seemingly irreconcilable assertions are being made. Again and again traditional Christianity failed Jefferson's personal "smell test" of truth and falsehood; it is not surprising that he rejected many of Christianity's central doctrines, such as the miracles of Jesus (which he actually cut out of his Bible). What is surprising is that much of what science has discovered about the universe fails Jefferson's test also. It turns out that the material universe contains its own paradoxes.

Light cannot be fully imagined; it presents us with a natural paradox. But this is because the nature of light is richer than our minds can fully comprehend.

For example, consider the science of light, an important branch of modern physics. Over centuries many scientists developed distinct ideas about light, ideas that would have passed Jefferson's truth test. **Sir Isaac Newton** (1642-1727), following the position of the Catholic priest and astronomer **Pierre Gassendi** (1592-1655), thought that light was a particle, which would explain why light can knock electrons off of metal plates. But light also flows around objects and reforms its patterns by "diffraction," an effect discovered by the Jesuit priest and scientist **Francesco Grimaldi** (1618-1663), which led to the hypothesis that light is a wave. The debate lasted for centuries until, in 1905, **Albert Einstein** resolved the issue by demonstrating that light is a "wavelike particle" called a *photon*. Later he explained the "wave-particle" paradox of light this way:

> **But what is light really? Is it a wave or a shower of photons?...It seems as though we must use sometimes the one theory and sometimes the other, while at times we may use either. We are faced with a new kind of difficulty.** ***We have two contradictory pictures of reality; separately neither of them fully explains the phenomena of light, but together they do.***[19]

Light cannot be fully imagined; it presents us with a natural paradox. But this is because the nature of light is richer than our minds can handle. The same is true of the Trinity, the Incarnation, the Eucharist, and many other articles of faith.

The Bohr–Einstein debates were a series of public disputes about quantum mechanics between Albert Einstein and Niels Bohr. Despite their differences of opinion, Bohr and Einstein had a mutual admiration that was to last the rest of their lives. The debates represent one of the high points of scientific inquiry in the first half of the twentieth century.

Since Einstein, many other natural paradoxes have been discovered by scientists, leading the physicist **Neils Bohr** (1885-1962) to introduce a scientific principle he called *complementarity*, i.e., that objects have properties which cannot be observed all at once because of the limitation of our point of view. Interestingly, he used a theological example to illustrate his scientific principle: the paradox that God is perfectly just and perfectly merciful.[20]

Notice that Einstein's explanation of light would not satisfy Thomas Jefferson, but considering that Einstein's insight is foundational to all modern physics shows that Jefferson had a far too simplistic "smell test" for truth. Reality is bigger than the human mind, even a mind as great as Jefferson's.[21] Both the wave and particle models of light are necessary to explain what light is, in a way similar to how we must hold in faith that God is both one and three, Jesus is both human and divine, etc. In the words of **Joseph Ratzinger**:

> **We can only speak rightly about [God] if we renounce the attempt to comprehend and leave him as the uncomprehended....What is true [of light] here in the physical realm as the result of the deficiencies in our vision is true in an incomparably greater degree of the spiritual realities and of God...Only by circling around, by looking and describing from different, apparently contrary angles can we succeed in alluding to the truth, which is never visible to us in its totality.**[22]

Science not only clarifies and makes the complex simple. When the truth requires it, it also reveals the complexity of physical reality, its paradoxes and mysteries. This is not so different from faith that, by recognizing the mysteries of God, clarifies the meaning of life, as it did for **St. Ignatius Loyola** at the Cardoner River. In the words of **C.S. Lewis** (1898-1963), "I believe in Christianity as I believe that the sun has risen: not only because I see it, but because by it I see everything else."[23]

By recognizing the mysteries of God, faith clarifies both the meaning of life and the universe as a whole.

F. Looking Forward: *Faith, Science, and Reason* in Outline

IN CHAPTER ONE we have laid out some general themes and a very broad picture of the relationship between modern science and the Christian faith. The rest of this text will focus on completing that picture, applying these themes, adding other important perspectives and principles, and treating major issues in a more thorough fashion. The contents have been inspired by the most common questions and misunderstandings that I have encountered in conversations and news stories, in questions from my own students and attendees at public presentations. Above all, the contents have arisen from my own personal quest to seek understanding of the Catholic faith in a way that thoroughly embraces scientific insights, allowing those insights to, in the words of St. John Paul II, draw me "into a wider world" where science is allowed to purify and strengthen my vision of the faith and my understanding of God.

THIS BOOK HAS THREE PARTS:

PART ONE: ***Seeing the Whole: Natural Science and Supernatural Faith*** is the longest part and is concerned with creating a strong foundation for understanding specific topics in the faith-science relationship:

- **Chapter Two:** ***Science and the Christian Faith: Understanding and Correcting Models of Conflict*** dispels misconceptions of the relationship between faith and science and offers a better way of framing the relationship.
- **Chapter Three:** ***The Christian Doctrine of Creation: A Wisdom Wider Than Science*** introduces and explains important concepts and principles that are essential to understanding God's relationship to the universe, concluding with the Christian doctrine of creation.
- **Chapter Four:** ***The First Creation Account and Modern Science: Uniting Perspectives*** explains the relationship between Genesis 1 and modern science, using Catholic principles of biblical interpretation and an exploration of the pagan context in which Genesis 1 was written.
- **Chapter Five:** ***Patroness or Persecutor? Sacred Tradition and Scientific Discovery*** lays out the broad historical picture of the Catholic Church's role in the advancement of modern science, including the tragic case of Galileo as an exception to an otherwise glorious history.
- **Chapter Six:** ***Evil, Prayer, and Miracles: Questions for God in the Light of Modern Science*** applies the philosophical and theological concepts explained in Chapter Three to three specific questions: the problem of evil, the necessity of prayer, and the reality of miracles.

PART TWO: ***The Mind of the Maker: Physics, Biology, and Human Origins*** has three chapters, all of which approach the discoveries of modern science from the perspective of God's relationship to the universe, beginning with the discoveries of modern physics and then proceeding to the issue of biological evolution:

- **Chapter Seven:** ***The Twist in the Tale: God and Modern Physics*** investigates important advances in modern physics (the Big Bang theory, discoveries of "fine-tuning" of the universe for life, and of symmetry and beauty in the laws of nature) and explains how to relate them to our faith in God as Creator.

- **Chapter Eight:** ***Going "Deeper Than Darwin": God and Biological Evolution*** investigates the contemporary theory of the evolution of life and both theological and scientific misunderstandings of evolution in order to reflect upon evolution in the light of faith.
- **Chapter Nine:** ***The Emergence of the Image: God and the Sciences of Human Origins*** sharpens the focus of Chapter Eight to consider what science has shown about the origins of our species, *Homo sapiens*, through investigating the evolutionary process. Genesis 2 will then be explored as the divine perspective on this natural process, as well as reflecting on how human evolution should be understood theologically.

PART THREE: ***In His Image: Human Personhood, Human History, and Modern Science*** also has three chapters, all of which engage science to better understand the Christian doctrine of the human person as created in the image of God:

- **Chapter Ten:** ***In His Image: The Human Person from the Divine Perspective*** offers a general explanation of what God has revealed about the human person.
- **Chapter Eleven:** ***Human Sin and Modern Science: The Tragic History of the Image of God*** examines the tragic presence of moral evil in human life, and brings evolutionary biology and psychology into dialogue with the theology of Original Sin, the figures of Adam and Eve, and the redemption of humanity through the love of Christ expressed in his life and Death.
- **Chapter Twelve:** ***From Evolution to Resurrection: Jesus Christ, the True Origin of Humanity*** completes the theological picture by considering how Jesus Christ has revealed the true meaning of being human, and what the final destiny of humanity is in God's plan.

VOCABULARY

Define the following terms (or identify the person's significance):

1. Reason
2. Wisdom
3. Faith
4. Religion
5. Universe (*unum in diversis*)
6. "How" Questions (Science)
7. "Why" Questions (Theology)
8. Scientific Method
9. Hypothesis (Science)
10. Theory (Science)
11. Order (Science)
12. Physical Determinism
13. Openness (Science)
14. Emergence (Science)
15. Obedience of Faith
16. Theology
17. Order (Theology)
18. *Logos* (Son, Mind)
19. Gospel
20. Openness (Theology)
21. Holy Spirit (Gift-Love)
22. Paradox (Natural)
23. Paradox (Supernatural)
24. Complementarity (Science)

"The eternal mystery of the world is its comprehensibility. The fact that it is comprehensible is a miracle."
—Albert Einstein (1879-1955)

STUDY QUESTIONS

1. How did St. John Paul II approach the relationship between faith and reason? Between faith and science?

Section A

2. Formulate another analogy that shows the difference between "how" and "why" explanations.

Section B

3. How do the differences between Miescher's discovery of DNA and St. Ignatius's discovery at the Cardoner River illustrate the "How/ Why" distinction?

Section C

4. Consider the descriptions of the universe as both orderly and open, as a balance of "symmetry and surprises." If the universe was only orderly, or only open, what would that mean for human existence?

Section D

5. How do theological order and natural order parallel each other?

6. Why do we appropriate natural and theological order to the Son-*Logos*?

7. How do theological openness and natural openness parallel each other?

8. Why do we appropriate natural and theological openness to the Holy Spirit (divine Gift-Love)?

Section E

9. Is it true that acknowledging paradoxes and mysteries is a flaw of faith, or is it the case that reality is richer than the human mind can fully comprehend? Why or why not?

"Struggling and questioning thought remains present, which ever and again has to seek its light from that essential light which shines into the heart from the Word of God."
—Cardinal Joseph Ratzinger (Pope Benedict XVI)

PRACTICAL EXERCISES

1. Reread the quote from St. John Paul II that begins the chapter. In reference to real-life experiences, what happens when a person chooses faith and rejects reason? Or vice-versa?

2. Watch the short film "Awe and Wonder: Scientists Reflect on Their Vocations" (3 minutes, 47 seconds: *mtfresources.org/videos*). Relate the perspective of these scientists to the story of St. Ignatius of Loyola. What does the awe and wonder in science have in common with the awe and wonder involved in a personal encounter with God?

3. Faith is a gift of God, but it also requires our cooperation with God's grace in order for it to be the certainty on which our lives are based. To deepen your cooperation with God's grace, ask God for the gift of faith. Say the following prayer once a day for the next week:

O my God, I firmly believe that you are one God in three divine Persons: Father, Son, and Holy Spirit.

I believe that your divine Son became man, and died for our sins, and that he will come to judge the living and the dead.

I believe these and all the truths which the Holy Catholic Church teaches because you have revealed them, who can neither deceive nor be deceived. Amen.[24]

Endnotes – Chapter One

1. Nicanor Austriaco, James Brent, Thomas Davenport, and John Baptist Ku, *Thomistic Evolution: A Catholic Approach to Understanding Evolution in the Light of Faith* (Tacoma, WA: Cluny Media LLC, 2016), 15-16.
2. Joseph Ratzinger, "Faith and Theology," in *Pilgrim Fellowship of Faith: The Church as Communion* (San Francisco: Ignatius Press, 2005), 24.
3. St. John Paul II, *Message to the Reverend George V. Coyne, S.J.*, Director of the Vatican Observatory, June 1, 1988, *inters.org/John-Paul-II-Coyne-Vatican-Observatory.*
4. Juan José Sanguineti, *Interdisciplinary Encyclopedia on Science and Religion*, "Universe," *inters.org/universe.*
5. Jonathan Sacks, *The Great Partnership: Science, Religion, and the Search for Meaning* (New York: Schocken Books, 2011), 2.
6. Florian Maderspacher, "Rags before the riches: Friedrich Miescher and the discovery of DNA," in *Current Biology* 14, no. 15 (August 2004), R608.
7. DotMagis Editor, "Cardoner Vision," *Ignatian Spirituality.* May 13, 2019.
8. Board on Science Education, *A Framework for K-12 Science Education: Practices, Crosscutting Concepts, and Core Ideas* (Washington, D.C.: National Academies Press, 2012), 50-53.
9. Board on Science Education, *A Framework for K-12 Science Education*, 84-85.
10. Albert Einstein, *Ideas and Opinions*, trans. by Sonja Bargmann (New York: Crown Publishers, 1954), 292.
11. Carsten Bresch, "What is Evolution?" in *Evolution and Creation*, ed. Svend Andersen and Arthur Peacocke (Aarhus: Aarhus University Press, 1987), 36-37, as quoted in Mariano Artigas, *The Mind of the Universe: Understanding Science and Religion* (Radnor, PA: Templeton Foundation Press, 2000), 65.
12. Artigas, *Mind*, 101-103.
13. Stephen M. Barr, *The Believing Scientist: Essays on Science and Religion* (Grand Rapids, MI: Eerdmans, 2016), 54-55.
14. Jamie Henzy, "Retroviruses, the Placenta, and the Genomic Junk Drawer," *schaechter.asmblog.org/schaechter/2014/06/retroviruses-the-placenta-and-the-genomic-junk-drawer.html.*
15. *Catechism of the Catholic Church*, no. 476 (hereafter abbreviated "CCC").
16. Joseph Ratzinger, "Faith and Theology," 25.
17. St. John Paul II, Encyclical *Dominum et Vivificantem* (On the Holy Spirit), no. 10.
18. Thomas Jefferson, "Letter to Francis Adrian Van der Kemp," July 30, 1816, *founders.archives.gov/documents/Jefferson/03-10-02-0167.*
19. Albert Einstein and Leopold Infeld, *The Evolution of Physics*, 18th print ed. (New York: Touchstone, 1967), 262-263.
20. Joseph Ratzinger, *Introduction to Christianity*, trans. by J.R. Foster and Michael J. Miller (San Francisco: Ignatius Press, 2004), 173 n. 5.
21. That Jefferson had a much better grasp on political philosophy than he did on Trinitarian theology should be obvious to all Americans.
22. Joseph Ratzinger, *Introduction to Christianity*, 174.
23. C.S. Lewis, "Is Theology Poetry?" in *The Weight of Glory: And Other Addresses* (New York: HarperCollins, 2001), 140.
24. James Socias, ed., "Act of Faith," in *Handbook of Prayers*, 8th Edition (Downers Grove, IL: Midwest Theological Forum, 2019), 62.

Chapter Two
Science and the Christian Faith: Understanding and Correcting Models of Conflict

Why do so many people today think that science and faith are in conflict? When did this rumor of conflict begin?

Are there better ways of thinking about the relationship between science and faith?

What false ideas keep the rumor of conflict alive today?

If methodical investigation within every branch of learning is carried out in a genuinely scientific manner and in accord with moral norms, it never truly conflicts with faith, for earthly matters and the concerns of faith derive from the same God.

—Vatican II, Pastoral Constitution *Gaudium et Spes* on the Church in the Modern World, 36

A. New Rumors About an Old Friendship

Have you ever encountered a rumor that you and an old friend are no longer on speaking terms? Perhaps someone heard about a disagreement between you and your friend, one that was settled weeks or even months ago. The person or persons at the source of the rumor concluded that what was a momentary, real conflict has actually become the status quo, and that you and your friend have actually become enemies for good.

If you have had this experience, then you have a solid insight into the very common and tragic misconception of incompatibility between the natural sciences and *the Christian faith*, the truth God has revealed in Sacred Scripture, Sacred Tradition, and the teachings of the Church. This misconceived understanding is often called the *warfare* or *conflict model* of science and faith. According to this model, science and religion hold no possibility of harmony because it is

assumed that they are rival, mutually exclusive ways of explaining the universe and that their practitioners are both aware of this and are actively fighting each other for supremacy. Many now believe that to gain scientific knowledge is a process that moves a person further away from belief in God. They assume that to be friendly with science means to lose one's acquaintance with religion and, therefore, one's Christian faith. Many also assume that belief in God, especially as he is revealed in Sacred Scripture and in the teachings of the Church, somehow replaces a scientific, rationally informed picture of reality, or at least makes it unnecessary.

The warfare model has become a deeply rooted assumption in the minds of many modern Westerners, and recent research reveals that the perspective of many young Western Catholics today has been shaped by it. A 2014 study from the Center for the Study of Religion and Society and the National Study of Youth and Religion (NSYR) by sociologist **Christian Smith** discovered the following:

- Seventy-two percent of all Roman Catholic emerging adults in the study adopted the "inherent warfare" model of science and religion; that is, they saw the two as contradictory and incompatible.
- Sixty-two percent of Roman Catholic emerging adults in the study said that their own views about religion have *not* been strengthened by the discoveries of science.
- Seventy-eight percent of Roman Catholic emerging adults in the study who have stopped practicing their faith cited the "conflict" of science and religion as one of the reasons why they no longer practice their faith.[1]

These findings were reinforced by a study released in 2016 by the Center for Applied Research in the Apostolate (CARA). The study focused on roughly the same age group as the NSYR, and it also identified the assumption of conflict between science and religion as the most common reason given by young people for no longer practicing their Catholic faith. A significant segment of these youth described the faith as "incompatible" with what they learned or are learning in their high school and university science education. Typical responses to questions were: "It [the Catholic faith] no longer fits what I understand of the universe," and, "As I learn more about the world around me and understand things that I once did not, I find the thought of an all-powerful being to be less and less believable."[2]

"God, Who is the first principle of all things, may be compared to things created as the architect is to things designed." —St. Thomas Aquinas

Many scientists have arrived at the conclusion that to be scientific necessarily excludes any kind of faith. One example is the famous biologist **E.O. Wilson** (1929-), who left behind his Baptist upbringing as soon as he discovered the theory of evolution in his scientific studies in college. "I knew the healing power of Redemption," he tells his readers in his book *Consilience*, "But...I chose to doubt."[3] Doubt about God, not faith in him, Wilson tells us, made it possible for him to arrive at a "truly scientific" outlook on the world.

It should not surprise anyone that, just as Wilson rejected faith in his quest to be scientific, so others have rejected contemporary science in an attempt to maintain a religious outlook. Debates have long raged over how much of the findings of modern science can be accepted by a genuine believer, especially in the area of biological evolution. Some believers have thrown doubt on scientific findings that seem to them to threaten what they find in the pages of the Bible. Some try to use *miracles* (that is, extraordinary interventions by God in the universe) to explain gaps in scientific data. Other believers have pointed to the inability of science to achieve absolute certainty as a sign that science is on shaky ground in all cases and, therefore, cannot be genuinely reliable. One example is the Discovery Institute, an organization that promotes Intelligent Design Theory (ID). ID is an attack upon evolutionary biology, which claims that the intervention of a divine intelligent designer was necessary for the existence of some features of living organisms, such as the human eye or the bacterial flagellum, the very complex, whiplike appendage that makes some bacteria capable of movement.

Chemist and historian of science Lawrence Principe rejects the warfare/conflict model: "During the sixteenth and seventeenth centuries and during the Middle Ages, there was not a camp of 'scientists' struggling to break free of the repression of 'religionists'; such separate camps simply did not exist as such."

The warfare/conflict model has become a rarely challenged principle in our society, one that powerfully shapes attitudes toward religion and faith, even among Catholics. However, it has no foundation in history, and it is largely the product of propaganda. In the words of **Lawrence Principe** (1962-), a chemist and eminent historian of science at Johns Hopkins University, "The idea that scientific and religious camps have historically been separate and antagonistic is rejected by *all* modern historians of science."[4]

Why, then, are so many people convinced that these two old friends, science and the Christian faith, are actually enemies? In order to discover the source of the warfare "rumor" we have to go no further than the late nineteenth century and the work of two American scholars, one a scientist, the other a historian. To understand why their promotion of the warfare model was so successful, we should begin by understanding the times in which they lived.

1. The Warfare Model in Its Historical Context

THE WARFARE MODEL OF SCIENCE AND FAITH emerged when three historical developments were unfolding at the same time in Europe and the United States. First, the various areas of study to which we now refer with the umbrella term "science," such as physics, chemistry, biology, etc., were being professionalized, taking on a whole new level of respectability and exciting popular enthusiasm through the benefits they were producing in the new technologies of the Industrial Revolution, such as steam engines and textile machines. The methodical study of the natural world through observation and experimentation was gaining its reputation as the cutting edge of human knowledge, which it has kept ever since.

As a result, science, as we define it today, began to stand out as a specific and separate pursuit, a status it had never enjoyed in previous centuries. This change in perception even involved a change in vocabulary. Before the nineteenth century, the word "science" referred to any knowledge demonstrated logically, including theological knowledge. The words "philosophy" and "science" were treated as synonyms, as in the title of a book published in 1821: *Elements of the **Philosophy** of Plants Containing the **Scientific** Principles of Botany*.[5] But by the late nineteenth century the terms "science" and "scientific method" began to be associated exclusively with the study of the physical universe through observation and experimentation. This change in perception added new words to the English vocabulary, terms such as "scientist" and "physicist," which were coined in 1833 by the Anglican theologian and natural philosopher **William Whewell** (1794-1866).[6] Sadly, the restriction of the word "science" to one kind of human knowledge left open the possibility that other areas of knowledge such as philosophy, art, morality, poetry, and theology could be considered as unfruitful, subjective flights of fancy by comparison.

GREAT MEN OF SCIENCE AND RELIGION (top) Sir Isaac Newton was a deeply religious man and studied the Bible intensely. (bottom) St. Thomas Aquinas wrote numerous works of theology and also wrote a treatise on the physical motions of the human heart.

Once this shift in perception and language occurred, the notion of possible conflict between science and faith could emerge. In previous centuries, many of the greatest minds in history produced works of both science and theology; both were considered "scientific" (meaning rational, founded on sound principles). **Sir Isaac Newton** (1643-1727), the genius who discovered the law of gravity, was a deeply religious man who studied the Bible almost as intensely as he studied the natural world. **St. Thomas Aquinas** (1224/25-1274), perhaps the greatest theologian in the history of the Church, wrote numerous works of theology and long commentaries on books of the Bible, but he also wrote a treatise on the physical motions of the human heart, as well as a commentary on **Aristotle's** (384-322 BC) *Meteorology*. Both would have been puzzled by the claim that science and religion are opposed to each other. They saw both as necessary for the attainment of wisdom.

The second development occurred exclusively in the United States: the rise of anti-Catholic bias in American society as a response to the influx of Irish and other Catholic immigrants beginning in the mid-1840's. While this phenomenon had nothing to do with the change in perceptions about science, it did create an intellectual environment in which bigotry and prejudice against Catholics were ripe to be exploited for social and political change. The majority of Catholic immigrants were poor and illiterate, which gave their religion an air of ignorance and superstition to non-Catholics. A largely successful attempt to forbid public aid to Catholic schools drew upon fears that Catholics secretly wanted to bring the entire nation under the control of the Pope by corrupting education. Therefore, a bias against the possibility of Catholics being open to the progress of knowledge ruled the day. False claims about the history of the Church and science could draw upon the fuel of anti-Catholic fears and hatred to promote the greatness of science to the detriment of religion.

The final development was a new suspicion of any Christian doctrines other than moral teachings. Terms such as "dogma" and "articles of faith" began to be used pejoratively to characterize foolishness and fear of progress. By the late nineteenth century, dogmas had begun to be seen by many as antirational, the products of blind faith. The belief that religion must be confined only to rules about behavior became a cherished ideal. Many thought that science should replace dogmas in a crusade to rescue religion from irrational ideas. The misconception of **Thomas Jefferson** that we addressed in Chapter One had become widespread—dogmas, because they involve the paradoxical and mysterious and go beyond scientific demonstration, must be rejected as absurd and even as the work of tricksters who wished to control the uneducated. The recognition that dogmas have to do with realities that are by nature unable to be fully comprehended, realities that are not in any way assertions about the universe and its laws but are the self-Revelation of God, was lost to view.

Science is the true savior of humanity, the Catholic Church is the enemy of progress, and divinely revealed truths are obstacles to free scientific investigation. With these assumptions, the situation was ripe for claims of conflict between science and faith, and they would not be long in appearing.

2. John William Draper and Andrew Dickson White

IN 1874, **John William Draper** (1811-1882), a successful American chemist and early innovator of photography, published his book entitled *History of the Conflict between Religion and Science.* He begins by making a generalized judgment: "The history of Science is not a mere record of isolated discoveries; it is a narrative of the conflict of two contending powers, the expansive force of the human intellect on one side, and the compression arising from [traditional] faith."[7] Shortly after this declaration, he qualifies it by proclaiming the innocence of Protestant and Greek [Orthodox] Christians, whom he claims have never opposed the advancement of knowledge and have always had "a reverential attitude to truth, from whatever quarter it might come." The true religious enemy of science, Draper then claims, is the Roman Catholic Church, which he indicts for rejecting science and engaging in violent means so as to maintain power over its adherents in its attempt to gain total political supremacy over all peoples:

St. Augustine is one of the Church's greatest theologians. He recognized that the Bible's description of natural phenomena must always be interpreted figuratively, in accordance with reason, and not literalistically.

> **In speaking of Christianity, reference is generally made to the Roman Church, partly because its adherents compose the majority of Christendom, partly because its demands are the most pretentious, and partly because it has commonly sought to enforce those demands by the civil power. None of the Protestant Churches has ever occupied a position so imperious—none has ever had such widespread political influence....But in the Vatican—we have only to recall the Inquisition—the hands that are now raised in appeals to the Most Merciful are crimsoned. They have been steeped in blood![8]**

Throughout the rest of the book, Draper alleges conflict after conflict between the Catholic Church and science while offering little or no evidence. He makes up details and presents them as facts. He rearranges sequences of events in order to support his position. He selects quotes that seem to support his case and refuses to give the context, even leaving out parts of quotes that call into question his interpretation of them.[9]

For instance, Draper condemns the Catholic bishop and theologian **St. Augustine** (354-430) for teaching that the sky is stretched out like a skin over a flat earth.[10] Actually, St. Augustine quotes Psalm 104:1-2 ("LORD my God, you are great indeed...you stretched out the sky like a skin") in order to demonstrate his principle that the Bible must be read figuratively, not literalistically, in its depictions of natural phenomena. He actually affirms the very position Draper accuses him of rejecting: "Rational arguments," St. Augustine concludes, "inform us that the sky has the shape of a hollow globe all round us."[11]

Draper ends the book with his own prophecy of doom for religion and victory for science:

> **As to the issue of the coming conflict, can any one doubt? Whatever is resting on fiction and fraud will be overthrown. Institutions that organize impostures and spread delusions must show what right they have to exist. Faith must render an account of herself to Reason. Mysteries must give place to facts. Religion must relinquish that imperious, that domineering position which she has so long maintained against Science.**[12]

Despite his fury and contempt for religion, especially Catholicism, or more likely because of it, Draper's book was an instant success. It outsold every other book in the series in which it was included. Since then it has been reprinted fifty times and has been translated into ten languages. Even today it remains readily available.[13]

Andrew Dickson White (1832-1918) was an American historian and the co-founder of Cornell University (1865), the first purely secular institution of higher learning in the United States. For this he was subjected to criticism for separating learning from religion, criticism that came mostly from competitors at Protestant institutions of higher learning. In response, White decided to write a book showing that both religion and science would be better off once "dogmatic theology," a subject *not* included in the curriculum at Cornell, was fully overcome. "I will give them a lesson which they will remember," he wrote to his friend Ezra Cornell in 1869.[14]

"There is nothing that has been created without some reason, even if human nature is incapable of knowing precisely the reason for them all."
—St. John Chrysostom

The "lesson" he gave to his opponents was a two-volume work, *History of the Warfare of Science with Theology in Christendom*, first published in 1896. He begins by praising Draper for "his work of great ability." He then goes on to repeat many of Draper's errors, including one that remains quite popular today: the flat-earth "dogma." White claims that, until Christopher Columbus's time, the majority of Christian thinkers had insisted on biblical grounds that the earth was flat, and that a flat earth was practically a dogma of the Church. In reality, only two Christian thinkers, **Lactantius** (ca. AD 250-325) and **Cosmas Indicopleustes** (sixth century AD) had ever claimed that the earth was flat. To make his argument, White misrepresents much more influential Christian thinkers, such as **St. Basil the Great** (AD 330-379) and **St. John Chrysostom** (ca. AD 309-407), as flat-earthers, and presents Lactantius and Cosmas as representatives of the official Christian position. To add a touch of drama, he adopts a fictional account of **Christopher Columbus** (1451-1506) struggling unsuccessfully to convince Catholic priests and professors at the University of Salamanca in 1487 that the earth is spherical:

Andrew Dickson White misrepresented the Salamanca debate. All parties at the University of Salamanca in 1487 agreed with Columbus that the earth is a sphere. What was debated was the size of the earth. Columbus thought the earth was small enough to reach Asia with sufficient supplies. His opponents thought the earth was much larger.

> **The warfare of Columbus the world knows well...how sundry wise men of Spain confronted him with the usual quotations from the Psalms, from St. Paul, and from St. Augustine; how, even after he was triumphant, and after his voyage had greatly strengthened the theory of the earth's sphericity...the Church by its highest authority solemnly stumbled and persisted in going astray.[15]**

Had White done his homework, he would have discovered that all parties at Salamanca *agreed* with Columbus that the earth is a sphere. What was debated at Salamanca was the size of the earth; Columbus thought it was small enough to get to Asia with sufficient supplies, and his opponents thought that it was much larger. (His opponents were right; it was much larger than Columbus thought, although neither they nor Columbus knew about what lay between Europe and Asia: the Americas and the Pacific Ocean.)[16]

The "one-two punch" of Draper and White has had a remarkable, long-standing effect on popular opinion, as we have seen from the statistics at the beginning of this chapter. Appealing to the prejudices of their day and riding the wave of scientific progress, they created the very conflict they claimed to resolve. The errors and misrepresentations they foisted upon their readers are now routinely repeated as historical facts by people who are not historians, finding new life in the work of science popularizers such as **Neil DeGrasse Tyson** (1958-), who in his 2014 TV series *Cosmos* falsely portrayed the Church as persecuting and killing the Italian monk **Giordano Bruno** (1548-1600) for a scientific idea (Bruno was actually executed for theological heresies).[17] In 2012, even U.S. President **Barack Obama** (1961-) repeated the flat-earth error in a jibe against political opponents: "If some of these folks were around when Columbus set sail, they probably would have been founding members of the Flat Earth Society. They would not have believed that the world was round."[18]

B. Fighting for the Friendship: Credibility and Affirmation[19]

WITH SUCH POWERFUL MISCONCEPTIONS ABOUNDING within popular opinion, the only remedy to the warfare approach to science and faith is to take a closer look at each of them, moving beyond the unfounded claims of Dickson and White. As we do so in this text, it will become apparent that the discoveries of science have not harmed the *credibility* of the Christian Faith (i.e., its harmony and compatibility with reason); rather, in many cases those discoveries indirectly support that credibility. It will also be demonstrated that the faith of the Church *affirms* and supports the value of the scientific investigation of the universe. For now, let us briefly summarize what we mean when we declare that science supports the credibility of the Christian faith, and that the Church thoroughly affirms science as a genuine and important exercise of human reason.

1. Credibility: The Self-Corrections of Science and the Progress of Theology

AS WE HAVE SEEN, IN THE NINETEENTH CENTURY a growing number of thinkers came to the conclusion that groundbreaking new scientific discoveries had damaged the credibility of the Christian faith, including belief in God. The answers to those challenges were not very clear at the time. In the twentieth century, however, the situation began to change. Theologians began to reconsider certain assumptions and to reflect upon the Christian faith in the light of new discoveries. Also, some of the conclusions of earlier scientific inquiry that had seemed difficult to reconcile with Christian belief were called into question and were even overturned by newer discoveries.

These newer discoveries, far from undermining Christian doctrines, actually began to point in a direction that made those doctrines more credible. (We will explore several examples later. One you may have already heard about is the *Big Bang theory*, which is now the generally accepted account of the beginnings of the universe. But there are other examples of discoveries that strengthen the credibility of Christian beliefs, and we shall discuss them at length in Chapter Seven.) In the twentieth century the story of science did not go in the direction that some had expected; there were several "twists in the plot," so to speak. These helped to overcome some of the challenges to the credibility of the Christian faith that had once seemed so formidable. There is an important lesson in all of this: while God's truth cannot change, the conclusions of science can and do, and often in quite unexpected ways. And our conception of God's truth theologically can and does progress in the light of new knowledge. This should teach us not to jump to hasty

The Big Bang theory is the prevailing cosmological model for the observable universe. Georges Lemaître (1894-1966), a Jesuit trained Belgian Roman Catholic priest, mathematician, astronomer, and professor of physics at the Catholic University of Louvain, was the first to identify that the recession of nearby galaxies can be explained by a theory of an expanding universe, which was observationally confirmed soon afterwards by Edwin Hubble.

conclusions about supposed "conflicts" that may later turn out to be illusory, based on inconclusive evidence or appearances.

These new discoveries of science began to change the minds of some people, and the notion of warfare between science and faith has begun to recede among scholars who have become more aware of the biased perspective from which it emerged. Over the course of the twentieth and twenty-first centuries, theologians began to incorporate scientific insights directly into their reflections upon the teachings of faith and to clarify the distinction between the two perspectives and the harmony between them. Also, among members of the scientific community, more and more believing scientists began to feel confident in the intellectual respectability of their faith. A powerful example can be seen in the Society of Catholic Scientists, which was founded by particle physicist **Stephen Barr** in June 2016. In the span of just three years, the total membership grew to over 1000 members and includes scientists from respected institutions across the United States, including Harvard University and the National Academy of the Sciences.[20]

Particle physicist Stephen Barr, author of *Modern Physics and Ancient Faith*: "Science has given us new eyes that allow us to see down to the deeper roots of the world's structure, and there all we see is order and symmetry of pristine mathematical purity."

2. Affirmation: Faith Fosters Science

THE MISCONCEPTION THAT SCIENCE AND RELIGION are enemies is also contradicted by the historical record, which shows that revealed religion, especially the Christian faith, has fostered the development of modern science. This would have surprised Dickson and White, but it is a historical fact. In studying ancient civilizations, such as Greece, China, Egypt, and the Aztec Empire of Mexico, historians have discovered that many of them had achieved some impressive results in science and technology (the practical application of mathematics and science). But of all the world's cultures and civilizations, only the Christian culture of Western Europe made the breakthrough to a total, lasting, and far-reaching scientific approach. It was from there that modern science spread to the rest of the world. This is well-documented in recent books such as **Edwards Grant's** *God and Reason in the Middle Ages* (2001) and **James Hannam's** (1970-) *The Genesis of Science: How the Christian Middle Ages Launched the Scientific Revolution* (2011).

That Christianity had a positive role to play in the history of science can appear to be a puzzling claim, especially to those who assume that Christian belief and natural science are inherently opposed. Why would a society based upon the Christian faith, a faith so many assume to be science's enemy, be the very society that formed the cradle for the natural sciences? The answer is so surprising that it is still often overlooked. According to some leading historians, it was the *centrality of the Christian faith* to European culture and learning which offered the right kind of cultural environment for modern science to emerge.

This makes more sense if we give a little thought to what the Bible teaches about God and the universe. Sacred Scripture insists that the universe reflects the wisdom and goodness of its Creator. Indeed, it was created by a God who, according to Christian belief, is himself Wisdom, Goodness, and the Source of all that is. Because of this, Christian cultures had confidence that the world could be understood and was worthy of understanding *on its own terms*. The world

"The journey is difficult, immense. We will travel as far as we can, but we cannot in one lifetime see all that we would like to see or to learn all that we hunger to know."
—Loren Eiseley

was the product of a Mind, and so could be understood by minds. God, according to Scripture, had given laws to the universe "which cannot be passed" (Ps 148:6). Since other civilizations lacked a strong notion of a personal, perfectly good, wise, and creative God, they also lacked a firm religious and cultural stimulus in their search for natural principles and laws in the universe.[21]

The scriptural and Christian belief that the universe is created by an all-good, all-powerful, and perfectly wise Creator implies that it can be understood, that it has an order which can be marveled at and a goodness that makes it valuable. It is this outlook which gave and still gives affirmation to science, and which nurtures it and encourages it to begin and continue its quest for more knowledge.[22] For those who are still mired in the warfare model, history has a wake-up call. Not only has the Christian faith been the friend of science, it actually helped to bring modern science to birth. And, as we shall see in Chapter Five, the Church and Christian believers have played an active and positive role in the development of science for at least 1500 years. In the words of the evolutionary anthropologist **Loren Eiseley**:

> **[Experimental science] began its discoveries and made use of its methods *in the faith, not the knowledge*, that it was dealing with a rational universe controlled by a Creator who did not act upon whim nor interfere with the forces He had set in operation. The experimental method succeeded beyond man's wildest dreams, but the faith that brought it into being owes something to the Christian conception of the nature of God. It is surely one of the curious paradoxes of history that science, which professionally has little to do with faith, owes its origins to an act of faith that the universe can be rationally interpreted, and that science today is sustained by that assumption.**[23]

C. Scientific Atheism and Literalistic Creationism: Misconceptions About the Universe and Science

AS WE CAN SEE, THE WARFARE MODEL does not do justice to history. It is also often fueled by misconceptions of the natural universe and of science itself, sometimes on the part of those who claim to support science, and also by some believers who seek to defend their faith without fully understanding it. It should not surprise us that those most responsible for spreading the warfare/conflict rumor are those who start from beliefs that require them to assume that science and faith are incompatible.

Understanding these belief systems is necessary for understanding why many today still hold science and faith to be at odds even when they understand the false historical foundations of the warfare model. To examine these we have to move beyond historical matters and consider some flawed philosophical and theological ideas about the universe and science.

1. Materialism, Reductionism, Scientism: What You See Is ALL You Get!

ONE SUCH BELIEF SYSTEM is *materialism*, the notion that "lifeless and mindless 'matter' alone is real."[24] Put another way, materialism is the conviction that *only* the material universe, that is, things that are capable of being seen, smelled, touched, heard, and tasted (or at least capable of being measured by instruments), exists. In the words of one such materialist, the evolutionary biologist **Richard Lewontin** (1929-):

> **We take the side of science *in spite* of the patent absurdity of some of its constructs, *in spite* of its failure to fulfill many of its extravagant promises of health and life, *in spite* of the tolerance of the scientific community for unsubstantiated just-so stories, because we have a *prior commitment*, a commitment to materialism....Moreover, that materialism is absolute, for we cannot allow a Divine Foot in the door.**[25]

Lewontin is clearly aware that the method of science can be entirely ruined by inserting supernatural causes ("a Divine Foot") to explain material realities. And, to that extent, he is correct; as a method, scientists must assume a *methodological materialism* in which they persist in seeking material explanations, never inserting God's miraculous activity into the gaps of our scientific understanding. The problem is that Lewontin and other materialists make the method of science into a mentality, a rigid ideology, an all-encompassing worldview, a cookie-cutter conception of reality. As with a cookie cutter, they assume that the "dough" of reality can all be fit within the scientific method; and since material things are the only things that fit the method of science, only material things are real. In the next chapter we will see how Catholic thinkers affirm the methodological materialism of science without embracing actual materialism, conceiving of God as the real Cause of all causes, not an alternative cause to material causes.

Closely related to materialism is *reductionism*, the idea that all real things are *only* the sum of their parts and that all explanations of material reality must move from the bottom up, from smaller entities and more fundamental physical forces to more complex entities and physical forces. In this belief system, what seems to be higher levels of existence (like animals and humans) are merely new collections of smaller elements, arranged in a different, more complex order, and are able to be explained entirely by reference to these smaller parts. Perhaps the most famous statement of reductionism came from the well-known American scientist **Carl Sagan** (1934-1996), who once said, "I, Carl Sagan, am nothing but a collection of atoms bearing the name 'Carl Sagan.'"[26] Of course, most people recognize that material creatures are made up of

Reductionism is the idea that all real things are only the sum of their parts and that all explanations of material reality must move from the bottom up. "Despite usage to the contrary, there is no necessary implication in the word 'spiritual' that we are talking of anything other than matter (including the matter of which the brain is made), or anything outside the realm of science." —Carl Sagan, *The Demon-Haunted World: Science as a Candle in the Dark*

To fully appreciate the flaws of reductionism, consider the mystery of a human being: "the immensity of the human spirit." —St. John Paul II

atoms, just as Sagan said. However, reductionism is the belief that creatures, humans included, can be fully explained in terms of their parts, that they are mere collections of smaller entities.

Reductionism is also based upon a crucial truth: that the scientific method must begin with reducing things to their most fundamental parts and the universe to its most foundational laws. As a method, scientists must assume a *methodological reductionism*, investigating what the parts contribute to the whole and attributing to these as much explanatory power as they actually have. But they must not stop there, and if they did all science would simply be reducible to physics. Chemistry and biology would simply become branches of physics, rather than distinct sciences, if reductionism were an accurate picture of reality.

To fully appreciate the flaws of reductionism, consider the mystery of a human being. It is possible to know a human being on many levels: one can study human biology or physiology, or the range of human emotions, or even human brain waves. But in such an attempt, we begin to realize that there are human activities, actions, accomplishments, phenomena, and desires that go beyond the purely material. As we realize this, what **St. John Paul II** once called "the immensity of the human spirit"[27] becomes apparent, an immensity and dignity that cannot be reduced to the material or biological level.

The reductionist and materialist ideologies can be summarized in one term—*scientism*, which can also be called *scientific atheism*. *Scientism* is the view that "[empirical] science alone can put us in touch with the ultimate depths of the world."[28] These scienti*st*ic (vs. scienti*f*ic) ideologies obviously allow no room for the Christian faith as a source of truth. As the Christian faith is concerned ultimately with God, who is spiritual and not material, those who deny that there are any immaterial realities reject the Christian faith. Since reductionists and materialists see science as the only way to gain knowledge of things as they really are, they consider religion to be inherently incompatible with scientific thought.

Scientism involves a logical flaw—it is based on an assertion that is not logically consistent. As we said above, scientism is the belief that only science, which observes and measures material realities, can put us in touch with truth. And yet the very statement "only science can put us in touch with truth" is not able to be verified by science. If you are having a hard time grasping this, think about this statement, which is similar because it is also logically inconsistent: "There is no such thing as absolute truth because all truth is relative." Just like the logically problematic claim of scientism, this sentence, too, supposes the very thing that it sets out to deny, because the very claim that "There is no such thing as absolute truth" is itself making a claim to be true in an absolute sense! In the same way, if the statement "only science can put us in touch with truth" is true, then it must be scientifically verifiable, or else it is self-defeating according to its own terms and scope. But that assertion cannot be observed or measured through scientific means. Thus, the foundational assumption of scientism claims a standard for truth that it itself cannot satisfy. No scientific facts defeat scientism; but no scientific facts prove it either. Those who interpret reality in this way cannot logically rule out other approaches to reality, such as belief in God.

2. Dogmas and Mysteries

AS WE HAVE INDICATED in regard to the warfare model, scientific atheism finds fault with the Christian faith because it involves *dogmas* and *mysteries*.[29] A closer look at both will help us understand why. It will also show that scientific atheism involves a flawed understanding of what Christians mean by dogmas and mysteries.

Dogmas (which are complete, authoritative definitions of *doctrines*) are truths revealed by Christ which, because they come from God himself, cannot be changed or challenged; only our understanding of them can progress.[30] An example of a dogma would be the Christian belief that the eternal Son of God became man in the womb of the Virgin Mary: the dogma of the Incarnation. Scientific atheism sees the believer's acceptance of dogmas as *antirational*. But this objection is incorrect. To believe in a dogma on God's own authority is perfectly rational—if God does exist and has really revealed it. And dogmas, once accepted on those grounds, can be rationally explored: we can examine them by means of our naturally derived knowledge in order to understand how they fit together to form a coherent and consistent picture of reality. As we noted in Chapter One, this rational exploration is called *theology*.[31]

Dogmas and Mysteries:
The Church teaches that what we believe as Christians and our act of believing it are in harmony with reason.

The Church teaches that what we believe as Christians and our act of believing it are in harmony with reason, and that God desires us to see the reasonableness of the things he has revealed, so that we can better understand the world, ourselves, and God himself. The Church, therefore, invites us to approach dogmas intelligently—to ponder them and penetrate more deeply into them, just as the Blessed Virgin Mary "kept all these things in her heart" (Lk 2:51). In the words of **Vatican I** (1869-1870), "The assent of faith is *by no means* a blind impulse of the mind."[32]

Mysteries are aspects of reality that transcend our ability to fully grasp them because they are so closely connected to the reality of God, who is infinite and beyond all attempts of comprehension by our finite minds. Scientific atheism sees the Christian respect for mysteries as antirational because it involves the assertion that some things transcend our intellectual capacity. To say that there are things that are beyond our full comprehension, according to scientism, is to give up on thinking, to end the struggle for deeper understanding. But that which lies beyond our mental grasp does not necessarily put an end to thought. In the words of physicist **Stephen Barr** (1953-):

> **[Divine mysteries] do not shut off thought, like a wall. Rather they open the mind to vistas that are too deep and too broad for our vision. A mystery is what cannot be seen, not because there is a barrier across our field of vision, but because the horizon is so far away. [To name something a mystery] is a statement not of limits, but of limitlessness. The reason that there are mysteries is that God is infinite and our intellects are finite.**[33]

In summary, the acknowledgment of mysteries does not close the human mind. Rather, mysteries open an infinite horizon for us to explore.

Materialism, reductionism, and scientism are *belief systems*, convictions about reality. They must be clearly distinguished from science as such. Science, which examines the elements of the visible world, is not the same thing as materialism, which holds that the elements of the visible world are the only things that really exist. Nor is it the same thing as reductionism, which says that all things are reducible to their physical, visible parts. Finally, the belief that only science can reveal the truth about reality (scientism) is not a requirement for the study of science, just as the study of paintings does not require denying that other forms of art are also valuable.

3. Literalistic Creationism: Making God in Our Image

IT WOULD BE UNFAIR TO PLACE THE BURDEN of the warfare/conflict misconception only upon the backs of those who embrace materialism, reductionism, and scientism. Another source of the rumor that science and faith are enemies is actually a very vocal group of believers. They are often referred to as *creationists* because of their belief that God created the universe exactly (or almost exactly) according to their interpretation of the First and Second Creation Accounts found in the Book of Genesis (Gn 1–3). One common belief among creationists is that the universe is only around 6000 years old, based upon their calculation of the dates and ages of certain people given in the Bible, rejecting modern Big Bang cosmology and the billions of years of cosmic history it reveals. Another common belief is that all species were originated by God at various points in time within the first week of the earth's existence through sudden and miraculous divine intervention, rejecting evolution and its natural explanation for the origins of living things over billions of years. Creationism flatly rejects the modern scientific consensus and does so on the authority of the Bible, and attacks "secular science" as atheistic and as lacking solid evidence for its claims.

Creationist Ken Ham: "God created 'the heavens and the earth' fully-formed and functioning in six days."

Ken Ham (1951-), the famous creationist who is responsible for the Creation Museum in Northern Kentucky, summarizes the creationist position as follows: "God created 'the heavens and the earth' fully-formed and functioning in six days, 6,000 years ago, at around 4004 BC. The context of Genesis 1, as well as other places in Scripture, make it clear these days were ordinary, 24-hour days. God's original creation was perfect, with no death or suffering."[34]

Creationism is a theological position; it claims to be the proper interpretation of the Bible and of the Christian doctrine of creation. As such, it has been rejected by the three most recent Popes. In 1981, **St. John Paul II** noted that the Bible does not wish to give us a "scientific treatise," declaring that the Bible wishes to teaches us theological truths, not scientific ones: "Any other teaching about the origin and make-up of the universe is alien to the intentions of the Bible, which does not wish to teach how heaven was made but how one goes to heaven."[35] In his Easter Vigil homily in 2011, **Pope Benedict XVI** declared that the creation account in Genesis 1 "is not information about the external processes by which the cosmos and man himself came into being."[36] And in 2014, **Pope Francis** (1936-) repeated the same rebuttal in greater detail:

> **When we read the account of Creation in Genesis we risk imagining that God was a magician, complete with an all-powerful magic wand. But that was not so. He created beings and he let them develop according to the internal laws with which He endowed each one, that they might develop, and reach their fullness...The Big Bang theory, which is proposed today as the origin of the world, does not contradict the intervention of a divine creator but depends on it. Evolution in nature does not conflict with the notion of Creation, because evolution presupposes the creation of beings that evolve.**[37]

In Chapter Three we will look more closely at what we mean by the word "creation" and God as Creator, and we will see that it shares nothing in common with the literalistic creationism of Ken Ham and others. For now these quotes should make it clear that Catholics who embrace creationism do not represent the Church's understanding of creation and run afoul of the teachings of the Popes, which should be observed as authoritative Catholic teachings. Arguing against well-established science simply by virtue of one's own interpretation of the Bible breaks faith and reason apart and fails to distinguish between science and theology.

Although it is just as false as scientism, creationism is based upon a crucial theological truth. The truth behind creationism is to be found in its insistence on the divine inspiration of the Bible, that through its human authors God reveals truth for the sake of our salvation. Creationists correctly recognize that God is not capable of error, and that his word given in Sacred Scripture cannot be wrong. Unfortunately, from this they draw a false conclusion: It is one thing to say that the purpose of the Bible is to reveal truth; it is quite another to say that it is directly concerned with the kinds of truth about the physical world that the natural sciences investigate. Unconsciously, "scientific creationists" have absorbed some of the errors of scientific atheism, ascribing to truths about the natural world a kind of ultimate importance, instead of realizing that the truths with which Scripture is primarily concerned are of a much higher order. By failing to distinguish between the "how?" explanations of science and the "why?" explanations of faith, creationists squeeze God into a simplistic mold that fails to distinguish between what they can imagine and the divine mystery of creation. God becomes an all-powerful agent doing things the way we would do them. They remake God into their own image, making him fit their finite perspective.

In Chapter Four, we will look more closely at the issue of *how* God's Word is without error in order to explain how it is possible to accept the findings of science and to also embrace Sacred Scripture as God's Word. We will examine how Sacred Scripture itself gives indications that it is not about giving an account of the scientific details of the material world, but rather shows itself open to changing views of the universe that become deeper and more accurate with time. In short, we will see that Scripture shows itself to be open to science.

D. Separation Anxiety: A False Solution to the Warfare Model

IN LARGE PART, ONE CAN TRACE THE OPINION that science and the Christian faith are irreconcilable to the groups we just examined. But, while they have fueled the rumor that science and faith are enemies, another group has attempted to dispel the rumor by asserting that science and faith have *no relationship*. In other words, while scientific atheists and creationists are spreading the rumor that science and faith are not on speaking terms because they are in conflict, this third group holds that they are not speaking because they have nothing in common to talk about.

(top) Nuclear physicist and theologian Ian Barbour, author of *When Science Meets Religion: Enemies, Strangers, or Partners?*, was a pioneer in the study of the integration of religion and science.

(bottom) Evolutionist and separationist Stephen Jay Gould, author of *Rocks of Ages: Science and Religion in the Fullness of Life*. Science defines the natural world, religion our moral world...separate spheres of influence.

In their anxiety to end the rumor that science and faith are irreconcilable, many thinkers—some of whom are scientists, some of whom are believers, and some of whom are both—have argued that science and faith are really too different to be in conflict. **Ian Barbour** (1923-2013) gives an excellent explanation of this position, which he calls the *Independence Model*—"Proponents of this view say there are two jurisdictions [i.e., science and faith] and each party must keep off the other's turf. Each must tend to its own business and not meddle in the affairs of the other."[38] We will refer to this approach as *separationism*, because it maintains that science and the Christian faith must always be kept separate in every way possible.

According to separationism, a person can embrace both scientific discoveries and religious customs and values without having to worry about contradictions because their jurisdictions never intersect. For separationism, the distinction we have made between "how?" and "why?" is hardened beyond a difference of perspectives into entirely different claims with no common ground.

One influential separator of science and faith was the biologist **Stephen Jay Gould** (1941-2002). Science, he told us, is about facts; religion is about "values and meaning." No war can exist between them, because they never address the same realities.[39] Gould's approach is attractive to many people. By separating science and all religious beliefs, including the Christian faith, into their own compartments and keeping them neatly tucked away from each other, Gould intended to resolve potential problems and conflicts before they can even begin.

However, this very tidy separationist approach has a fatal flaw—it involves a complete misunderstanding of the Christian faith.

1. Getting the Facts Right About the Christian Faith

CONTRARY TO THE VIEW HELD BY THE SEPARATIONISTS, the Christian faith is not just interested in values and meaning but in facts as well. The problem with separationism can be explained in a single sentence: ***The Christian faith considers facts as having value and meaning, and values and meaning as factual.*** Let us look more closely at what this sentence means, and why it makes the separationist approach to science and faith a dead end.

The Christian faith considers facts as having value and meaning. The full value of facts can only be understood in the light of faith in God. Faith in God involves the recognition that all things are *theocentric*—that is, they are centered on God because (a) they are created by God, and (b) they are created for a purpose known to God. To know about a thing without knowing (a) and (b) is to only know it in a limited sense. This does not mean that science must accept things on faith—as a method, it must not. But it does mean that the Christian faith and science really do talk about many of the same realities, contrary to separationism. The Christian faith, like science, also reveals certain facts, and calls us to put our faith in them. The Incarnation of the Son of God, who became man in the womb of the Virgin Mary, is proclaimed by both Scripture and the Church to be a real event. It is a historical fact, something that really happened in history, although it is certainly not a fact that can be ascertained through the scientific method.

The Coronation of the Virgin
The Christian faith, like science, also reveals certain facts, and calls us to put our faith in them.

This is also true of other elements of faith as well, such as the belief that God is a Trinity of Persons, that Jesus rose from the dead, and that his mother was assumed body and soul into heaven. If science is about facts, and religion is only about values and meaning, then the Christian faith could never teach that such beliefs actually are true.

The Christian faith considers values and meaning as factual. That is, they are not mere opinions, which change from person to person. Values and meaning are not human daydreams projected onto a neutral landscape of facts which science lays out for us. The statement "murder is evil" is no less true than the statement "the water molecule contains two hydrogen atoms." Its truth just happens to be known in a different way than by looking into a microscope.

The objectivity and factuality of values and meaning has often been overlooked by the modern world, but has never been overlooked by the Catholic Church. In the words of **Pope Benedict XVI**:

> **We must again learn to understand that the great ethical insights of mankind are just as rational and just as true as—*indeed more true than*—the experimental knowledge of the realm of the natural sciences and technology. They are more true, because they...have a more decisive significance for the humanity of man.**[40]

At a conference on the human genome project, **Cardinal Camillo Ruini** (1931-) expressed exactly this point in relation to science's ability to map out the entire genetic information present in human beings. The map of the human genome is being drawn, he told his audience, just at the point when it seems that humans may have lost the map of the meaning and value of life itself.[41] The point is clear—there is a real map to life, just as there is now a real map of the human genome. Science and the Christian faith both really tell us about *what is*—not just what we happen to feel or imagine.

Cardinal Camillo Ruini
"To know man better from the scientific point of view is not automatically the same as knowing more about the value and meaning of his existence."

In an effort to make peace between science and religion, separationists actually make them strangers. In the process, they correctly understand science, but entirely misunderstand the Christian faith.

E. Looking Ahead

WE HAVE LOOKED AT SOME MISTAKEN IDEAS of the relationship between science and religion: materialism, reductionism, scientism, creationism, and separationism. The first four want to put science and faith into a no-holds-barred cage match, while the last wants to put each in its own little airtight box so they can do no harm to each other. But what is the right relationship? There must be a way of looking at the universe that respects both science and the Christian faith, a way that unites facts, values, and meaning: the "how" and the "why." Can we really let science be science, let faith be faith, and yet still find places where they meet and shed light upon each other? If not, then even if science and the Christian faith seem to be friends, their friendship is false because they are incapable of actually relating positively (or at all!) to one another.

For this task a wisdom wider than modern science, a more foundational use of reason, is necessary. **St. John Paul II** identified *philosophy* as that wider wisdom, and as the bridge that connects science and faith: "The contemporary vision of the cosmos, the concept of time and space, the ever-multiplying discoveries of physics, of chemistry, of biology...demand...a renewal of philosophical thinking among Christians."[42] While science only studies material reality, the scope of philosophy is much larger, including the most universal characteristics of reality and our ability to inquire into this reality and to understand it. Science studies this or that material cause-effect relationship; philosophy studies causality in all its forms. Science studies all the various kinds of existing material beings; philosophy studies being, existence itself. Philosophy is so crucial that the Catholic Church considers it to be an essential part of "the normal exercise of the life of faith in human minds."[43]

A scientific bridge between science and faith would only get us back to material reality, and so it could not shed light on the dogmas of faith. The dogmas of faith, being divine and mysterious, can shed light upon the meaning of material reality, but do not in any way include their own interpretation or connection to scientific discoveries. Philosophy serves as a middle ground, and it is through philosophical reflection on both material reality and ultimate reality that science and faith can find a common ground. In the next chapter we will tap into this wider wisdom and learn the philosophical principles that both distinguish and unite science and the Christian faith and help us to understand God's relationship to the universe as Creator.

VOCABULARY

Define the following terms (or identify the person's significance):

1. **The Christian Faith**
2. **Warfare/Conflict Model**
3. **Science (pre-Whewell definition)**
4. **William Whewell**
5. **John William Draper**
6. ***History of the Conflict Between Religion and Science***
7. **Andrew Dickson White**
8. ***History of the Warfare of Science with Theology in Christendom***
9. **Credibility**
10. **Affirmation**
11. **Technology**
12. **Materialism**
13. **Methodological Materialism**
14. **Reductionism**
15. **Methodological Reductionism**
16. **Scientism (Scientific Atheism)**
17. **Dogma (Doctrine)**
18. **Mystery**
19. **Literalistic Creationism**
20. **Independence Model**
21. **Separationism**
22. **Stephen Jay Gould**
23. **Theocentric**
24. **Philosophy**

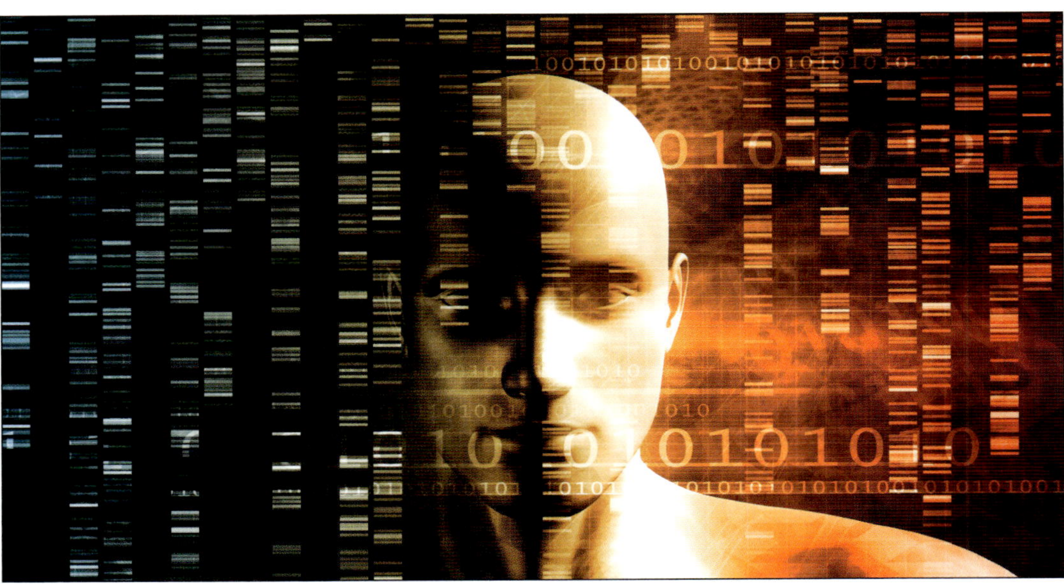

"The map of the human genome is being drawn just at the point when it seems that humans may have lost the map of the meaning and value of life itself." —Cardinal Ruini

STUDY QUESTIONS

Section A

1. How is the relationship between the Christian faith and science much like a human relationship that is plagued by false rumors? What contemporary evidence substantiates this claim?

2. List and briefly describe the three elements of the social context in which the conflict thesis originated.

3. How does John William Draper reveal his anti-Catholic bias in his book? How can bias against a racial, religious, or cultural group create an obstacle to good history-writing?

Section B

4. What is the truth about the historical relationship between the Christian faith and modern science? What roles do each play in the relationship?

5. Distinguish between outright materialism and methodological materialism. How is the latter required by science based on its object of study? Is this a problem from the perspective of faith? Explain.

6. Distinguish between outright reductionism and methodological reductionism. How is the latter required to an extent by science based on its object of study? Is this a problem from the perspective of faith? Explain.

7. Explain the two key elements of the Christian faith which scientism rejects. Why is this rejection misguided?

8. Why is scientism a flawed position from the perspective of logic?

Section C

9. Summarize the response of the three most recent Popes to literalistic creationism. What do these responses have in common?

10. What motivates literalistic creationists to reject modern science? How is this a misunderstanding of a crucial theological truth?

Section D

11. Why is separationism a false approach to "reconciling" the Christian faith and science from the perspective of facts?

12. Why is separationism a false approach to "reconciling" the Christian faith and science from the perspective of values and meaning?

Rev. Dr. William Whewell (1794-1866) English polymath, scientist, Anglican priest, philosopher, theologian, and science historian. He researched ocean tides, published works in the disciplines of mechanics, physics, geology, astronomy, and economics. As a wordsmith, Whewell contributed the terms *scientist* and *physicist* (and many more) to the English vocabulary.

PRACTICAL EXERCISES

1. The various positions on the relationship between faith and science discussed in this chapter are present in our society today, and reveal a widespread disagreement about that relationship. Speak with someone outside of your class about the relationship between faith and science. List the various positions, and ask him or her what position most closely resembles his or her own and why. Without judging or identifying the person, explain the reasons for his or her answer to the class.

2. Watch the video "Science and Religion: The Draper-White Conflict Thesis" (4 minutes, 59 seconds, *mtfresources.org/videos*). What role does fear play in the context within which Draper and White originated their conflict thesis? Do you think fear plays a role in current discussions about science and religion?

3. Watch the atheist propaganda video "Top Ten Creationist Arguments" (7 minutes, 55 seconds, *mtfresources.org/videos*). In light of our consideration of the "How/Why" distinction, the conflict/warfare model, and literalistic creationism, consider the tangle of anti-God rhetoric and anticreationism arguments in this video. Must the correct scientific explanations given as responses to creationism also be considered as disproving the existence of God? Why or why not?

John William Draper (1811-1882)
Draper alleges conflict after conflict between the Catholic Church and science while offering little or no evidence.

Andrew Dickson White (1832-1918)
The errors and misrepresentations White and Draper foisted upon their readers are now routinely repeated as historical facts by people who are not historians.

Endnotes – Chapter Two

1. This presentation was given on February 14, 2014 at a symposium for diocesan bishops and diocesan superintendents of Catholic education entitled "Science and Human Dignity" and cosponsored by the USCCB and the Institute for Church Life, University of Notre Dame, South Bend, IN. The video of the presentation is available at: *youtu.be/OaS1SV7xwWQ*.
2. Mark Gray, "Young People Are Leaving the Faith. Here's Why," *Our Sunday Visitor Newsweekly* (August 27, 2016), available at: *www.osvnews.com/2016/08/27/young-people-are-leaving-the-faith-heres-why/*.
3. E.O. Wilson, *Consilience: The Unity of Knowledge* (New York: Knopf, 1998), 6.
4. Lawrence M. Principe, "The Warfare Thesis" Lecture, *Science and Religion*, downloaded from *www.thegreatcourses.com/courses/science-and-religion.html*.
5. Sydney Ross, "Scientist: the story of a word," *Annals of Science* 18:2 (1962): 69.
6. Ibid., 71-72.
7. John William Draper, *History of the Conflict between Religion and Science*, Vol. XII, The International Scientific Series (New York: D. Appleton, 1874), vi.
8. Ibid., x-xi.
9. Principe, "The Warfare Thesis."
10. Draper, 63.
11. St. Augustine, *De Genesi ad Litteram*, Book II.21.
12. Draper, 367.
13. Principe, "The Warfare Thesis."
14. Andrew Dickson White, "Letter to Ezra Cornell," August 3, 1869, as quoted in James R. Moore, *The Post-Darwinian Controversies: A Study of the Protestant Struggle to Come to Terms with Darwin in Great Britain and America* (Cambridge: Cambridge University Press, 1979), 35.
15. Andrew Dickson White, *History of the Warfare of Science with Religion*, Vol. I (New York: D. Appleton, 1894), 48.
16. Matt J. Rossano, "How the Myth of the Flat-Earth Dogma Started the Religion-Science War," *The Huffington Post Blog* (September 9, 2016), available at *www.huffingtonpost.com/matt-j-rossano/starting-a-war-with-a-fla_b_707471.html*.
17. Ted Davis and Stephen Snobelen, "New Atheists and the 'Conflict' between Science and Religion," BioLogos, January 05, 2017, *biologos.org/blogs/ted-davis-reading-the-book-of-nature/new-atheists-and-the-conflict-between-science-and-religion*.
18. Brad Johnson, "Obama: GOP Candidates 'Would Have Been Founding Members Of The Flat Earth Society'," YouTube, 15 Mar. 2012, *www.youtube.com/watch?v=Rsz3uLxTwQs*.
19. John F. Haught, *Science and Religion: From Conflict to Conversation* (New York/Mahwah: Paulist, 1995), 9. [Haught's original terminology is "confirmation" and "credibility"; I have altered the former term to "affirmation."]
20. See *www.catholicscientists.org*.
21. Stephen M. Barr, *Modern Physics and Ancient Faith* (Notre Dame: University of Notre Dame Press, 2003), 66-68; cf. Wilson, 31.
22. Haught, *Science and Religion*, 22.
23. Loren Eiseley, *Darwin's Century: Evolution and the Men Who Discovered It* (Garden City, NY: Anchor Books: 1961), 62 [italics mine].
24. John F. Haught, *God After Darwin: A Theology of Evolution* (Boulder, CO: Westview, 2000), 1.
25. Richard C. Lewontin, "Billions and Billions of Demons," *The New York Review of Books*, January 9, 1997, *www.nybooks.com/articles/1997/01/09/billions-and-billions-of-demons/*.
26. W. Norris Clarke, *The One and the Many: A Contemporary Thomistic Metaphysics* (Notre Dame: University of Notre Dame Press, 2001), 247.
27. St. John Paul II, "Address to a group of scientists gathered to honor the centenary of the birth of Albert Einstein" (September 28, 1979), *inters.org/John-Paul-II-deep-harmony*.
28. John F. Haught, *Deeper than Darwin: The Prospect for Religion in an Age of Evolution* (Boulder: Westview, 2003), 32.
29. Barr, *Modern Physics*, 11-15.
30. CCC 88, 94.
31. Barr, *Modern Physics*, 11-12.
32. *Dei Filius*, 3: DS 3009, as quoted by Barr, *Modern Physics*, 12.
33. Barr, *Modern Physics*, 14-15.
34. Ken Ham, "Creation," *answersingenesis.org/creation/*.
35. St. John Paul II, Address to the Pontifical Academy of the Sciences, October 3, 1981, *www.ewtn.com/library/PAPALDOC/JP2COSM.HTM*.
36. Pope Benedict XVI, Easter Vigil Homily, April 23, 2011, *w2.vatican.va/content/benedict-xvi/en/homilies/2011/documents/hf_ben-xvi_hom_20110423_veglia-pasquale.html*.
37. Pope Francis, Address to the Pontifical Academy of the Sciences, October 27, 2014, *w2.vatican.va/content/francesco/en/speeches/2014/october/documents/papa-francesco_20141027_plenaria-accademia-scienze.html*.
38. Ian G. Barbour, *Religion and Science: Historical and Contemporary Issues* (New York: HarperCollins, 1997), 84.
39. Stephen J. Gould, *Dinosaur in a Haystack* (New York: Harmony, 1995), 48.
40. Joseph Ratzinger, *A Turning Point for Europe? The Church in the Modern World—Assessment and Forecast* (San Francisco: Ignatius Press, 1994), 35-36.
41. "Genome Known, but Meaning of Life Lost," in *Zenit: The World Seen from Rome Daily Dispatch*, November 28, 2005. Available from *www.zenit.org*.
42. St. John Paul II, "Address to a Colloquium on Science, Philosophy and Theology," September 5, 1986.
43. Ibid.

Chapter Three
The Christian Doctrine of Creation: A Wisdom Wider than Science

How do our models of the universe affect our conception of God?

What is the Christian understanding of God as Creator?

How does human creativity help us understand God as Creator of the universe?

Though we speak much we cannot reach the end,
and the sum of our words is: "He is the all."
Where shall we find strength to praise him?
For he is greater than all his works. (Sir 43:27-28)

With these words **Ben Sira** (second century BC), the Jewish author of the Old Testament Book of Sirach, set a standard for Christian theology. Christians believe that God is the perfect, unlimited source of all truth, goodness, and beauty, and so he is able to be completely present to the universe as the cause of its existence and of all its beings, laws, and physical causes. In the words of this divinely inspired author, God should be called "the ALL" (Sir 43:27), because God is the cause of everything in a way more profound and more essential than physical, material causes.

And yet, the author of Sirach tells us, God is also greater than all his works, wholly different from them, and so cannot be understood as being and acting in the same way that creatures exist and act. God's relationship to the universe is not like the relationships his creatures have with each other. He doesn't have a "role" to play in the universe, for he is the Creator of everything in it. He is infinitely greater than all things, even as he is more intimately close to them than they are to themselves.

"The King of kings and Lord of lords, who alone has immortality and dwells in unapproachable light, whom no man has ever seen or can see. To him be honor and eternal dominion. Amen." (1 Tm 6:15-16)

Other passages in Sacred Scripture make it very clear that our limited human conceptions can never fully express this mystery of God's relationship to his creatures. **St. Paul** described God as the one "who alone has immortality and dwells in unapproachable light, whom no man has ever seen or can see" (1 Tm 6:16). The prophet **Isaiah** reveals God's perspective on divine mercy:

> "My thoughts are not your thoughts,
> neither are your ways my ways, says the LORD.
> For as the heavens are higher than the earth,
> so are my ways higher than your ways
> and my thoughts than your thoughts." (Is 55:8-9)

The humility involved in this Christian understanding of God is beautifully represented in a fictional dialogue written in 1444 by the philosopher, theologican, and bishop **Cardinal Nicholas of Cusa** (1401-1464). He called this work "On the Hidden God" (*De Deo Abscondito*). In it a pagan approaches a Christian whom he finds at prayer. When the pagan asks the Christian to identify the God he worships, he receives a startling answer:

> The *Pagan* spoke: I see that you have most devoutly prostrated yourself and are shedding tears of love—not hypocritical tears but heartfelt ones.
> Who are you, I ask?
>
> *Christian*: I am a Christian.
>
> *Pagan*: What are you worshiping?
>
> *Christian*: God.
>
> *Pagan*: Who is [this] God whom you worship?
>
> *Christian*: I don't know.
>
> *Pagan*: How is it that you worship so seriously that of which you have no knowledge?
>
> *Christian*: Because I am without knowledge [of Him], I worship Him.[1]

Nicholas of Cusa
German philosopher, theologian, jurist, and astronomer. One of the first German proponents of Renaissance humanism.

The paradox is obvious—only a God who *cannot* be fully known, who is inexpressible Truth, could be the true God and worthy of our adoration.

In this chapter, we will see how this humble approach to God was replaced by new and faulty conceptions of God during the Scientific Revolution. These conceptions ultimately led to the warfare model discussed above and to scientific atheism. Then we will consider how to return to the orthodox Christian conception of God with the help of the philosophy of **St. Thomas Aquinas**. In his thought we will see that the Christian approach to God represents an important framework for science because of its respect for the integrity of creation, which is expressed in St. Thomas's distinction between the primary causality of God and the secondary causality of creatures, commonly known as *the principle of double agency*. This is the most important philosophical principle for the harmony between science and faith, and shall be explained in depth. For now, simply note that our distinction between "how" and "why" explanations will be deepened by a closer look at the concept of existence, with St. Thomas as our guide.

We will also consider a conception of God that can help us to better understand God's relationship to the universe in the true, Christian sense: the relationship of an author to a novel or a play. Lastly, we will move from philosophy to theology, and begin to reflect upon the Christian doctrine of God as Creator, whose only motive for causing the universe is to communicate his goodness.

As we will see, God's infinite love, not merely his perfect knowledge (omniscience) or power (omnipotence), is the foundation of all creation.

To begin, let us go back to the Scientific Revolution to see how a great scientific genius misunderstood God's relationship to the universe.

A. Scientific Atheism in Context: Newton's Laws and Newton's Flaws

1. Newton's Laws: The Man Who Embodied the Scientific Revolution

"NATURE AND NATURE'S LAWS LAY HID IN NIGHT: God said, 'Let Newton be!' and all was light." The great English poet **Alexander Pope** (1688-1744) wrote this epitaph to be inscribed on the tomb of **Sir Isaac Newton** (1643-1727), and captured in two lines the immense importance of Newton to the history of modern science. In the words of particle physicist **Stephen Barr**,

> **One could almost say that Sir Isaac Newton *was* the Scientific Revolution... Newton was a towering peak. There was no rival to him in physics until the twentieth century. One may think of everything that went before Newton as having set the stage for his great breakthroughs, and everything that came after him—until the twentieth century—as having exploited those breakthroughs.**[2]

No student today makes it through high school without encountering Newton's *universal laws of motion and his universal law of gravity*. What makes these ideas so important can be guessed from the word *universal* that is used to describe them. For the first time in history a human being had discovered laws that describe all earthly and celestial motion and that allow all physical cause and effect relationships to be understood with mathematical formulas. With Newton, science broke through descriptions of individual phenomena in the material universe to a deep understanding that unified the way we think about the earth, the solar system, and beyond.[3]

Unlike the apple which fell and bumped his head in the famous event that first caused him to ponder the law of gravity, Newton's immense breakthrough did not fall out of the sky. His thought rested upon a shift in thinking that had already occurred in the centuries prior to his birth. Scientific pioneers whom Newton greatly admired, such as **Galileo Galilei** (1564-1642), **Johannes Kepler** (1571-1630), and **Rene Descartes** (1596-1650), had found it very effective to think of the universe in mechanical and mathematical terms in order to better understand it. Newton recognized that their successes came not only from their genius but also because they worked from this kind of approach, and so he set out to describe all natural phenomena the way one might describe a clock or an engine.[4] His enormous success set science firmly upon this path of mechanical thinking, a path it was to follow exclusively for more than one and one-half centuries.

Newton set out to describe all natural phenomena the way one might describe a clock or an engine. His enormous success set science firmly upon this path of mechanical thinking.

Thinking of the universe as a machine is a great example of *scientific modeling*, a process by which scientific thinkers use something they understand to model things they do not understand. In this case Newton and his predecessors chose for their model one of the greatest technological innovations of medieval European culture: the mechanical clock, a device that could tick away accurately for years thanks to its hidden gears, cogs, and wheels. It was a stroke of genius, and the mechanistic "clock" conception of the universe greatly benefited every area of the natural sciences. For example, much of what we know about anatomy comes from modeling living organisms as machines, an idea first proposed by Descartes.[5] In the words of **Lawrence Principe**, "In living organisms, the levers and pulleys were to be revealed by anatomy and the new microscope. Individual organs became mechanical devices; the heart, a pump, the kidneys, filters, and indeed the whole body, a mass of plumbing and rigging."[6]

But while extremely helpful, a scientific model is, still, only a model. The universe is not a machine, nor is it a living organism, even though they both have qualities that can be effectively modeled as such. No one model can capture everything about the universe, nor should a scientific model of the universe be simply turned into a theological model. But this is something that is easy to overlook, as even the great Isaac Newton unfortunately did.

2. Newton's Flaws and the Rise of Scientific Atheism

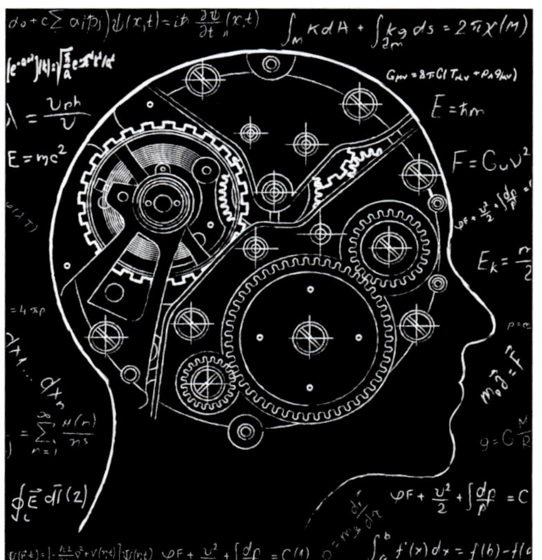

FOR ALL HIS GREATNESS AS A SCIENTIST, Newton was much less gifted as a theologian and a philosopher. A devoutly religious man who wanted to speak of God as insightfully as he spoke of the universe, Newton unwisely adopted the same approach in theology as he did in science. Just as he described the universe using the model of a clocklike machine, he described God as an all-powerful clockmaker, engineer, or mechanic, whose primary connection to all things was that of a craftsman who puts parts together in ingenious designs.[7] He believed that God did this through the instrument of space and that he occasionally had to "rewind" the clock of the universe, giving the planets occasional adjustments to keep them in line in their orbits around the sun.[8] He insisted that the universe occupied infinite space and time, and if there were ever a time that space did not exist, then neither would God have existed.[9] This made the Creator of space dependent upon the existence of space, which is absurd.

Newton also involved God in the universe by reference to gravity. Gravity involves the immediate action of things upon each other without physical contact; however, because of Newton's universal application of the "clock" model for a scientific understanding of the physical universe, he was unable to conceive of gravity outside of this mechanistic framework. So Newton supposed that gravity must be a force produced by God acting directly within the universe, since it was unclear what other origin it could possibly have.[10] This gave God a constant role in the universe and seemed to be irrefutable evidence against atheism, evidence that would later be explained away when Einstein showed that gravity is not a mechanistic force at all, but is the effect of the curvature of space and time upon material objects.

Charles Darwin's evolutionary biology challenged the role Newton and others had assigned to God within the universe.

Newton's theological ideas would become almost as influential as his scientific breakthroughs. As later scientists began to be able to explain things that Newton could not, they imagined that they had replaced God with natural explanations. Actually, they had just squeezed Newton's clockmaker "God of the gaps" *out of* the gaps, where Newton had placed him. So, for example, the great French scientist **Pierre Simon Laplace** (1749-1827), when asked by his emperor, Napoleon Bonaparte, about why he never mentioned the Creator in his five volume work on astronomy and celestial mechanics, reportedly responded: "Sire, I had no need of that hypothesis."[11]

Another gap was closed in 1859 when a natural explanation for living things was given by **Charles Darwin** (1809-1882) and his evolutionary biology. Up to that time, many thought that the origins of living things required divine miraculous intervention, that is, a clockmaker who not only put parts together but who mysteriously made his machines capable of sense and motion. It seemed to many that God's existence had been challenged, that God no longer had a "role" to fill. Eight years after Darwin first published his theory, the atheist poet **Matthew Arnold** (1822-1888) would mourn the loss of faith in his poem "Dover Beach," comparing it to the ebbing away of seawater at low tide:

> **The Sea of Faith**
> **Was once, too, at the full, and round earth's shore**
> **Lay like the folds of a bright girdle furled.**
> **But now I only hear**
> **Its melancholy, long, withdrawing roar,**
> **Retreating, to the breath**
> **Of the night-wind, down the vast edges drear**
> **And naked shingles of the world.**[12]

And yet the only thing that had really been challenged by these new scientific discoveries was the role Newton and others had assigned to God *within* the universe. As we observed above, looking for roles for God to fill *within the universe* is a misconception of who God is, as we shall see in more detail below when we discuss the principle of double agency.

Newton's clockmaker God is very different than the understanding of God that is at the heart of Christianity.

Newton's clockmaker God is very different than the understanding of God that is at the heart of Christianity. As we saw above, traditional Christian thought understood God as entirely other and different than the universe, not filling any physical roles but causing all things to exist. But for Newton and many who followed him, God was assumed to be an explanation for *how* the universe works. As we learned in Chapter One and will further examine in the next section on the thought of St. Thomas Aquinas, this is bad theology. In the words of **St. John Paul II**: "The theological teaching of the Bible, like the doctrine of the Church . . . does not seek so much to teach us the *how* of things, as rather the *why* of things."[13]

Over the rest of the seventeenth and through the following two centuries, new, flawed theologies began to emerge, all of which were based upon the error of trying to make God fit the mechanistic model of the universe. Some, such as Thomas Jefferson and some of his contemporaries, adopted *deism*, putting God at the beginning of the universe to set up the machine and then restricting God's present action simply to legislating values and morality and his future action to the punishment and reward of behavior in the afterlife. Other thinkers, such as the American poet and philosopher **Henry David Thoreau** (1817-1862) began to merge God and the universe, a belief system called *pantheism*, positing the universe to be God's "body." But these half-baked theologies were easily debunked; nonetheless, the descent of Western culture into widespread materialism, reductionism, and atheism began.

What had happened can easily be summarized in the following way: *Newton and his followers had turned his model of the universe into a mentality, reducing all of reality, including God, to fit into the mold of his mechanical model.* This model fits the goals of science very well, and even today remains essential to science, but it was too small for theology and too narrow for the attainment of true wisdom. Despite his unlimited power, Newton's God is a tiny god, acting the way material beings and forces act. A God who intervenes to rewind the clock of the universe, and makes things attract each other through direct divine power, is a God that is doing things that natural forces can do all on their own, not the God who is the Source of nature and its laws.

Newton failed to recognize that the truth about God requires that we recognize the limitations of our scientific and theological models. Ironically, even the truth about the universe requires more than is offered by the mechanistic model, as would be discovered in the profound scientific achievements of the twentieth century. Science has pushed beyond the confines of this single model in a way that hearkens back to conceptions of the universe that were either unknown or rejected by theologians during the Scientific Revolution. To forge a better perspective, let us examine a different way of modeling God's relationship to the universe.

B. Expanded Wisdom: Connecting the Cosmos to the Creator

1. The Art of Analogy

HOW CAN WE MODEL GOD'S RELATIONSHIP to the universe in a way that respects the integrity of the natural world and also does justice to what God has revealed to us about himself? Since God is greater than the universe and everything in it, we can only do so by creating a limited comparison in which there are similarities but also differences. Such a comparison is called an *analogy*, and the two things compared are called *analogues* of each other. An analogy exists when a property that is shared by two or more subjects—such as beauty, strength, or goodness—is used to show some similarity between them.[14] Every analogy involves both similarity and difference, but what makes any analogy a good analogy is awareness not only of the similarity it reveals but also the difference between the things compared. This is especially true of theological analogies; God is infinitely greater than any of his creatures, and so the dissimilarity between God and creatures will always be greater than the similarity.

Despite the infinite difference, the Christian faith teaches that there are real similarities between God and creatures, and so Christian theology thrives on finding good *analogues*, things comparable to God, among creatures, using them to explore divine mysteries. We find numerous analogies in Sacred Scripture in which the characteristics of God's creatures are used to help reveal something about God. In the Book of Wisdom, for example, beauty in nature is given as a quality that is *analogous*, similar to, divine beauty: "From the greatness and the beauty of created things their original author, *by analogy*, is seen" (Wis 13:5). In other words, there are things in the world that delight us by their beauty and grandeur, and *by analogy*, these things show us God who is the "author of beauty," although only imperfectly: "Far more excellent is the Lord than these" (Wis 13:3).[15]

The incredible order we see in the universe is the product of the wisdom of God, and so it is helpful to think of God as the Source of order in the way an ingenious mechanic, inventor, or engineer produces a sophisticated machine.

Returning momentarily to Newton and the many who followed him, we can say that the real problem with their machine-maker/engineer model of God is that they did not limit their suggestion of similarity with the recognition of difference. They had what is called a *univocal* conception of God, in which they claimed to describe God *in the same way* ("univocal," meaning "one voice") that one might describe an apple tree or a galaxy. In their univocal theology, God is not like an all-powerful engineer, he *actually is* an all-powerful engineer who puts things together and maintains them the way human engineers do. Had Newton used the engineer model of God as an analogy, this would have been fine; many great theologians before him had done so. As we saw in Chapter One, the incredible order we see in the universe is the product of the wisdom of God, and so it is helpful to think of God as the Source of order in the way an ingenious mechanic, inventor, or engineer produces a sophisticated machine. The problem is not the model Newton used. The problem was his expansion of that model into an exhaustive description.

An analogical, Christian approach is humble before the mystery of God, suggesting insights but never total comprehension. A univocal approach tries to *resolve* the mystery of God into something fully understandable to the human mind. The art of analogy is the art by which we can begin to understand God, as well as acknowledge that he is ineffable, inexpressible Truth.

In order to create a proper analogy between God and creatures, we must note the infinite difference between them. To grasp that difference, we must go all the way "down," beyond nature, to the very concept of existence. To do so, we need the help of a wisdom wider than science, the wisdom of philosophy.

2. Philosophy and Existence: The Principle of Double Agency

SO FAR IN THIS BOOK I HAVE OFFERED the "how" and "why" distinction several times between the knowledge science gives about the universe and the knowledge given by Divine Revelation, faith, and theology. But philosophy offers a third kind of knowledge about God and the universe—God is not only the "why" behind the universe but also the reason "that" it exists at all. God is "He who Is," and as such he causes all things that exist to exist, regardless of whether such things existed in the universe's first moments or exist even today or will a million years from now. So, in order to think about God, we must ask the question, "What is existence?" Thankfully, the branch of philosophy called *metaphysics*, which deals with the most fundamental truths about reality, tackles this question as its primary object of study.

Creation of the Animals, Genesis 1:24.
The most basic relationship between God and the universe is that God is the Giver of existence to all things.

Existence is the first, most fundamental "property" of every being, which is why we call them "beings." Even something I imagine, such as a unicorn, has a kind of existence—the unicorn exists as something thought and imagined by human beings—it has *mental being*. My dog Sophie, by contrast, is not simply something I imagine—she has *real being*. The first and most basic thing about Sophie, the one thing she shares in common with the whole universe and everything in it, is obviously not her cuteness nor her dogginess. It is her *existence*, her *being*—if Sophie did not exist, then she would not be a part of the universe at all. All things, even thoughts, are connected by existence and share in it as a common characteristic in different ways. Whatever else a thing is, it is only *what* it is *because* it is. *If you can say something true about being, about existence, then you have said something true about every existing thing in a single statement.*

Sophie has real being, but she *is not* Being itself. If Sophie were Being itself, then everything that ever existed would have to share in, or participate in, Sophie, just as we would say that all things, including Sophie, insofar as they truly exist, participate in Being itself! But there was a time not long ago when Sophie did not exist. Her being is something that she *has*, not something she *is*, because if Sophie *is* by nature her being or her existence, then it would pertain to the nature of Sophie to always exist, to always be, which she clearly did not just a few years ago and will not in the years to come. And she did not give existence to herself—she exists "only if" she is given existence. Existence comes to all things from without—it is like a gift.

You may be asking, "What is "Being itself"? A being like Sophie is something that *has* being, but what *is* Being? From where do all beings get their existence? To be Being itself is to exist necessarily, and to be the uncaused Cause, the source of being for all things, because all things do not and cannot give themselves existence. It is illogical to say that any given finite thing can give existence to itself, since it would have to first exist, in order to give itself existence, which is self-contradictory. Being itself is "the infinite fullness of pure unlimited existence, and the one ultimate Source of all being."[16] *God is Being subsisting in itself.*

St. Thomas Aquinas teaches us that God causes all things to be, and so God is rightly called the *Primary Cause*.

We are not far from theology here; this philosophical insight is also revealed in Sacred Scripture. When Moses asked God for his name, the LORD responded, "I AM WHO I AM" (Ex 3:14). And, when the Son of God becomes incarnate, he tells those Jews who were skeptical of his authority and origins, "Truly, truly, I say to you, before Abraham was, I am" (Jn 8:58).

Above and beyond any other consideration, the most basic relationship between God and the universe is that God is the Giver of existence to all things. God is not simply perfect in himself. He also makes all things, and all the perfections of those things, *real*. This means that God truly does cause all things, but not in the way Newton supposed. He causes them not by crafting them like a watchmaker but by thinking of them and so willing them to exist.

The great philosopher and theologian, who most fully developed this insight to explain God's relationship to the universe, was **St. Thomas Aquinas**. According to St. Thomas, God causes all things to be, and so God is rightly called the *Primary Cause*. But in causing all things to be, God causes them in such a way that they are able to be causes of each other in various ways. For example, parents are the real biological causes of their children, giving them a particular *kind* of existence as this or that kind of animal. But it is God who gives *being* to both the parents and their offspring. God causes all dogs to be real, but Sophie's dog parents really did cause Sophie to be the kind of dog that she is. The universe is made up of *secondary causes*, which are the very kinds of causes studied by scientists. St. Thomas taught that God set things up this way so that creatures could share in his own goodness, by being causes like (but not exactly like!) God himself: "The Primary Cause, by the preeminence of its goodness, gives other beings not only their existence, but also their existence as causes."[17]

This means that, for every cause and effect relationship in the universe, there are at least two causes: God the Primary Cause and whatever secondary cause or causes are involved. It also means that God and those secondary causes can really be called causes, but only in entirely different and complementary ways, such that they are *never* in competition with each other. This is called *the principle of double agency*. St. Thomas explains this in one of his greatest works, the *Summa Contra Gentiles*:

> **[An] effect is not attributed to a natural cause and to divine power in such a way that it is partly done by God, and partly by the natural agent; rather, it is wholly done by both... [for the] same God who transcends the created order is also intimately... present within that order as upholding all causes in their causing.[18]**

Principle of double agency: "wholly done by both." God causes things in a way that no creature can cause them, and creatures cause things in their own genuine way.

The key words in this quote are "wholly done by both"—God causes things in a way that no creature can cause them, and creatures cause things in their own genuine way that is *really and truly their own*. God is not the immediate source of "how" answers about the universe (although God certainly does know all of the answers as Creator!); "how" questions can only be answered with reference to the inner workings of his creation by his creatures. Likewise, no creature can answer the question of its very existence; that question can only be answered by God the Creator. God holds all creatures in being even as they cause each other.

We might be tempted to ask, "*How* does God cause creatures to exist and the universe to be real?" But, this is dead-end thinking. "How" answers involve processes that occur in time and can be studied by science. But God is eternal and unchanging; time is something he creates; his reality is a perfect *NOW* with no past or future. In his perfect eternity God wills his creatures to be, and because he does so, they are. No process is involved in divine creation, as we will see in more detail later. As St. Thomas says, God is "the cause hidden from every human being."[19]

St. Thomas explains God's relationship to the natural world with an analogy which brings to mind Newton's clockmaker/mechanic model of God but with a crucial difference: "It is clear that nature is nothing but a certain kind of art, i.e., the divine art, impressed upon things.... It is as if the shipbuilder were able to give to timbers that by which they would move themselves to take the form of a ship."[20] Here, God is not inserted as a "how" answer, as he is in Newton's theology; St. Thomas does not give God a role in "building" the universe. Instead, creatures (pictured here as wooden timbers) are caused to exist by God *with* the ability to bring about what God intends.

Why does anything exist at all?
The more science can explain, the more it shows God's majesty as Creator.

In another work St. Thomas uses the analogy of a great teacher to explain why it is fitting that God makes the world in such a way that its cause and effect relationships are real:

> **It is a greater perfection for a thing to be good in itself and also the cause of goodness in others, than only to be good in itself. Therefore God so governs things that He makes some of them to be causes of others...; as a teacher, who not only imparts knowledge to his pupils, but also gives them the capacity to teach others.[21]**

From God's perspective, it wasn't enough for him to cause creatures to exist; he wanted to establish them in real causal relationships with each other. And so, unlike Newton, St. Thomas recognizes that God is not the cause of this or that force or thing, such as gravity or the human eye, but of "the all," establishing the universe as a vast system of real causes and effects, all with their own integrity. The cosmos is not a thing that God must maintain by intermittently interfering with the universe's natural development, nor by miraculously producing this or that natural phenomenon.

We can now see how the principle of double agency is so hospitable to science, unlike literalistic creationism. The principle of double agency preserves scientific and theological explanations from bleeding into, substituting for, or competing with, each other. Scientists rightly become upset when believers try to stick God into the processes of the universe as a "how" explanation; recall **Richard Lewontin's** commitment to materialism to avoid "a Divine Foot in the door," which we learned about in Chapter Two. And, yet, materialism is not necessary to protect the integrity of the natural world. In the Christian understanding, God is the cause of the existence, the reality, of all things, not an all-powerful, magical substitute for natural causes. He answers the ultimate questions: "Why does anything exist at all?" and, "Why is the universe orderly and yet open?" not questions like, "How did mammals evolve?" or, "How did the universe develop during the Big Bang?" Science takes care of those questions, and the more science can explain, the more it shows God's majesty as Creator.

For their part, many believers become upset when atheists, such as **Christopher Hitchens** (1949-2011), reject the existence of God because they assume that science has squeezed the "God of the gaps" *out of* the gaps, as it were, in our knowledge of how the universe works. "Thanks to the telescope and the microscope, religion no longer offers an explanation of anything important," declared Hitchens, as if that settles everything.[22] That is a problem for Newton's God, but not the God of Christianity. If we truly understand God in St. Thomas's way we would expect, like the Christian in **Nicholas of Cusa's** dialogue, not a God who explains this or that natural phenomenon, but who, beyond our greatest genius and wildest dreams, is the ultimate reason for the existence of all things, constantly upholding them in being, allowing and enabling them to cause each other in a beautiful, sometimes perplexing, always amazing, universe. Any being that could be detected with Hitchens's telescope or microscope would be too small and too creaturely to be Truth and Being Itself.

3. The Mind of the Maker: God as Playwright

AS NOTED ABOVE, NO ONE ANALOGY can be fully sufficient for understanding the Creator. So let us add another analogy to our repertoire that highlights God as the transcendent Creator who is greater than everything that he has made, based on the principle of double agency. Here it is: As a playwright is the author of a play, so God is Creator of the universe. The mystery of imagination involved in creating a play has much to add to our understanding of God the Creator.

The universe has a real existence distinct from God. It has real cause-and-effect relationships that can be understood in their own right.

A playwright creates a play not primarily through physical activity, but by conceiving of it in his or her mind. Whether or not the play is ever written, it exists in the mind of the playwright. By causing the play and everything within it to exist through creative genius, a playwright like **William Shakespeare** (1564-1616) makes a world that we also can mentally inhabit, characters we can love or hate, cause and effect relationships that sometimes delight, sometimes shock or sadden. Therefore, the playwright is "the All" to his play; nothing of it would be were it not for the playwright. Every part of it is conceived by the playwright; he or she is the origin of it in its entirety. In a similar, but much greater way, God is Creator of the universe by thinking and loving it into existence in its entirety. In the words of **St. John the Evangelist**, "All things were made through him, and without him was not anything made that was made" (Jn 1:3).

Yet, from the perspective of its events and characters, a play also has a real independence from the playwright's mind. It can be thought about and studied and enjoyed by anyone who reads it or sees it performed, without even knowing who wrote it. The things that happen in the play have their own real causes within the play. It makes no sense to ask, "Did Juliet accept Romeo's offer of marriage because Shakespeare wrote the play that way, or because she freely chose Romeo to be her husband?" These are two very different questions, and they must both be answered not only separately but also affirmatively. Shakespeare did not accept Romeo's offer of marriage; Juliet did so herself. But Shakespeare did conceive of Romeo and Juliet as well as their love for each other.

In a similar way, the universe has a real existence distinct from God. It has real cause-and-effect relationships that can be understood in their own right. It makes no sense to say, "Did the Big Bang cause the universe, or did God cause the universe?" Both explain the universe in their own way; or, as St. Thomas might say, "The universe is wholly done by both but differently." The event of the Big Bang is the beginning of the universe in time, but God is the origin of the universe and the Big Bang from eternity.

We are *in* the story but not entirely *of* the story—we can both live it and know it, although only imperfectly, because the "play" of the universe has not yet reached its conclusion.

Just as a playwright is responsible for the "All" of his play, he is also greater than his play and everything in it. The internal time of the play has no application to the activity of the author. Shakespeare's real life wedding, for example, has no place in *Romeo and Juliet*. Even his creation of the play, his invention of the characters, his thinking out the plot, etc., are not themselves part of the play; they make the play possible, they aren't scenes within it. Also, the playwright can write other plays, create different characters, etc.[23] In a similar way, God is not dependent upon the universe in any way; rather, it is entirely dependent on him. God's own inner life is the perfect fullness of existence, and creation is the sharing in his perfections out of the infinite abundance of his love.

As we said above, no analogy is properly understood if we note similarity without also noting the differences. So let us note some very important differences between a playwright and his or her play, on the one hand, and God and the universe on the other. For one thing, it takes time for a playwright to produce a play. But God is eternal; time is a part of his universe, but he transcends time. To conceive of his play a playwright must use his or her brain, with neurons firing across synapses. The brain is the first "instrument" used to produce the play. But God has no physical parts; he is Perfect Truth, creating the universe simply by knowing and willing it. To communicate his play a playwright must take up a quill or type on a keyboard—both physical activities. But physical activity is something that is part of creation, not of the Creator, who is pure Spirit. God simply wills it, and the universe and all creatures come to be in the manner that God has so ordained.

Moving to theology, there are other differences that can be appreciated in the light of what God has revealed. First, while the saga of *Romeo and Juliet* is completely dependent on Shakespeare, as history and the universe are upon God, Shakespeare is not part of his play. Yet the Author of the universe has not created a story in which he is not involved. The climax of history is the moment when he enters the universe, when God becomes man in Jesus Christ. And the fulfillment of history will be when Jesus returns in glory. This brings out another important difference: unlike the story of *Romeo and Juliet*, the play of the universe is an unfinished one—for humanity, the last dramatic scene has yet to occur.

Another difference is that the characters in *Romeo and Juliet* do not have the ability to read their own story. They only think, feel, and act in imagination—when the story is not being written or read or at least thought about, they do not exist as anything but ink on a page. But the amazing characters in our story—real human beings—do have the ability to read their own story. We can both participate in the drama of the universe, but can also read that drama through reflection, understanding it through science, philosophy, and theology. We are *in* the story but not entirely *of* the story—we can both live it and know it, although only imperfectly, because the "play" of the universe has not yet reached its conclusion.

Finally, God has revealed the reason why he is authoring the universe, the greatest secret of all—his desire to communicate his goodness to us and to unite us to himself in love. This is the widest wisdom—it is at the heart of the Christian doctrine of creation, to which we now turn.

Christians believe that the world is created *ex Trinitate*, "by the Trinity," that is, by all three divine Persons equally and in complete unity—the Father, Son, and Holy Spirit.

C. The Widest Wisdom: The Christian Doctrine of Creation

THE DOCTRINE OF CREATION refers to God, by a love, power, and wisdom that are absolute and unimaginable, bringing into being things distinct from himself. Creation is the beginning of God's Revelation of himself, in which his reality is manifested to his creatures in their very coming to be and continuing in existence. It is the basis of all other Christian doctrines, and is referenced in the very first line of the Christian profession of faith, the **Nicene Creed**, which is professed every Sunday in the Mass: "I believe in one God, the Father almighty, maker of heaven and earth, of all things visible and invisible."[24]

The Christian belief in a Creator God has four distinctive elements:

- First, Christians believe that God creates the world *ex nihilo*, "from nothing."
- Second, Christians believe that God creates the world *cum tempore*, "with time."
- Third, Christians believe that God creates the world *cum libertate*, "freely."
- Fourth, Christians believe that the world is created *ex Trinitate*, "by the Trinity," that is, by all three Persons equally and in complete divine unity.

These elements of the Christian doctrine of creation have been solemnly professed by the Catholic Church at three Ecumenical Councils: **Lateran IV** in 1215, **Florence** in 1442, and **Vatican I** in 1869-1870. *Ecumenical Councils* are assemblies at which bishops from the whole world come together to authoritatively teach in union with the Pope regarding matters of faith and morals—there have been only twenty-one in the two millennia of Church history. Catholics recognize the teachings of the bishops gathered in Ecumenical Councils that are affirmed by the Pope as having "*the charism of infallibility*" from the Holy Spirit. Thanks to this special and unique grace, bishops assembled in Ecumenical Councils together exercise freedom from error in matters of faith and morals, and their teaching requires the unswerving "assent of faith," since God has definitively spoken through them.[25] Therefore, the four elements listed above are integral to the Christian faith and are divinely revealed truths. Let us look at each element to theologically complete the philosophical understanding we have achieved so far.

1. Creation, Not Change: Creation *ex Nihilo*

I HAVE SHARPLY DISTINGUISHED between "how" and "why" questions and answers throughout the first few chapters of this book. The reason for this distinction is the Christian doctrine of creation *ex nihilo*—"from nothing." God uses no preexisting material to create the universe, so no "how" explanations are possible to describe the act of creation; his act of creation causes matter, space, time, and even the very laws which govern the universe to exist and, without this divine action, there would literally be "no thing," as well as no space and no time, whatsoever. In the words of **Lateran IV**,

Creation *ex nihilo* is not a change. Every change involves going from one real state to another. Creation *ex nihilo* refers to the bringing into existence of something wholly new and previously nonexistent.

> **We firmly believe and openly confess that there is only one true God... [who is] the one principle of the universe, Creator of all things invisible and visible, spiritual and corporeal, who from the beginning of time and by His omnipotent power *made from nothing* creatures both spiritual and corporeal, angelic, namely, and mundane, and then human, as it were, common, composed of spirit and body.**[26]

Creation *ex nihilo* is not a change. Every change involves going from one real state to another, as when a sperm and ova unite and cease existing, contributing their genetic material to an entirely new state of being, an embryo. The Big Bang may have been a change from one state to another through a cosmic explosion, but, in the divine act of creation, God causes something to exist out of nothing, and nothing is, by definition, not a state of being. In the words of philosopher **William Carroll**, "Whenever there is a change there must be something that changes . . . [by contrast Divine] creation . . . is the radical causing of the whole existence of whatever exists . . . any thing left entirely to itself, wholly separated from the cause of its existence, would be absolutely nothing."[27]

G.K. Chesterton
"It may be that He [God] has the eternal appetite of infancy; for we have sinned and grown old, and our Father is younger than we."

God, in one divine action from all of eternity, creates and sustains all that exists in its existence and nature, regardless of whether it was the cosmic explosion of the Big Bang and the celestial formation of the billions of galaxies that are flying through space or the evolution of planetary life and the formation of the earth's majestic mountain ranges. Time and space are not determinative factors when it comes to God's divine activity of creation, "for a thousand years in thy sight are but as yesterday when it is past" (Ps 90:4) for God. No one captured this mystery more beautifully than **G.K. Chesterton** (1974-1936):

> **A child kicks his legs rhythmically through excess, not absence, of life. Because children have abounding vitality, because they are in spirit fierce and free, therefore they want things repeated and unchanged. They always say, "Do it again"; and the grownup person does it again until he is nearly dead. For grownup people are not strong enough to exult in monotony. *But perhaps God is strong enough to exult in monotony.* It is possible that God says every morning, "Do it again" to the sun; and every evening, "Do it again" to the moon. It may not be automatic necessity that makes all daisies alike; it may be that God makes every daisy separately, but has never got tired of making them. It may be that He has the eternal appetite of infancy; for we have sinned and grown old, and our Father is younger than we.**[28]

Chesterton's poetic imagery is true—with unlimited divine youthfulness and energy God creates every daisy, causes every sunrise, because God is holding all things in existence through his perfect, eternal act of creation *ex nihilo*. In the words of the Letter to the Hebrews, "By faith we understand that the world was created by the word of God, so that what is seen was made out of things which do not appear" (Heb 11:3).

2. From Beginning to End: Creation *cum Tempore*

ALONG WITH CREATION *EX NIHILO*, the Church's doctrine of creation includes the assertion that the universe was created "with time." In the words of **Lateran IV** above, which were repeated by **Vatican I**, God creates "from the beginning of time." This phrase should be interpreted as identifying *every moment* as the result of the divine act of creation. Since God transcends time, his creative act is itself timeless. The term "with time" (*cum tempore*) has also been used by the Church and her theologians to emphasize that time only exists in relation to creatures, not God. It is a feature of the universe and is itself a created reality that simultaneously accompanies the creation of physical matter.[29]

Creation *cum tempore* means that every moment is the moment of creation, from the first moment of the universe's existence until now. All things are being brought into existence out of nothing by God *right now*. For God, who transcends time, to create at the first moment of the universe is no different than what God is doing at this moment. Right now, as much as at any time in the past, God is saying, "Let there be light," "Let the waters bring forth swarms of living creatures," etc. God's act of creation is not a historical event that happens within time, but it is instead a metaphysical reality describing the universe's dependence on God's eternal act of creating, which transcends time.[30]

Sacred Scripture often refers to "the beginning" to indicate this element of creation (Gn 1:1; Sir 16:16; Jn 1:1). It also refers to God as existing and acting "before the foundation of the world" (Jn 17:24; Eph 1:4; 1 Pt 1:20). Such phrases should be interpreted carefully, lest they lead us to assume that God is in time, rather than the Creator of it. God as "the beginning" is not pointing to something God did "back then" but to God as the timeless origin of all things. The Big Bang is not the moment of creation. Rather, the Big Bang, the present moment, and every moment in between them and every moment to come, are all equally the moment of creation.

The Big Bang, the present moment, and every moment in between them and every moment to come, are all equally the moment of creation.

To help us understand this, recall our playwright analogy. The opening lines of Shakespeare's *Romeo and Juliet* are: "Two households, both alike in dignity, In fair Verona, where we lay our scene, From ancient grudge break to new mutiny, Where civil blood makes civil hands unclean." That is the *beginning* of *Romeo and Juliet*; it references a point in time when the play begins in Shakespeare's fictional Verona. But Shakespeare is the *origin* of those lines and everything else in *Romeo and Juliet*. When Sacred Scripture speaks of God acting "in the beginning" or before it, it is pointing to God as the origin of the universe and history, not to some moment in the past.

It is a doctrine of the Christian faith that the universe has a temporal beginning, as indicated by the words "at the beginning of time" quoted above from **Lateran IV**. This is a topic we will consider in Chapter Seven. But creation *cum tempore* refers primarily to the fact that God transcends time and that all moments of time rely on him as their origin.

3. A Freely Created Universe: Creation *cum Libertate*

IN THE FIRST CREATION ACCOUNT we read that God said, "Let us make man in our image, after our likeness" (Gn 1:26). This very human image of God mulling over the prospect of making human beings points to divine freedom, that God freely created humans and the entire universe. In the words of Psalm 135:6-7, "Whatever the LORD pleases he does, in heaven and on earth, in the seas and all deeps." In the same vein, **Vatican I** states:

> **[The] one true God, by his goodness and almighty power, [brought things into being] not with the intention of increasing his happiness, nor indeed of obtaining happiness, but in order to manifest his perfection by the good things which he bestows on what he creates, [but] by *an absolutely free plan*.**[31]

The act of creation is perfect because it is divine. God has pledged himself to bringing his creation to its fullest possible perfection.

Let us reflect on what this implies. First of all, it means that God is free to either create the cosmos or not create it. It also means that God is not obligated to create the best possible universe. God is not forced to create one possible universe out of all possible universes because it is "best." This shows God's radical difference from us—as creatures with a capacity to develop toward perfection, there is always a tendency to choose the best, and choosing the best is always preferable and sometimes morally necessary. But God cannot be perfected and is not perfected through creating—he is already perfect Goodness. Also, the idea of "the best universe" is very problematic. Any estimation of what the best universe would be is limited by our own finite, personal viewpoint.[32] We are part of the universe, and a part cannot know the whole well enough to make such a judgment.

The important distinction to make here is between the act of creation and the product of that act, which is the universe and all things, including human beings and angels. The act of creation is perfect because it is divine. But the object resulting from the act of creation, insofar as it is finite, is necessarily imperfect. So, the universe is imperfect, but it corresponds perfectly to what God freely wills to create.[33] Furthermore, God has pledged himself to bringing his creation to its fullest possible perfection. In the words of the *Catechism*:

> **With infinite power God could always create something better. But with infinite wisdom and goodness God freely willed to create a world "in a state of journeying" towards its ultimate perfection. In God's plan this process of becoming involves the appearance of certain beings and the disappearance of others, the existence of the more perfect alongside the less perfect, both constructive and destructive forces of nature. With physical good there exists also physical evil as long as creation has not reached perfection.**[34]

The perfect freedom by which God creates also means that the universe was created out of perfect love. God, who is *Love* (1 Jn 4:8), chose to make this universe, and he did so without being under any coercion or divine necessity, which means that God did not *have* to create in order to be God. The International Theological Commission, the Pope's theological "think tank," emphasizes the personal nature of this free choice of God, who makes the whole universe for humanity: "[The doctrine of creation] teach[es] us that the existing universe is the setting for a radically personal drama, in which the triune Creator calls out of nothingness those to whom He then calls out in love."[35] This brings us to our final element.

4. Love Is the Reason: Creation *ex Trinitate*

FOR THE WORLD TO HAVE ITS BEGINNING IN GOD THE CREATOR means that it has its origin from the Trinity. It is not simply from the Father—the Father, Son, and Holy Spirit create together. In the words of the **Council of Florence**,

> **Most firmly [this council] believes, professes and preaches that *the one true God, Father, Son and Holy Spirit, is the creator of all things that are*, visible and invisible, who, when he willed it, made from his own goodness all creatures, both spiritual and corporeal, good indeed because they are made by the supreme good, but changeable because they are made from nothing, and it asserts that *there is no nature of evil* because every nature, in so far as it is a nature, is good.**[36]

In Chapter One, I related the universe's order and openness that we see through science to the work of the Son and the Spirit. The Son-*Logos* is the "Mind" or "Reason" to whom we attribute the orderliness of the universe. The Holy Spirit, the Gift-Love of God, is the one to whom we attribute its openness. To the Father, who eternally begets the Son and from whom the Spirit eternally proceeds, is attributed the very power by which the universe exists. It should be noted that, though we attribute these various actions to one of each of the Three divine Persons, creation is a unified action on the part of the whole divine Trinity.

The Holy Trinity is a perfect communion of love, which means that the universe is the product of divine love and goodness. **St. Thomas Aquinas** teaches that there are two kinds of love: the love that is justice and the love that is mercy. This distinction is very helpful in understanding what kind of love God manifests by creating the universe:

Jesus speaks to St. Faustina Kowalska:
"Let the greatest sinners place their trust in My mercy. They have the right before others to trust in the abyss of My mercy. My daughter, write about My mercy towards tormented souls. Souls that make an appeal to My mercy delight Me. To such souls I grant even more graces than they ask. I cannot punish even the greatest sinner if he makes an appeal to My compassion, but on the contrary, I justify him in My unfathomable and inscrutable mercy. Write: before I come as a just Judge, I first open wide the door of My mercy. He who refuses to pass through the door of My mercy must pass through the door of My justice." (*Diary*, 1146)

> **When a person's love is caused by the goodness of the one he loves, then that person loves out of justice—it is just that he love such a person. When, however, love causes goodness in the beloved, then it is a love springing from mercy. The love with which God loves us produces goodness in us; hence mercy is . . . *the root of divine love.*[37]**

Justice is the giving to another what is due to him or her. When I love and respect a great person, such as a saint, I am not being merciful to him or her; I am being just. Similarly, when I give my children my time and attention, I am not being merciful to them, I am simply being just to them—I am giving them what is theirs by right. These should be called love, but each is an example of loving out of justice, because love is what is due. In these cases, those who receive love have a right to it.

But what about when I forgive an offense committed against me and am friendly to a person who has hurt me? What about when I refuse to retaliate with insult or injury and, instead, offer a kind word? Or, when I give to the poor, helping them to have a better life? This is a love that actually causes goodness where it is absent, "a love springing from mercy."

Nothing can be good unless it exists, and nothing is owed to something that doesn't exist. As we have already seen, God creates the universe *ex nihilo*, out of nothing. He causes good things to exist not out of any justice to them but out of something like mercy. Therefore, divine mercy, "the root of divine love," is the reason for the universe and everything in it. The great English mystic **Julian of Norwich** (1342-after 1416) portrays this beautifully in a vision she was given in prayer:

> **The Holy Spirit showed me a little thing, the size of a hazelnut, lying in the palm of my hand, and to my understanding it was as round as any ball. I looked upon it and thought, "What may this be?" And I was answered, "It is everything that exists." I marveled how it could endure, for I thought it would certainly fall into nothingness because of its littleness. And I was answered, *"It lasts and always shall, because God loves it, and all things have being through the love of God."*[38]**

Creation *ex Trinitate* is the heart of the Christian doctrine of creation. Nothing is unless it is created, and everything created exists because of God's inexhaustible, merciful love. Machinists sometimes create because they have some need, as do some playwrights. But God had no need to create, no hunger to fill by creating. Rather, the universe is the product of love overflowing, and merciful love is therefore the foundation and deepest meaning of all things, which is the same mercy with which the world is redeemed by Christ on the Cross.

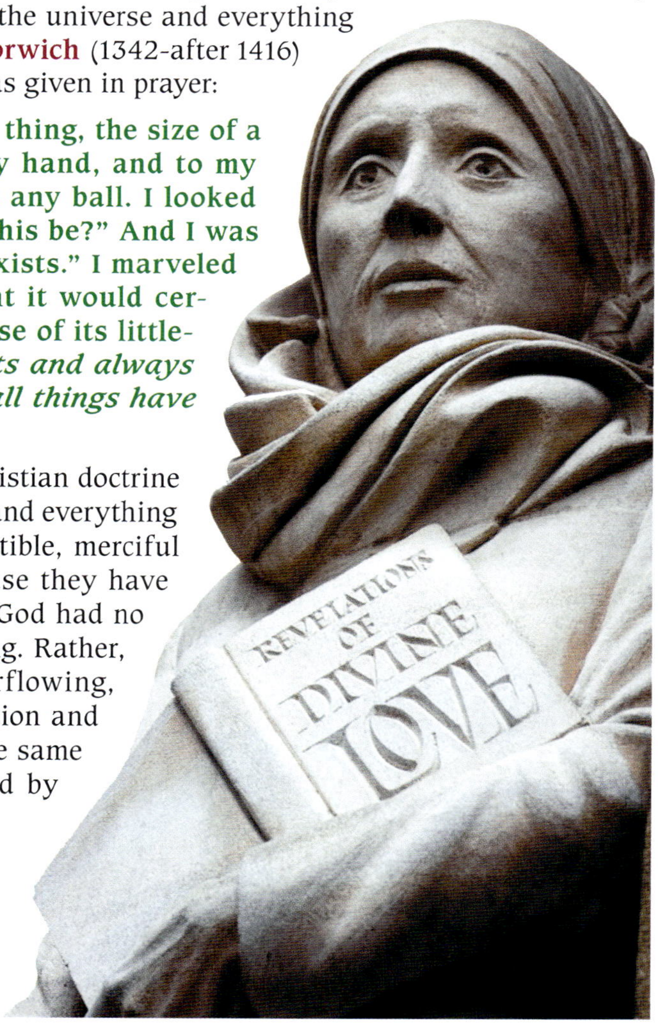

Julian of Norwich lived in a time of turmoil, but her theology was optimistic and spoke of God's love in terms of joy and compassion. *Revelations of Divine Love* "contains a message of optimism based on the certainty of being loved by God and of being protected by his Providence."—Pope Benedict XVI

God creates the universe *ex nihilo*, out of nothing. He causes good things to exist not out of any justice to them but out of something like mercy.

D. Looking Forward: The Sources of Divine Revelation

SO FAR, MY APPROACH to the harmony between modern science and the Christian faith has largely stayed at a general level. In the next two chapters, we will consider this relationship more specifically in regards to Sacred Scripture (Chapter Four) and Sacred Tradition (Chapter Five).

In Chapter Four, we will focus on the **First Creation Account**, the six-day story of creation with which the Bible begins, to better understand how the picture of the origins of the universe given by science and faith are not rival explanations but ones that differ and complete each other.

In Chapter Five, we will turn from **Sacred Scripture** to **Sacred Tradition**, as it is embodied in the Church's history, with reference to important events, ending with a closer look at the life of **Galileo** and his condemnation by the Inquisition, which stands out as an exception to an otherwise glorious history of openness to scientific discovery on the part of the Catholic Church.

Finally, in Chapter Six we will apply the concepts we developed in this chapter to three issues that are at the heart of personal spirituality—**the reality of evil, the power of prayer, and the possibility of miracles.**

VOCABULARY

Define the following terms (or identify the person's significance):

1. **Ben Sira**
2. **Nicholas of Cusa**
3. **Sir Isaac Newton (Science)**
4. **Clockmaker God (Newton)**
5. **Deism**
6. **Pantheism**
7. **Analogy (Analogous)**
8. **Analogue**
9. **Univocal Conception of God**
10. **Existence**
11. **Mental Being (Existence)**
12. **Real Being (Existence)**
13. **St. Thomas Aquinas**
14. **Being Subsisting in Itself**
15. **Primary Cause (God)**
16. **Secondary Cause (Creatures)**
17. **Principle of Double Agency**
18. **Ecumenical Council**
19. **Charism of Infallibility**
20. **Creation *ex nihilo***
21. **Change**
22. **Creation *cum tempore***
23. **Creation *cum libertate***
24. **Creation *ex Trinitate***
25. **Justice**
26. **Mercy**

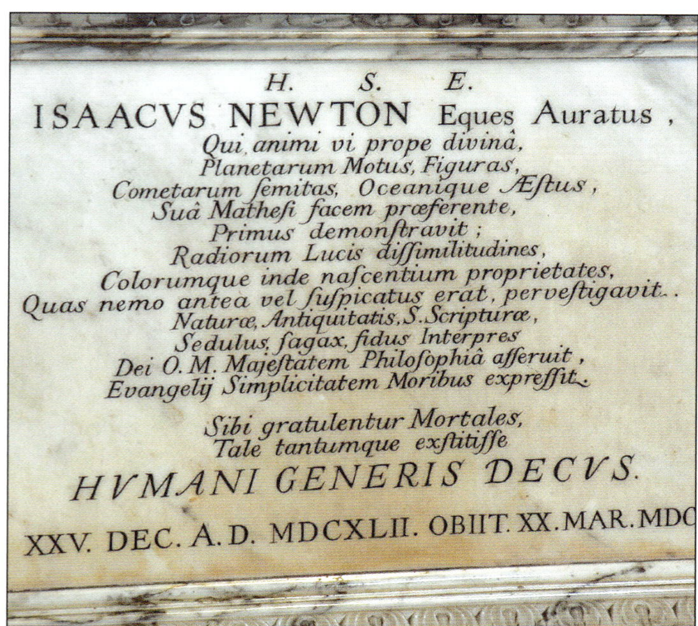

Sir Isaac Newton Monument at Westminster Abbey inscription:
"Here is buried Isaac Newton, Knight, who by a strength of mind almost divine, and mathematical principles peculiarly his own, explored the course and figures of the planets, the paths of comets, the tides of the sea, the dissimilarities in rays of light, and, what no other scholar has previously imagined, the properties of the colours thus produced. Diligent, sagacious and faithful, in his expositions of nature, antiquity and the holy Scriptures, he vindicated by his philosophy the majesty of God mighty and good, and expressed the simplicity of the Gospel in his manners. Mortals rejoice that there has existed such and so great an ornament of the human race!"

STUDY QUESTIONS

1. The quote from the Book of Sirach that begins the chapter asserts two things about God's relationship to the universe. Identify each and refer them to the parts of the quote that suggest them.

Section A

2. Why is Isaac Newton rightly celebrated as one of the greatest scientists of all time?

3. What model did Newton use to understand the universe? Was this model original to him?

4. What are the benefits of scientific modeling, and what are its limitations?

5. Critique Newton's theology of God's relationship to the universe from a) the perspective of the quote from Sirach and b) the absurd conclusions to which it led him.

6. Describe the chain of thinking that Newton's univocal theology set in motion.

Section B

7. Summarize St. Thomas Aquinas's Principle of Double Agency. How does it overcome models of conflict/warfare such as creationism and scientific atheism?

8. Which characteristics of the analogy of a playwright for God as Primary Cause/Creator make it helpful? What are the limits of the playwright analogy?

Section C

9. Distinguish between divine creation and temporal change with reference to the doctrine of creation *ex nihilo*.

10. Distinguish between divine creation and the beginning of time with reference to the doctrine of creation *cum tempore*.

11. Critique the idea that God must create the "best possible world" with reference to the doctrine of creation *cum libertate*.

12. Justify the assertion that the universe is the product of divine love with reference to the doctrine of creation *ex Trinitate*.

13. What is "love springing from mercy," and why is it appropriate to identify this kind of love as the love with which God creates with reference to the doctrine of creation *ex nihilo*?

Along with other influential errant thinkers, Henry David Thoreau (1817-1862) began to merge God and the universe, a belief system called *pantheism*.

"At its most general, pantheism may be understood positively as the view that God is identical with the cosmos, the view that there exists nothing which is outside of God, or else negatively as the rejection of any view that considers God as distinct from the universe."
—Stanford Encyclopedia of Philosophy

PRACTICAL EXERCISES

1. Read the following biblical passages, each of which uses analogical language to describe God:

   - Psalm 10:3-4
   - Psalm 14:2
   - Psalm 16:6, 11

   In a few sentences for each, describe the analogy being used, how it is helpful, and its limits.

Endnotes – Chapter Three

1. Nicholas of Cusa, *De Deo Abscondito*, 1, 6, in Jasper Hopkins, ed. and trans., *A Miscellany on Nicholas of Cusa* (Minneapolis, MN, Arthur J. Banning Press, 1994), 300-311.
2. Stephen M. Barr, *A Student's Guide to Natural Science* (Wilmington, DE: ISI Books, 2006), 33.
3. Ibid., 34-42.
4. Amos Funkenstein, *Theology and the Scientific Imagination: From the Middle Ages to the Seventeenth Century* (Princeton, NJ: Princeton University Press, 1986), 30.
5. Rene Descartes, *Meditations on First Philosophy*, med. 6.
6. Lawrence Principe, "God the Watchmaker" Lecture, *Science and Religion*.
7. Funkenstein, 96.
8. Ibid., 95.
9. Christopher Insole, "Kant's Transcendental Idealism and Newton's Divine Sensorium," *Journal of the History of Ideas* 72:3 (2011): 416-417, quoting Isaac Newton, "De Gravitatione et Aequipondio Fluidorum" (1684/85), 89-169, in *Unpublished Scientific Papers of Isaac Newton*, ed. Rupert Hall and Marie Boas Hall (Cambridge: Cambridge University Press, 1962).
10. Funkenstein, 94.
11. F. Antommarchi, *Mémoires du docteur F. Antommarchi, ou les derniers momens de Napoléon*, vol. 1, (Paris: Barrois L'Ainé, 1825), 282.
12. Matthew Arnold, "Dover Beach" (1867), *www.poetryfoundation.org/poems/43588/dover-beach*.
13. St. John Paul II, "Address to a Colloquium," September 5, 1986.
14. W. Norris Clarke, *The One and the Many*, 46.
15. Quote from the *New American Bible, Revised Edition*; italics added.
16. Ibid., 47.
17. St. Thomas Aquinas, *De Veritate* 11.1.
18. St. Thomas Aquinas, *Summa Contra Gentiles* III.70.8.
19. Ibid., III.101.1.
20. St. Thomas Aquinas, *In Physicorum*, II.8.14, no. 268.
21. St. Thomas Aquinas, *Summa Theologiae* I.103.6 resp.
22. Christopher Hitchens, *God is Not Great: How Religion Poisons Everything* (New York: Hachette Book Group, 2009), 282.
23. Stephen M. Barr, *The Believing Scientist: Essays on Science and Religion* (Grand Rapids, MI: Eerdmans, 2016) 124-126.
24. *Roman Missal*, Third Edition. The Order of Mass, no. 18.
25. CCC 888-892.
26. Paul Halsall, ed., "The Canons of the Fourth Lateran Council (1215 AD)," *Medieval Sourcebook: Twelfth Ecumenical Council: Lateran IV 1215*, can. 1, *sourcebooks.fordham.edu/basis/lateran4.asp*.
27. William E. Carroll, "Creation, Evolution, and Thomas Aquinas," Catholic Education Resource Center, *www.catholiceducation.org/en/science/faith-and-science/creation-evolution-and-thomas-aquinas.html*.
28. G.K. Chesterton, *Orthodoxy*, Moody Classics new ed. (Chicago: Moody Publishers, 2009), 92.
29. Paul Haffner, *Mystery of Creation* (Herefordshire, UK: Gracewing, 1995), 52.
30. Austriaco, et al., *Thomistic Evolution*, 65-66.
31. Vatican I, Dogmatic Constitution *Dei Filius* on the Catholic Faith, chap. 1, no. 2-3, *www.ewtn.com/library/councils/v1.htm#4*.
32. Haffner, *Mystery of Creation*, 56-57.
33. Ibid., 57.
34. CCC 310.
35. International Theological Commission, "Communion and Stewardship: Human Persons Created in the Image of God," July 23, 2004, no. 66, *www.vatican.va/roman_curia/congregations/cfaith/cti_documents/rc_con_cfaith_doc_20040723_communion-stewardship_en.html* (hereafter abbreviated C&S.).
36. Ecumenical Council of Florence, *Bull of Union With the Copts* (1442), *www.ewtn.com/library/COUNCILS/FLORENCE.HTM*.
37. St. Thomas Aquinas, *In Ephesios*, 2.2.
38. Julian of Norwich, *Revelations of Divine Love*, chap. 5.

Chapter Four

The First Creation Account and Modern Science: Uniting Perspectives

How should Christians understand the authority of the Bible regarding history and science? What kind of truth does God teach us through the Bible?

How do we integrate truth statements from different perspectives into a fuller understanding of reality?

Is the First Creation Account in the Book of Genesis a religious obstacle to modern science? What kind of literature is it, and what principles should we apply in our interpretation of it?

Does the divine message of the Bible affirm science as something that God desires?

The Bible itself speaks to us of the origin of the universe and its make-up, not in order to provide us with a scientific treatise, but in order to state the correct relationships of man with God and with the universe. Any other teaching about the origin and make-up of the universe is alien to the intentions of the Bible, which does not wish to teach us how heaven was made but how one goes to heaven.

—St. John Paul II, Speech to Scientists, October 3, 1981

New biblical discoveries, especially when they confirm the historical authenticity of biblical stories, fascinate the popular imagination. Every so often the news and social media will highlight an archaeological discovery that touches upon some detail of the Old Testament or of the life of Jesus and the early Church. One such discovery was made in July 2014 in the Northern Iraqi city of Mosul, which in biblical times was Nineveh, the capital of Assyria. The Islamic State (ISIS) blew up a Sunni mosque that, according to legend, contained the tomb of the prophet Jonah, a monument which was completely destroyed by the blast. Underneath the rubble they discovered stone sculptures of a goddess, images of combat, and cuneiform inscriptions, an ancient writing system, dating back to 600 BC. These inscriptions identified the remains as belonging to the ancient palace

Assyrian King Tiglath-Pileser III (named *Pul* in 2 Kings 15:19) ruled 745-727 BC. He created Assyria's first professional standing army and brutally conquered most of the world known to the Assyrians before his death.

of Sennacherib, the Assyrian king whose invasion of the kingdom of Judah ended unsuccessfully, and miraculously so, at the walls of Jerusalem, as documented in the Second Book of Kings (chs. 18-19), the Second Book of Chronicles (ch. 32), and the Book of the Prophet Isaiah (chs. 36-37). Ironically, ISIS had blown up a monument to a prophet honored by all Jews, Muslims, and Christians, and had uncovered one to a pagan and a fierce enemy of God's People.

All Christians should take interest in such discoveries because they help to bring the Bible to life for us. They remind us that the events of our salvation history really happened and involved momentous things, some of great triumph, others of great tragedy. Just think: The prophet Isaiah, who gave us the Christmas prophecy: "A young woman shall conceive and bear a son, and shall call his name Immanuel [that is, *God is with us*]" (Is 7:14), is the same Isaiah who prophesied to Hezekiah, the king of Judah, that he should trust in the Lord in the face of Sennacherib's invasion (cf. Is 37:33-35). Hezekiah lived to celebrate the prophecy of Isaiah about the failed invasion; we live now to celebrate, every Advent and Christmas, the prophecy of Isaiah about the virgin birth of Immanuel, Jesus Christ.

Sennacherib's Prism details the events of Sennacherib's campaign against Judah. The cuneiform journal dates from ca. 690 BC. The text of the prism boasts how he [Sennacherib] destroyed forty-six of Judah's cities and trapped Hezekiah in Jerusalem "like a caged bird."

However, some Christians get excited about such stories not only because they bring the Bible to life but because they see them as necessary to confirm every minute detail of biblical assertions taken at face value, literalistically. These Christians hold the Bible not only to be God's Word to us but also to be flawless in every single detail. For such believers, the Bible is God's Word without any trace of the usual cultural characteristics of other ancient writings and even modern writings such as hyperbole, poetic license, metaphor, allegory, imagery, etc. They assume that what makes the Bible special is that it is not like other human writings, as if finding humanity in the Bible would make it less divine. They measure its divinity by the accuracy of its facts. When a biblical detail receives external confirmation, they point to it as proof that its spiritual message must be true as well, as if the facts uphold divine mysteries and as if details are the foundation of faith and morals. Since it is impossible for God to be mistaken or to lie, every geographical and historical detail must be defended as true without qualification.

When we move from historical facts to scientific ones, facts about the beginnings of the universe, the way life came to exist in all its diverse forms, etc., these same Christians

Jonah Preaching in Nineveh. "He cried, 'Yet forty days, and Nineveh shall be overthrown!' And the people of Nineveh believed God; they proclaimed a fast, and put on sackcloth, from the greatest of them to the least of them" (Jon 3:4-5).

left: The minaret of the Mosque of the Prophet Jonah. *right:* After the destruction by ISIS in 2014. When built, the mosque replaced an Eastern Christian Church believed to be the burial place of Jonah and called Jonah's Tomb.

apply the same standard—if the Bible says it, it must be taken to be true, regardless of what common sense or modern science says. If science seems to agree, it is proof of the Bible's divine authority. If science disagrees, then the science is wrong. Thus, the creationist misconception of faith and science begins to emerge.

St. John Paul II lamented this rigid approach to biblical truth in the following words:

> **A false idea of God and the incarnation presses a certain number of Christians . . . to believe that, since God is the absolute Being, each of his words has an absolute value, independent of all the conditions of human language. . . . However, that is where the illusion occurs and the mysteries of scriptural inspiration and the incarnation are really rejected, by clinging to a false notion of the Absolute.**
>
> **The God of the Bible is not [a God] who, crushing everything he touches, would suppress all differences and all nuances. On the contrary, he is God the Creator, who created the astonishing variety of beings "each according to its kind," as the Genesis account says repeatedly (see Genesis 1). Far from destroying differences, God respects them and makes use of them (See 1 Corinthians 12:18, 24, 28). Although he expresses himself in human language, he does not give each expression a uniform value, but uses its possible nuances with extreme flexibility and likewise accepts its limitations.[1]**

This brings us to the topic of this chapter: How should Catholics approach the relationship between the Bible and science? Is the purpose of the Bible to give us a scientific understanding of things, to correct our scientific mistakes? Should a believing scientist use the Bible as a tool for evaluating his or her findings—if they agree with the Bible they are true; if they don't, then it's back to the laboratory to try again? Or, should believers reject scientific findings if they perceive a difference between what science is saying and what the Bible is saying? It is easy to see how such confusion quickly leads to conflict, because in the end every new scientific discovery becomes a test of the truth of the Bible: One to be rejected if it is seen as different than what the Bible says or to be celebrated if it is seen as agreeing with what the Bible says.

The Catholic Church offers a different, and better, approach to the authority and truth of the Bible, which is one that does not lead to conflict between faith and science but that helps us understand the deepest meaning of the world God created. Before we consider that deeper meaning in the **First Creation Account** found in Genesis 1-2, let us begin by understanding the Catholic approach to Sacred Scripture so that we can apply it to that important biblical text.

The Great Isaiah Scroll is one of the original seven Dead Sea Scrolls discovered in the Qumran Caves in 1947. It is the largest and best preserved of all the biblical scrolls and the only one that is almost complete. The fifty-four columns contain all sixty-six chapters of the Hebrew version of the Book of Isaiah. Dating from ca. 125 BC, it is one of the oldest of the Dead Sea Scrolls.

A. Science and the Catholic Church's Teaching About the Bible

THE CATHOLIC CHURCH TEACHES that Sacred Scripture, firmly, faithfully, and without error, teaches the truth that God, for the sake of our salvation, wished to see confided in it.[2] Another way of saying this is to say that, thanks to God's gift of grace to the human authors of the Bible, which we call *divine inspiration*, the Bible contains no error *from the perspective of saving truth*. Let us explore what we mean when we use the word "perspective" to characterize the truth of the Bible.

Different perspectives lead us to make different kinds of assertions. From the perspective of chemistry, the study of compounds, I am an organic (carbon-based) compound, a collection of atoms including about 65% oxygen, 18.5% carbon, 9.5% hydrogen, and so on. From the perspective of biology, the study of life and living organisms, I (Chris Baglow) am a mammal and a member of the hominin species *Homo sapiens*. From the perspective of socioeconomics, the study of economic activity and processes, I am a member of the working middle-class with a household of a certain size. From the perspective of the Catholic faith, I am a baptized and confirmed member of the Body of Christ, a Catholic husband, father, and theologian.

Notice that from each of these perspectives I am being viewed in different ways that are not at all in competition with each other. Knowing my socioeconomic status in no way affects the truth of my biological classification. Both perspectives are valid; they are not rival versions of truth. If one of the above statements about me happened to be erroneous, it would not affect the truth of the others. If I were a secret millionaire, I would not really be a member of the middle class, but I would still be a mammal.

The Prophet Isaiah by Raphael

Let us go back now to what the Church teaches about the Bible. She teaches that, from the perspective of saving truth, the Bible contains no error—it never misleads us on our path to salvation. She says that I come to understand this saving truth only when I read the Bible as a whole and in light of the Person and the teaching of Jesus Christ and under the guidance of her leaders, the Pope and the bishops. When I do this, then I will find three things that are essential to salvation. First, I will find teachings about who and what God is, how he sees the whole universe and the reasons for his creating it, what his plan is for humanity's eternal happiness and fulfillment—these are teachings that must be believed since they are teachings of faith. Such teachings are also given in summary form in the Creed we profess every Sunday: "I believe in one God, the Father Almighty," etc. Second, I will find teachings about what it means to live a life pleasing to God in which I realize his plan for my happiness, making me the kind of person he created me to be—these are teaching to be obeyed, or teachings of morals.

Finally, I will find all this within the literary heritage of his chosen people: their poems, songs, and historical records. There I learn about the people of Israel, the children of Abraham, and above all about the life, Death, and Resurrection of Jesus Christ and his founding of a new People of God open to all of humanity, the Church. This literary heritage includes narratives of historical events. Of these, the Church identifies some that are guaranteed to be historically sound in all their major elements—the accounts of what Jesus Christ did and taught for the sake of our salvation, including the ways in which he manifested his divinity—through being born of the Virgin, through miraculous signs, and through his Resurrection. In the words of **Vatican II**, "Holy Mother Church has firmly and with absolute constancy held, and continues to hold, that the four Gospels . . . whose *historical character* the Church unhesitatingly asserts, faithfully hand on what Jesus Christ, while living among men, really did and taught for their eternal salvation until the day he was taken up into heaven."[3]

St. Matthew and the Angel

So, from the perspective of saving truth we find in the Bible, without error, truths of faith and morals. We also find some important historical details about God's chosen people and above all about the life, Death, and Resurrection of his Son that are essentially connected to faith and morals. And this is the only claim the Church makes about the Bible's freedom from error. She does not assert that the Bible is guaranteed to be without error from other perspectives. Why not? Because the books of the Bible are truly human as well as truly divine, and the divine comes to us in and through the real human authors with all of their cultural and personal limitations and imperfections because they, too, inspired by the Holy Spirit, are true authors of Sacred Scripture.

In 2014, the Pontifical Biblical Commission, the Pope's special think tank on the Bible, said it this way: "Not everything in the Bible is expressed in accordance with the demands of the contemporary sciences, because the biblical writers reflect the limits of their own personal

"For he willed to make them Christians, not mathematicians."—St. Augustine

knowledge, in addition to those of their time and culture."[4] If there was no science of chemistry in their ancient culture, then we should not seek truth from the perspective of chemistry. If there were not strict, universally agreed upon rules of history-writing in that culture that required exact details given in exact chronological order, relying on firsthand witnesses, then we will find various imperfections in the details of the historical narratives. But, if we are waiting for the Bible to give us a science lesson or a modern-style historical documentary, then we are reading it for the wrong reasons.

This truth is summed up eloquently in the *YouCat*, the official catechism given to young people by **Pope Benedict XVI** at World Youth Day in 2011. Question 15 is entitled "How can Sacred Scripture be truth if not everything in it is right?" Here's the answer it gives:

> **The Bible is not meant to convey precise historical information or scientific findings to us. Moreover, the authors were children of their time. They shared the ideas of their cultural environment and sometimes were also held back by its errors. Nevertheless, everything that man must know about God and the way of his salvation is found with infallible certainty in Sacred Scripture.**[5]

Why did the Holy Spirit not correct the limitations of the biblical authors? **St. Augustine** (354-430), the great Catholic bishop, philosopher, and theologian, captures the reason: "One does *not* read in the Gospel that the Lord said: 'I will send you the Paraclete [the Holy Spirit] who will teach you about the course of the sun and the moon.' For he willed to make them *Christians*, not *mathematicians*."[6]

It should be easy to relate this to our main issue, which is the relationship between the Bible and science. To seek to confirm the truth of the Bible by science is like trying to confirm whether a person is a baptized Catholic by analyzing a blood or tissue sample! Equally misguided would be the endeavor to evaluate a scientific idea as true or false by checking to see if it agrees or disagrees with the Bible. From the perspective of faith, morals, and some important historical truths closely related to them that are necessary for our salvation, the Bible never misleads us.

1. The Bible: God Reaching Down, Humanity Reaching Up

SINCE THE BIBLE IS FREE FROM ERROR regarding salvation, there can be no doubt about the importance of the Bible for the life of faith. From the very beginning of the Church's history, Sacred Scripture has always been recognized and revered as the Word of God. The *Catechism of the Catholic Church* strikingly formulates the importance of Sacred Scripture for faithful believers, comparing its veneration to that of the Eucharist, which is the Real Presence of Jesus Christ: "The Church has always venerated the divine Scriptures as she venerated the Body of the Lord: *both* nourish and govern the whole Christian life [italics mine]."[7] A perfect illustration of this truth can be seen at Mass, during which only three things are raised up: the consecrated Host, the precious Chalice, and the Book of the Gospels.

Like the Eucharist, Sacred Scripture is divine.

Thus, similar to the Eucharist, Sacred Scripture is divine. And yet the Eucharist is not simply divine; it is also a human reality. Jesus Christ, who is really present in the Eucharist, is the Word who became flesh. He is fully God and fully human, a unity of both in his one divine Person. It should not surprise us, then, that the Bible has God as its Author, but he is its Author only through human instruments: "God is the author of Sacred Scripture because he inspired its human authors; he acts in them and by means of them."[8] God "writes" the books of the Bible by divinely inspiring members of his people to compose them. What this means is that the Bible reflects a long and storied human process—it has a history. **Pope Benedict XVI** once put it this way:

> **Scripture is not a meteorite fallen from the sky.... Certainly Scripture carries God's thoughts within it; that makes it unique and constitutes it an authority. Yet it is transmitted by a human history. It carries within it the life and thought of a historical society that we call the "People of God..."[9]**

The Bible reflects, therefore, two histories at once, which are really in the end just one salvation history: It is the history of God reaching down to humanity with his truth and his saving grace, and it is the history of humanity reaching back up, striving to understand and live according to the truth that God reveals, despite their rather frequent failures to do so.

This important fact—that Scripture is divine and human, the divine Word in human words—must guide us as we approach the relationship between Sacred Scripture and modern science and, in particular, as we approach the First Creation Account found in the Book of Genesis. This will help us to avoid two opposite errors that lead to dead ends and misconceptions. The first error is *creationism*, which defends the divinity of the First Creation Account but loses sight of its humanity. The opposite error, popular with those who embrace materialism, reductionism, and scientism, is to see *only* the human aspects of the First Creation Account and therefore to dismiss it as the product of prescientific ignorance. If we instead take an approach that respects both the human and the divine elements of the First Creation Account—with the understanding that the divine truth comes to us *through* the human author's words and expressions—then we will understand it properly and see that its truth allows us, and indeed encourages us, to be open to modern scientific insights.

If we take a "both/and" approach, respecting both the divine and human aspects of the First Creation Account, then we will understand how its truth is not a barrier to our openness to modern scientific insights. Ultimately, a "both/and" approach means embracing at once all three of the following points:

1. **The First Creation Account tells us, without error, the truth about God the Creator and the deepest truth about why God created the universe;**
2. **The First Creation Account tells us this truth using poetic and symbolic language and images, which is the product of ancient Near-Eastern authors;** ***and***
3. **The First Creation Account is not a scientific treatise, but something more essential: It is a testament to God's wisdom in creating and to the goodness of the universe he created.**

B. "In the Beginning...": The First Creation Account (Genesis 1:1–2:4a)

THE FIRST CREATION ACCOUNT is a piece of literature that is familiar to many people but is not often studied with care and attention. It must be read closely and in full in order to be understood.

Chapter One

1 In the beginning God created the heavens and the earth.

2 The earth was without form and void, and darkness was upon the face of the deep; and the Spirit of God was moving over the face of the waters.

3 And God said, "Let there be light"; and there was light.

4 And God saw that the light was good; and God separated the light from the darkness.

5 God called the light Day, and the darkness he called Night. And there was evening and there was morning, one day.

6 And God said, "Let there be a firmament in the midst of the waters, and let it separate the waters from the waters."

7 And God made the firmament and separated the waters which were under the firmament from the waters which were above the firmament. And it was so.

8 And God called the firmament Heaven. And there was evening and there was morning, a second day.

9 And God said, "Let the waters under the heavens be gathered together into one place, and let the dry land appear." And it was so.

10 God called the dry land Earth, and the waters that were gathered together he called Seas. And God saw that it was good.

11 And God said, "Let the earth put forth vegetation, plants yielding seed, and fruit trees bearing fruit in which is their seed, each according to its kind, upon the earth." And it was so.

12 The earth brought forth vegetation, plants yielding seed according to their own kinds, and trees bearing fruit in which is their seed, each according to its kind. And God saw that it was good.

13 And there was evening and there was morning, a third day.

14 And God said, "Let there be lights in the firmament of the heavens to separate the day from the night; and let them be for signs and for seasons and for days and years,

15 and let them be lights in the firmament of the heavens to give light upon the earth." And it was so.

16 And God made the two great lights, the greater light to rule the day, and the lesser light to rule the night; he made the stars also.

17 And God set them in the firmament of the heavens to give light upon the earth,

18 to rule over the day and over the night, and to separate the light from the darkness. And God saw that it was good.

19 And there was evening and there was morning, a fourth day.

20 And God said, "Let the waters bring forth swarms of living creatures, and let birds fly above the earth across the firmament of the heavens."

21 So God created the great sea monsters and every living creature that moves, with which the waters swarm, according to their kinds, and every winged bird according to its kind. And God saw that it was good.

22 And God blessed them, saying, "Be fruitful and multiply and fill the waters in the seas, and let birds multiply on the earth."

23 And there was evening and there was morning, a fifth day.

24 And God said, "Let the earth bring forth living creatures according to their kinds: cattle and creeping things and beasts of the earth according to their kinds." And it was so.

25 And God made the beasts of the earth according to their kinds and the cattle according to their kinds, and everything that creeps upon the ground according to its kind. And God saw that it was good.

26 Then God said, "Let us make man in our image, after our likeness; and let them have dominion over the fish of the sea, and over the birds of the air, and over the cattle, and over all the earth, and over every creeping thing that creeps upon the earth."

27 So God created man in his own image, in the image of God he created him; male and female he created them.

28 And God blessed them, and God said to them, "Be fruitful and multiply, and fill the earth and subdue it; and have dominion over the fish of the sea and over the birds of the air and over every living thing that moves upon the earth."

29 And God said, "Behold, I have given you every plant yielding seed which is upon the face of all the earth, and every tree with seed in its fruit; you shall have them for food.

30 And to every beast of the earth, and to every bird of the air, and to everything that creeps on the earth, everything that has the breath of life, I have given every green plant for food." And it was so.

31 And God saw everything that he had made, and behold, it was very good. And there was evening and there was morning, a sixth day.

Chapter Two

1 Thus the heavens and the earth were finished, and all the host of them.

2 And on the seventh day God finished his work which he had done, and he rested on the seventh day from all his work which he had done.

3 So God blessed the seventh day and hallowed it, because on it God rested from all his work which he had done in creation.

4a These are the generations of the heavens and the earth when they were created.

The beauty of this poetic passage has been celebrated for millennia, but more background is necessary to fully grasp its truth. Many scientific atheists dismiss this story as a primitive myth, the product of "a Bronze Age desert kingdom." Ironically, they have this dismissive attitude, in many cases, not because they know more history than theologians do but because they know far less. They see the apparent human limitations of the men who set down these words so long ago. Yet they do not really understand the human history and context in which the story was originally written. For if God really acts *in and through* the human, as we noted above, and not merely alongside the human, then one cannot hear the divine voice unless one truly understands the human voice through which God speaks. There is a further irony: Scientific atheists dismiss the First Creation Account as "myth" without realizing that it was actually written in order to correct the myths of pagan peoples by reorienting their myths toward the one true God. In order to understand this, let us imaginatively place ourselves within the story *behind* the story—a story both human and divine, a story about the People of God.

1. The Babylonian Background to the First Creation Account

MUCH BIBLICAL SCHOLARSHIP HAS BEEN DEDICATED to understanding the context in which the First Creation Account was written, and most scholars suggest that, due to its language and style, it took its final form around the middle of the sixth century BC. Although no one knows the name(s) of the inspired author(s), some creative thinking can help us establish a possible, but not certain, scenario for its final composition.

Imagine that you are a Jew living more than 500 years before Christ. You are a priest, a duty of religious leadership bestowed by God upon your family line, a duty that you take as the primary purpose of your life. Your responsibilities are vital: offering sacrifices, leading the congregation in prayer, and maintaining a close adherence to the Law given by **Moses**, whom God raised up long ago to lead his people out of slavery in Egypt and into a land "flowing with milk and honey" (Dt 26:9)—the Promised Land.

But you are no longer living in that land. It has been devastated by an invading empire. You, and all of God's people, have been forcibly removed from it, and have been deported to live in the land of the very empire that took it from you—Babylon. The Temple, the place of God's presence, has been reduced to rubble. You now have a new duty—you must help your people hold on to their faith in God and to the way of life he gave to them, and you must do so against all odds.

It is in that place, during that terrible time which generations to come will call the Exile (597-539 BC), that you and your children hear these unsettling words:

When in the height heaven was not named,
And the earth beneath did not yet bear a name,
Apsu, Fresh-Water, the Father of the Gods,
And Tiamat, Salt-Water, Chaos, the mother of the Gods,
Mingled their waters together...

Then, in the midst of heaven, the gods were created...

These words begin the *Enûma Eliš* (ē-nooh-mah eh-lēsh), the Babylonian story of the world's creation and the central myth of the Babylonian religion.[10] It begins with a father god, *Apsu*, and a mother god, *Tiamat*, attempting to kill their own children. It continues with them instead being killed by their offspring and with the leader of those offspring, *Marduk*, making the earth and sky out of his mother's body parts. It ends with Marduk killing the dragon *Kingu*, Tiamat's lover and the commander of her army. As the blood of the dragon drips out, it is collected so that human beings can be formed out of it. Marduk then makes them to be slaves to all the gods, including the sun-god, the moon-god, and the star-gods.

From the *Enûma Eliš* creation story: Marduk killing the dragon Kingu.

It is a story of violence and death, filled with deeds that are the polar opposite of the way the one true God, YHWH, acts. Slowly, but surely, a response is growing within you and within the other priests to this dreadfully warped picture of divinity and of the origin of human beings and the universe. Thanks to you, a different story will be heard by the people, a story with a very different beginning: "*Bereshit bara Elohim et hashamayim ve'et ha'arets*"—"In the beginning the LORD-God [not Marduk] created the heavens and the earth..."

C. The Divine Message of the First Creation Account

1. The Message: God, the Creator of the Cosmos

PERHAPS IT IS ONLY WITH THE BLOODY EVENTS of the *Enûma Eliš* still floating in our minds that we can best interpret all of the amazing details of the First Creation Account, which is also known as the Priestly Creation Account because it was probably composed by Jewish priests during or after the Babylonian Exile. In this beautiful picture of the origin of the world, the violence of the *Enûma Eliš* is utterly rejected while many of its details are preserved and reinterpreted. We see a theologically enlightened and, indeed, an inspired people responding to superstition and ignorance regarding the nature of God, the universe, and humanity.

The earth is the product of an unbelievably large and well-orchestrated set of events. The one God makes all that exists according to his divine wisdom and power.

Now that we have this background, we can get a better understanding of the account's true meaning. Scholars tell us that this meaning is communicated to us in two ways: both by certain important assertions and in the order these assertions are made. We must look at both the message and the medium, both the statements in the story and the structure of the story, to catch its total meaning. Let us give our attention first to the message itself. We can summarize it as follows: *The universe was created by a God who is one, who is all-powerful, who is perfectly intelligent, and who is perfectly good.*

The clearest element of the creation drama of the First Creation Account is that it has a single actor. In contrast to the *Enûma Eliš*, there is only one God. Everything else that exists has God as its source. In the Babylonian religion, the sun, moon, and stars were all considered to be gods who had to be worshiped. In this story, they are lights that God turns on to illuminate the earth and to measure time for the sake of humanity. God has no rival in the universe or in any of its parts. Just as no stream can rival the spring from which it flows, so no creature can be compared with the Creator. Because the universe and all that it contains have been created by God out of nothing, they cannot be themselves divine.

Perhaps the most interesting element of the account is the way creation comes about. The earth is not the gory, dismembered corpse of a slain goddess, the aftermath of a divine brawl. It is the product of a well-orchestrated event—there is one God, and he makes all that exists according to his deliberate intention.[11] The universe exists because God wills it to be. His *astonishing power* is infinitely greater than that of Marduk. God does not have to exert himself in the making of the universe. He just speaks his Word and the universe springs into being, so that the universe can be defined simply as "the event of God's personal word."[12] He burns no calories nor flexes any muscles in the series of events, because calories and muscles are part of the creation, not of the Creator. Nothing disrupts his perfect tranquility, and a fundamentally good, well-ordered creation pours out of his own tranquility as he wills it to do so.

If there is anything active about God in the account, it is his mind. Just as the *Enûma Eliš* is saturated with violence, the Genesis account is saturated with intelligence, with *divine rationality*. God is a profound architect, structuring and setting up a masterpiece of design. As the Scripture scholar **Michael Duggan** writes:

> **There is no confusion; light is distinguishable from darkness, the land from the sea. Vegetation is abundant and guarantees a rich array of food for humanity. The categorization of animals, fish and birds reflects [an] appreciation for order.**[13]

The universe God creates is good, a reflection of its *perfectly good Creator*. This goodness is both manifested in its order and explicitly declared by God. Seven times he sees and declares its goodness, a number that in the Bible symbolizes completion and perfection.

Creation of Adam in the Paradise

At verse 26, with the creation of his image, man and woman, God's goodness and rationality reach a peak of intensity in his creative action. The authors portray God in deep reflection and planning only once—when he creates human beings. It is as if God is looking into a mirror as he speaks. Only human beings are called God's image and likeness. While God sees each part of his creation as good, only after man and woman are present in it does he call it "very good." The message is clear—humans are not the spawn of Kingu's blood, but the reflection of God himself, "man and woman equally and in union with each other."[14] God sees the goodness of all that he creates, but he speaks directly to his human creation, describing his will for them and the tasks they must fulfill. Only they are given the command to subdue the earth, and only they are given dominion over all the other creatures. In every way humans are a part of the creation but nonetheless a very unique part. *Humans are the summit of God's creation.*

The Creator's oneness, power, rationality, and goodness are clear from the symbolism of the account. Now we can look at the account's structure and see how it enriches the story and deepens its message.

2. The Medium Has a Message: Reading the "Shape" of the First Creation Account

BIBLICAL SCHOLARS WHO HAVE LOOKED CAREFULLY at the First Creation Account have some important details to add to our understanding of it that we might otherwise overlook. The rationality and goodness of the production of the universe by God has a more fundamental layer than just the events of the account. It also has a deeper order below its surface—*symmetry* (i.e., equality of measure) and proportion even characterize the way the story is told. The medium reinforces the written message and even carries its own message.

First, the six days of making (Gn 1:1-31) actually interact with each other, making two columns of events. When the days are considered in two sets, Days 1-3 and Days 4-6, each day in the first set matches the corresponding day in the second. On Day 1, God makes light; on Day 4, he makes lights (sun, moon, and stars). On Day 2, he makes sky and sea; on Day 5 he makes birds (sky creatures) and fish (sea creatures). On Day 3 he makes the dry land and vegetation (green plants and fruit trees); on Day 6 he makes the land creatures and humans who eat these plants and fruits.

Note that what is stressed in this symbolic structuring is not so much what is made first, second, and third, but that each part of creation corresponds to other parts. The whole thing *fits*, and fits together perfectly. Horizontally (that is, among its creatures), the universe is symmetrically interdependent, just as it is vertically dependent upon God.

Looking even more closely, we can detect *another* layer of meaning—*the universe God is creating is being set up precisely to support life.* In the first three days, things are created that correspond to things created in the last three days. On Day 1 and Day 4 God makes light and the sources of light that benefit all living things. On Day 2 he makes sky and sea; on Day 5 the life forms that inhabit sky and sea. On Day 3 he makes land; on Day 6 the life forms that inhabit land. The fitting together of Days 1-3 with Days 4-6 reveals that the nonliving universe is made for the benefit of living creatures. As we shall see in Chapter Seven, this layer of meaning fits beautifully with what modern science has discovered, namely that the structure of the universe in its fundamental laws seems specifically designed to bring about and support living things.

If the two sets of days run side-by-side perfectly like two columns, the seventh day is the arch that completes their unity: the *Sabbath*, God's day of rest (Gn 2:1-4a). This particular aspect of the story offers a detail that science itself cannot teach or know about. It is that the universe is ordered toward fulfillment, rest, and worship. God's rest is reflected in his later command to his people to keep the Sabbath (which Christians will later honor on the "eighth day" of Christ's Resurrection) holy, that is, to order the Sabbath toward the One who gave rise to all things through intelligence and love.

The Sabbath, the majestic arch that binds all parts of the creation into one, is a clue for man as to what God's creation is all about.

The Sabbath, the majestic arch that binds all parts of the creation into one, is a clue for man as to what God's creation is all about. At least 1000 years after Genesis was written, **St. Benedict of Nursia**, the father of Western monastic life, captured this idea in his great Rule of Life, in which he says, "*Operi Dei nihil præponitur*"—"Nothing should be put before the service of God."[15] In other words, all the columns of creation are oriented toward the arch, which is the possibility of finding fulfillment in God. As the Christian mystic Meister Eckhart once put it, "God enjoys himself, and wants us to join him."

The medium is the message, or at least, it is a vital part of the message—God's architectural masterpiece, the universe, is a unity in diversity that reflects God's glory so that man can know God in it and serve him through it for the sake of man's own happiness.

3. The Big Picture: A Symbolic Cosmogony

THE FIRST CREATION ACCOUNT is filled with other symbolic details that deserve to be mentioned. God speaks ten times in the account, which calls to mind the Ten Commandments. This symbolizes the truth that the universe is created as a space for human goodness, for the sake of goodness. God does not create the universe as an amoral reality to be exploited; rather, the order we see in the world is a sign to us that God calls us to live virtuously, according to what is good and true.

God only deliberates when he creates human beings. This is symbolic of the uniqueness of human beings, who like God also deliberate. Of all the creatures known to the human authors of the account, only human beings are capable of rationality as the image of God's own perfect reason, a detail we shall explore in Part III. Also, God never beholds his human creatures, nor declares their goodness simply by virtue of their existence, even though he does declare that creation is "very good" only after humans have been created. In other cases (see verses 4, 12, 10, 18, and 25), God makes things, beholds them, and their goodness is proclaimed. But, with human beings, God only gives them their mission. The symbolism is clear; although by virtue of their creation by God human beings are "very good," in the final analysis human goodness is not simply up to God, but to God and to us. God has given a command, and the human response (obedience or disobedience) has yet to be given. In the account, our *moral* goodness is a question in suspense—it is up to us to freely cooperate with the Creator and to thereby realize the goodness by which and in which God has created us.

God Creates Adam
The literary genre of the First Creation Account is a *symbolic cosmogony*, an account of the beginning and development of the universe that uses symbolism to show its deepest meaning and our place within it.

These symbolic details, along with the many others we have identified, help us to identify the literary genre of the First Creation Account as a *symbolic cosmogony*, an account of the beginning and development of the universe that uses symbolism to show its deepest meaning and our place within it. Unlike the Big Bang Theory, which is a *scientific cosmogony* that involves careful calculation to give us details about time, space, matter, and energy, and the *Enûma Eliš*, a misguided, anti-Christian, antihuman, and *mythological cosmogony* in which symbolism is secondary and powerful gods and goddess have sex and kill each other and make the universe in the process, the First Creation Account is *primarily* symbolic, a great work of poetic imagination that captures a truth deeper than other modes of human writing can convey.

D. Obstacle or Origin? The First Creation Account and Modern Science

THE PICTURE OF CREATION DRAWN by the authors of the First Creation Account seems a perfect picture; in fact, it seems almost too perfect to some. As we noted above, many dismiss it as a religious daydream. "Nice try," they say, "but scientifically speaking, it is simply a primitive, unenlightened myth." In the words of the late Christopher Hitchens, "How can it be proven . . . that this book was written by ignorant men and not by any god? Because man is given dominion over all beasts, fowl and fish. But no dinosaurs or plesiosaurs or pterodactyls are specified, because the authors did not know of their existence."[16]

Yet we have already seen in Chapter Two that the biblical understanding of the universe was a major element of the cultural environment in which modern science was born and (as we will see in Chapter Five) thrived. In rejecting it outright, scientific atheists are sawing away at the very branch that they themselves are sitting on. The notion of an all-good, all-powerful, intelligent Creator implies that the universe he created has discoverable limits, order, and value. Without limits, order, and value, scientific investigators would have nothing to investigate.

So, what are the difficulties raised by those who wish to dismiss the creation account? The devil is in the details. Here are a few problems that are often pointed out:

- **The Superdome Sky**—Genesis 1:6 describes the sky as an upside-down bowl which has been submerged in water, having water on all sides and above it. But, of course, we now know that the sky is not shaped like a bowl.
- **The Order of Production**—God makes light before he makes the sun, but how could there be light without a source of light? God makes plants before he makes the sun. The problem is obvious: how could they grow?
- **The Duration of Creation**—Although the sun and moon are not created until the fourth day, it seems as if the whole production of the universe occurs in seven, twenty-four hour periods. Modern science, however, has shown the earth itself to be at least 4.5 *billion* years old and the universe to be 13.7 billion years old.

The details of the account are clearly "contradicted" by modern science if they are taken literalistically. There are two ways that believers have tried to answer this challenge: by trying to harmonize and correlate the Bible and science or by reading the First Creation Account in the context of the rest of the Bible. The first approach is incorrect and dangerous; the second helpfully illustrates the principles we have already discussed. Let us examine both.

The biblical understanding of the universe was a major element of the cultural environment necessary for science to be born and to thrive.

Concordists have tried to create a harmony between every detail of the First Creation Account and this or that cosmogony offered by science, only to have that science later proven to be false.

1. Concordism: Losing the Forest for the Trees

IN RESPONSE TO THE GROWTH of scientific understanding of the details of the beginning of the universe and of the earth, some believers have tried to create a harmony between every detail of the First Creation Account and this or that cosmogony offered by science. This is called *concordism*, and believers who have attempted to match up details in this way have fallen into two serious mistakes.

First, the concordists are trying to hit a moving target: Science is a progressive enterprise, and over time it corrects itself in substantial ways through new discoveries and the corresponding development of new theories or the nuancing of old ones. In Parts II and III of this course we will look at some important ways that it has changed in the last century. As a result, concordists in the past succeeded by great ingenuity in matching the Bible to this or that scientific calculation of the origins of the universe and of life, only to have that science later proven to be false. Here is the tragic irony: What was an attempt to strengthen faith in God actually resulted in jeopardizing that faith—the divine truth of the Bible was incorrectly tied to a discarded theory.[17]

A classic and somewhat humorous example occurred in the case of **Archbishop James Ussher**, a seventeenth-century Anglican theologian, who attempted to reconcile the six-day creation account with the physics of **Sir Isaac Newton**. In his strained attempt at harmonizing the dates found in the Bible with science, he concluded that the creation began in the year 4004 BC on Sunday, October 23, at 9:00 am.[18]

The second mistake involved in concordism is even more significant than the first. In artificially trying to tie the symbolic cosmogony of the Bible to a modern, scientific account, concordism actually misses the whole point of the First Creation Account by treating truths communicated through a symbolic cosmogony as if they were truths ascertained by way of scientific investigation. By trying to directly correlate the First Creation Account with a modern, scientific understanding, the truth of the symbolic cosmogony is overlooked because one is approaching it on scientific terms rather than on its own terms.

2. Dealing with Details: What God Is NOT Telling Us in the First Creation Account

THE BEAUTY OF THE SIX-DAY ACCOUNT can be appreciated by anyone with a taste for ancient literature and poetic description, and its meaning can be discovered through its symbolism and structure, as we saw above. But to interpret what it means also requires discovering what it does not mean, which requires reading it in the context of the entirety of Sacred Scripture.

The Bible, the Christian faith tells us, is a unity—although it is a library of many books from the perspective of its human authors, it is theologically one Book because God inspired its many parts to be read in light of each other and in light of the teaching of the Church. As **Cardinal Joseph Ratzinger**—before he was elected Pope Benedict XVI—pointed out, "[The First Creation Account] is not, from its very beginning, something that is closed in on itself.... Hence, the theme of creation is not set down once in only one place..."[19] There are several other creation accounts in the Bible, including a much older one that immediately follows the First Creation Account and is called the Second Creation Account (cf. Gn 2:4b-25). By reading these other accounts alongside the First Creation Account, we discover that details change from one account to another (as the authors of the later accounts would obviously have realized), showing that, even to the authors themselves, such details were not given for their own sake but to serve the more fundamental and important truths that God is conveying in the Bible. These details simply serve as different ways of grasping hold of that deeper message.

The dome sky, the exact sequence of events, and the duration of creation pertain to the *literary dimension* of the creation story with its poetic style typical of that period and form of literature.

For instance, whereas in the First Creation Account man is created last, in the Second Creation Account God creates man before the other living things (cf. Gn 2:4b-7). If the details of the order of creation in the First Creation Account were supposed to be taken as factual, it would make no sense for the second story to be included. Clearly, we are dealing with the literary dimension of the story when we deal with such poetic details as the dome sky, the exact sequence of events, and the duration of creation.

Here is another example. In the First Creation Account, the message is proclaimed using the details of pagan mythology in order to correct them, to purify them of religious errors, and to orient them toward God. But Psalm 104, a great psalm of praise to the Creator, narrates God's production of the universe using different details. For instance, it speaks of the sun and moon only after the man and animals. Birds and fish are referred to separately from each other, while in the First Creation Account they are created together on Day 4.

Another example of the openness of Scripture to new ways of expressing revealed truth can be found in the Book of Wisdom. The human author refers to his desire and prayer for the gift of wisdom. He then describes the wisdom he is given *in scientific terms*: "It is he who gave me unerring knowledge of what exists, to know the structure of the world and the activity of the elements; the beginning and end and middle of times..." (Wis 7:17-18a). Here, a biblical author, inspired by God and writing centuries after the Book of Genesis was written, goes on a quest for knowledge concerning the "beginning." If the details of the Book of Genesis were to be taken as if they were scientific textbook facts, why would this inspired biblical author seek knowledge of the actual details? As a Jew, he revered the *Torah* (including Genesis) as God's Word. His desire for and openness to new insights leave no doubt that "sticking to the old images such as the seven days"[20] *is to miss the picture for the frame that holds it.*

Therefore, **Cardinal Ratzinger** concludes:

> **Thus we can see how the Bible itself constantly readapts its images to a continually developing way of thinking, how it changes time and again.... In the Bible, the images [e.g., the six days, the sky dome, etc.] are free and they correct themselves accordingly. In this way they show, by means of a gradual and interactive process, that they are only images, which reveal something deeper and greater.**[21]

Does this mean that the Bible is wrong? Obviously not. It means that Sacred Scripture has something to teach every age of history, regardless of the level of science any age may have reached. Its truth is "deeper and greater" than science, and it adopts the cosmogony of its age to express that truth. That is why, even in Scripture, the details vary from creation account to creation account.

God Separates Light From Darkness
The creation of light, of earth and sky, of celestial lights and living things is the result of an intelligent plan.

Of course, reason urges us to ask whether the beautiful picture we find in Scripture is true. Has science overthrown the "deeper and greater" truth to which the human images in Scripture are pointing? Has God's eternal reason (which Scripture calls his wisdom and his Word) been shown to be absent from creation—or has it instead been confirmed to be magnificently pervasive throughout it? Is divine rationality really the final word on the universe? For now we can say this: The more deeply the sciences have penetrated the universe, the more its rich and wonderful rationality has been revealed. **Albert Einstein**, perhaps the greatest scientist of the twentieth century and even of human history, was himself taken aback by this fact. "In the laws of Nature," he declared, "there is revealed such a superior Reason that everything significant which has arisen out of human thought and arrangement is, in comparison with it, the merest empty reflection."[22]

Here the notion of the six days from the First Creation Account can be rediscovered as having an enduring significance even today in our scientific age. The process described there—the creation of light, of earth and sky, of celestial lights and living things—is the result of an intelligent plan, not haphazard but ordered. Its deeper, greater truth is confirmed every time scientists uncover newer and deeper levels of the order of nature—from the vast order uncovered by astronomy all the way down to the minute order found in subatomic particles.

3. The Final Word on Creation: The Creating Word Is God's *Logos*

ONE OF THE FINAL CREATION ACCOUNTS given in Sacred Scripture was written by **St. John the Evangelist**. It is found in the New Testament in Chapter One of his Gospel. In it and through it we reach down so deeply into the truth of the universe that we are allowed to reach right into the identity of the Creator:

1 In the beginning was the Word [*Logos*], and the Word was with God, and the Word was God.

2 He was in the beginning with God;

3 all things were made through him, and without him was not anything made that was made.

4 In him was life, and the life was the light of men.

5 The light shines in the darkness, and the darkness has not overcome it.

6 A man named John was sent from God.

7 He came for testimony, to testify to the light, so that all might believe through him.

8 He was not the light, but came to testify to the light.

9 The true light, which enlightens everyone, was coming into the world.

10 He was in the world, and the world was made through him, yet the world knew him not.

14 And the Word became flesh and dwelt among us, full of grace and truth; we have beheld his glory, glory as of the only Son from the Father.

16 And from his fullness have we all received, grace upon grace.

17 For the law was given through Moses; grace and truth came through Jesus Christ.

18 No one has ever seen God; the only Son, who is in the bosom of the Father, he has made him known.

St. John the Evangelist
"The light shines in the darkness, and the darkness has not overcome it." (Jn 1:5)

As we have already seen, the Greek word *Logos*, which is usually translated "Word," also means "Mind" or "Reason." So, this famous passage also bears this meaning: "In the beginning was Reason, and Reason was with God, and Reason was God. He was in the beginning with God. All things came to be through him . . . " Thus, divine rationality, the blueprint of the universe, becomes flesh, that is, becomes human, in Jesus Christ. All things flow, not from a divine *what*, but a divine *Who*—the Son, the perfect image of the Father who is one with and equal to the Father, brings the universe about as an expression of God's goodness and wisdom.

The Father, Son, and Holy Spirit love one another from all eternity, and the universe is a freely chosen overflow of that love. It is created by the Father, the power behind its existence, for and through the Son, the source of its rationality and order, in the Divine Love they share—the Holy Spirit, who is the source of its openness. How far we have come from the *Enûma Eliš*, with its foreboding, terror-filled chaos of murderous deities and demons, can be seen in the words of the Christian mystic Meister Eckhart, who once declared that "the world is created out of the laughter of the Trinity."

E. Is Science in Accord with Scripture?

NOW THAT WE HAVE A BETTER UNDERSTANDING of what we mean by the truth of the Bible regarding creation and see that its truth is not scientific truth, let us turn things around. Instead of looking for scientific truth in the Bible, let us see if perhaps the Bible can offer us a perspective that welcomes a scientific approach to reality. For a believer, this is the most important issue. If the Bible truthfully tells us all we need to know about God for the sake of our salvation, perhaps it can tell us whether or not God desires us to engage in science. Is science something God desires? Is it good, bad, or indifferent to the salvation of those human beings who are scientists?

Food Science brings together multiple scientific disciplines from fields such as chemistry, physics, physiology, microbiology, and biochemistry with the intent of growing more and better food for the good of all humanity.

Let us start by asking, "What do we have to believe about the universe before we can hope to become scientists?" First, we must believe that the universe is fundamentally orderly and rational. This is necessary so that we have both a reason to believe that our investigation has the possibility of being successful and that what we find out one day will still be true on the next day—if we believed otherwise then we wouldn't bother to study the universe. Second, we must believe that this order is open to the human mind, for otherwise there would be no point in trying to figure it out. Third, however, we must believe that this order is not an order so obvious that it could be found out by pure thought but that it is rather an order that can only be found out through experimentation—we cannot understand it unless we experience it.

In addition to these beliefs about the universe itself, the development of science as it emerged from the Scientific Revolution depended on certain moral convictions, such as the value of freely sharing the fruits of scientific discoveries with fellow researchers. Furthermore, once it became clear that scientific understanding can be applied to grow more food or cure diseases, then its further development was encouraged by the assumption that one should work for the common good of humanity.

Therefore, the progress of science historically, and even today, depends on three assumptions:

- The universe is orderly and rational (it has laws);
- The universe requires investigation in order to be understood (no sofa science allowed!);
- Knowledge, including scientific knowledge, should be shared for the good of humanity.

Let us compare these beliefs to what we learn in the Bible, starting with the order and rationality of the universe. Every time a scientist seeks to discover how the universe works, he or she assumes that its order is reliable and that it is not a chaotic, unknowable mess. Before this idea found application in science, it was taught by God in the Bible, as we have seen in the First Creation Account. We read in the Book of Wisdom 11:21 that the Creator arranged everything in the universe by measure, number, and weight, a verse that was often quoted by the pioneers of the Scientific Revolution. Compare this idea to the saying of Galileo Galilei (1564-1642) that God wrote the universe in the language of mathematics. In short, scientists rely upon and investigate an order that the Bible teaches comes from divine wisdom, whether they realize it or not.

But our universe is not a necessary one; the order of the universe is not a rigid order of pure necessity. There are a great many things about the universe that can't be predicted by working out the math but instead require careful experimentation to discover. The picture of God and the universe given by the Bible supports this assumption of science, namely, that we must investigate the universe in order to understand it. The Bible teaches not only that God's order and rationality is reflected in the universe he created but also that he created the universe with perfect freedom. The universe indeed has an order, but it is an order that is freely chosen by God. "Whatever the LORD pleases he does, in heaven and on earth, in the seas and all deeps" (Ps 135:6-7). He could have made the universe in many different ways but chose to make it this way. Because God is free in creating the universe, we have to take the universe on its own terms—we have to explore it to know it. Experimentation, whether this or that scientist realizes it, is necessary because God creates the universe with divine freedom (creation *cum libertate*).

Galileo said that God wrote the universe in the language of mathematics. Because God is free in creating the universe, we have to take the universe on its own terms—we have to explore it to know it.

If the Bible only taught these things, then it would teach enough for us to say, "Yes, it seems as if God created a universe that would require something like science to be understood." But science requires more than just the right assumptions about the universe. It requires that certain values be in place, such as a willingness to share scientific discoveries across cultures, the belief that knowledge must be freely shared. This is enjoined by the author of the Book of Wisdom: "I learned without guile and I impart without grudging; I do not hide her wealth, for it [Wisdom] is an unfailing treasure for men; those who get it obtain friendship with God" (Wis 7:13-14b). The Bible teaches that knowledge is meant to be shared, not hoarded. By the time of the Scientific Revolution, Europe had developed a culture of sharing knowledge through a university system. Universities are the historical embodiment of the biblical idea that we should share the riches of truth with all people, and it was in the Christian universities of Europe that modern science was born.

However, all of this pales in comparison to the command of God in Genesis 1:28: "Be fruitful and multiply, and fill the earth and subdue it; and have dominion over the fish of the sea and over the birds of the air and over every living thing that moves upon the earth." In other words, God commands that human beings have oversight of the world he created. It is not an optional exercise, but an integral one. In the Second Creation Account (Gn 2:19-20), God parades the animals before Adam so that he can name them all—this is symbolic of the urge for discovery and understanding that fuels all science. Adam is portrayed as the first investigator of nature.

The biblical message is clear. We are not simply here to make things or to do stuff. We are placed on earth to behold and understand the good, beautiful, and true things which God has made to communicate his love to us so that we may better know, love, and serve him in return. Science is one important way that we accomplish God's will for us as it is expressed in Sacred Scripture. The testimony of Sacred Scripture is that science is a noble project, something God wills for his human creatures. In the words of **Cardinal Joseph Ratzinger**, before he was elected Pope Benedict XVI: "Scientific knowledge is, so to speak, the adventure that he [God] has left to *us ourselves*."[23]

God commands that human beings have oversight of the world he created. God parades the animals before Adam so that he can name them all—this is symbolic of the urge for discovery and understanding that fuels all science. Adam is portrayed as the first investigator of nature.

F. The Whole Picture

FOR THE SAKE OF SUMMARIZING, let us go back to the three points with which we began this chapter. Noting that Scripture was both human and divine, we developed a *holistic* (a complete, "both/and") approach to Scripture that respects both science and faith:

1. **The First Creation Account tells us, without error, the truth about God the Creator and the deepest truth about why God created the universe.** We have seen that the story does exactly that: It reveals that the universe has an all-powerful, all-good, perfectly intelligent God as its source (reflected in the logically ordered and perfectly symmetrical "six days") and its unifying summit (the "seventh day"). Its plain message and its structure both point confidently to a creation that flows from eternal reason and reflects it.
2. **The First Creation Account tells us this truth using poetic and symbolic language and images, the product of ancient Near-Eastern authors.** In regard to this aspect of the First Creation Account, we see that, when we read it in the light of the rest

of Sacred Scripture, we do not need to strain the details to fit modern scientific discoveries. These details are not there to give us an exact, scientific cosmogony; they are images that are open and freely adaptable to new contexts, especially to the context of new knowledge. Here, we should remember that this principle is an ancient one; we can see it in Scripture itself in the Book of Wisdom.

3. **The First Creation Account is not a scientific treatise, but something more essential: It is a testament to God's wisdom in creating and to his divine goodness of the universe he created.** In regard to the First Creation Account, we saw that the total story, even in its prescientific details, gives a wonderful way of approaching the vastness of the universe "in a nutshell"—all of its beauty, its vastness, and its incredible detail boils down to the glory of its Creator offered freely to humanity, finding its summit in the fulfillment which God offers it in a Sabbath rest and worship that ultimately leads to union with himself. The gift is great, but the Giver is even greater.

If the purpose of the First Creation Account had been to give us scientific knowledge about how the universe began, how stars and planets formed, and how life started on earth, we would have to judge it a miserable failure. But that was obviously not the purpose. The priests of the Jewish people had other things on their minds during their woeful exile in Babylon besides physics, chemistry, astronomy, geology, and biology. Their concerns were primarily religious. And so, if we think of the details of the First Creation Account as scientific details, we will be reading into them a kind of meaning of which the authors never dreamed nor intended.

The details do indeed have meaning. They were painstakingly chosen and arranged so as to teach religious truths, not scientific ones. What mattered to the authors was not whether the moon was made by the condensation of a dust cloud, as once was thought, or by the impact of a large object striking the earth, as is now thought, or by some other mechanism; what mattered to them was just that it was made, that it is a part of God's creation and not itself a god. They were not proposing a theory about how the universe is ordered but were instead calling attention to the gigantic fact that it is ordered and that its orderliness points to a divine plan. The pattern of the six days is not the kind of pattern that the modern physicist would capture with an equation or a graph, but it is the kind of pattern that reveals a purpose. And the authors had something to tell us about that purpose. The universe does not only exist for its own sake, but it exists so that there could be life. And life does not exist only so that there could be plants and animals, but it exists so that there could be rational beings made in the image of God. And these beings have not been made only for themselves, but they have been made for a relationship with God, a relationship which is expressed in the notion of a Sabbath rest that symbolizes completion and eternal happiness: the eternal rest we shall have with God, the rest of which St. Augustine spoke when he said, "Our heart is restless until it rest in Thee."[24]

The details of the First Creation Account do indeed have meaning. They were painstakingly chosen and arranged so as to teach religious truths, not scientific ones.

G. Looking Ahead

AS OUR THOROUGH EXAMINATION REVEALS, Sacred Scripture is not only compatible with science, but it fosters it and offers it a transcendent goal and framework within which to operate and understand the nature of its own work. What is true of biblical cosmogony is also true of other prescientific details. Throughout this text, we will return to Sacred Scripture: miracles, the Second Creation Account in Genesis, and many other biblical topics will emerge as we continue our quest to rediscover the Christian faith on the frontiers of modern science.

The Bible is not simply a divinely inspired Book; as we saw at the beginning of this chapter, it is also the Book of the Church. God's Book is certainly compatible with science, but is it compatible with the Church and her teachings? For some people, the fact that the Catholic Church is pro-science is almost as surprising as the fact that Scripture is pro-science. There is a reason for this; while she has defended and promoted science for centuries, the Catholic Church also has a serious blemish on her history, one that explains why many in modern society consider her to be a harsh persecutor of scientific pioneers.

To understand the Church's support for science, we must understand how God reveals himself through the Church's life and consciousness, which is called Sacred Tradition. We must also look into the past and explore the marvelous history of the Church's support of the sciences. Then we must look directly at that blemish on that history, and into the life of a scientist whose name is almost a synonym for both scientific discovery and persecution—**Galileo Galilei**.

The Prophet Isaiah and the Seraphim (Is 6:6-7).
Sacred Scripture is not only compatible with science, but it also fosters it and offers it a transcendent goal and framework within which to operate and understand the nature of its own work.

VOCABULARY

Define the following terms (or identify the person's significance):

1. Divine Inspiration
2. Saving Truth (Bible)
3. Perspective
4. Sacred Scripture (Divinity)
5. Sacred Scripture (Humanity)
6. Holistic Approach (Both/And)
7. Genesis 1:1–2:4a
8. Babylonian Exile
9. *Enûma Eliš*
10. Apsu
11. Tiamat
12. Marduk
13. Kingu
14. Divine Unity (First Creation Account)
15. Divine Rationality (First Creation Account)
16. Divine Goodness (First Creation Account)
17. Human Beings (First Creation Account)
18. Symmetry (Structure of First Creation Account)
19. Cosmogony
20. Concordism
21. Archbishop James Ussher
22. Genesis 2:4b-25
23. Psalm 104
24. Wisdom 7:17-18a
25. *Torah*
26. John 1:1-18
27. *Logos* (John 1:1-18)
28. Assumptions of Modern Science
29. Wisdom 11:21
30. Psalm 135:6-7
31. Wisdom 7:13-14b
32. Genesis 2:19-20

The Destruction of Solomon's Temple and Jerusalem by King Nebuchadnezzar II and the Exile of Judeans to Babylon. This deportation is dated at 588-587 BC. After the fall of Babylon to the Persian King Cyrus the Great in 539 BC, the exiled Judeans were permitted to return to Judah if they chose to.

STUDY QUESTIONS

1. How does the opening quote from St. John Paul II guide us in reading the First Creation Account?

2. How is the expectation of finding any and all kinds of truths in Sacred Scripture related to the conflict/warfare model of science and faith?

Section A

3. What does the Catholic Church teach about biblical truth?

4. How does the concept of *perspective* help to distinguish biblical and theological truths from other kinds of truth?

5. What three kinds of truths are to be found in Sacred Scripture?

6. Refute the assertion that Sacred Scripture teaches empirical scientific truths by reference to the Pontifical Biblical Commission and *YouCat*.

7. Does the divine and human status of Sacred Scripture have any important implications for the issue of modern science and Sacred Scripture?

8. What three principles should guide one's approach to interpreting and understanding the First Creation Account?

Section B

9. What is the historical background of the First Creation Account?

10. Briefly summarize the *Enûma Eliš* account of creation, and describe the vision of the universe and humanity that it presents.

Section C

11. What is the message about God in the First Creation Account? What is its message about the world and humanity?

12. What theological truths are symbolized by the structure of the First Creation Account?

13. Distinguish between the three kinds of cosmogony mentioned, and identify the genre of cosmogony found in the First Creation Account.

Section D

14. Why do some scientific thinkers dismiss the First Creation Account? What misunderstanding about biblical truth does their dismissal reveal?

15. Why is concordism a faulty approach to reconciling Scripture and science? Give two reasons which show that concordism is the wrong approach for believers to use in defending Sacred Scripture as God's Word.

16. What is God NOT telling us through the First Creation Account? Why are the prescientific details of the account not a threat to the truth of Sacred Scripture?

17. Refute the creationist assertion that the Bible teaches scientific truths by reference to the Second Creation Account, Psalm 104, or Book of Wisdom.

18. How does the Prologue to St. John's Gospel complete the understanding of divine creation given in the First Creation Account?

Section E

19. What does modern science assume about the universe? Explain how Sacred Scripture includes the same assumptions by reference to specific passages.

PRACTICAL EXERCISES

1. Watch the video "Science and Genesis" (11 minutes, 46 seconds, *mtfresources.org/videos*). How does the video reflect upon both the human and divine aspects of the First Creation Account? What additional details does it add to the understanding developed in this chapter?

2. Consider each of the following Scripture verses. Explain what each has to say about the "deeper, greater truth" of creation: Isaiah 40:12-14, 18-20; Isaiah 42:25-31; Job 28:20, 23-28; Psalm 95:1-7; Psalm 8; Sirach 24:1-7; Wisdom 13:1-7; Romans 1:18-21; Colossians 1:15-18; and Hebrews 1:1-3.

James Ussher (1581-1656) was the Church of Ireland Archbishop of Armagh and Primate of all Ireland between 1625 and 1656. He is most famous for his chronology "Annals of the Old Testament, Deduced from the First Origins of the World" published in 1650, which (through his interpretation of historical timelines) established the exact time and date of Creation. Ussher's chronology is used to support "Young Earth Creationism," which holds that the universe was created thousands of years ago rather than billions.

Endnotes – Chapter Four

1. John Paul II, Address to the Pontifical Biblical Commission, April 23, 1992, no. 8.
2. Vatican II, Dogmatic Constitution *Dei Verbum* on Divine Revelation, no. 11 (hereafter abbreviated *DV*).
3. *DV* 19; cf. Acts 1:1.
4. Pontifical Biblical Commission, *The Inspiration and Truth of Sacred Scripture: The Word that Comes from God and Speaks for God for the Salvation of the World*, trans. by Thomas Esposito and Stephen Gregg (Collegeville, MN: Liturgical Press, 2014), no. 63.
5. Christoph Schönborn, ed., *YouCat: Youth Catechism of the Catholic Church* (San Francisco, CA: Ignatius Press, 2011), q. 15.
6. St. Augustine, *De actis cum Felice Manichaeo*, I.10 (P.L. 42.525).
7. CCC 141; cf. *DV* 21.
8. Ibid., 136.
9. Joseph Ratzinger, "What in Fact is Theology?" in *Pilgrim Fellowship of Faith: The Church as Communion*, trans. by Henry Taylor (San Francisco, CA: Ignatius Press, 2005), 33.
10. For a complete translation online, go to *www.sacred-texts.com/ane/enuma.htm*.
10. Michael Duggan, *The Consuming Fire: A Christian Guide to the Old Testament* (San Francisco, CA: Ignatius Press, 1991), 74.
12. Duggan, *The Consuming Fire*, 74.
13. Ibid., 75.
14. Ibid.
15. As quoted in Joseph Ratzinger, *'In the Beginning…': A Catholic Understanding of the Story of Creation and the Fall*, trans. by Boniface Ramsey (Grand Rapids, MI: Eerdmans, 1986), 27-28, 38.
16. Hitchens, *God is Not Great*, 90.
17. Haffner, *Mystery of Creation*, 11.
18. Ibid.
19. Ratzinger, *In the Beginning*, 8-9.
20. Ibid., 15.
21. Ibid.
22. Ibid., 23. The original quote may be found in *Dear Professor Einstein: Albert Einstein's Letters to and from Children*, ed. by Alice Calaprice (Amherst, NY: Prometheus Books, 2002), 127-129.
23. Joseph Ratzinger, *God and the World: A Conversation with Peter Seewald*, trans. by Henry Taylor (San Francisco, CA: Ignatius Press, 2002), 121.
24. St. Augustine, *Confessions*, Book I.1.

Nebuchadnezzar II, King of Babylon ca. 605-562 BC, was the longest-reigning and most powerful monarch of the Neo-Babylonian Empire.
The prophecies of Jeremiah, Ezekiel, and Daniel, and the last chapters of Kings and Chronicles centered around his life and oppression of Judah and God's people.

Chapter Five

Patroness or Persecutor? Sacred Tradition and Scientific Discovery

What is Sacred Tradition, and why must we take it into account in order to understand the relationship between faith and science?

What common themes do we find among great Christian theologians that are significant for the harmony of faith and science?

What are the most important moments in Church history in regard to the harmony of faith and science?

What important contributions have Catholic scientists made to the progress of science throughout Church history?

What really happened to Galileo, and what significance does it have for understanding the Church's attitude toward science and scientists?

You will know them by their fruits. Are grapes gathered from thorns, or figs from thistles? So, every sound tree bears good fruit, but the bad tree bears evil fruit. A sound tree cannot bear evil fruit, nor can a bad tree bear good fruit....Thus you will know them by their fruits. (Mt 7:16-18,20)

Beautiful is what we see.
More beautiful is what we comprehend.
Most beautiful is what we do not comprehend.
—Blessed Nicholas Steno, 1673

American Catholics live in a culture deeply influenced by the Protestant doctrine that the Bible stands alone as the self-sufficient, fully complete source for discovering Divine Revelation, commonly called the doctrine of "*sola Scriptura*" (Scripture alone). "If the Bible says it, I believe it!" is a common slogan among many American Christians. Behind this slogan is the assumption not only that Sacred Scripture alone is our source for discovering divine truth but also that Sacred Scripture is *perspicuous*—it is abundantly clear and easily understood by every Christian thanks to the interior illumination of the Holy Spirit. Hence, another common and equally cheesy slogan: B.I.B.L.E., that is, "*Basic Instructions Before Leaving Earth*"!

The Catholic Church, in conjunction with the various Protestant denominations, also venerates Sacred Scripture as the Word of God. But she does so with a crucial difference—she teaches that Sacred Tradition, the living relationship between Christ and his Church made possible by the

Holy Spirit, is also a necessary source for discovering divine truth equal with, and inseparable from, Sacred Scripture. In the words of Vatican II:

> **There exists a close connection and communication between Sacred Tradition and Sacred Scripture. For both of them, flowing from the same divine wellspring, in a certain way merge into a unity and tend toward the same end.... Consequently it is not from Sacred Scripture alone that the Church draws her certainty about everything which has been revealed. Therefore both Sacred Tradition and Sacred Scripture are to be accepted and venerated with the same sense of loyalty and reverence.[1]**

Sacred Tradition and Sacred Scripture "flow from the same divine wellspring." Sacred Tradition is manifested through the works of great thinkers, men and women we call Fathers and Doctors of the Church.

Because the Church's very existence at any and every moment depends upon Christ's union with and the Spirit's activity within her, Sacred Tradition is nothing less than the *very life and consciousness* of the Church, her deepest self-identity.[2] Like your own life and consciousness, or mine, it is manifested in all the important acts and events of the Church's past and present. Sacred Tradition is nothing less than Jesus Christ, the Word of God, living within his Church throughout history and in the *here and now*.

Contrary to the creators of the B.I.B.L.E. slogan, Sacred Scripture is not a basic, easily understood instruction manual; it cannot be truly and fully understood without relying upon the help of Sacred Tradition. As noted by the great Dominican theologian, **Yves Congar**, everything God wishes to reveal to us can be found in Sacred Scripture *except* for its meaning, which can only be found when Scripture is read in light of Sacred Tradition.[3] Whenever the two are separated, our grasp of divine truth is obscured or diminished.

When we apply this to our current topic, then, we see that even the openness to science that we discovered in Sacred Scripture does not suffice to reveal the openness of the Christian faith to scientific investigation. We must also consider what we find in the Church's history, following the Lord's guidance in the Sermon on the Mount—"You will know them by their fruits" (Mt 7:16). Has the Church been a patroness (that is, a "sponsor" and a "supporter") of the sciences, or has she been a persecutor of scientists? As we will see, the Church is a patroness of the sciences—

her history is full of examples of her sponsorship and support of the sciences. First, she has formally nurtured the sciences in her teaching and in her actions. Second, members of the Church throughout her history have been inspired to enter into the scientific arena and have made momentous contributions to the progress of scientific understanding.

In this chapter we will take a tour of the Church's history, considering the thought of great Catholic theologians who embraced the harmony of faith and reason in regard to the natural world. We will learn about important Catholic "moments" that preceded the Scientific Revolution and which paved the way for science, as well as great moments since that give evidence of the Church's embrace of scientific progress. In the longest section, we will analyze the data of Sacred Tradition in practice, recounting a dazzling array of Catholic scientists—men and women, priests and bishops—who from ancient times participated in the progress of scientific knowledge as authentic, sometimes even saintly, Catholic believers. Finally, we will squarely and honestly face a true embarrassment in the Church's history, which modern historians refer to as "the Galileo Affair." What happened in this case requires careful consideration. But, as we shall see, the Galileo Affair was really a rare exception to an otherwise excellent relationship.

A. Science and the Witness of Sacred Tradition

1. Setting the Stage: The Golden Threads of Theological Insight

AS NOTED ABOVE, ONE OF THE WAYS IN WHICH SACRED TRADITION is manifested is through the works of great thinkers whom the Church has celebrated for their insights into divine truth, men and women we call Fathers and Doctors of the Church. Finding the ways in which they agree with each other across the ages is key to finding the "golden threads" of divine truth running through the various ages, cultures, and crises in which they lived and wrote. Across history we see two such "threads" that help reveal the witness of Sacred Tradition regarding science and nature:

1. Faith and Reason Together: The great thinkers of the Church's history show a common commitment to embracing well-demonstrated facts about the universe and the established scholarly insights of the age in which they lived, utilizing them for the benefit of deepening our understanding of Divine Revelation. At no point do we find them rejecting reason wholesale for the sake of faith; rather, they let reason inform their faith where it is appropriate and helpful for the sake of the integrity of the faith itself.

In his commentary (written AD 414) on the Book of Genesis, for example, **St. Augustine of Hippo** relied on established astronomical observations to come to the conclusion that the First Creation Account must be a symbolic cosmogony and not an actual scientific treatise. In the First Creation Account, each day ends with "evening came and morning followed." He

St. Augustine of Hippo (AD 354-430)
"In matters that are so obscure and far beyond our vision, we find in Holy Scripture passages which can be interpreted in very different ways without prejudice to the faith we have received." (*De Genesi ad Litteram*)

realized that the six days mentioned could not possibly be "days" in the way we think of actual, twenty-four hour days because it was well-known that the time of night and day are different in various parts of the world:

> **But if I say that [the days are twenty-four hour periods], I am afraid I will be laughed at by those who know for certain... that during the time when it is night with us the presence of light is illuminating those parts of the world past which the Sun is returning from its setting to its rising.... So then, are we really going to station God in some part [of the world] where evening can be made for him, while the light withdraws from that part to another?[4]**

St. John Henry Newman (1801-1890)
"We can believe what we choose. We are answerable for what we choose to believe." (*Letter to Mrs. William Froude*, June 1848)

Over 1450 years later, in 1870, the Catholic priest and cardinal **St. John Henry Newman** would make a similar judgment in light of Darwin's theory of evolution, namely, "that [life] began in some common ancestor," and the age of the earth, which scientists of his day had speculated to be anywhere from 20 million to 400 million years old (and not 6000 years old, as had once been assumed). In response to these new hypotheses, Newman was entirely open, noting the distinction between primary and secondary causality that we learned in Chapter Three: "If second[ary] causes are conceivable at all, an Almighty Agent being supposed, I don't see why the series [of living things] should not last for millions of years [rather than] thousands."[5]

Eight decades later, in 1951, **Pope Venerable Pius XII** would celebrate the Big Bang Theory and its description of a universe that is billions of years old as helping us to see the opening command of God in the First Creation Account in a new way: "... It seems that the science of today, by going back in one leap millions of centuries, has succeeded in being a witness to that primordial *Fiat Lux* ['Let there be light'], when, out of nothing, there burst forth with matter a sea of light and radiation, while the particles of chemical elements split and reunited in millions of galaxies." Although it seemed to some that Pius XII was trying to prove the existence of God from the Big Bang, he was careful to clarify that proofs for the existence of God were "outside the sphere of the natural sciences."[6]

Pope Venerable Pius XII (1876-1958)
"True science discovers God in an ever-increasing degree—as though God were waiting behind every door opened by science." (*Address to the Pontifical Academy of Sciences*, November 1951)

In all three cases, to which many more can be added, we see great Catholic thinkers giving the discoveries of science a kind of "veto power" in interpreting biblical texts[7]—when new scientific knowledge is achieved, it then serves to help us understand how to better interpret Sacred Scripture, which is never held as a reason to reject new knowledge. Sacred Tradition teaches us that reason should always inform and strengthen our faith.

2. The Integrity of Nature: The great thinkers of the Catholic tradition are very careful to avoid *supernaturalism*, which in this case means relying on divine, miraculous intervention as an explanation for how the universe works, often called the *"God of the Gaps"* error. Instead, these thinkers emphasize the wisdom of God in establishing the universe in such a way that it could bring about the ends he intended for it according to its own secondary causality. For them, the universe itself is a miracle because it exists and is able to do God's will. They avoid suggesting miracles as divine micromanagement of the universe, and they reject the temptation to see God as constantly tinkering with or "fixing" the universe through miraculous intervention.

St. Thomas Aquinas (1224/25-1274)
"To scorn the dictate of reason is to scorn the commandment of God."
(*STh* I-II, q. 19, art. 5)

Once again, **St. Augustine's** commentary on Genesis is a prime example. Inspired by his reverence for God's perfect wisdom, Augustine found the idea of separate creative acts on God's part to be problematic when trying to explain the origins of living things, even human beings. If God is perfect, his creative act must also be perfect, lacking nothing, requiring no additional divine acts to complete it. According to Augustine, God created the universe as already having everything necessary to be life-producing. For example, he taught that all living things, human beings included, naturally existed in the universe from its first moment, not as actual, already existing organisms but as *rational seeds*, which he identified as existing in "the very fabric, as it were, or texture of the elements... [requiring only] the right occasion actually to emerge into being."[8] Although he had no idea of common descent from an original ancestor, nor of natural selection and genetic variation, the integrity of nature as the source of life that Darwin would eventually champion was already being celebrated by this Father and Doctor of the Church one and one-half millennia before him.

Charles De Koninck (1906-1965)
"I fail to see why Natural Selection must be understood as devoid of purpose." (*Darwin's Dilemma*)

Following Augustine, **St. Thomas Aquinas** would later teach that "in the first founding of the order of nature *we must not look for miracles*, but for what is in accordance with nature."[9] Once evolutionary biology suggested centuries later that human beings have an evolutionary origin connecting them to all living things on earth, the twentieth-century Catholic philosopher **Charles De Koninck** dismissed creationists who considered such an idea to be an affront to the Creator and to the special dignity of human beings. He made it clear that the temptation of inserting miraculous explanations is actually bad theology, not simply bad science, because it deforms the natural order that all created things in the physical universe share in common. "Creationism," he observes, "which opens the world directly to God... implicitly rejects what is essential to the universe: the unity of order."[10] He also chastises those who find the idea of human evolution unacceptable:

> **If man and the ape have... a common ancestor, how would that detract from human dignity? Why prefer that he came from the mud?... is it not a sin... for man to deny his humble origins...? Is it not rather his glory to be the goal of these immense efforts of the world [to produce him]?[11]**

These examples represent a thorough commitment to the integrity of nature due to the perfection of divine wisdom and power. They show how very different the Catholic way of honoring the Creator is from literalistic creationism. Although not all went as far as St. Augustine or St. Thomas Aquinas in offering alternative speculations about the biblical narratives, the great thinkers of the Catholic tradition sought to appreciate as much as possible the causality of creatures. They did this not to get God out of the picture but to glorify him, because God is most profoundly at work, and his divine wisdom and power are most acutely manifest, when the universe is able to do his will just as he intended. As we saw in Chapter Three, God is not one cause among many. He is the cause of all causes; the more a creature can do, the more it shows forth the power of God. Creationism incorrectly squeezes God into the picture of nature, whereas Catholicism gives the whole picture to him, frame and all.

In summary, these two "golden threads" which run through the history of the Church show that the Church's theological priorities favor a harmony between faith and science. The emphasis on balancing faith and reason allows for reason to have a profound impact on faith; the emphasis on the integrity of nature due to divine perfection encourages confidence that the universe can be understood by assuming that natural explanations exist and ought to be pursued.

Keeping these "golden threads" in mind, we can now proceed on our "tour" of the evidence of Sacred Tradition to the formal teachings of the Church offered by the *Magisterium*. The Magisterium is the teaching authority of the Church; this is exercised by the bishops in union with the Pope so that the truths revealed by God can be faithfully proclaimed, defended, and clarified in every age.

"The Father begetting, the Son begotten, and the Holy Ghost proceeding; consubstantial and coequal, co-omnipotent and coeternal, the one principle of the universe, Creator of all things invisible and visible, spiritual and corporeal, who from the beginning of time and by His omnipotent power made from nothing creatures both spiritual and corporeal, angelic, namely, and mundane, and then human, as it were, common, composed of spirit and body." (Canon I of the Fourth Lateran Council, 1215)

2. Great Catholic Moments in Faith and Science: The "Prenatal Period"

SCIENCE AS A FORMAL, SYSTEMATIC, MATHEMATICAL STUDY of the natural world is a rather recent development, and it did not fully blossom until the latter half of the second Christian millennium. But the Church's patronage predates the birth of modern science. In fact, certain moments in Catholic teaching actually laid the groundwork for the birth of modern science, which occurred during the "prenatal period" just before the emergence of the modern scientific approach to the universe.

As we saw in Chapter Three, it was at the **Fourth Lateran Council** (Lateran IV) that the Church first solemnly taught that God created the world "out of nothing" (*ex nihilo* in Latin) and that his creation, unlike God himself, had a beginning in time.[12] Both of these ideas are biblical,[13] and both are favorable to a scientific outlook.

Pope Innocent III (1160/61-1216) presided over the Fourth Lateran Council, which gathered at Rome's Lateran Palace beginning November 11, 1215. It is sometimes called the "Great Council" due to the presence of 71 patriarchs and metropolitan bishops, 412 bishops, 900 abbots and priors, and representatives of several monarchs.

First, by teaching that the universe was created out of nothing, the Church dispelled a popular idea, already rejected by the Greek philosophers but still common among uneducated medieval Europeans, that the world was somehow divine, magical in itself, and not subject to discoverable principles and laws. At the time of the council many pagan ideas persisted that attributed magical properties to rivers, lakes, trees, etc. But recognizing that the world is thoroughly the product of God's creative will allowed people to approach the universe scientifically and not as if the forces in it had their own wills, powers, and mysterious personalities.[14]

The Lateran IV declaration that the universe had a real starting point, a beginning in time, was another crucial ingredient in the soil that the seeds of modern science needed to germinate and grow. Many in the ancient world thought that the universe was caught up in an ongoing cycle, like a great hamster wheel in which all events repeat themselves over and over again. But the Revelation that there was a real beginning encouraged believers to think in terms of real starting points, to look for causes in the past for things in the present, and to discover patterns that are there not simply because the "Great Cycle" always brings them back but because they have some real relationship to other things.[15]

God made the world out of nothing, and so the world was free to be itself—not a disguised form of divinity. And it had a beginning in time, which meant that cause and effect relationships were of the utmost importance in understanding it from its beginning to its end. *These key beliefs created important questions. The first shoots of medieval science grew out of the intelligent attempt to answer those questions.*

Only sixty-two years after Lateran IV, another teaching moment in Church history contributed further to the birth of science. In the year 1277 **Bishop Stephen Tempier** of Paris rejected the

Aristotelian idea that the universe could not be different than we find it to be, that it "had" to be the way it is or not at all. For example, the Aristotelians said that a true "vacuum" is an absolute impossibility because no one had ever observed one. But this kind of limit on God, Bishop Tempier said, contradicts the doctrine of God's omnipotence. Since God is all-powerful, he could have made a world where vacuums exist. This teaching stimulated people to think about vacuums and how they would behave if they did in fact exist (which we now know that they do!).

Similarly, Tempier condemned the Aristotelian idea that there could not possibly be other worlds. So questions such as whether other worlds exist or whether vacuums exist could not be answered except by seeing what God had actually chosen to create and then reasoning from there in the pursuit of new knowledge. It is true that Tempier rejected many ideas that would later be accepted by the Church as orthodox, such as the idea that the rational soul is the substantial form of the human body. But by rejecting these other Aristotelian ideas, Tempier pushed Western thought away from the idea that we can know what the universe is by *pure logic without experimentation*.[16] Because God is free in creating the world, we have to take the world on its own terms—we have to explore it to know it.

(top) *Bishop Stephen Tempier* (d.1279) was Chancellor of the Sorbonne in Paris from 1263 to 1268 and bishop of Paris from 1268 until his death. (bottom) *Jean Buridan* (ca.1300-1358/61) was a priest and professor at the Sorbonne for his entire career, focusing on logic and the works of Aristotle. With his concept of *impetus*, he sowed the seeds of the Copernican revolution in Europe.

Results of scientific importance were quick to follow. Only fifty-three years after Tempier's decree, in 1330, **Jean Buridan**, a priest and professor at the Sorbonne in Paris, proposed the principle of *impetus*—the notion that God set in motion the heavenly bodies but that they remained in motion without further divine (or angelic) action. Here we see a Christian thinker boldly speculating about the way the world works without being held back by previous notions. Stepping out as he did, he moved science forward; with Buridan we are one step away from a law you may well be familiar with from your own physics (or physical science) classes: "a body, once in motion, tends to remain in motion." That is **Sir Isaac Newton's** First Law of Motion, a foundation stone for modern physics.[17]

3. The Church and the Growth of the Scientific Age

THE CHURCH DECLARED THESE TEACHINGS before the scientific age began. When science finally got going, it found the Church ready to embrace it. One of the most important moments in this long history occurred at the **First Vatican Council** (Vatican I) in 1869-1870, particularly in Vatican I's Dogmatic Constitution on the Catholic Faith, entitled *Dei Filius*.

This important proclamation asserted a number of teachings of significance for the relationship between the Christian faith and the sciences. As we saw in Chapter Three, it repeated earlier statements that the world was created out of nothing, in time, and as an act freely undertaken by God.[18] But it also helped to reinforce the "rule of thumb" regarding how a believer should approach the difficulties that may arise in the "dialogue" between science and faith: "There can never be a real conflict between faith and reason, since the same God who reveals mysteries and infuses faith has bestowed the light of reason on the human mind, and God cannot deny himself, nor can truth ever contradict truth."[19] In other words, science, which comes from the use of God-given reason, and the Christian faith, which comes to us through the Church established by God, cannot really be at odds. If they seem to be, then we have not fully understood one or the other.

The **Second Vatican Council** (Vatican II), which met 1962-1965, would apply what Vatican I had decreed in general about the relationship of faith and reason to the sciences in particular. In this regard, it taught specifically about "the legitimate autonomy of science," i.e., the freedom of science to engage in scientific discovery and speculation without artificial constraints:

> **There are "two orders of knowledge" which are distinct, namely faith and reason; and... the Church does not forbid that "the human arts and disciplines use their own principles and their proper method, each in its own domain"; therefore "acknowledging this just liberty," this Sacred Synod affirms the legitimate autonomy of human culture and *especially of the sciences*.**[20]

Now that the Church's teaching has been considered, let us look at her actions. In this regard, we have a picture that paints a thousand words.

4. The Pontifical Academy of Sciences

IN 1603, THE *ACADEMY OF THE LYNX-EYED* (*Accademia dei Lincei*) was founded in Rome under the patronage of **Pope Clement VIII**. The purpose of the Academy was to develop "a method of research based upon observation, experiment, and the inductive method"—in other words, a truly *scientific* method. Its unusual name was coined by **Federico Cesi**, the Roman prince who started the Academy, and referred to his desire that the scientists who worked there would have eyes as sharp as wildcats in order to penetrate the secrets of nature, on both the tiniest and the largest of levels.[21] It predates all other existing scientific societies, including the English Royal Society and the French Academy of the Sciences.[22] In 1611, **Galileo** was inducted and quickly became its greatest member and president. The Academy published at least two of his works before it closed with the death of Cesi in 1630.

Federico Cesi (1585-1630) was an Italian prince, scientist, and naturalist. In 1603, at the age of eighteen, with three friends, he founded the *Accademia dei Lincei*, or the Academy of the Lynx-Eyed. Cesi chose the sharp-eyed lynx (inset) as their symbol. The academy's motto: "Take care of small things if you want to obtain the greatest results" (*minima cura si maxima vis*).

It was re-founded in 1847 by **Blessed Pius IX** and renamed as the *Pontifical Academy of New Lincei*. In 1937 it received its present name from **Pope Pius XI** —the *Pontifical Academy of Sciences* ("pontifical" refers to the Pope, who is also known as the Roman *Pontiff*). Its goal is "the promotion of the progress of the mathematical, physical, and natural sciences, and the study of related... questions and issues."[23] Since 1908, it has had forty-five Nobel Prize winners among its members.

As should be expected on the basis of the Church's teaching regarding the legitimate autonomy of the sciences, the Pontifical Academy of Sciences enjoys autonomy as a scientific organization.[24] It includes scientists without regard to their membership in the Catholic Church, recognizing that all human beings are capable of reason and, therefore, of good science. As of 2017, members included the renowned physicist **Stephen Hawking**, a self-proclaimed atheist, and **Francis Collins**, the Evangelical Christian and geneticist who led the team that mapped the entire human genome.

Through supporting and maintaining this internationally esteemed Academy, the Church offers a clear example of her love and respect for the sciences. It is clear from its existence that the Church shares the biblical perspective on science as something God desires of his human creatures. As we shall see in the next section, it is a call to which many Catholics have responded through the centuries, some of whom have forever changed the trajectory of science and the world through their discoveries. Let us turn to these great Catholics now.

B. Catholic Scientists Throughout the Ages[25]

IF OUR TOUR OF THE EVIDENCE of Sacred Tradition were only to show us openness to scientific insights on the part of the Church, but no or just very few actual scientists within the Church, it would be rather empty. Perhaps there is no better way to see the witness of Sacred Tradition regarding science than to observe how many great scientists the Church has had within her ranks throughout history. Stretching back to ancient times and forward to the present day, Catholic men and women have understood God's call to include investigating the natural world, and have made major contributions to science. They had significant firsts to their credit, and some were founders of entire branches of science: acoustics, hydraulics, stratigraphy, fossil study, crystallography, genetics, and Big Bang cosmology. An impressive number could even be considered *game changers*, scientists who either founded whole branches of science or whose original discoveries advanced understanding for all ages to come. The following is an incomplete chronological list of some of the most important Catholic scientists. For a more complete list see the Appendix, "More Catholic Scientists Throughout the Ages" (pp. 297 ff.).

John Philoponus (490-ca. 570)
"If an arrow or a stone is projected by force in a void, the same will happen much more easily, nothing being necessary except the thrower."

John Philoponus (Lay person: Astronomy, Physics, 490-ca. 570) was a theologian and natural philosopher in Alexandria, Egypt. One major contribution lay in his passionate denunciation of the widespread pagan belief that the stars were unchanging, divine entities. He saw that they were changeable and different from each other in numerous ways. Against the scholarly opinions of his day he correctly theorized that the sun was made of the same fire that we see in earthly fires, that the space above the earth might be a vacuum, and that light actually moves.[26] He also realized, contrary to the thought of Aristotle, that the weight of an object does not affect the time it takes for it to fall—in other words, heavier objects fall at the same rate as lighter ones.[27] These were all revolutionary ideas for his time, and 1000 years later he was still being recognized for his genius. In fact, the principle of impetus, proposed by Jean Buridan as mentioned above, was first proposed by Philoponus.[28]

St. Albert the Great, also known as Albertus Magnus, (Dominican Friar, Bishop: Biology, 1200-1280) is famous for being the teacher of St. Thomas Aquinas. He emphasized in his writings the importance of an experimental approach to science, and he practiced what he preached by doing a great amount of original observational work in botany and zoology, especially in the classification of plants, flowers, and fruits; in animal reproduction and embryology; and in the study of insects. For example, he was the first to distinguish between thorns and prickles on the basis of their formation and structure, to note the influence of light and heat on the growth of trees, to establish that sap is tasteless at the root of a plant but becomes flavored as it ascends, and to discover that ants lose their sense of direction when their antennae are removed. The *Complete Dictionary of Scientific Biography* calls his work *On Vegetables and Plants* "a masterpiece for its independence of treatment, its accuracy and range of detailed description, its freedom from myth, and its innovation in systematic classification."[29]

St. Albert the Great (1200-1280)
"Natural science does not consist in ratifying what others have said, but in seeking the causes of phenomena."

Nicholas Oresme (Bishop: Physics, Astronomy, 1329-1392) was the most brilliant scientist of the Middle Ages. Oresme was not only very original but also remarkably broad in his interests and accomplishments. He made contributions to musicology, psychology, physics, and mathematics, and is considered the greatest economist of the Middle Ages.

Nicholas Oresme (1329-1392)
"The heavenly bodies move with such regularity, orderliness, and symmetry that it is truly a marvel; and they continue always to act in this manner ceaselessly, following the established system, without increasing or reducing speed and continuing without respite, as the Scripture says: Summer and winter, night and day they never rest."
(*Le livre du ciel et du monde*,1377)

In mathematics, Oresme discovered the rules for combining "exponents," and he even discussed fractional and irrational exponents. He developed the use of simple graphs to plot physical quantities, thus anticipating by three centuries some of the ideas of Cartesian "analytic geometry." He used such graphical methods to prove the "Merton theorem," which gives the distance traversed by a uniformly accelerating body. Oresme proposed that the speed of a falling body is proportional to the time it has fallen, which Galileo re-discovered almost three hundred years later. Oresme argued that the apparent motion of the stars could be explained by the earth's rotation on its axis, and the analysis by which he refuted common physical objections to this was superior in some ways to those later given by Copernicus and Galileo because he understood how to decompose motion into horizontal and vertical components.

Interestingly, Oresme and his teacher, Jean Buridan, were the first in Church history to propose that the sun, not the earth, might be at the center of the universe (no one had a concept of a solar system distinct from the universe until after the Scientific Revolution). Although they incorrectly concluded that the e arth was at the center (*geocentrism*), they showed that no physical arguments existed that could refute the position that the sun was at the center (*heliocentrism*), paving the way for Copernicus, who used an analogy he discovered in Buridan's writings to make his argument for the earth's motion around the sun.[30]

Historians of science rightly admire the boldness of Copernicus and Galileo in suggesting that the earth was in motion and that the sun, rather than the earth, was at the center of the universe, and rightly disapprove of those who attempted to repress this idea. Yet, it is not often mentioned that Copernicus got the idea from a priest (Buridan) and a bishop (Oresme), who investigated it over a century before he did.

Astronomer Copernicus, Conversation with God by Matejko.
"I am aware that a philosopher's ideas are not subject to the judgment of ordinary persons, because it is his endeavor to seek the truth in all things, to the extent permitted to human reason by God."
(*De revolutionibus orbium coelestium*, 1543)

Nicolaus Copernicus (Lay person: Founder of Modern Cosmology, 1473-1543) was the great Polish astronomer who speculated that the sun, not the earth, was at the center of the universe. It was his great book, *De Revolutionibus Orbium Cœlestium* ("On the Revolutions of the Heavenly Spheres"), that sparked the Scientific Revolution. Contrary to widespread opinion, Copernicus received no resistance in his lifetime from Church officials. *De Revolutionibus* was read and taught in universities and was never banned by the Church, although it was suspended in 1616 and then revised in 1620 by Church censors to make his heliocentrism appear hypothetical, for reasons we shall explore when we consider Galileo.

Christoph Clavius (Jesuit Priest: Mathematics, Astronomy, 1538-1612) made his great contribution by combining astronomical observation and mathematical genius to give us the calendar we use today. Our calendar is called the *Gregorian calendar* after **Pope Gregory XIII**, who promulgated it in 1582 after appointing Clavius to revise the less accurate "Julian" calendar that had been in use. Clavius' ability to produce the calendar was fueled by his incredible abilities in math. He was "the first to use a decimal point, some twenty years before it became common; the first to use parentheses to collect terms; and the first to use the plus (+) and minus (–) signs in Italy." Through these he made computation much more efficient for astronomers, paving the way for many future discoveries.[31]

Christoph Clavius (1538-1612)
"Clavius' commentary on Euclid became the standard textbook for the seventeenth century and his books on arithmetic, geometry, algebra, harmonics, and astronomy were used in all the European Jesuit schools, as well as many other schools." (Joseph F. MacDonnell, S.J.)

Clavius would be only the first of many Jesuits to make contributions to science. The Jesuit Order was founded in 1540, and within a few decades its members were already at the forefront of scientific research. They were among the leaders in astronomy in the 1600s and for quite a while after that. In fact, at the time of the American Revolution, 30 out of the world's 130 astronomical observatories were operated by the Jesuit Order.

Marin Mersenne (Minimite Priest: Founder of Acoustics and Architect of the European Scientific Community, 1588-1648) was a French priest of the Minimite Order. In our day, scientists and mathematicians learn about new developments in their fields and share their discoveries with other researchers in several ways: through professional journals, at international conferences, and, more recently, by the Internet. However, in the 1600s, when the Scientific Revolution began, there were no professional journals; there were no international conferences; and, of course, there was no Internet. What they did have, at least in France, was Marin Mersenne.

Marin Mersenne (1588-1648)
"The sciences have sworn among themselves an inviolable partnership; it is almost impossible to separate them, for they would rather suffer than be torn apart." (*Les Préludes de l'Harmonie Universelle*, 1634)

Mersenne carried on volumes of correspondence with the leading scientists of his day. They would inform him by letters of their new results and he would disseminate the information by letters to other scientists. His convent in Paris became a meeting place of scientists. In 1653 Mersenne organized the *Academia Parisiensis* (the Paris Academy), one of the earliest scientific organizations in Europe. He was thus one of the "architects of the European scientific community."[32]

Today, Mersenne's name is most well known in the mathematical world because of so-called "Mersenne prime numbers." But Mersenne's really significant contributions to science lay elsewhere, in particular in the sciences of optics and acoustics. In optics, Mersenne contributed to the theory and design of reflecting telescopes. Although he never manufactured one, he improved the basic design. Mersenne made even greater contributions to the study of sound and vibrations. One of the basic facts taught in college physics courses is how the frequency of vibration of a string is related to its length, its mass-per-unit-length, and its tension. These relationships were first discovered by Mersenne. He also measured the speed of sound and showed that it was independent of frequency and loudness. For these and other discoveries Mersenne has been called the "father of acoustics."

Bl. Nicholas Steno (1638-1686)
"One sins against the majesty of God by being unwilling to look into nature's own works."

Blessed Nicholas Steno (Bishop: Founder of Stratigraphy and Fossil Study, 1638-1686), also known as Niels Stensen, was a remarkable figure in many ways. He made fundamental contributions to four branches of science: anatomy, paleontology, geology, and crystallography. While still in his twenties, he was already recognized as one of the leading anatomists in Europe. His anatomical studies greatly increased knowledge of the glandular-lymphatic system. Various parts of the human body are named after him, including Stensen's duct, Stensen's gland, Stensen's vein, and Stensen's foramina. He also did important work on heart and muscle structure, brain anatomy, and embryology. He was a Dane by birth, but he eventually ended up in Florence, where he worked in a research institute that included some of Galileo's pupils.

In 1666, while he was dissecting the head of a Great White shark that had been caught near Livorno, he noticed that the teeth of the shark bore a strong resemblance to the so-called tongue-stones that were common on the island of Malta. He realized that the tongue-stones were actually ancient shark teeth. This mystified him because these teeth (as well as seashells) were very often found high up on cliffs and mountaintops. Unraveling this mystery led him to develop, after much further investigation, a detailed theory of the origin of fossils and of sedimentary rock that was very controversial at that time, but was essentially correct. He is thus regarded as the founder of the study of fossils and of the branch of geology called "stratigraphy." Steno's theory of how geological strata were laid down allowed people to begin to understand the extended nature of the history of the earth and of life.

The study of geology led Steno to the study of crystals, where he discovered the basic fact, known as *Steno's*, or *Stensen's, Law*, that in all crystals of the same mineral the angles are the same.

Steno was raised as a Lutheran, but after a deep study of theology and early Church history, he converted to Catholicism. He left scientific research to become a priest, and was soon elevated to the rank of bishop. In his last public lecture as a scientist, he offered to history one of the greatest descriptions of the relationship between nature, our grasp of truth, and the absolute mystery of God:

> **Beautiful is what we see.**
> **More beautiful is what we comprehend.**
> **Most beautiful is what we do not comprehend.**

As bishop, he was known as an ardent advocate for the poor, for whom he sold all of his belongings, even his bishop's ring. He practiced rigorous asceticism, constantly praying and fasting. On October 23, 1988, he was beatified by Pope John Paul II.

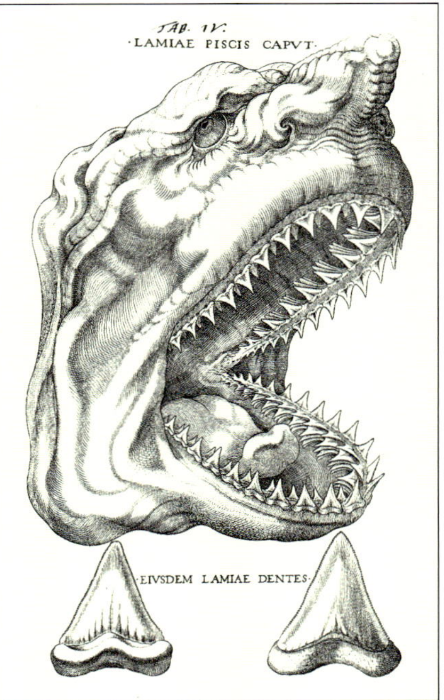

Illustration from Steno's 1667 paper *Elementorum myologiae specimen* comparing the teeth of a shark he dissected with a stony object then known as a "tongue-stone."

Angelo Secchi (1818-1878)
Craters on both the moon and Mars are named after Secchi. He discovered three comets. He invented the heliospectrograph, star spectrograph, and telespectroscope.

Angelo Secchi (Priest: Astronomer, 1818-1878) continued the great tradition of Jesuit astronomy into the nineteenth century. He is one of the founders of modern astrophysics. He pioneered the study and classification of stars using *spectroscopy*, or color classification. Before his contribution it was thought that, besides their position in the sky, we would never be able to discover the "stuff" of stars, i.e., their material composition. Secchi challenged this by attaching a prism to his telescope, allowing him to classify the stars by the colors they emitted, which revealed their chemical constituents. His classification of stars was the standard model for two decades until a somewhat improved one was developed at Harvard University in the early twentieth century. Perhaps nothing so dramatizes the positive relationship between faith and science as the fact that Secchi did much of his research using a telescope that was set up on the roof of *San Ignazio*, one of the most beautiful churches in the city of Rome, right above the sanctuary where he and his fellow Jesuits celebrated Mass.

Gregor Mendel (Augustinian Priest: Founder of Genetics, 1822-1884) is universally honored as the founder of the science of genetics. He was the first ever to discover the basic principles of *heredity*, the passing on of characteristics (traits) genetically from one generation to another.[33] Mendel was the son of a peasant who entered the monastery in Brno, in what is now the Czech Republic, at the age of 21. He was sent to study at the University of Vienna, where he excelled in physics, mathematics, chemistry, and plant physiology. He took his learning into the classroom but also into the garden, where he spent most of his time from 1854 onward conducting a careful, private research program on heredity. He focused on pea plants because he could easily control their propagation. In 1865 he delivered his resultsin lectures that were largely ignored by the scientific community, both at that time and in a later publication. Mendel had created an entirely new way of studying heredity that would not be appreciated in his lifetime. He is reported to have said, "Though I have had to live through many bitter moments in my life, I must admit with gratitude that the beautiful and good prevailed. My scientific work brought me much satisfaction, and I am sure it will soon be recognized by the whole world."[34] Around the year 1900 his work was finally appreciated and it became foundational to the new science of genetics. In the 1930's it would revolutionize evolutionary biology as well.

Gregor Mendel (1822-1884)
"The seed of supernatural life, of sanctifying grace, cleanses from sin, so preparing the soul of man, and man must seek to preserve this life by his good works." (Easter Sermon)

Georges Lemaître (1894-1966)
Lemaître was the first theoretical cosmologist ever nominated for the Nobel Prize in Physics (1954) for his prediction of the expanding universe.

Georges Lemaître (Priest: Founder of the Big Bang Theory and of Modern Cosmology, 1894-1966), a Belgian priest, was one of the two originators of the *Big Bang Theory*, now accepted as the authoritative account of the beginnings of the universe. One might say that the Big Bang Theory was too revolutionary for Einstein, even though it was based on Einstein's own theory of gravity, the Theory of General Relativity. Einstein published his theory in 1916. In 1922, a Russian mathematician **Alexander Friedmann** and, independently a few years later, Fr. Lemaître found solutions of Einstein's theory that described a universe in which space itself is expanding. Einstein and others at first resisted the idea, but in 1929 the astronomers **Edwin Hubble** and **Milton Humason** confirmed that the universe is indeed expanding, and physicists began to accept Lemaître's idea. Lemaître also served as the Director of the Pontifical Academy of Sciences. His great discovery will be discussed in more detail in Chapter Seven.

Miriam Michael Stimson (1913-2002)
Using a potassium bromide technique she developed, Stimson was able to not only confirm the structure of DNA nucleotide bases but also study how they were connected in the DNA double helix structure.

Miriam Michael Stimson (Dominican Sister: Biochemistry, Genetics, 1913-2002) was a chemist who taught at Siena Heights University in Adrian, Michigan, where she also ran a laboratory that she put together in a converted bathroom. She researched cancer there for over thirty years and in the process began to unravel the mystery of DNA. Using the method of ultraviolet analysis of DNA that she pioneered, **James Watson** and **Francis Crick** would discover its double helix structure; after they did, she developed another method of analysis using infrared light to prove that Watson and Crick were right. Because of her groundbreaking work she became only the second woman in history (**Marie Curie** was the first) to be invited to lecture at the Sorbonne in Paris, which she did in 1953.[35]

1. Summary

THROUGH OUR TOUR OF HISTORY we see that important Catholic scientists have existed since the first millennium of the Christian era. With them there is no doubt that a commitment to science is in the very spiritual DNA of the Church, part of her very life and consciousness. And our chapter could end here were it not for an episode in 1633 that is now taken by conflict theorists as the representative case for the relationship between the Church and science. To correct this misconception, we now turn back to the 1600s and the life of **Galileo Galilei**.

C. A Misleading Moment: The Galileo Affair[36]

OF ALL THE GREAT CATHOLIC SCIENTISTS listed above, none was greater than **Galileo Galilei** (1564-1642). His insights into the workings of the universe using mathematics and the power of careful experimentation have led many to call him "The Father of Modern Science." As he forged this new path, he found himself on trial and then condemned for his claim that an earlier thinker (Copernicus) was right when he asserted that it is the earth that moves around the sun. The court that condemned him was none other than the *Roman Inquisition*, the Church's legal body for prosecuting crimes involved in denying truths of the Catholic faith.

Based upon our tour of Sacred Tradition up to this point, the Galileo Affair is striking for how out of place it seems compared to the rest of Church history, especially compared to the long list of scientists who made major contributions not only without any ecclesial penalties but with unqualified appreciation and encouragement and even the declaration of sainthood in some cases. Why was the same not the case with Galileo? To understand this, we will consider the events of Galileo's life and troubles in four parts: the situation before Galileo, his first encounter with the Inquisition (1615-1616), his trial (1633), and his vindication, not only scientifically but also theologically, in the centuries after his death.

1. The Situation Before Galileo

THE GALILEO AFFAIR really begins with **Nicolaus Copernicus**, the great Catholic scientist who, relying on the work of **Jean Buridan** and **Nicholas Oresme**, proposed two innovations to the view of the cosmos held universally at the time. First, Copernicus proposed that the sun is at the center of the universe, a position called *heliocentrism*; he also proposed that the earth was orbiting around the sun and moving around its own axis while it did so (called *geokineticism*). At the time Copernicus himself was in Holy Orders as a canon, an administrative position. Although he only published his ideas in 1543, the last year of his life, his position had been well known for three decades.

Most astronomers did not accept Copernicus's position, to which there were several objections. One was ordinary sense experience. From our vantage point on earth, it seems as if the sun is orbiting the earth as the center around which it moves (*geocentrism*). A second was based on the scientific presuppositions of Aristotle, whose ideas about gravity had not yet been swept away as they would later be by Newton. Aristotle thought that all things tend to move to the center of the cosmos. Thanks to his influence, many in Galileo's time thought that the earth had to be the center, since things with weight move toward it when

The Galileo Affair really begins with Nicolaus Copernicus.

dropped. Why do they not fall upwards if the sun is the center? Finally, if Copernicus was right, then stars should seem to change positions according to the earth's motion, a phenomenon called *stellar parallax*. Yet, this phenomenon had never been observed, and it would not be until 1838.

Among theologians there were some who called into question Copernicus's idea based on certain passages of Scripture, especially Joshua 10:12-14, where we are told that God made the sun stand still in the sky for the sake of an Israelite victory in a battle against the Amorites. But by no means was this seen, at least within Copernicus's lifetime, as an irresolvable theological obstacle, nor was it one that called into question his faithfulness as a believer. Yet, it would be this very passage that would begin the Galileo Affair.

2. Galileo's First Encounter with the Inquisition (1615-1616)

BY 1609 GALILEO HAD BECOME CONVINCED that Copernicus was right. By then he had developed his famous telescope and had seen things, such as sunspots, the moons of Jupiter, and the phases of Venus, that seemed to him to clearly prove the sun to be at the center. Even more convincing to Galileo was the consistency between Copernicanism and the laws of motion he had discovered.

Galileo Galilei (1564-1642)
This portrait was painted of Galileo by Sustermans in 1636 when Galileo was 78. Sustermans was the court painter to the Medici family for three generations.

Galileo's Copernicanism was known to his patrons, the Medici family, who ruled Florence and all of Tuscany, Galileo's homeland. Over breakfast in December 1613, **Fr. Benedetto Castelli**, Galileo's pupil, was asked by the **Grand Duchess Christina de' Medici** if Galileo's idea contradicted the Joshua story of the Old Testament. The duchess seemed to be satisfied with the explanation Castelli gave to show that it did not, and Galileo followed up with a letter to Castelli (and one to Christina herself) in which he explained why he believed there was no contradiction. "I do not think it necessary to believe that the same God who has furnished us with senses, language, and intellect would want to bypass their use and give us by other means the information we can obtain with them," he wrote to Castelli.[37] He also went on to reinterpret the Joshua passage. Perhaps, he speculated, the sun stopped moving on its own axis, therefore shutting down the movement of the rest of the cosmos. If this is what the passage means when it refers to the sun "standing still," Galileo wrote, then it is not contrary to a heliocentric model of the universe.

But there were others in Florence who were quite upset about Galileo's heliocentrism. In December 1614 **Fr. Tommaso Caccini**, a Dominican friar, preached a sermon on the Joshua passage in which he criticized Copernicus and Galileo by name. In January 1615 another Florentine Dominican, **Fr. Niccolò Lorini**, complained about Galileo to the Inquisition. The Inquisition officials had concerns about three expressions they found in the copy of Galileo's letter to Castelli that Lorini had forwarded with his complaint. In their copy, for example, Galileo says that Scripture "perverts" certain things, a poor word choice indeed. But two of the "bad expressions," including that one, were only to be found in Lorini's copy and not in any of the others.

Galileo Before the Inquisition in Rome by Cristiano Banti.

Galileo decided to go to Rome in order to defend himself and his ideas before the Inquisition in a voluntary hearing in December, informally known as the Hearing of 1615. It quickly became clear to the Inquisition that there was no good evidence against Galileo. The case was dismissed with two qualifications. First, Copernicus's *De Revolutionibus* was suspended from publication until certain expressions in it were corrected. Second, **St. Robert Bellarmine** (1542-1621), an important theologian and a member of the Inquisition, was asked to meet with Galileo and to warn him to abandon his opinions about Copernicanism being literally true and to not teach it as such any longer. Bellarmine did so, and Galileo agreed to abide by the warning, although the full extent of what Galileo agreed to would become a matter of great controversy at his trial in 1633 (and remains a mystery even today). At the very least, Galileo did agree to only use the heliocentric model as a convenient fiction, useful for calculating planetary positions, which all recognized as a technical benefit of heliocentrism regardless of their opinion of its actual truth. Bellarmine issued Galileo a certificate stating that Galileo was not under any suspicion or investigation. Finally, Galileo met with **Pope Paul V** (1550-1621), who assured Galileo of his support.

At this point we must ask, "Why was this an issue for Galileo when it was not for Copernicus?" The Protestant Reformation, a movement that had torn the Church apart for over a century by this time, is probably the main reason. Protestant reformers had produced novel interpretations of the Bible that separated Scripture from the witness of Sacred Tradition and undermined central teachings of the Church on major points such as the Eucharist. In short, Galileo lived at a time when the authority to interpret the Bible was a hot issue and when many Catholic theologians were extremely suspicious of surprising new interpretations of the Bible.

Interestingly, and despite the atmosphere of anxiety, Cardinal Bellarmine followed the principle of "faith and reason together." In a letter to a friend of Galileo, the Carmelite priest **Paolo Antonio Foscarini** (1565-1616), Bellarmine wrote "if there were a true demonstration that the sun is at the center of [the universe]...then one would have to proceed with great care in explaining the

St. Robert Bellarmine (1542-1621)
In his judgment of Galileo in 1616, Cardinal Bellarmine followed the principle of "faith and reason together."

Scriptures that appear contrary, and say rather that we do not understand them..."[38] In other words, Galileo claimed that he had demonstrated heliocentrism, and Bellarmine denied it on the basis not of faith but of reason. In this regard, Bellarmine was right and Galileo was wrong.

Galileo had advanced three "proofs" of heliocentrism, two of which he had discovered using his telescope. First, he had observed that Venus shows phases like the moon, which would be impossible unless it orbited the sun. That proved that Venus orbits the sun, but it did not prove that the earth did. In fact, some models that were well-known at the time, such as that of the Danish astronomer **Tycho Brahe** (1546-1601), had Venus and Mercury orbiting the sun while the sun orbited the earth. For this reason, evidence of Venus' phases were inconclusive with respect to the superiority of either heliocentrism or geocentrism. Second, Galileo had discovered the satellites of Jupiter, showing that orbital motion could happen around a different body than the earth. But this only proved that such a thing could happen, not that the earth is actually orbiting the sun. Finally, Galileo's favorite "proof" was his idea that the tides were caused by the motion of our planet. However, the German astronomer **Johannes Kepler** (1571-1630) had already explained the tides by reference to the moon's gravitational pull, an idea Galileo rejected but that was actually correct.

In other words, we must not be quick to either condemn Bellarmine in this situation or to champion Galileo. In the words of **Lawrence Principe**, "Imagine the utter confusion that would result if the Scriptures had to be reinterpreted for every possible unproven scientific system. Bellarmine was holding out for a sound proof, and Galileo just didn't have one."

In June 1616 Galileo left Rome and went home to Florence, his good standing in the Church and in public opinion intact, with just a warning not to hold, teach, or defend Copernicanism. He continued work on his many scientific projects and published a work on comets in 1621. Then, in 1623, Galileo received what he thought was very good news—his close friend **Cardinal Maffeo Barberini** had been elected to the papacy and had taken the name **Urban VIII**. This brings us to the next phase of the Galileo Affair.

3. The Trial of Galileo (1633)

TO CALL URBAN VIII (1568-1644) a "huge fan" of Galileo would not be an overstatement. He had read Galileo's work *On Sunspots* with great appreciation. A celebrated poet, he had even written a poem in Galileo's honor that he cleverly entitled "Dangerous Adulation," which may have been a "wink and nod" at the warning Galileo received in 1616. In early 1624, Galileo would travel to Rome to visit him and would be received for six private audiences over the course of several days. During this time the Pope gave permission to Galileo to write about heliocentrism in a work that Galileo planned to entitle *On the Tides*. The Pope instructed Galileo to speak only hypothetically and added an additional qualification, namely, that Galileo include an argument the Pope had thought of himself. Because of his omnipotence, Urban argued, God could have created the world in such a way that the cause of the tides could never be discovered by human beings. In other words, perhaps we'll never know the cause of the tides because God made it to be inherently mysterious and unknowable.

In light of all that has been discussed so far in this book, it should be obvious that Urban's argument is not a very good one, to say the least. It essentially devastates cause and effect in the natural world, or at least our ability to discover it. One might assume that Urban's folly must be defended by Catholics because of the Catholic belief in papal infallibility. But, actually, Catholics do not believe that the Pope is infallible in whatever he says about anything, only in matters of faith and morals, and only when he is offering a solemn formal definition after having carefully investigated the faith of the Church. Galileo, whose whole career shows his dedication to investigating natural causes with confidence that such causes can be discovered, probably wasn't sure whether to laugh or to cry when he heard it. Nevertheless, he agreed and returned to Florence to begin writing.

By 1630 *On the Tides* was ready for printing and distribution, although a breakout of the Black Plague in central Italy postponed its publication. In 1631 Galileo changed the title to *A Dialogue on the Two Chief World Systems*, a suggestion that may have come from Urban himself. It was finally published in Florence in February 1632, and it received immediate praise but also began to stir rumors. Instead of defending Galileo, Urban exploded in anger, telling the Tuscan ambassador "I have been deceived!"

Why the Pope's sudden change of attitude? There seems to have been two reasons. First, Galileo had included the Pope's argument as he had requested, but he did so in a way that humiliated the Pope. He wrote the *Dialogue* as one between three characters: *Salviati*, who is Galileo's mouthpiece and represents the Copernican position; *Sagredo*, who plays the part of an impartial questioner; and *Simplicio*, literally "Simpleton" or "Fool" in Italian, who represents the geocentric position. Foolishly, Galileo placed the Pope's argument on the lips of Simplicio the fool! Since it did not become an issue at his trial, it is not clear why he did this. But it was clearly a very unwise choice.

Galileo Before Members of the Holy Office in the Vatican, 1633 by Joseph-Nicolas Robert-Fleury.

Pope Urban VIII (1568-1644)
The Pope was almost certainly motivated by a combination of personal humiliation and political expediency.

Second, it seems that Urban was made aware only after the publication of the *Dialogue* that in 1616 Galileo had been warned not to defend the Copernican system *even hypothetically*, which he does vigorously throughout his work. Urban hadn't known beforehand about this warning. The panel that examined the case of Galileo concluded that Galileo "may have been deceitfully silent about this injunction" when he sought the Pope's permission. It seems that Urban felt both humiliated and manipulated, and allowed for Galileo to be formally tried by the Inquisition.

Galileo was summoned for questioning and traveled to Rome in January 1633. Although fictional accounts portray him as being thrown into a dungeon, at no point was Galileo subjected to imprisonment; he stayed at the palace of the Tuscan ambassador until his questioning began in April and throughout the trial.

In his pretrial hearing the question that the inquisitors had was simple: In writing the *Dialogue*, did Galileo violate his 1616 agreement with Bellarmine? He was asked specifically why he didn't get written permission to write the *Dialogue* and why he had not informed the Pope of Bellarmine's warning. Galileo claimed that he did not remember such restrictive language and presented the certificate he received from Bellarmine. The Inquisition then presented him with the copy they had from their files, with much more severe language than Galileo's copy, restricting Galileo from defending heliocentrism in any way whatsoever. This document should have borne signatures from both Galileo and Bellarmine, and yet it was unsigned by either, while Galileo's copy bore both signatures. Since Bellarmine had died twelve years earlier, there was no way to confirm the validity of the certificate.

At this point Galileo backed down. He claimed that he never imagined that his book was actually defending heliocentrism, and so had not thought that Bellarmine's warning was relevant. He even said that he really didn't think heliocentrism was true. The inquisitors accepted this explanation. They proposed a plea bargain to avoid going to trial. The offer was this: Galileo would admit that he had inadvertently broken his agreement and then be acquitted. Galileo made the admission, but Urban refused to accept the settlement. He demanded that Galileo be formally arrested (though not imprisoned), formally interrogated and sentenced, that he make a public abjuration, and that his book be banned but that he not be punished in any other way.

On June 21, 1633, the inquisitors handed down the sentence of "vehement suspicion of heresy" against Galileo. The following day he recited his *abjuration*, i.e., his solemn renunciation, of heliocentrism. He did not, as some writers have romantically suggested, mutter the words, "*E pur si muove*" ("And yet it moves"). It has been suggested by some that by the time of his abjuration Galileo had finally admitted to himself that he had not discovered sufficient proof of heliocentrism. In the opinion of **William Wallace**, an expert on the Galileo Affair, "Galileo knew in his heart that he had not demonstrated the earth's motion; he was too good a [scientist] for that. And once he admitted this to himself, the work of the special commission [of the Inquisition] was over."[39] Therefore, it is not clear that we should attribute dishonesty or perjury to Galileo.

Unfortunately, it is extremely difficult to avoid attributing the sin of vengeance to his alienated friend, Pope Urban VIII. While Urban may have not known about the earlier agreement, which seems unlikely, he certainly did encourage Galileo to write and at least up to that point saw no theological reasons why he should not. And, when Galileo backed down, Urban refused his plea and made sure he was tried and convicted. The Pope was almost certainly motivated by a combination of personal humiliation and political expediency, not by any theological principle, to put Galileo "in his place." The Galileo Affair had much more to do with a papal abuse of power than it had to do with Scripture or science.

4. The Rest of the Story: From the 1600s to the Present Day

JUST AS MANY TODAY are not aware that Galileo had not conclusively proven heliocentrism, there are also many who do not know the whole story of what happened after his condemnation in 1633. Three of the ten cardinals who judged Galileo failed to sign the verdict, including Urban's nephew, **Cardinal Francesco Barberini** (1597-1679). Galileo was placed under permanent house arrest, yet had a servant and "every convenience," according to a friend who observed his arrest. And he was allowed to continue scientific research as long as he did not defend heliocentrism. In fact, it was during his house arrest that he published his greatest contribution to science, namely, his book on mechanics and gravity.

Not until 1687, when **Isaac Newton** published his Laws of Motion and his Law of Gravity, did scientists have the theoretical tools they needed to resolve the dispute between heliocentrism and geocentrism. However, it was not until the discovery in 1728 of the phenomenon called "the aberration of light" that there was direct experimental evidence of the truth of the heliocentric theory. In 1757 **Pope Benedict XIV** (1675-1758), at the urging of the great Jesuit astronomer **Roger Boscovich** (1711-1787), removed the "corrected" version of Copernicus's book from the *Index of Prohibited Books*.

Galileo (on the right) *with his disciple Vincenzo Viviani.* In 1639, at the age of seventeen, Viviani became an assistant to Galileo. After his condemnation in 1633, Galileo was confined to the Villa Il Gioiello in Arcetri, Italy. Viviani assisted him there until Galileo's death in 1642. From 1655 to 1656, Viviani edited the first edition of Galileo's collected works. Despite becoming blind in 1638, Galileo continued to write some of his most significant works.

The most important moment occurred between 1789 and 1792 when the astronomer **Giovanni Guglielmini** (1763-1817) showed that heavy objects dropped from a very tall tower actually deviate slightly to the east because of the turning of the earth. In 1806 another astronomer, **Giuseppe Calandrelli** (1749-1827), measured the stellar parallax of the star Alpha in the Lyra constellation and so demonstrated the earth's annual motion around the sun.[40] After these discoveries were made known to the Church, the prohibition against Copernicanism was entirely removed in 1820, and in 1822 Galileo's *Dialogue* was removed from the *Index*.

The last chapter of the Galileo Affair, his theological vindication, was "written" over 150 years later by St. John Paul II in a speech to the Galileo Commission in October 1992.

The last chapter of the Galileo Affair, his theological vindication, was "written" over 150 years later by **St. John Paul II**. In November 1979, thirteen months after his election to the papacy, the Pope gave a speech to the Pontifical Academy of Sciences in which he praised Galileo's greatness and noted the injustice of his condemnation; in his words, "...the former had to suffer a great deal—we cannot conceal the fact—at the hands of men and entities of the Church."[41] In 1984 he appointed his own special commission to reexamine the Galileo case. In 1992 the commission explicitly acknowledged that Church officials had erred in condemning Galileo. In his formal response, St. John Paul II would refer to Galileo as the "inspired founder" of experimental science and actually called Galileo a *better theologian* than those who condemned him. In his own words: "Galileo, a sincere believer, showed himself to be *more perceptive*... than the theologians who opposed him."[42]

What made Galileo more perceptive? The Pope goes on to say that his opponents failed to recognize what was obvious to Galileo himself, as we saw in his letter to Castelli: "...the Bible does not concern itself with the details of the physical world... which is the competence [i.e., the proper domain] of human experience and reasoning."[43] Galileo had not contradicted the Bible by promoting heliocentrism because the Bible, as God's Revelation, is not about such details. As Galileo wrote to Castelli, "I do not think it necessary to believe that the same God who has furnished us with senses, language, and intellect would want to bypass their use and give us by other means the information we can obtain with them." It was his adversaries, not Galileo, who committed the real theological mistake in the whole sad affair. Not recognizing the liberty that Sacred Tradition had always given to science, they condemned a *scientific hypothesis* as a *theological error*.

The Galileo Affair was a tragedy, an exception to the rule of the Church's long history of openness to the natural sciences and their ability to enlighten us with a better and truer understanding of the physical universe. But it is a rare conflict in an otherwise glorious history of harmony. Our tour of the various manifestations of Sacred Tradition has shown that the openness and encouragement of a scientific approach to the universe that we found in Sacred Scripture has been repeated and magnified throughout Church history.

VOCABULARY

Define the following terms (or identify the person's significance):

1. *Sola Scriptura*
2. Perspicuity of Scripture
3. Sacred Tradition
4. Faith and Reason Together
5. Venerable Pius XII (Age of the Universe)
6. Integrity of Nature
7. Supernaturalism
8. "God of the Gaps" Error
9. Rational Seeds (St. Augustine)
10. Magisterium
11. Lateran IV
12. Stephen Tempier
13. Jean Buridan (Theory of Impetus)
14. Vatican I (*Dei Filius*)
15. Vatican II (*Gaudium et Spes*)
16. Autonomy
17. Academy of the Lynx-Eyed
18. Federico Cesi
19. Pontifical Academy of Sciences
20. John Philoponus
21. St. Albert the Great
22. Nicholas Oresme
23. Nicolaus Copernicus
24. *De revolutionibus orbium coelestium* ("On the Revolutions of the Heavenly Spheres")
25. Christoph Clavius
26. Marin Mersenne
27. Blessed Nicholas Steno (Niels Stensen)
28. Angelo Secchi
29. Gregor Mendel
30. Georges Lemaître
31. Miriam Michael Stimson
32. Galileo Galilei
33. Geocentrism
34. Geokineticism (Copernicanism)
35. Heliocentrism (Copernicanism)
36. Stellar Parallax
37. Joshua 10:12-14
38. Benedetto Castelli
39. Christina de' Medici
40. *Letter to Castelli* (Galileo)
41. Tommaso Caccini
42. Niccolò Lorini
43. Hearing of 1615 (Galileo, Inquisition)
44. St. Robert Bellarmine (*Letter to Foscarini*)
45. Paolo Antonio Foscarini
46. Tycho Brahe
47. Johannes Kepler
48. Maffeo Barberini (Urban VIII)
49. *A Dialogue on the Two Chief World Systems*
50. Trial of Galileo (1633)
51. Giovanni Guglielmini
52. Giuseppe Calandrelli

STUDY QUESTIONS

1. What is Sacred Tradition, and why is it essential to understanding Divine Revelation?

2. Given the importance of Sacred Tradition, explain why the history of the Church's relationship to science and scientists helps us understand the message of the Bible regarding science.

Section A

3. Briefly describe the principle of "faith and reason together" from Sacred Tradition, and explain how it should affect our interpretation of Sacred Scripture.

4. Briefly describe the principle of "the integrity of nature" from Sacred Tradition, and provide an example of its application by a great Catholic thinker.

5. How did the Lateran IV teaching that God created the universe *ex nihilo* help to stimulate scientific thought?

6. How did the Lateran IV teaching that the universe had a first moment in time help to stimulate scientific thought?

7. How did Tempier's condemnation of the idea that God had to create the world exactly as it is help to give birth to modern science's experiential and experimental method?

8. What rule of thumb did Vatican I offer to the relationship between faith and science?

9. How did Vatican II foster the growth and progress of the sciences?

10. What is the significance of the Pontifical Academy of Sciences?

Section B

11. What does the history of priest-scientists throughout the ages reveal about the Church's attitude toward science?

Section C

12. What is "the Galileo Affair"? Why is it a blemish on the Church's relationship with science?

13. What are some of the different issues that led to Galileo's condemnation?

14. What was the theological error committed by those who opposed Galileo, according to St. John Paul II?

Danish astronomer Tycho Brahe (1546-1601) had Venus and Mercury orbiting the sun while the sun orbited the earth.

German astronomer Johannes Kepler (1571-1630) explained the tides by reference to the moon's gravitational pull.

PRACTICAL EXERCISES

1. Watch the video "The most groundbreaking scientist you've never heard of—Addison Anderson" (4 minutes, 32 seconds, *mtfresources.org/videos*). What does the video celebrate about Niels Stensen? What does it not mention? Create a script completing the video and the picture it gives of this great Catholic and scientist.

2. Watch the video "A Vatican scientist, Part I" (5 minutes, *mtfresources.org/videos*) about Br. Guy Consolmagno, S.J., astronomer and Director of the Vatican Observatory. How does Consolmagno explain the relationship between science and religion? What is the traditional Catholic approach to science, as he describes it?

3. Watch the video "A Vatican Scientist, Part II" (4 minutes, 2 seconds, *mtfresources.org/videos*) about common mistakes made in relating science and religion. Relate Consolmagno's explanation to the principle of the integrity of nature, as well as the distinction between "how" and "why" explanations that we have discussed in previous chapters.

4. The Church continues to be the subject of prejudice when it comes to her relationship to science and scientists. Create a list of steps by which a high-school student can help dispel popular misconceptions about the Church.

5. *To the presenter or teacher:* This assignment involves colored construction paper, black markers, scissors, and glue. Assign to each student in your class one of the Catholic scientists described in Section B of this chapter or in the Appendix (pp. 297 ff.). Have students search the internet for a picture or pictures of the individual and create a small poster (8½ x 11), using print-outs of the picture(s), prominently featuring his or her name, date, status in the Church (i.e., monk, bishop, lay woman, etc.), and his or her scientific contribution. After these are completed, hang them in your classroom, on a school bulletin board, or in a school hallway.

6. *To the presenter or teacher:* Bring a scientist or a group of scientists to your classroom for a short presentation to address the following questions: "What makes for successful science? What qualities do successful scientists incorporate into their scientific work?" Then have students revisit Section B of this chapter and the Appendix (pp. 297 ff.) and evaluate the Catholic scientists provided, choosing one which they think exemplifies successful science and the qualities of successful scientific work.

The courtyard of the Pontifical Academy of Sciences, headquartered in the Casina Pio IV in the heart of the Vatican Gardens.

The purpose of the Academy is to develop "a method of research based upon observation, experiment, and the inductive method," in other words, a truly scientific method.

It includes scientists without regard to their membership in the Catholic Church, recognizing that all human beings are capable of reason and, therefore, of good science.

Since 1908, it has had forty-five Nobel Prize winners among its members.

Endnotes – Chapter Five

1. Dogmatic Constitution *Dei Verbum* on Divine Revelation, no. 9.
2. Aidan Nicholas, *The Shape of Catholic Theology* (Collegeville, MN: Liturgical Press, 1990), 176-177.
3. Yves Congar, *The Meaning of Tradition*, trans. by A. N. Woodrow (San Francisco, CA: Ignatius Press, 2004), 127.
4. St. Augustine, *De Genesi ad Litteram* 1.10.21; cf. 4.26.43.
5. St. J.H. Newman, Letter to Pusey, *Letters & Diaries* (Oxford: Oxford University Press, 1973), 25.137.
6. Pius XII, Address of November 22, 1951 to the Pontifical Academy of Sciences, *inters.org/pius-xii-speech-1952-proofs-god.*
7. Carroll, "Creation, Evolution and St. Thomas Aquinas."
8. St. Augustine, *De Trinitate* 3.9.16. Cf. De Genesi, 3.9.16; 5.23.45.
9. St. Thomas Aquinas, *Summa Theologiae* I.67.4 ad 3.
10. Charles De Koninck, *The Cosmos*, 235-254, in *The Writings of Charles De Koninck*, Volume One, ed. and trans. by Ralph McInerny (Notre Dame, IN: University of Notre Dame Press, 2008), 31.
11. Ibid., 292.
12. DS 800, as quoted in CCC 327.
13. On the teaching that the universe was created out of nothing, see 2 Mc 7:28; on the idea of the universe being created in time, see the great words which begin the Book of Genesis (Gn 1:1) and the Gospel of St. John (Jn 1): "In the beginning..."
14. Paul Haffner, *Creation and Scientific Creativity: A Study in the Thought of S.L. Jaki* (Front Royal: Christendom Press, 1991), 41.
15. Ibid.
16. Ibid., 60.
17. Haffner, *Mystery of Creation*, 160.
18. Vatican I, *Dei Filius*, 1: DS 3002; cf. CCC no 293.
19. Vatican I, *Dei Filius*, 5-6: DS 3017.
20. Vatican II, Pastoral Constitution *Gaudium et Spes* on the Church in the Modern World (hereafter abbreviated *GS*), 59.
21. Marcelo Sorondo, *The Pontifical Academy of Sciences: A Historical Profile*, The Pontifical Academy of Sciences Extra Series 16 (Vatican City: 2003), 8.
22. Ibid., 8.
23. Ibid., 1-2. Cf. Pontifical Academy of Sciences, *Statutes* of 1976, art. 2, §1.
24. Ibid., 18.
25. (*Author's note: This section was partially created by Stephen M. Barr and Dermott Mullan. It was originally an account of priest-scientists from the Middle Ages to the 20th century, but has been expanded.*)
26. David Bentley Hart, *Atheist Delusions* (New Haven, CT: Yale University Press, 2009), 69.
27. James Hannam, *The Genesis of Science* (Washington, D.C.; Regnery Publishing, 2011), 172.
28. Ibid., 179.
29. Henryk Anzulewicz, "Albertus Magnus, Saint," in *Complete Dictionary of Scientific Biography*, Vol. 19 (Detroit, MI: Charles Scribner's Sons, 2008), 36–40.
30. James Hannam, "Medieval Christianity and the Rise of Modern Science, Part 2," *BioLogos* (October 31, 2012), *biologos.org/blogs/archive/medieval-christianity-and-the-rise-of-modern-science-part-2*.
31. C. Sigismondi, "Christopher Clavius astronomer and mathematician," *Il Nuovo Cimento, arxiv.org/pdf/1203.0476v1.pdf.*
32. A.C. Crombie, "Mersenne, Marin," in *Complete Dictionary of Scientific Biography*, Vol. 9, 316.
33. Vítězslav Orel, Staffan Müller-Wille and Robert Olby, "Mendel, Johann Gregor," in *Complete Dictionary of Scientific Biography*, Vol. 23, 97.
34. Ibid.
35. Sam Kean, *The Violinist's Thumb and Other Tales of Love, War and Genius as Written by Our Genetic Code* (New York: Back Bay Books, 2012), 95-102; cf. Jun Tsuji, *The Soul of DNA* (Ocala, FL: Llumina Press, 2004).
36. The following account of the Galileo Affair is largely a condensed and adapted version of two excellent lectures on Galileo by Lawrence Principe, Drew Professor of the Humanities at Johns Hopkins University in the Department of the History of Science and Technology and the Department of Chemistry: "Church, Copernicus and Galileo" and "Galileo's Trial," *Science and Religion*, downloaded from *www.thegreatcourses.com/courses/science-and-religion.html*. Direct quotations from Galileo's works, St. Robert Bellarmine, and other documents are taken from Galileo Galilei, et al., *The Essential Galileo*, ed. and trans. by Maurice Finocchiaro (Indianapolis: Hackett Publishing, 2008).
37. Galileo, "Letter to Castelli" in *Essential Galileo*, 106.
38. Bellarmine, "Letter to Foscarini" in *Essential Galileo*, 147.
39. William Wallace, "Galileo's Trial and the Proofs of the Earth's Motion," *Catholic Dossier* (1995): 12.
40. Ibid., 12-13.
41. St. John Paul II, Address of November 10, 1979, to the Pontifical Academy of Sciences, *inters.org/John-Paul-II-deep-harmony.*
42. St. John Paul II, Address of October 31, 1992, to the Galileo Commission, *inters.org/John-Paul-II-conclusion-galileo-affair.*
43. Ibid.

Chapter Six
Evil, Prayer, and Miracles: Questions for God in the Light of Modern Science

What role does humility play in understanding both natural and supernatural realities?

Does the reality of evil create an obstacle for reconciling faith and science?

Does the necessity of prayer contradict the idea of God as the unchanging Source of being, the Creator of all things?

Does belief in miracles contradict the commitment of science to discovering natural causes?

> Job answered the LORD:
> "I know that thou canst do all things,
> and that no purpose of thine can be thwarted....
> I have uttered what I did not understand,
> things too wonderful for me, which I did not know....
> I had heard of thee by the hearing of the ear,
> but now my eye sees thee;
> therefore I despise myself,
> and repent in dust and ashes." (Jb 42:1-6)

In theology and philosophy, just as in science, a good explanation not only sheds light, but it also creates new questions. Brilliant insights deepen our understanding, but that deepening never resolves the mysteries at the heart of reality. In the words of physicist **Peter Hodgson**, "In [both science and faith] there is detailed knowledge that guides our lives, one in the natural world and the other in the supernatural world, and in each there is a mystery at its heart."[1]

One great scientist who knew this was **William Thomson** (1824-1907), known to history as **Lord Kelvin**. Kelvin was one of the great pioneers of electrical theory after whom the standard measurement of electric current, the *Kelvin (ampere) balance*, was named. As the story goes, he once made an anonymous tour of an electrical equipment factory. Kelvin

"Then the LORD answered Job out of the whirlwind: 'Who is this that darkens counsel by words without knowledge?... Where were you when I laid the foundation of the earth?'" (Jb 38:1-4)

listened patiently to a young factory apprentice as he explained elementary facts about amps and volts. Once he was done, Kelvin asked him, "Please tell me what electricity is." The young man fell into an awkward silence. "Don't let that worry you," Kelvin remarked, "no one knows what electricity is."[2] No one in his day understood electricity better than Kelvin, and yet Kelvin also humbly recognized that his understanding was only a glimpse, not unlimited comprehension.

Theologians and philosophers are not exempt from this humility of Kelvin; in fact, it is an even greater necessity for those contemplating the mysteries of faith and the absolute mystery of God. Consider **St. Thomas Aquinas**, the greatest theologian of the Middle Ages and perhaps of all Church history, who at the end of his life had a remarkable spiritual experience while celebrating Mass on the Feast of St. Nicholas in 1273, the year before his death. He abruptly stopped writing afterwards, and when a fellow friar urged him to finish, he exclaimed, "Everything that I have written seems like straw compared to those things that I have seen and have been revealed to me."

Given the examples of Kelvin and St. Thomas, it should not be surprising that as we have explored numerous important theological issues in the light of science, we have also raised new questions that have been left unexplored. These questions are essential not only to the relationship between faith and reason, but also to everyday life and religious experience, and must be given special consideration before we continue.

In Chapter Three, we explored God's relationship to his creation, celebrating the whole universe as a work of divine love. And yet the universe, life, and especially human life, give evidence of imperfections that cause oceans of suffering and death for God's creatures. The *problem of evil* seems to call into question that the universe is a product of divine love, and the misery and destruction we see all around lead many to reject the existence of God altogether. This is not a new problem, but modern science has made it even clearer by helping us understand the fragility of all life and has shown that our very sun is destined to fizzle out, along with the entire universe, which will expand until it is so spread out that it will whisper away. This leads us to our first critical question: How can we reconcile the doctrine of God the Creator with the presence of evil in creation?

St. Thomas Aquinas, the greatest theologian of the Middle Ages and perhaps of all Church history: "Everything that I have written seems like straw compared to those things that I have seen and have been revealed to me."

The necessity of prayer is also a critical issue for understanding faith in the light of science. Throughout the text we have celebrated holy men and women for whom prayer was essential to their heroic lives of holiness. We have considered **St. Ignatius of Loyola**, **Julian of Norwich**, and **St. John Henry Newman**, to name just a few. We also explored the doctrine of creation *cum tempore* ("with time") and noted that time is just a feature of the physical universe, not of God's reality, since he is timeless and unchanging. But these lead us to other critical questions: If God is unchanging, why did these great saints offer prayers to God in petition for their needs? Why does Jesus, the Son of God, teach us to pray daily for our needs ("Give us this day our daily bread" [Mt 6:11])? If God respects the integrity of nature and is eternal and changeless, why would we assume that he would grant our needs in response to our prayers?

Finally, *the reality of miracles* confronts us with other critical questions for faith in the light of science. Miracles are hard to reconcile with the fact that Sacred Tradition shows an avoidance of supernaturalism and respects the integrity of nature, that God does not create by inserting a "Divine Foot" in the door of nature. And yet the Christian faith does not simply profess belief in a Creator but also that the same God who creates the universe also redeems it through becoming one of us. When God became man, incredible signs and wonders occurred. As Catholics profess in the Creed, Jesus "by the Holy Spirit was incarnate of the Virgin Mary" and that he "rose again on the third day in accordance with the Scriptures." In both cases, as well as in Jesus's many deeds of healing and power, things occurred that cannot be explained simply by referring to natural causes. These marvels have been followed by countless others in the history of the Church. Isn't belief in the miracles of Jesus and the saints just one more "God of the Gaps" error?

The Resurrection
The problem of evil, the necessity of prayer, and the reality of miracles involve mysteries of faith. The key to avoiding contradiction while embracing mystery is to know both the power and limits of human reason.

The problem of evil, the necessity of prayer, and the reality of miracles involve mysteries of faith, and so the critical questions they raise cannot be fully resolved simply by reasoning about them apart from it. At the end of Chapter One we saw that science itself involves paradoxes and mysteries, just as faith does. And, just as **Einstein** shed light upon the scientific mystery of the nature of light, theology and philosophy can help us answer our critical questions about evil, prayer, and miracles.

But we must also adopt the humility of Kelvin and St. Thomas as we proceed. In the use of our powers of reason, two conditions of darkness can occur: mysteries beyond us that show reason's limits and contradictions below us that disturb and injure truth. The key to avoiding contradiction while embracing mystery is to know both the power and limits of human reason, to go only as far in exploring as reality permits, and to leave the rest to wonder and humble speculation.[3] We will know that we are successful when absurdities are resolved but mystery remains and when we are invited into awe and wonder at the nature of reality and the absolute mystery of God.

In the liturgical calendar the Church observes two seasons, *Advent* and *Lent*, in which she confronts evil through prayer and prepares to celebrate two miracles that are at the heart of the Christian faith: the Incarnation of the Son of God and the Virgin Birth of Jesus celebrated at Christmas and his Resurrection celebrated at Easter. These two seasons and the great feasts to which they lead will serve as helpful reference points to guide our reflections.

A. "The Cry of the Poor": Divine Providence and the Mystery of Evil

St. Teresa of Calcutta answered "the cry of the poor."
The mystery of evil is an insoluble misery without the ability to recognize the redemptive power of Christ to transform evil and suffering into redemption and joy.

THE PROBLEM OF EVIL IS IMMENSE; it touches all of creation. At the same time, the doctrine of creation *ex nihilo* implicates God in the existence of all things, as we explored in Chapter Three. And so all things, even our thoughts and own free actions, are locked in a paradox; both have God for their source and yet also have the capacity for evil. **St. Paul**, recognizing the imperfections of creation, speaks of the whole of creation groaning in pain (Rom 8:22). God, Creator, and Source of existence for all things, made real the freedom of the Nazi concentration camp guards, for instance, just as he made real the freedom of **St. Teresa of Calcutta** (lovingly known as Mother Teresa) as she gave herself to the poor. So we must face the question: How can we claim God as the source of all things when evil and suffering permeate all of creation?

1500 years ago, **St. Augustine** asked this more poignantly than anyone, reflecting upon the evil he found in himself. We now make his questions our own:

> **Who made me? Was it not my God, who is not only good, but Goodness itself? Whence came I then to will to do evil, and to be unwilling to do good, that there**

might be cause for my just punishment? Who was it that put this in me, and implanted in me the root of bitterness, seeing I was altogether made by my most sweet God? . . .

Where is evil then, and when did it start, and how has it crept into the world? What is its root, and what is its seed?[4]

1. Defining Evil

MANY PHILOSOPHERS BEFORE ST. AUGUSTINE pondered the problem of evil, and they made some progress in understanding, especially the pagan philosophers **Plato** (ca. 424-ca. 347 BC) and **Plotinus** (AD 204-270). And yet it was **St. Augustine** himself who would be the first to offer to history a clearer perspective on evil, often referred to as the *privation theory of evil.* He saw that evil was not a being and, therefore, not a subsistent reality, a "thing," of divine creation. Rather, evil is a lack or absence, the *privation*, of a good that should be present. Not all privations are evil. A rock is not able to see, but we do not feel compassion for it as we do for a blind person or animal because it is not in the nature of a mineral to see. Every created nature is finite; even if a creature has all that is natural to it, it does not have the infinite range of perfections that only belong to God, the Source of all being and goodness.

Interestingly, it was precisely the realization of God as Creator of all things that allowed Augustine to conclude that evil "is not any *thing* found in nature."[5] Augustine's insight was formally proclaimed as a doctrine of the Catholic faith by the **Council of Florence** (1431-1449), as we saw in Chapter Three: "[This council] asserts that *there is no nature of evil* because every nature, in so far as it is a nature, is good." The evil that causes us to suffer and creation to groan is not a creature of God, not something willed into being by him. It exists precisely when a creature or (in the case of human beings) a thought, word, or action lacks something that it ought to possess. God is not its source, although he does permit it.

St. Paul Healing the Cripple at Lystra
Physical evil is evil that does not involve personal fault. The evil that causes us to suffer and "creation to groan" is not something willed into being by God. It exists precisely when a creature lacks something that it ought to possess.

Augustine and the Catholic philosophical tradition recognize two kinds of evil. The first kind, *physical evil,* is evil that does not involve personal fault, although personal fault is sometimes the cause of it. Physical blindness is an example—blindness is the nonexistence, the privation, of sight in a creature whose nature it is to see. Many physical evils occur as a matter of course because of physical good. Cancer happens because mutations that drive evolution (which is good) also drive disease (which is evil). Underwater earthquakes and their tsunamis create human deaths and property destruction (evil) because geological processes (good) that form beautiful tropical islands (good) also deprive the earth's crust of stability, which causes evils for creatures whose lives depend upon that stability.[6] The same is true with all biological life. As **Aristotle** keenly observed, the generation of new life often requires *corruption*, which literally means "destruction." The conception of a new human being requires the corruption of the ovum and sperm, which cease to exist when they combine to form the zygote. And in order to sustain their lives, animals destroy other living things by consuming them; hence, "The life of the spider [good] is the death [evil] of the fly."

Any time we observe an example of physical evil and try to identify it, we discover that it is impossible to "find" evil until we come to some negative, some absence. The purely positive properties of any thing cannot be called evil, even if those positive properties are the cause of evil. For example, a deadly *virus* consists of genetic material and a coating of protein. None of these positive components are evil; indeed, all living things are made up of genetic material and proteins. The evil of a deadly virus is not any part of it; rather, the *privation* of health and life it causes is the true evil. As proof of this, consider that the very viruses that may cause sickness can also be directly involved in great good. As we noted in Chapter One, it seems that a *retrovirus*, a kind of virus that inserts its DNA into cells of other organisms, inserted its DNA into the DNA of our evolutionary ancestors millions of years ago. What would normally have meant sickness and death became the genetic component for the mammalian placenta upon which all human infants depend in the womb. But no evil can also be good and be a positive cause of goodness—this would be a contradiction. The virus is not the evil; the absence of health and the negation of life it might cause is the true evil. Therefore, the late Jesuit philosopher **W. Norris Clarke** called evil "a hole in being"[7]; it is the lack of what ought to be present, the nonexistence of some good.

The evil of the concentration camps involved the absence of the proper respect for human life and dignity.

The second and more tragic kind of evil St. Augustine identified as *moral evil*, evil in which rational creatures knowingly and freely deprive their own thoughts, words, and actions of the good that ought to be present within them. Once again, it is the "hole" within these that make them evil. Adultery is an example. Its evil does not consist in the bodily pleasure or personal intimacy involved in the sexual act, both of which are good as such. The evil of adultery is the nonexistence of sexual fidelity when this fidelity ought to be present. This lack of loving fidelity to a spouse corrupts the good of sex from within, rendering it an inherently immoral action. The evil of the crimes of the Nazis in the concentration camps involved the absence, in their thoughts, words, and deeds, of the proper respect for the human life and dignity of the Jewish people that they imprisoned, tortured, and killed. The absence of compassion, kindness, and justice is what made Auschwitz evil, not the concrete walls of the gas chambers or the gases used there for horrific purposes.

One reality closely associated with evil is often confused for it but actually needs special consideration: pain and emotional suffering. The feeling of *pain* is actually a positive presence, not a privation; it tells us that there is something wrong in our bodies (*physical pain*) or within our relationships, actions, or attitudes (*emotional pain*). Without them we could not function, and so these important "messenger services" actually aid us rather than deprive us.[8] Many a hand would be irreparably burned if the pain of the fire and heat from the stove burner did not alert us to its destructive presence! It would be hard to count how many times pain has saved any person's life or well being, even though from the perspective of pleasure it is never preferable. Pain is rightly ordered response to physical and moral evil. It is not an evil in itself.[9]

Finally, to call evil a privation is not to declare it to be nonexistent or powerless. It is a lack where something truly ought to be present, and so it is always a privation, a hole, in something real. Because of this it is powerfully destructive simply by virtue of what it "takes away" and disfigures. *Physical* and *moral evil* are the source of all suffering for human beings, and those who suffer from them (and is there anyone who does not?) can rightly be called "poor" in some real way. Psalm 34:7 tells us "[the] poor one cried out and the LORD heard, and from all his distress he saved him." Our question is if the Lord is the poor one's Creator, why must he need to cry out in the first place?

2. The Mystery of God and the Reality of Evil

WE CAN NOW TURN TO OUR CRITICAL QUESTION, "Why does God, the source of all things, create a universe in which physical evil is actually a part of its functioning and in which moral evil permeates human life?" The classic argument, proposed centuries ago by the English philosopher **David Hume** (1711-1776), runs as follows:

> **God by nature must be both omnipotent (all-powerful) and omnibenevolent (all-good). Now if God is omnipotent, he *could* prevent all evil. And if he is all-good, he *would* do so, since it is the characteristic of a good person to prevent evil wherever possible. But in fact he does not prevent all evil, even though he could, but allows a vast amount of it, both physical and moral, as is evident in the world around us. Therefore, it follows that God is either not omnipotent or omnibenevolent. In either case such a being could not be God; therefore, there is no God.[10]**

Evil is powerfully destructive simply by virtue of what it "takes away" and disfigures. The possibility to choose evil rather than good is at the heart of what occurred with our first human parents.

It seems almost an insult to those who suffer in a world weighed down with evil to disagree with Hume, as if denying God's existence is a necessary part of showing compassion to the suffering. But denying the existence of ultimate Goodness is no compassion at all.

Hume's argument is inadequate, not because he does not make valid points, but because he is missing an important alternative. A good person is not always obliged to prevent any and all evil; it may be that a good person allows a lesser evil to occur so that a greater good may be achieved through it, as a parent does when they allow their children to suffer failures in order to learn responsible judgment and valuable lessons without which they would be worse off than not. In a similar way, when we consider the universe and human life, we realize that the possibility of goodness is deeply reduced and diminished without the possibility of evil.

As for the universe, its integrity would simply be annihilated if God were to miraculously suspend the stable operation of the many forces and laws that undergird the entire cosmos whenever necessary in order to prevent every physical evil. Given this stable operation, on which the evolution of the universe and of life depends, it is inevitable that living organisms will occasionally act spontaneously (or be acted upon) in ways that bring them into conflict with this stable operation and so cause them injury, with pain and suffering as a result. As noted above, most physical evils occur because of physical goods—recall the geological processes example. The lion (good) could not be itself unless it killed and consumed the gazelle, which is good for the lion but evil for the gazelle. Therefore, much of the beauty and majesty of our universe would be missing were God simply to halt every physical evil.

The absence of physical evil in the universe would also mean a universe in which life would not freely develop, and in which everything would operate according to a single, static pattern. That would translate into a world in which there would be nothing surprising in nature—neither evolution nor emergence—and in which human beings could not choose to impose their own patterns on things. It would be a world without freedom. It would be a completely regimented world in which we could not have any meaningful activity of our own. In the words of W. Norris Clarke:

> **But, the objector might ask, would it not be even better to make a world wherein no physical evil were possible? But would this really be better in the long run? We would never be challenged to learn from experience, since we would never get hurt no matter what we did, and, worst of all, virtues would disappear since not needed.... We would remain like simple, spoiled children... in a word, quite unlike the human beings we know and admire today.**

The Expulsion from the Garden of Eden
Adam and Eve were capable of choosing against God not simply because of their free will but also because the fullness of God's reality had not yet been bestowed upon them; there was still a higher awareness and love that they had not yet experienced.

When we come to the greatest tragedy of all, the moral evil of human beings, we are faced with the same dilemma. There would be no human freedom in a world in which God prevented all moral evil. In such a universe it would also be the case that human beings acting morally, with goodness in mind, could accomplish no good freely as real causes of goodness. God would not simply be the Absolute Source of all things, he would also prevent us from collaborating with him in the fulfillment of his desire to perfect the world he created, and to make moral masterpieces of our own lives. But, if he enables us to freely cooperate, he must also enable us to freely choose to reject goodness, and so moral evil must be allowed if moral goodness is to be possible.

This possibility to choose evil rather than good is at the heart of what occurred with our first human parents, who freely chose to disobey God, to choose a lesser good, rather than to choose the good that had been presented to them, which led to their fall from grace and original justice. They were capable of choosing against God not simply because of their free will but also because the fullness of God's reality had not yet been bestowed upon them; there was still a higher awareness and love that they had not yet experienced. However, in the time to come, when the blessed stand before and behold the full reality of God "face to face," free will will remain, but it will not be possible to choose sinfully, since the goodness of God's very being will be so abundantly evident and clear. We will freely and consistently choose God all the time, every time, which is itself the perfection of our free will.

Crucifixion
"God, who became a lamb, tells us that the world is saved by the Crucified One, not by those who crucified him." (Pope Benedict XVI)

We do not want a divine dictator who would destroy our freedom, we want a Heavenly Father who does not violate the universe and human freedom, a God who deals with us in love, not simply in power. Here, we can define love as "willing the good of the other as other," for their own sake and not for the sake of one's self. **Pope Benedict XVI** captured this point beautifully in his first homily as Pope by showing the unloving, totalitarian lie behind the false promise of a universe with no evil, a lie that has been foisted upon human beings by "ideologies of power," ideologies such as Nazism and Marxism:

> **It is not power, but love that redeems us! This is God's sign: he himself is love. How often we wish that God would show himself stronger, that he would strike decisively, defeating evil and creating a better world. All ideologies of power justify themselves in exactly this way; they justify the destruction of whatever would stand in the way of progress and the liberation of humanity. We suffer on account of God's patience. And yet, we need his patience. God, who became a lamb, tells us that the world is saved by the Crucified One, not by those who crucified him. *The world is redeemed by the patience of God. It is destroyed by the impatience of man.*[12]**

Perhaps the Christian solution to Hume's argument lies precisely in the fact that God's work of creation and redemption is not yet complete. God wills a perfect world, and he is actively working to bring the universe and history to its perfect completion. In the words of 2 Peter 3:13, "According to his promise we wait for new heavens and a new earth in which righteousness dwells." From this perspective of faith, we can say to Hume: "Yes, God is all-good and all-powerful, and, yes, evil is present in 'vast amounts.' Therefore, God *will* defeat all evil." Indeed, he is already powerfully and mysteriously doing so by enabling his creatures to be themselves and mercifully forgiving them when they fail, working through holy men and women to transform the world through their free cooperation with him. God would not allow any evil unless he could and would bring some greater good from it.

This free cooperation and the transformation of the universe does not come simply from good intentions shared among a few; it comes from the loving Sacrifice that God took upon himself when he became human in order to accomplish our liberation from evil, sin, and death. The ultimate answer that God gives to our question is the life, Death, and Resurrection of Christ, which we annually celebrate in the seasons of Advent and Christmas, Lent and Easter. First, in his life Christ overcame moral evil in himself by being the perfect example of the fullness of human goodness with no moral evil whatsoever. In the words of Sacred Scripture, Jesus, the High Priest who offered himself in sacrifice for our sins, is not "unable to sympathize with our weaknesses, but... in every respect has been tempted as we are, yet without sin" (Heb 4:15).

The Nativity
God became a human being in order to accomplish our liberation from evil, sin, and death.

Second, in his Sacrifice on the Cross, Jesus overcame moral evil not only in himself but in all human beings—past, present, and future—by becoming an inexhaustible source of forgiveness to those who have sinned and the one who reconciles all human beings to each other and to God.

Finally, through the miracle of his Resurrection, Christ overcame all physical evil and took our human nature into an indestructible life, preparing the coming of a new creation, a new heavens and earth, with no evil whatsoever. This is why **St. Paul** calls the risen Christ "the firstborn of many brothers and sisters" (Rom 8:29), because he offers us the way to join him, body and soul, in a universe to come that is perfectly fulfilled and transformed into the Kingdom of God. This is why, after the consecration at Mass, when Christ is truly present—Body, Blood, Soul, and Divinity—we sing "Save us, Savior of the world, for by your Cross and Resurrection, you have set us free."[13] By his Cross, all moral evil is overcome; by his Resurrection, all physical evil is put to an end.

Christians do not deny the existence of evil; in fact, they see it for what it is, a hole in God's good creation. Science is put to the task of finding solutions to various evils, and it has greatly improved human life through medical therapies, agricultural innovations, and technological advancements, all of which are rightly celebrated as progress and as God's providential will for his human creatures. But evil will always be present in the world until it is fulfilled, and the way to overcome it fully is to walk daily with Christ crucified and risen through life. This means we must be willing to suffer patiently out of love, recognizing that one's suffering is precious to God, not because he wishes us to suffer, but because such love is his own attitude to our universe, a love that overcomes all evil. Through loving God and loving like God, our suffering in the face of evil is transformed into *sacrifice*, which is not misery, but a joy-filled hope that, in response to the cry of the poor, the Lord "will wipe every tear from their eyes, and death shall be no more, neither shall there be mourning nor crying nor pain..." (Rev 21:4) in the new creation, where God "will be all in all" (1 Cor 15:28).

B. "Ask and It Will Be Given": Divine Eternity and the Necessity of Prayer

WITH THE MYSTERY OF EVIL OBSERVED AND CLARIFIED, we can now turn to the very "cry" of those afflicted by it: prayer, and specifically *petitionary prayer*, the kind of prayer in which we ask God for things we need, which naturally flows forth from our encounters with evil and suffering. There are many other kinds of prayer: prayer of thanksgiving, prayer of praise and adoration, and prayer of repentance, to name a few other kinds. But, our critical question has to do with our asking God for things we want and need, and God's ability to answer. Jesus said, "Ask, and it will be given you; seek, and you will find; knock, and it will be opened to you" (Mt 7:7). How can God, who is eternal and unchanging, answer the requests he encourages and even commands us to offer? And, if God is all-knowing, why does he instruct us to give him information by offering our needs to him?

The purpose of prayer is not to change God but to change us, to connect us more deeply and authentically to God, the source of our being.

Or, consider this riddle about Zeus, the pagan Greek god of the sky, which comes from a pagan source but is equally applicable to Christian prayer. The mother of two daughters first visits one of her children, who asks her to pray to Zeus for rain so that her garden will grow. Then she visits the second, who begs her to pray for sunshine because she is planning a journey.[14] What does Zeus (or, in reality, the one true God) do with contradictory requests? Does he grant one and not the other based on the merits of those in need? Or, does he do so arbitrarily?

These puzzling questions show how often we think in very human ways about prayer and the divine response to prayer. In our ordinary way of thinking, God answers prayers in the way a friend or neighbor might respond to a request for a favor, or a first responder to a call for help in an emergency. First, the responder becomes aware that there is a need. Then that person does something in his or her power to help, fills our need or rescues us from our distress.[15] But this cannot be the way it is with God. God, who perfectly knows all things, does not have to become aware of things unknown to him. And God, who is eternal and unchanging, does not "begin" doing things; to be eternal means to have no beginning, nor to change from inactivity to activity. We imagine God responding in this way not because that is how prayer works but because as creatures within time we cannot imagine the mystery of his eternity. Yet if we are to answer our critical question, we must begin to think beyond our ordinary thoughts, to adopt a wisdom wider and deeper than our normal notions.

The Virgin in Prayer
The Church teaches that intercessory prayer is powerfully effective.

Based upon the understanding of God we developed in Chapter Three, we can begin to move beyond contradiction into a deeper appreciation of the mystery of prayer and why it is essential to the Christian life. The principle of double agency developed by **St. Thomas Aquinas** teaches us that God is already the source of all of our actions, including our prayers. This means that although our prayers fully originate with us in one way, they also fully originate with God in another: Prayer is "wholly done by both" God and the person praying, as St. Thomas would say. It is not that we pray first and then God responds, but that as soon as we pray, the prayer itself is already God's action in us and for us. As one of the Prefaces, the prayer said at Mass at the beginning of the Eucharistic Prayer, describes our prayers of thanksgiving, "You have no need of our praise, yet our thanksgiving is itself your gift."[16] It is as if the first responder is the very one who dials 911 *and* makes the rescue! In the words of **C.S. Lewis**, "'God did (or said) it' and 'I did (or said) it' can both be true.... The deeper the level within ourselves from which our prayer, or any other act, wells up, the more it is His, but not at all the less ours. *Rather, most ours when most His.*"[17]

This helps us to understand the first, and most important, reason that God wants us to tell him our needs and desires even when he already knows them, and when they seem to contradict those of others (as when one prays that a hurricane will avoid their area, while another prays for it to avoid theirs, when it cannot avoid both). The purpose of prayer is not to change God but to change us, to connect us more deeply and authentically to God, the source of our being. God purifies our desires when we pray sincerely and with humble trust. St. Thomas Aquinas imagines salvation and happiness as a great chain of light hanging from heaven and stretching to earth, and prayer as the way a person climbs it—notice that it is the person praying that is changed, not God:

> **If we take hold of this chain and move ourselves hand over hand toward the top, we will seem to pull the chain downwards, but really we will not bring it down.... Rather, we ourselves will be raised into the greater splendor of that luminous chain.... Before all acts, but most especially before theological work, it**

> **is beneficial for us to begin with prayer, not as if we were to draw down divine power which is everywhere present and nowhere contained, but as drawing and uniting ourselves to him through recollection and supplication.[18]**

If prayer does not change God and only changes us, then why do we thank God for "answered" prayers? Once again the principle of double agency helps us to transcend our ordinary way of thinking. The distinction between the primary causality of God and the secondary causality of creatures has been key so far to understanding how God acts in the natural world. For example, God causes all living creatures on our planet to exist through a process we call "evolution," through the secondary causality of random genetic mutation, natural selection, etc. God provides the food we eat and the air we breathe through the secondary causality of plant and animal growth and a stable, oxygen-rich atmosphere. We should think of petitionary prayer as yet another secondary cause that at times God uses to accomplish what he intends. It is just as much a part of the unfolding of his divine plan as everything else is.

The Repentant Peter
God allows our prayers to cause things that might otherwise not be accomplished.

In other words, God allows our prayers to cause things that might otherwise not be accomplished, just as the activity of bees is necessary for the pollination of the myriad of different flowers that exist, without which the flowers would fail to reproduce and spread across fields and forests. He does so through his eternal decree and unchanging will to bring the universe and his creatures to fulfillment, which we call *divine providence*. St. Thomas explains why this does not mean that God is changed by our prayers, because it is his unchanging will that some things be caused by prayer:

> **The cause of some things that are done by God is prayers and holy desires.... [P]rayers are efficacious [effective; successful] before God, yet they do not destroy the [unchangeable] order of divine providence, because whatever request is granted already falls under the order of divine providence. To say we should not pray...because his providence is [unchangeable], is like saying that we should not walk in order to get somewhere, nor eat in order to be nourished, which is completely absurd![19]**

C.S. Lewis's point above, i.e., that the deeper the level within ourselves from which we pray, the better our prayer is, might help us understand why the Church teaches that the intercession of the saints in heaven, especially the Blessed Virgin Mary, is so powerfully effective. The deeper one is completely united to God, the more it is the case that one's prayers are in keeping with God's will; imperfectly on earth but perfectly in heaven. Among all human beings, the saints are "most his," and so uniting our prayers to theirs and seeking their intercession is something that God eternally desires of us. God has revealed that all of the faithful are united in Christ's

The spiritual goods and happiness that the saints have, they wish to share with us, and God eternally desires that the whole human family be united in what is called "the Communion of Saints." Just as he wishes us to share our goods with the poor, the saints help us by taking up our cause as God empowers them to do so.

Mystical Body, the Church, which transcends the boundaries between life and death, heaven and earth. The spiritual goods and happiness that the saints have, they wish to share with us, and God eternally desires that the whole human family be united in what is called "the Communion of Saints." Just as he wishes us to share our goods with the poor, the saints help us by taking up our cause as God empowers them to do so.

Finally, let us connect the mystery of prayer to the mystery of evil that prayer so often addresses. In the section on the problem of evil, we noted that God would never allow evil unless he could bring a greater good from it. God has revealed that his plan for the universe is to perfect it, to offer the perfect fullness of life, everlasting happiness, and the complete conquest of all physical and moral evil. As we read in the Chapter 21 of the Book of Revelation:

1 I saw a new heaven and a new earth; for the first heaven and the first earth had passed away, and the sea was no more.

2 And I saw the holy city, new Jerusalem, coming down out of heaven from God, prepared as a bride adorned for her husband;

3 and I heard a loud voice from the throne saying, "Behold, the dwelling of God is with men. He will dwell with them, and they shall be his people, and God himself will be with them;

4 he will wipe away every tear from their eyes, and death shall be no more, neither shall there be mourning nor crying nor pain any more, for the former things have passed away."

5 And he who sat upon the throne said, "Behold, I make all things new." Also he said, "Write this, for these words are trustworthy and true."

God's will for his creatures is the fullness of life in a new heaven and earth beyond any evil. And yet he wills this to occur with our cooperation. In light of this, prayer is one essential way in which we begin to allow that transformation to occur within ourselves and within those whose lives we touch. Just as in the Eucharist, in which bread and wine are substantially changed, prayer is the desire that the whole world become the reality hidden in the Eucharist: humanity risen and glorified, and the physical universe transformed according to God's will for it.

Our consideration of the tragedy of evil and the necessity of prayer now sets the stage for our final critical issue, the reality of miracles. Let us consider a miracle of healing from our own day to set the stage.

C. Miracles: Signs and Wonders at the Crossroads of Faith and Science

UNDER NORMAL CIRCUMSTANCES, the beginning of the year 2000 would have been a wonderful time in the life of **Elisabeth Comparini Arcolino**, a Brazilian mother of three children who had recently learned that she was expecting her fourth child. But, during an emergency visit to the hospital in the sixteenth week of her pregnancy, Elizabeth's happiness was troubled by tragic news. Her baby's placenta had torn, resulting in a total loss of amniotic fluid, the watery substance that creates the unborn baby's necessary growth environment. She was told by the examining physician that the baby had absolutely no chance of survival and was advised to have an abortion.

The Arcolino family at the canonization of St. Gianna Molla.
Elisabeth is third from left; Gianna Arcolino is fifth from left in the arms of her father.

At that very moment **Diogenes Matthes**, her diocesan bishop, was at the hospital visiting a friend. He was summoned to Elizabeth's room, where he urged her to consult another physician. But there was a slight problem with his advice, at least for eyes without faith: the bishop recommended a physician who had died 38 years earlier!

What the bishop advised Elisabeth was that she join with him in praying for the intercession of Blessed **Gianna Beretta Molla**, an Italian wife, mother, and physician who had died to save the life of her own unborn child. In late 1961, Molla was newly pregnant when she learned that she had a tumor in her uterus that was threatening both her own life and the life of her baby. Rather than have an abortion, or even a morally acceptable hysterectomy, she chose the path riskiest to herself and safest for her baby—an operation to remove the tumor. Her heroic desire to save the baby was fulfilled but only at the sacrifice of her own life—Molla died on April 28, 1962, at the age of 39 due to an infection she would have avoided had she not had the surgery.

One miracle had already been attributed to the intercession of Gianna Molla, and due to her remarkable love and witness as a Catholic mother, **St. John Paul II** had beatified her in 1994. This meant that she was one miracle short of the two miracles required for her canonization as a saint, giving Bishop Matthes his idea: "You don't kill life inside the mother," the bishop told Elisabeth. "This is the time for Blessed Gianna Beretta Molla to intercede for the life you are carrying." At home the bishop began praying to Molla, saying, "The time for your canonization has arrived. Intercede to the Lord for the grace of a miracle and save the life of this little baby."[20]

St. Gianna Molla and her children.
The Arcolino family, including Gianna Marie, were in Rome along with thousands of other pilgrims for Molla's canonization.

Elisabeth took the bishop's advice and began to ask Gianna for her intercession. She turned out to be the "specialist" Elisabeth needed. Despite the lack of amniotic fluid—and in an event without scientific explanation—Elisabeth delivered a healthy baby girl by Caesarean section on May 31, 2000. She and her husband named their child Gianna Marie after the woman of faith and of science on whose prayers they had relied.[21] After a careful investigation that included scientists and doctors, St. John Paul II accepted the miracle as authentic. Four years later, on May 16, 2004, the Arcolino family, including Gianna Marie, were in Rome along with thousands of other pilgrims for Molla's canonization. Gianna Beretta Molla, believer, scientist, and pro-life hero, is now St. Gianna Molla. She has joined the ranks of the extraordinary men and women throughout history who have been recognized by the Church as saints.

The story of the Arcolino family and their heavenly physician brings us to our final critical issue of this chapter—miracles—and to our question regarding the integrity of nature. If the Church acknowledges the possibility of miracles such as this, how can we say that the Christian faith upholds the integrity of nature? Does God insert himself into ordinary events and so violate the order he established in the universe? To answer our questions, we must first understand the definition of a miracle.

1. Miracles in the Light of Faith

THE FRENCH THEOLOGIAN **Rene Latourelle** offers a precise definition of a *miracle* as "a religious wonder that expresses, in human beings and the universe, a special and utterly free intervention of God, who uses it to give human beings a sign of the presence of his message of salvation in the world."[22] Recalling the miracle that saved the pregnancy of Elisabeth Arcolino, we can see that each of these elements was present:

1. A "Religious Wonder": The Arcolino baby's survival transcended the ordinary course of things in nature. But this escape from death was not a simple wonder; it was one related directly to the prayers made by Elisabeth, her bishop, and others. It came after humble, trusting, persevering prayer; it came from the mediation of Jesus Christ shared with his holy and heroic servant, the pro-life, pro-baby hero St. Gianna. In this event we can clearly see a harmony between the wonder of the baby's miraculous cure and the calling on God, through **St. Gianna**, to which God "responded." This is the nature of all miracles: They are not simply wonders, but *religious wonders*, God's answer to the cry of those who place their trust in him.

2. A Sign of God's Message of Salvation: The Arcolino healing miracle was not simply a mysterious, inexplicable blessing for the baby and her family. It was also a picture that painted a thousand words, an action that taught many things at once. It made known that God's saving power is real. It showed God's love and care for all human beings, including the unborn, a very important message for our age in which many societies have legalized the destruction of unborn children. Finally, it confirmed the heroic holiness and the presence in heaven of Gianna Molla so that the Church could recognize her for the assistance that she can offer to the Church's members on earth. God, the greatest teacher, taught several lessons all at once in this marvelous event.

The Arcolino pregnancy miracle was, quite fittingly, a miracle *pregnant* with meaning. It was not divine micromanagement of the universe but a message to his human creatures of his blessing and salvation.

3. A Special and Free Divine "Intervention": God continuously acts in the world to bring about the fulfillment of his plan through the secondary causality of creatures within the normal course of nature. All pregnancies are God working through natural causes to bring new human life into the world. But a miracle is somewhat different than this normal course of divine providence. A miracle is a singular (i.e., one-time) "intervention" of God for an express purpose. In such an intervention, God is not acting in violation of nature; he is enabling natural causes to have effects that transcend their ordinary capacity. A miracle is a "violation" of nature if and only if nature is something that does not first already exist within the eternal "let there be" of God, who is nature's true and only Author and foundation. It is not that God sets aside natural causes; rather, natural causes are empowered to do what they cannot ordinarily do. The Arcolino healing did not occur through the violation of nature; the injured placenta and amniotic sac was enabled by God to do what it ordinarily does but had become incapable of doing. In the words of the International Theological Commission, in miracles "particular actions of God bring about effects that transcend the capacity of created causes acting according to their natures" in a way that is "non-disruptive."[23] In a miracle, God does not overrule a natural cause, he rather enables it to do what it cannot ordinarily do under given circumstances.

All pregnancies are God working through natural causes to bring new human life into the world. The Arcolino healing miracle showed God's love and care for all human beings, including the unborn.

The term "divine intervention" is the most common way of describing a miracle, but it only signifies what a miracle seems to be from our ordinary, limited perspective. We must treat this word with the same care that we applied to our understanding of prayer. From the perspective of God's plan of salvation, his plan to perfect the universe; it is helpful to think of miraculous signs and wonders not as "interventions" by God suspending natural causes and doing for them what they cannot do themselves, but as nature finally being able to do what God ultimately intends thanks to his special assistance.

Miracles only make sense if we place them in the context of God's plan for the universe. Thanks to God's loving providence, and not simply by its own power, the universe is journeying to a fulfillment in which physical and moral evil will be no more. If this is the case, then miracles are streams of light breaking through the ordinary, temporary, imperfect "former things" (Rev 21:4), the advent of a new set of laws for the universe through which the material universe will perfectly radiate the higher, spiritual realities of love and freedom. A miraculous physical healing points to the day when our human nature will no longer suffer from illness.

One person who saw miracles in this way was the great Catholic novelist **Flannery O'Connor** (1925-1964). In response to a friend for whom miracles were an obstacle to accepting the Christian faith because they seemed to violate natural laws, O'Connor took the reverse perspective:

> **For my part I think that when I know what the laws of the flesh and the physical really are, then I will know what God is. We know them as we see them, not as God sees them. For me it is the virgin birth, the Incarnation, the resurrection which are the true laws of the flesh and the physical. Death, decay, destruction are the suspension of these laws.... The resurrection of Christ seems [to me] the high point of the law of nature.[24]**

In a similar fashion, the Catholic convert and poet **Richard Crashaw** (1612-1649) interpreted the Miracle of Cana, where Jesus turned water into wine, precisely as the water "blushing" in the presence of its Lord and Maker![25] When the new order of things begins to break through, we discover *all* that nature can do when God is fully present to it and when it is conformed to God's will for it. God reaches "downward" to creation so that nature can reach "upward" to God.

Wedding Feast at Cana
"The water 'blushing' in the presence of its Lord and Maker!"

To understand this, **C.S. Lewis** invites us to consider novel writing as an analogy for God's creative activity with which we are already very familiar. If an author writes a story in which characters are in a completely ordinary plot, and it ends up in a tragedy or a complicated mess, then it would ruin the story to include something wondrous and strange that comes out of the blue to rescue them. That is not what one expects in a "normal" plot. But, if an author writes a novel in which the wondrous and strange is really at the heart of the plot, then it would be entirely different; the author *must* include the wondrous and strange in order to avoid ruining the story! Perhaps our problem as modern people is in thinking that there is no mystery already latent within creation itself, that it is merely "there" and devoid of God's all-embracing presence, which is in truth the Reality that makes possible all created realities.

All miracles are assisted by science; if a scientific explanation is found, then there is no need for a miraculous explanation. God has revealed to us that the universe as we know it is not completely ordinary. It is being taken over by a new kind of reality that goes beyond it and transforms it, the order of grace and salvation, a new heavens and a new earth.[26] Miracles are the plot twists of God's great book—history and the universe—which bring them closer to their magnificent and surprising conclusion. With this in mind, as Flannery O'Connor saw clearly, it becomes obvious who the central character is—the man whose very existence was a miracle, who performed countless miracles of healing and power, and whose death was followed by the greatest miracle of all, his Resurrection and Ascension into heaven. If miracles are at the heart of God's story, then Jesus of Nazareth is clearly its main protagonist, its central figure.

2. The Miracles of Jesus

THE FIRST MIRACLE in the life of Christ is the *Incarnation*, the assumption of a fully human nature, body and soul, by the divine *Logos* in order to achieve our salvation and reunion with God.[27] Unlike any other human being, Christ is "conceived by the Holy Spirit, born of the Virgin Mary," a human child without a human father. The Christian faith teaches that the Son, who from eternity is truly God, became true man in his Incarnation.[28] In the words of St. Paul, "When the time had fully come, God sent forth his Son, born of woman" (Gal 4:4). This event occurring in the *fullness of time* reveals to us that what happened in the womb of Mary is the central turning point of all of human history. **C.S. Lewis** shows us how the Incarnation gives a new dimension to the things we see all around us in the natural world:

> **In this descent [of God's Son]... everyone will recognize a familiar pattern: a thing written all over the world. It is the pattern of all vegetable life. It must belittle itself into something hard, small, and deathlike, it must fall into the ground: thence the new life re-ascends. It is the pattern of all animal generation too. There is descent from the full and perfect organisms into the spermatozoon and ovum, and in the dark womb a life at first inferior in kind to that of the species which is being produced: then the slow ascent to the perfect embryo, to the living, conscious baby, and finally to the adult.... The pattern is there in nature because it was first there in God.[29]**

The Incarnation of Jesus
The Christian faith teaches that the Son, who from eternity is truly God, became true man in his Incarnation.

The Incarnation reveals that all the "descent" around us points to the miracle in which God himself descends to us in order to re-ascend with us and as one of us for our salvation.

In his earthly life, Jesus performed many miracles. Some of these miracles had natural effects which Lewis calls *nature miracles*, such as turning water into wine. In these miracles Jesus did "small and up-close" what God does "large and everywhere." God, through the secondary causes of plant biology and organic chemistry, "changes" water into wine gradually in vineyards throughout the world. At the Wedding Feast of Cana (Jn 2:1-11), Jesus does the same in an instant.

We can say the same of Jesus' many healing miracles. Every time a person recovers from an illness, God heals him or her through the secondary causes of natural biological processes, as well as through antibiotics and other medicines. Jesus, in his miracles of healing, does quickly and flawlessly what the body does slowly and imperfectly; in him, "the power that always was behind all healings puts on a face and hands."[30] Through these and many other nature miracles, such as the calming of the storm at sea, he reveals that he is the God who created and sustains the universe, not merely a king but *the Lord*.

Other miracles performed by Jesus involved things that never happen in the normal course of nature, such as when he raised the dead; walked on water; and was transfigured before Peter, James, and John. **C.S. Lewis** calls such an act of power a *miracle of the New Creation*. Such miracles show that in the new creation, as described in Revelation 21:1-5, matter will be made obedient to spirit in a way that we cannot begin to imagine. Jesus' raising of Lazarus or of the widow's son from death prefigures the glorious and irreversible resurrection of all the dead, what is called the *resurrection of the body*.

Finally, after suffering the agony of betrayal, a physical torture, a separation from all whom he loved, a gruesome death and descent into hell, the third day after his execution found Jesus alive and among his disciples in a way that they could never have foreseen. He was clearly beyond the ordinary limits of human bodily life, not limited by space and time any longer. But he was still himself and fully human; he could still eat food, touch, and be touched. Therefore, the *Catechism of the Catholic Church* declares:

> **Christ's humanity can no longer be confined to earth and belongs henceforth only to the Father's divine realm. . . . In his risen body he passes from the state of death to another life beyond time and space. At Jesus' Resurrection his body is filled with the power of the Holy Spirit: he shares the divine life in his glorious state, so that St. Paul can say that Christ is "the man of heaven."**[31]

Jesus Walks on Water
C.S. Lewis calls these acts of power *miracles of the New Creation.*

In summary, we see that all the miracles of Jesus have a message to share with us. They are not merely for show. They are not there to violate nature or to cancel it out but to signal its transformation in a new and glorious reality that God has prepared for those who love him. They are clues to the meaning of the universe.

The Raising of Lazarus
Jesus' raising of Lazarus or of the widow's son from death prefigures the glorious and irreversible resurrection of all the dead, what is called the *resurrection of the body.*

3. The Integrity of Nature Revisited

WE CAN NOW FACE OUR CRITICAL QUESTION DIRECTLY: If miracles are real, then what about the integrity of nature? A proper theological account of miracles shows the difference between the veneration of the miracles of Christ and the saints, on the one hand, and an utter disrespect for nature and natural causes on the other, which would lead one to be wholly disinterested in the regularity of natural causes and the inherent order that the sciences investigate.

First, a miracle only makes sense in the context of faith, and faith is the domain of human persons. To posit miracles at the beginning of the universe or at the origins of life (as creationists do) makes no sense, for there were no human beings to receive the divine sign, the religious wonder, of a miracle at that time. Also, miracles do not replace the natural processes and patterns in nature by inserting God's direct action as an explanation for the ways things normally occur.

As moments of salvation and divine signs that teach, miracles are singular events by definition; when they occur, they cause astonishment precisely because they are not the way things usually happen.

Finally, to acknowledge the reality of miracles is not to picture God as "tuning up" or nudging the universe to do what he failed to make it capable of doing in his creative act. In a miracle, God does not violate nature; he ennobles it, showing its greatest possibilities when it is fully united to him. Water "blushes," the seas and storms obey, dead bodies are filled with life, and a new indestructible kind of life is revealed in the age to come. In miracles, God is eternally responsive to the cry of his people in ways they could never anticipate, and they usher in a new reality that awaits them and the whole universe.

D. Looking Forward

The Ascension
In a miracle, God does not violate nature; he ennobles it, showing its greatest possibilities when it is fully united to him.

SO FAR, AND ESPECIALLY IN THIS CHAPTER and the previous four, we have approached the relationship between science and faith from one side, the side of faith as embodied in theology. Starting with important historical and philosophical foundations, we have considered the Christian doctrine of creation, Scripture, Sacred Tradition, and our critical questions largely from the perspective of faith. Our consideration of science has been mostly in response to theological issues, and we have only pursued scientific matters as far as necessary to clarify the harmony science has with the Christian faith.

But this is only half of the task that the Church sets before the faithful in regard to science. In the words of **St. John Paul II**:

> **Only a dynamic relationship between theology and science can reveal those limits which support the integrity of either discipline, so that theology does not profess a pseudo-science and science does not become an unconscious theology. Our knowledge of each other can lead us to be more authentically ourselves....We [scientists and theologians] need each other to be what we must be, what we are called to be.**

A "dynamic relationship" between science and theology, which he also calls a "relational unity,"[32] requires that we let the sciences "speak freely" by exploring scientific findings more thoroughly than we have done so far in order to see how they can stimulate a deeper understanding of faith. It means to go as far as possible to the frontiers of modern science so as to reflect more deeply, to do "theology on the cutting edge" of science.

Therefore, in Part II we will turn first to science and only then to theological matters, approaching discoveries in physics, evolutionary biology, and the sciences of human origins to better understand the picture of the universe and of life that they reveal, reflecting theologically on what we find and how it helps us understand God as the Creator.

VOCABULARY

Define the following terms (or identify the person's significance):

1. William Thomson (Lord Kelvin)
2. Privation
3. Privation Theory of Evil
4. Council of Florence (Evil)
5. Physical Evil
6. Corruption
7. Virus
8. Moral Evil
9. David Hume
10. Petitionary Prayer
11. Divine Providence
12. St. Gianna Beretta Molla
13. Miracle (Rene Latourelle)
14. Incarnation
15. Fullness of Time
16. Nature Miracle (Jesus)
17. Miracle of the New Creation (Jesus)
18. Resurrection (Jesus)
19. Resurrection of the Body

C.S. Lewis (1898-1963)
"I believe in Christianity as I believe that the sun has risen.
Not only because I see it, but because by it I see everything else."
(*Is Theology Poetry?* 1945)

STUDY QUESTIONS

1. What do the examples of Lord Kelvin and St. Thomas Aquinas teach us about a proper approach to reality?

2. What is the difference between mystery and contradiction?

Section A

3. Briefly explain the critical question that the problem of evil poses for faith in the light of science.

4. What is physical evil, and how can it be said that any such evil is not a thing but a privation?

5. What is moral evil, and how can it be said that any such evil is not a thing but a privation?

6. Rephrase the argument of Hume against the existence of God based on the reality of evil. What alternative does he exclude?

7. If God eliminated all physical evil, what kind of universe would result? What about moral evil?

8. How does Jesus Christ overcome all moral evil and all physical evil?

Section B

9. Briefly explain the critical question that the necessity of prayer poses for faith in the light of science.

10. How do most believers think about prayer, and why is it deficient?

11. How does the principle of double agency help us understand the necessity of prayer more adequately?

12. What is the most important reason that God commands us to pray?

13. Does God work through prayers to bring about his will? Explain with reference to the intercession of holy men and women.

Section C

14. Briefly explain the critical question that the reality of miracles poses for faith in the light of science.

15. Explain Latourelle's identification of every miracle as a religious wonder, using the Arcolino pregnancy miracle as an example.

16. What are the implications of the fact that a miracle is always a special and free intervention of God?

17. Explain Latourelle's identification of every miracle as a sign of God's message of salvation, using the Arcolino pregnancy miracle as an example.

18. Why is divine intervention an insufficient term for describing a miracle?

19. What does the presence of miracles in human history reveal about God and his plan? Use the example of the writing of a novel to explain.

20. What is the significance of the Incarnation in light of how it reveals the deepest meaning of the natural process of the generation of living things?

21. What is the meaning of the nature miracles of Jesus? What do they reveal?

22. What is the meaning of the new creation miracles of Jesus? What do they reveal?

23. What will the general resurrection, as revealed in Jesus' Resurrection, involve for the natural world?

PRACTICAL EXERCISES

1. Watch the video "Why is There Disorder in the Universe?" (5 minutes, 13 seconds, *mtfresources.org/videos*) by Bishop Robert Barron on the problem of evil. How does the story of Job help us see the mystery involved in this problem?

2. Watch the video "Bishop Barron on Hell" (7 minutes, 2 seconds, *mtfresources.org/videos*). How does his explanation of hell stem from the Christian understanding of evil as a privation?

3. Research the miracles that have occurred at Lourdes and have been approved by the Church. Apply Latourelle's definition of a miracle to these events. How does it measure up to the standard set by Latourelle?

4. Have you or anyone you know ever experienced an event that seemed miraculous? Apply Latourelle's definition of a miracle to the event. How does it measure up to the standard set by Latourelle? If it does not, why should God still be given thanks for it regardless?

Flannery O'Connor (1925-1964)
"You will have found Christ when you are concerned with other people's sufferings and not your own."

"The resurrection of Christ seems [to me] the high point of the law of nature." —Flannery O'Connor

Endnotes – Chapter Six

1. Peter Hodgson, *Science and Belief in the Nuclear Age* (Naples, FL: Sapientia Press, 2005), 115.
2. Ibid., 115.
3. Charles Journet, *The Meaning of Evil*, trans. by Michael Barry (New York: P.J. Kenedy & Sons, 1963), 25-26.
4. St. Augustine, *Confessions*, Book VII, ch. 3.5; ch. 5.7.
5. St. Augustine, *City of God*, Book XI, ch. 22.
6. Nicanor Austriaco, "Three Critical Questions for Science and Religion" (Lecture, Science and Religion Seminar, Institute for Church Life, University of Notre Dame, South Bend, IN, June 18, 2014).
7. W. Norris Clarke, *The One and the Many*, 278-279.
8. Ibid., 280.
9. Ibid., 280.
10. Adapted from Ibid., 283.
11. Ibid., 285-286.
12. Benedict XVI, Inaugural Homily, April 24, 2005, *w2.vatican.va/content/benedict-xvi/en/homilies/2005/documents/hf_ben-xvi_hom_20050424_inizio-pontificato.html*.
13. *Roman Missal*, Third Edition. The Order of Mass: The Eucharistic Prayer, Eucharistic Prayer I, no. 91.
14. Joseph Ratzinger, *Dogma and Preaching: Applying Christian Doctrine to Daily Life*, Michael Miller and Michael J. O'Connor, trans., First unabridged edition (San Francisco: Ignatius Press, 2011), 109.
15. Michael J. Dodds, *Unlocking Divine Action: Contemporary Science and Thomas Aquinas* (Washington, D.C.: The Catholic University of America Press, 2002), 244.
16. *Roman Missal*, Third Edition. The Order of Mass: The Eucharistic Prayer, Common Preface IV, no. 75.
17. C.S. Lewis, *Letters to Malcolm Chiefly on Prayer*, as quoted in Dodds, 245.
18. St. Thomas Aquinas, *In de div. nom.* III, l. un., 239, 243-244, as quoted in Dodds, 246-247.
19. St. Thomas Aquinas, *ScG* III.96.8.
20. "A Pro-Life Icon to be Canonized: Gianna Molla Gave Her Life for Her Unborn Daughter," *Zenit: The World seen from Rome* (*www.zenit.org/english/visualizza.phtml?sid=53575*).
21. Ibid.
22. Rene Latourelle and Rino Fisichella, eds., *Dictionary of Fundamental Theology* (New York: Crossroad, 1994), 702.
23. ITC, *Communion and Stewardship*, no. 70.
24. Flannery O'Connor, *The Habit of Being: Letters of Flannery O'Connor*, selected and edited by Sally Fitzgerald (New York: Farrar, Straus & Giroux, 1979), 100.
25. Paul Haffner, *Mystery of Creation*, 104.
26. Ibid., 98-99.
27. CCC 461.
28. CCC 461.
29. C.S. Lewis, *Miracles: How God Intervenes in Nature and Human Affairs* (New York: Macmillan, 1960), 112.
30. Ibid., 140.
31. CCC 645-646; cf. 1 Cor 15:35-50.
32. St. John Paul II, Message to the Reverend George V. Coyne, S.J., Director of the Vatican Observatory, June 1, 1988.

Part II

The Mind of the Maker: Physics, Biology, and Creation

Chapter Seven
The Twist in the Tale: Modern Science *Versus* Scientific Atheism

How can the discoveries of modern physics relate to Christian doctrine?

What is the Big Bang Theory, and does it prove the existence of God?

How can the discoveries of modern physics help us to better appreciate the truth about God the Creator?

What is beauty, and how is beauty involved in our scientific understanding of the universe? Does the beauty of the universe tell us anything about the Creator?

"What is God? The mind and reason of the universe. What is God? Everything that we see, because in all things we see his wisdom and assistance, and so we confess his greatness, which is so great that we cannot think of anything greater."

—Venerable Louis of Granada, 1584

A. Marvels Beyond All Expectations

Einstein's official portrait after receiving the 1921 Nobel Prize in Physics.

In the Spring and Summer of 1919 the eyes of the world were focused on France. The battles of World War I that had killed 13.5 million people were over, and representatives of the great powers had converged upon the palace of Versailles, once the home of the French monarchy, to negotiate terms of peace. It was a moment of incalculable importance for humanity. But another momentous event was also taking place—expeditions of astronomers and physicists were making their way to Sobral, Brazil, and to the West African island of Principe in order to view a total solar eclipse that was to occur on May 29. Just as the Treaty of Versailles would forever affect the future of international relations, the findings of these astronomers would forever affect our understanding of the universe.

What the astronomers wanted to observe was not the eclipse but a cluster of stars positioned very near the sun; only during an eclipse, when the sun's intense radiance is blocked out by the moon, would these stars "come out" and be observable. Nor were they primarily interested in the stars themselves, which form a cluster called the Hyades. They were testing a new theory that predicted that gravity attracts light as well as ordinary matter. Their goal was to see if the light from these stars would be deflected slightly as it passed close by the sun on its way to the earth. They would be able to detect this deflection by observing if the positions of these stars appeared to be slightly shifted from their actual position in the sky. If they appeared out of place, this would confirm the bold new gravitational theory, a possibility so revolutionary that it would be well worth their efforts and travel.

Any new theory of gravity was bold, since the old one—proposed by none other than **Sir Isaac Newton**, the greatest physicist the world had yet known—had passed every experimental test for 232 years. The scientists set up their observation sites, gathered their data, and returned to Europe. On November 6, at a special meeting in London of the Royal Society, one of the oldest and most prestigious scientific organizations in the world, they stunned their audience with their report. The next day, the *Times of London* ran the following headline:

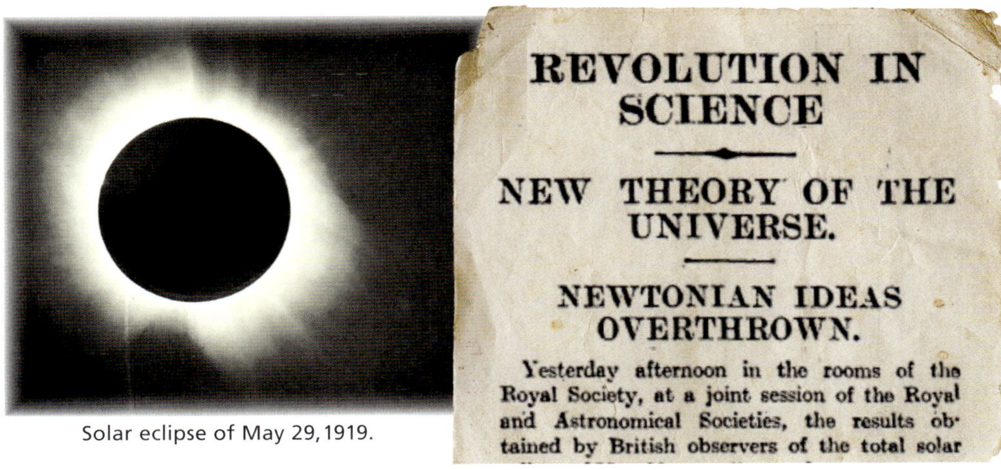

REVOLUTION IN SCIENCE

NEW THEORY OF THE UNIVERSE.

NEWTONIAN IDEAS OVERTHROWN.

Yesterday afternoon in the rooms of the Royal Society, at a joint session of the Royal and Astronomical Societies, the results obtained by British observers of the total solar

Solar eclipse of May 29, 1919.

Within hours, the news raced around the world. The scientist who had proposed the new theory—the *General Theory of Relativity*—became a household name. Indeed, his name, **Albert Einstein**, is probably better known than that of any other scientist who has ever lived either before or after his rise to prominence. And rightly so, for his theoretical breakthroughs opened a whole new era in the physical sciences and would allow other scientists to illuminate some of the greatest secrets of the universe, including many of the mysteries of the universe's origin.

This new scientific era, now a century old, would be full of surprises. From the time of **Nicolaus Copernicus** up until the end of the nineteenth century, the trend of scientific discoveries had seemed to some people to be leading away from the traditional Jewish and Christian conception of the universe. Indeed, as we saw in Chapter Three, throughout the nineteenth century atheism became more common among scientists and intellectuals generally, partly because of what they thought science was saying (and partly for other reasons). But, in the twentieth century, scientists would make discoveries that were totally unanticipated; there was one "twist in the plot" after another. Many people came to see that the old "scientific atheism" was based on outdated scientific ideas. In this chapter, we will look at three "twists in the tale" of the physical sciences that have occurred since Einstein's great breakthroughs. In each case, we will see that they have helped to deepen our understanding of God's creation and what he has revealed through Sacred Scripture and Sacred Tradition. In order to really appreciate the first of the three plot twists, we have to take a philosophical pause and ask two "big questions" about God and the universe.

In physics there are four fundamental interactions (or forces) known to exist: electromagnetic, gravitational, weak interactions, and strong interactions. Fundamental interactions are the interactions that do not appear to be reducible to more basic interactions.

B. A Perpetual Universe?

WHAT IF THE UNIVERSE JUST STRETCHED BACK INFINITELY, such that there was neither a starting point to it nor a first moment? Would the universe be uncaused, or would it still need a Creator?

These are incredible questions; they are so big that most usually never even attempt to ponder them. But, the question of "beginning, or no beginning" has been asked about the universe many times throughout the history of Western civilization. Most ancient philosophers, such as the Greek philosopher **Aristotle** (384-322 BC), held that the universe has always existed in some form or another, that its history and time itself are infinite. In the nineteenth century this ancient idea made a comeback. As scientists delved deeper and deeper into the secrets of the physical universe, it seemed to many that the universe was a perfectly interlocking system, a machine that had operated endlessly, without a first moment. Twin theories—*the law of the conservation of mass* and *the law of the conservation of energy*—seemed to support this view. The law of the conservation of mass states that when matter undergoes changes (for example, in chemical reactions) the total amount of mass in the universe does not change. The law of the conservation of energy states that energy can neither be created nor destroyed but only converted from one form to another. These principles seemed to imply that matter and energy must have always existed which, if true, would imply that the universe itself had always existed.[1]

1. God and the Limits of a Perpetual Universe

THE ISSUE OF WHETHER THE UNIVERSE did in fact have a beginning is the first plot twist we will consider. For now, let us suppose, for the sake of argument, that it did not and see where that leaves us. Many people think that the statement "the universe never had a beginning" is an atheistic one. To say that something is without a beginning seems to necessarily imply that it is uncaused; and if the universe is uncaused, then it has no Creator. But if it were true that the universe had no first moment, would that really mean that it is uncaused? The answer is "no"—at least according to **St. Thomas Aquinas**.

St. Thomas's approach to this difficult question shows how our faith never stops us from thinking critically about all of the possibilities, even ones that contradict our faith. For even though he believed, as a matter of faith, that the universe did have a beginning, he was willing to consider the idea of a perpetual universe from a purely philosophical point of view. His conclusion was that reason by itself could not settle the question of whether the universe (or to use his term, the "*mundi*" or "the world") had a beginning or not. We only know that the universe had a beginning, he reasoned, because God has revealed that it does. In his words, "By faith alone do we hold, and by no demonstration can it be proved, that the world did not always exist.... The reason of this is that the newness of the world (*novitas mundi*) *cannot* be demonstrated on the part of the world itself."[2]

Even though St. Thomas Aquinas believed, as a matter of faith, that the universe did have a beginning, he also realized that "having a beginning" and "being created" are not the same thing.

On the other hand, St. Thomas believed that human reason by itself, i.e., without the aid of Divine Revelation, *must* arrive at the conclusion that the universe has a Creator. Obviously, then, for him the universe must have a Creator *whether or not it had a beginning*. In other words, "having a beginning" and "being created" are not necessarily the same thing.

How did Aquinas arrive at the conclusion that a perpetually existing universe would still need a Creator? He did so by observing that the universe could have been caused to perpetually exist by God, that is, it could have always been because God caused it to always be. Even so, it would still need God to explain its existence. As an analogy, let us return to our image of the universe as a play. A play has a beginning and an end. But, the reason we say a play has an *author* has to do with the fact that *it exists at all*. Even if a play had a beginning and no end, or an end and no beginning, it would need an author, since the fact of the play cannot explain the reason for its existence. As we noted in Chapter Three, the opening lines of Shakespeare's *Romeo and Juliet* are: "Two households, both alike in dignity, In fair Verona, where we lay our scene..." That is the *beginning* of *Romeo and Juliet*; it references a point in time when the play begins in Shakespeare's fictional Verona. But, Shakespeare is the *origin* of those lines and everything else in *Romeo and Juliet*, and so it is with God the Creator and the universe. Anything that exists, but might not have existed, has to have its existence explained. There must be a cause or explanation of its existence, regardless of whether it has a beginning or not.

In the same way, we might reasonably entertain the possibility that the universe may or may not have had a beginning, just as we might entertain the possibility that it may or may not have an end. But, the reason we say that God creates it has to do with the fact that it exists at all. Even if the universe had no beginning and no end, or an end and no beginning, it still requires a Creator. We have already considered the idea that the universe's sheer existence requires a Creator in general in Chapter Three, but let us delve more deeply.

2. A Metaphysical Moment

LET US START WITH A BASIC OBSERVATION: None of the beings in our experience (e.g., ourselves, plants, planets, atoms, molecules, animals, etc.) are self-sufficient. All of them need certain conditions to be in place in order for them to exist at any given moment.[3] As we look around us, we see that beings depend upon other beings outside of themselves in order to exist. For example, beings depend upon other beings that came before them in order to come into existence. This is especially obvious in the case of animals, which have parents who generated them. The parents are causes of their offspring's existence. Such causes, which produce effects in such a way that those effects can continue to exist even after the causes themselves have ceased to exist, can be called "*nonsimultaneously acting causes*." But, this kind of causality is *not* what St. Thomas was focusing on when he constructed his argument for a Creator.

The existence of the earth is a *present condition* for the existence of its gravitational field—the earth is the *simultaneous cause* of its gravity.

There is a second kind of dependency in which a cause *keeps* a thing existing in the present moment. You needed to have parents to come into existence, but you do not need them to exist right at this moment—your parents are not holding you in existence at this moment (except financially, perhaps!). But there is another kind of causality, in which the effect would cease to exist should the cause cease to exist or stop its causal activity. Let us call these "*simultaneous causes*" or "*simultaneously acting causes*." For example, the earth is causing its "gravitational field" to exist *right now*. The existence of the earth is a *present condition* for the existence of its gravitational field—the earth is the *simultaneous cause* of its gravity. A gravitational field is an example of something that depends on another thing, distinct from itself, in order to exist, in such a way that this dependence is simultaneous with the ongoing existence of that distinct thing.[4]

Apply the same idea to yourself—you are a being that relies on other beings as conditions for your existence. Air, temperature within a certain range, the existence of the water molecule—without any one of these, you would not exist. They exist, therefore you can exist—they are simultaneously acting causes of your existence. They each have simultaneously acting causes that make it possible for them to exist—for instance, the existence of the water molecule relies on the stability of the proton, which makes the atomic elements (such as hydrogen and oxygen) capable of existing.

Now let us apply this analysis to all of reality: can all beings be conditioned, dependent on the ongoing existence of others for their existence? The answer is "no." Think about it—for A to exist, B must exist, for B to exist, C must exist, and so on. But, this chain of simultaneously acting causes cannot be an unending one, because then the whole chain would never get to a being which makes A (or B, or C, etc.) actually exist. Nor can the chain of simultaneously

God is the origin of the chain of being—all things ultimately depend on his necessary existence for their own existence at every moment, no matter how many moments there have been or will be.

acting causes go around in a circle—A depending on B, B on C, and C on A—because A cannot be making other things exist while also depending on those very things for its own existence. In either scenario, there would be no ultimate reason for the existence of the whole chain of causes, and, if this were the case, there would be no reason, no intelligibility, in any part of the chain. If there is no uncaused Cause, then no things in the chain could actually exist. There has to be at least one "thing" that currently exists which does not depend on another thing for its existence, a being that is totally *unconditioned* in its existence. This being has to be the ongoing reason for the existence of the whole chain, the thing that all other things depend on for their existences, the condition for all other beings. It has to be self-sufficient, self-explanatory, and uncaused, or else it, too, is conditioned and dependent.[5] In short, for any conditioned thing to exist *right now*, there has to be a God, who is "to all things the cause of being *right now*."[6] God, as the uncaused Cause, always remains wholly transcendent and wills creation into existence as its divine simultaneous cause in the here and now in a way that is different than that of created simultaneous causes. It is precisely because God transcends the universe and is not part of it that makes the existence of a fundamentally conditioned universe possible.

In summary, the preserving power which holds all things in being, right here and right now, "can ultimately only be something that is not in turn held in being by something else."[7] Our investigation of what we can observe through our common human experience leads us to God, if we patiently and intelligently consider the way the cosmos works.

To return to our big question, we would be led right to God even if the universe was ever-existing. Even if the great chain of *nonsimultaneously* acting causes stretched back infinitely, "a father being a cause of a son and another person the cause of that father, so on, endlessly,"[8] there must be a beginning to the chain of *simultaneously* acting causes which make anything exist in the present moment. God is the origin of that chain—all things ultimately depend on his necessary existence for their own existence at every moment, no matter how many moments there have been or will be.

Our consideration of a perpetually existing universe still leaves the questions: "Did the universe have a first moment? Is its history infinite or finite?" These questions lead us to one of the greatest stories of modern physics, the discovery of the Big Bang, the first "twist in the tale" of twentieth-century physical science. It has to do with one of the implications of Einstein's theory of gravity that he himself found hard to accept and indeed resisted for years. This implication would hit the scientific community like an explosion—literally.

C. Starting Things Off with a Bang

ABOVE WE OBSERVED THAT MANY PEOPLE equate a perpetual universe with atheism—if the universe has no beginning, they assume that it is also uncaused. As we learned from St. Thomas Aquinas, this jump is philosophically unjustified. Even a perpetual universe would be "contingent" and therefore need an ultimate cause. But the Christian faith tells us more than this. It says not only that the universe has a Creator but that it had an actual beginning in time, an actual first moment at which it appeared out of nothing, thanks to God's will and power. The Book of Genesis begins with the words, "In the beginning..." as does the Gospel of St. John in its own retelling of the creation account. So, at the beginning of the twentieth century, it seemed to some that if the scientific evidence that pointed to the universe's perpetual existence had not disproved God's existence, at the very least it had weakened the authority of the Bible and called into question the teachings of the Catholic Church.

Among those who believed in a perpetually existing universe was the great **Albert Einstein**. Though by his own account, he was "religious" in some sense, and often spoke of God, his conception of God and God's relation to the world made it hard for Einstein to accept the idea of a first moment, a temporal beginning to the universe. The great irony is that it was his own General Theory of Relativity that played a key role in bringing back the idea of a beginning.

To understand why, we must look more closely at the theory that made him famous and the equations he used to demonstrate it.

1. Einstein's Equations

IN EINSTEIN'S THEORY OF GRAVITY, things attract each other by warping the space (actually the space *and time*) near them. The way matter warps space and time is described by a set of equations, now called "Einstein's Equations." These remain among the fundamental equations of theoretical physics in our own day.

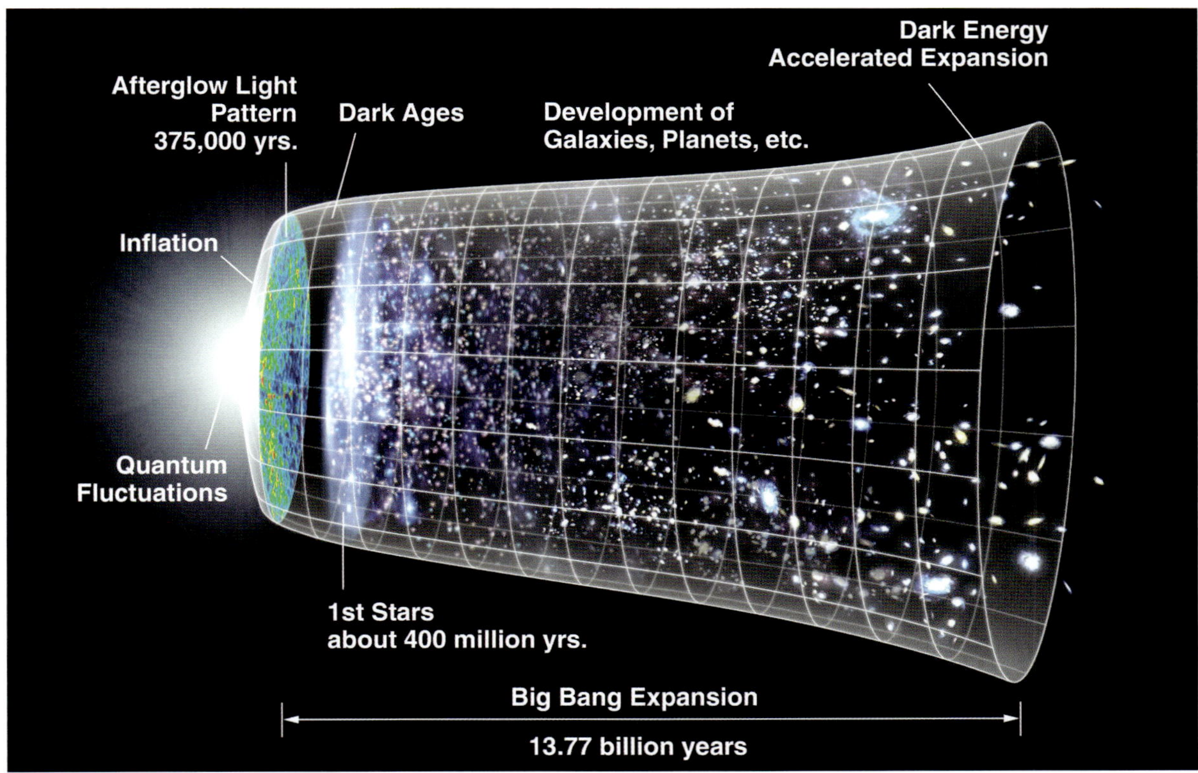

A representation of the expansion of the universe over 13.77 billion years.

The logic that led Einstein to these equations back in 1916 left a certain ambiguity. There was a "term" that could be included in the equations or left out; it did not seem to make much difference either way. Today this term is called the "cosmological constant." Einstein thought the theory would be simpler and more elegant without this term, so he originally decided to leave it out. However, Einstein noticed something that disturbed him. His equations could only describe a universe that was expanding or contracting, not a stable universe that could exist for infinite time into the past and future. He therefore put the cosmological constant back into the equations, thinking that it would allow the theory to describe a stable, eternal universe. Later, the physicist **Arthur Eddington** (1882-1944) showed that, even with the cosmological constant, the expansion or contraction of the universe was an unavoidable implication of Einstein's equations.

Had Einstein believed what his theory was telling him, instead of running away from it, he could have *predicted* the discovery of both the expansion of the universe and "the Big Bang," which was discovered by astronomers years later. His philosophical belief in an eternal universe made him miss the most important implication of his own theory. He later reproached himself severely for this blindness, as he saw it, and called it the biggest blunder of his life.[9]

2. Fr. Lemaître and the "Primeval Atom"

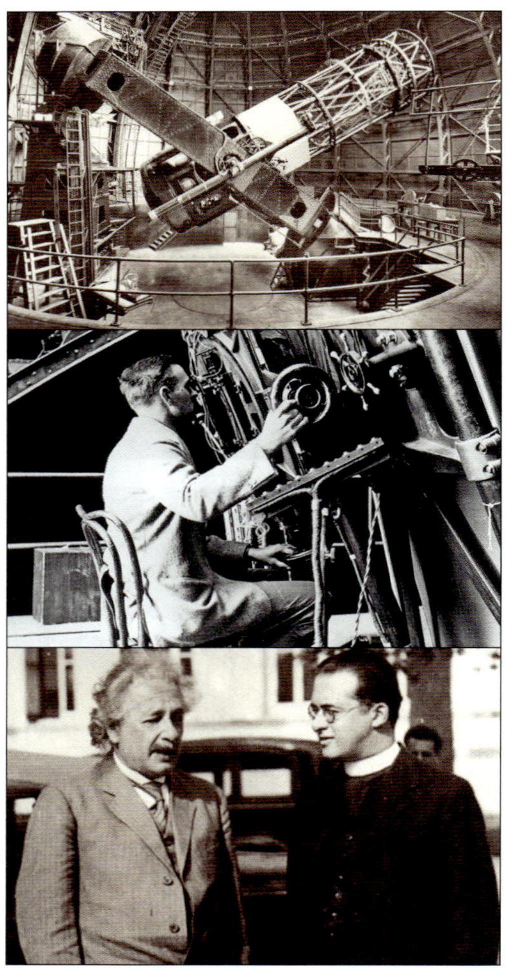

(top) The 100 inch Hooker telescope used by Edwin Hubble. In the 1920s it was the largest telescope in the world.
(middle) Edwin Hubble ca. 1922 studying the stars through the Hooker telescope.
(bottom) Albert Einstein and Fr. Lemaître.

THE SCENE NOW SWITCHES FROM EUROPE TO AMERICA. The last name of **Edwin Powell Hubble** (1889-1953) is known to many Americans from the famous Hubble Space Telescope. But he did not invent this telescope; it was named in his honor because of a great discovery he made in the 1920's using another telescope, one located at the Mt. Wilson Observatory in California. Hubble peered into space and discovered that other galaxies were moving away from our own. His observations showed that this expansion really was occurring and at incredibly high speeds. The expansion was so massive and so fast that some other galaxies were actually millions of light-years away.[10]

At the same time mathematicians and physicists were taking Einstein's insights in the very direction that he himself dismissed—toward a universe that is expanding from a "beginning"—two thinkers independently discovered that Einstein's Equations can describe such a universe: One was a Russian mathematician named **Alexander Friedmann** (1859-1925), the other was a Belgian physicist and Catholic priest named **Georges Lemaître**. As we saw in Chapter Five, it was Lemaître who saw the significance of Hubble's discovery and related it to his own theoretical work with Einstein's equations. In 1927, Lemaître proposed that the universe had started out very small and has been expanding for billions of years. If that were so, then all of the matter in the universe must originally have been concentrated in a super-dense mass, which Lemaître called the "primeval atom." It was the explosion of this "atom," said Lemaître, which had led to the expansion of the universe that Hubble would observe in 1929. In his words, "At the origin, all of the mass of the universe would exist in the form of a unique atom; the radius of the universe, though not strictly zero, being relatively small. The whole universe would be produced by the disintegration of this primeval atom."[11] Thus was the "*Big Bang Theory*" born.[12]

While he originally told Fr. Lemaître that although his math was "correct" and his grasp of physics was "abominable," Einstein eventually accepted that we live in a dynamically expanding universe; however, it is not clear if he ever accepted the idea of a first moment, a beginning. He revealed his change of mind in 1933 in a way that displayed his great humility and character: After listening to a lecture in which Fr. Lemaître explained his ideas on the beginnings of the universe, Einstein stood up and applauded enthusiastically.

The Big Bang Theory in its standard form says something much more profound and strange than that stars and galaxies and matter had a beginning. It says that *space and time themselves* had a beginning. What Hubble saw was that the distance between galaxies was increasing. The obvious interpretation of this is that galaxies are moving *through space* away from each other. But what is actually going on, as Fr. Lemaître understood, is that the space between the galaxies is *stretching*. Space itself is like a stretchable fabric, and, so, the amount of space is actually growing. If you followed this stretching process backwards in time, one would find that space itself was smaller in the past. And if you followed it far enough back you would find that the amount of space would go to *zero* at the very moment of the Big Bang. Space would shrink to a zero-state. If you could run the film of the universe's history backwards, the entire universe—the matter *and the space*—would seem to "wink out" altogether at the Big Bang.

It gets even stranger: Since Einstein's theory says that space and time are part of one fabric called "spacetime," accordingly, *there was no time either* before the Big Bang. In fact, it is meaningless (in the standard Big Bang Theory) even to say "before the Big Bang." There is no such thing as "before the Big Bang" since "before" implies a time previous to the Big Bang, and there was no time previous to the Big Bang. Strange as it may seem, the Big Bang was "a day without a yesterday," as Fr. Lemaître referred to it.

The Triumph of St. Augustine

This is a mind-boggling idea, but one person understood it very well 1600 years ago—**St. Augustine**. St. Augustine's autobiography, *The Confessions*, contains a very famous discussion of the nature of time. It is so profound that physicists who work in the field called "quantum cosmology" frequently quote from it.[13] Even the eminent twentieth-century philosopher and mathematician **Bertrand Russell** (1872-1970), an atheist and no friend of religion, praised St. Augustine for his "admirable relativistic theory of time."[14]

St. Augustine was answering the taunts of pagans who believed that the universe was perpetual. The pagans mocked the Christian belief that the universe had a first moment by asking, "What was God doing for all that time before he created the world? Why did he wait for an infinite time doing nothing before he got around to creating the world?" St. Augustine gave his answer in the form of a long prayer: "You [O Lord] created . . . time, and no time could pass by before you created it. But if there was no time 'before' you created heaven and earth, why do they ask what you did 'then'? There was no 'then,' where there was no time."[15] This is very similar to the answer that a modern physicist would give: There was no "then" before the Big Bang as it is understood in Einstein's Theory of General Relativity. The nineteenth-century idea of time in physics was the same as the ancient pagans' idea of time. The idea of time in the standard Big Bang Theory is St. Augustine's idea of time, the Christian idea of time.

To sum up: When we talk about "the beginning," we really mean not just the beginning of the universe but the beginning of time. As taught by the **Fourth Lateran Council** in 1215 and the **First Vatican Council** in 1870, God created the universe "from the beginning of time" ("*ab initio temporis*").

3. The End of the Debate

EINSTEIN WAS VERY UNCOMFORTABLE WITH THE IDEA of a beginning precisely because it sounded too biblical; as he told Fr. Lemaître, "it suggests too much the (theological) idea of creation."[16] He was not alone. **Arthur Eddington**, who had been on one of the 1919 expeditions that proved Einstein's theory, responded to Lemaître's theory by declaring, "The notion of a beginning is repugnant to me.... I simply do not believe that the present order of things started off with a bang." An eminent scientist named **Walther Nernst** (1864-1941) even wrote that the foundations of science would be undermined by denying that the universe and time had always existed. In fact, the idea of an ever-existing universe persisted for many years after Hubble's discovery that the universe is expanding. In 1959, two-thirds of American astronomers and physicists still believed that the universe had no beginning. It is generally admitted that the scientific community was slow in accepting the Big Bang Theory in part because of a widespread prejudice in favor of a perpetual universe. This prejudice was one reason (although not the only one) that a new hypothesis emerged that explained the expansion of the universe without a beginning. This so-called "Steady State Theory" eventually fell by the wayside as the evidence against it and in favor of the Big Bang Theory accumulated.[17]

Robert Wilson and Arno Penzias in 1978 in front of the Holmdel Horn Antenna, which detected a "whisper" from the Big Bang.

It is a strange story how the Big Bang Theory ended up being confirmed. In 1948, two students realized that the Big Bang, if it had occurred, must have been unimaginably hot due to the enormous squeezing of the matter—one second after the Big Bang the temperature of the universe would have been ten *billion* degrees centigrade! This had an interesting consequence: the universe just after the Big Bang would have been filled with intense radiation, much of it in the form of light, and a residue of that radiation would remain even now in the form of microwaves, filling the universe with a faint "afterglow" of the Big Bang.

Curiously, this idea was ignored. Almost two decades would pass before anyone would follow it up. When finally someone made the decision to look for this radiation, they were too late—it had already been discovered accidentally. The two scientists who found it, **Arno Penzias** and **Robert Wilson**, did not use a telescope but a radio detector. **Stephen Barr** described their process of discovery in the following way:

> **They found a noise, or static, that seemed to come equally from all directions in the sky. At first they thought that it was a problem with the device itself, or some local interference—they even considered the possibility that heat given off by bird droppings inside the antenna was responsible. Eventually, however... the true significance of what they were seeing was realized. They were hearing a whisper from the Big Bang.[18]**

Penzias and Wilson were awarded the Nobel Prize in Physics in 1978 for this discovery. Since then, several other pieces of evidence have confirmed their discovery, and very few now dispute the Big Bang Theory. Calculations made by scientists suggest that this event, apparently the first moment of our universe, happened almost 14 billion years ago. Physicists agree that all of the stars and galaxies that we observe were once packed into an almost "infinitely dense... point of pure energy."[19]

4. Going Out with a Bang: Modern Science *Versus* Materialism

THE DISCOVERY OF THE BIG BANG WAS A REVOLUTION in science. However, the revolution involved a battle not simply over science but over the materialistic assumptions of many in the scientific community. The significance of the Big Bang has been compellingly described by the astrophysicist **Robert Jastrow**: "For the [modern materialist] scientist . . . the story ends like a bad dream. He has scaled the mountains of ignorance; he is about to conquer the highest peak; as he pulls himself over the final rock, he is greeted by a band of theologians who have been sitting there for centuries."[20]

Jastrow's point is that the Big Bang was more than just a glimpse into the first moments of the universe. It also represented a major crack in the materialist, reductionist worldview of scientific atheism because it suggests that the physical universe does not contain its own explanation entirely within itself. The materialist ideology reduces the explanation of things to merely giving an account of how they arose from whatever existed beforehand. They explain what happens today by what happened yesterday. But, what if there were a "day with no yesterday," as the Big Bang Theory suggests? The Big Bang forces upon us deeper questions about the mystery of the universe, questions such as why the universe exists at all, and why it is the way it is.[21]

5. Theology on the Cutting Edge: The Big Bang and Faith

ELSEWHERE IN HIS BOOK, Robert Jastrow makes another provocative declaration: "Now we see how the astronomical evidence leads to a biblical view of the origin of the world. The details differ, but the essential elements in the astronomical and biblical accounts are the same; the chain of events leading to man commenced suddenly and sharply at a definite moment in time, in a flash of light and energy."[22]

Is Jastrow correct? Should the Big Bang be understood, as it is by some, as proving the existence of God and the divinely inspired truth of the Bible? The answer is "no." **St. John Paul II** once cautioned that we should not be too hasty in our use of the Big Bang Theory in this way.[23] In 1985, he said that "to desire a scientific proof of God would be equivalent to lowering God to the level of the beings of our world, and we would therefore be mistaken methodologically in regard to what God is. Science must recognize its limits and its inability to reach the existence of God: it can neither affirm nor deny his existence."[24] We cannot find a proof of God's existence through scientific discovery. Science studies the material world, and God is not part of the material world. That doesn't mean that believing scientists cannot affirm God's existence, but when they do so they do so through either faith or arguments from philosophy, not through any scientific method.

Fr. Lemaître himself was extremely concerned about the danger of believers drawing hasty theological conclusions from his theory; he knew that it was subject to further revision.[25] In fact, today theoretical physicists explore other scenarios besides the standard Big Bang Theory. In the words of particle physicist **Stephen Barr**:

> **That the Big Bang theory is correct, however, does not necessarily settle the question of whether the universe had a beginning. There remains the possibility that the explosion that occurred 14 billion years ago was only the beginning of a certain part of the universe or a certain phase in its history, rather than the beginning of the universe as a whole. In fact, over the years many scenarios and theories [in which the Big Bang is not the Beginning] have been proposed.**

In these scenarios, such as the bouncing universe, the cyclic universe, and "eternal inflation" models, the Big Bang was not the beginning of time, space, and matter, but it was merely the beginning of a particular phase of the history of the universe.[26]

Many contemporary Catholic theologians and philosophers would agree with **St. Thomas Aquinas** that the existence of a first moment in time cannot be absolutely proven through reason unaided by faith, because it is impossible to see past something that is supposed to be the first moment to verify that it is truly first. In the words of **Fr. Paul Haffner**, a priest and physicist, the beginning of the universe "is like a safe with a combination-lock and the combination is locked inside the safe."[27] The words "In the beginning..." will always remain a matter of faith because of the limitations of human reason. Simply put, temporal creatures such as ourselves, "locked" within the universe's history, can only say, "This is as far back in time as our science allows us to go."

The *Helix Nebula* (called the *Eye of God* by some) in the constellation of Aquarius lies about 700 light-years away. (image from the Hubble Space Telescope)

So, if it is not a slam-dunk proof of either God's existence or a beginning, then why is the Big Bang Theory important for theology? Three reasons stand out. First, the Big Bang Theory is important because it may suggest that more than science is needed to explain the universe. As St. John Paul II once observed, the problem of the universe's beginning requires "[the kind of] human knowledge which rises above physics and astrophysics and is called *metaphysics*."[28] When one runs up against what might be the very limits of time and space, one has to confront the issue of a Cause that transcends time and space. Once again, this does not mean that the moment of the Big Bang is necessarily the beginning. But, since it is as far back as we can currently observe, it does raise the question of not only the historical beginning but also of the *origin* of the universe—what causes it to exist at all?

Second, the Big Bang Theory shows that the idea of a beginning can be made sense of scientifically, something that was not at all clear before Einstein's theory. It shows that it is not "unscientific" to ponder an act of power and creativity that is not the mere unfolding of a process *within* the realm of matter, space, and time, but actually brings matter, space, and time into existence out of nothing.

Third, the Big Bang Theory shows us that time—like space and matter—is not a necessary feature of existence but merely a feature of the physical universe. Therefore, where there is no universe, there is also no time. Or, put in theological terms, time itself is something created, such that it only exists as a result of creation. This supports the traditional concept, clearly formulated by St. Augustine, of God's "timelessness," his eternity. God, transcending the universe, also transcends time. *Time*, the measurement of change, does not apply to God who, being perfect, never changes. The Big Bang, as potentially the first moment in time, draws the mind to marvel with St. Augustine at the eternal mystery of God who is outside of time.

Now we can move to the next plot twist, which emerged when scientists began to theorize about the kind of events that must have happened *after* the Bang.

D. Curious Coincidences: The Setting of the Stage

THE BIG BANG THEORY OF FRIEDMANN AND LEMAÎTRE sent physics in a new direction. It is the foundation on which all of modern cosmology, which is the study of the universe as a whole and how it develops, is built. At the same time, enormous strides were being made by particle physicists in understanding the basic forces of nature, the subatomic particles of which matter consists, and the mathematical laws that govern them. Scientists could then begin to explore such fundamental questions as how matter originated and how it became formed into galaxies and stars. Strange and surprising discoveries awaited them, and many of these findings had something in common—they seemed to reveal a universe that had been "fine tuned" for the possibility and existence of life, including human beings.

These surprising discoveries are commonly referred to as *anthropic coincidences*. The word "anthropic" comes from the Greek word *anthrōpos*, which means "human being." An anthropic coincidence is defined as a feature of the universe that is exactly what is needed for the existence of life but yet seemingly could have been otherwise.[29] Had such features been otherwise, *human beings would not exist*. Let us look at three examples of anthropic coincidences.

1. Gravity and the Big Bang

AS COSMOLOGISTS STUDIED THE MATHEMATICS of the Big Bang, a remarkable feature of the universe's very first moments came to light. Scientists had understood since the time of **Isaac Newton** that all massive objects are attracted to each other by gravity. So, as all of the energy in the universe flew apart at fantastic speeds just after the colossal explosion of the Big Bang, the attraction of gravity was trying to pull it all back together. There was therefore a competition between the outward impetus from the explosion and the inward force of gravity. This competition had to be very precisely balanced, otherwise one of two disasters would have happened. Had the gravitational attraction been too strong, it would have quickly halted and then reversed the expansion, and the matter would have come crashing back together while the universe was still very tiny and new. On the other hand, had the gravity been too weak, the matter would have spread out much too quickly and stars and galaxies would not have been able to form. We would either have had no universe or one that would not support life. As Harvard astrophysicist **Owen Gingerich** puts it, "The balance between the energy of expansion [i.e., the force of the explosion] and the braking power of gravitation had to be extraordinarily exact..."[30]

Two colliding galaxies succumb to immense gravitational forces. The two galaxies will probably merge to form a single galaxy.

Why so exact? The reason is that near the time of the Big Bang both the outward speed of expansion and the inward pull of gravity were vastly greater than they are now. (The outward speed was much greater back then because gravity has had 10 billion years since then to slow it down. The gravitational pull was much greater because all the matter was much more densely packed.) The gravitational pull in the moments after the Big Bang was so great that if it had not been in precise balance then it would have collapsed the universe in a tiny fraction of a second.

How exact was the balance? One way to measure it is by the temperature of the explosion. Imagine that you could have set the temperature of the Big Bang as you set the temperature of your oven. Most digitally controlled ovens will allow you to set it to a single degree. For baking a cake, this is more than enough. An oven whose temperature could be set to within a hundredth of a degree, say, would be much more sophisticated—you might find such a thing in a research laboratory, but not in a kitchen. But, for the Big Bang to happen in such a way that life as we know it could result, the "dial" had to be set not to an accuracy of a hundredth of a degree, or a millionth, or even a billionth, but to *thirty decimal places*, that is, to 0.000000000000000000000000000001 of a degree. Otherwise, this "cake"—this universe that was able to bring forth living things—would have been ruined. The balance necessary for our life-producing universe was so exact that it is unbelievably improbable. And yet exactly what needed to happen *did* happen.

2. The Strong Nuclear Force and the Building Blocks of Life

A SECOND ANTHROPIC COINCIDENCE has to do with the origins of the building blocks of life, the formation of atoms. As scientists analyzed the process of the Big Bang and the events that followed it, much attention was focused on the structure and formation of atoms and atomic elements—hydrogen, carbon, oxygen, etc. None of the atomic elements existed at the very beginning of the universe. A few were constituted shortly after the Big Bang; all of the others were either formed within stars as they burned or in post-Big Bang explosions of stars called *supernovas*. These supernova explosions also served to spew the elements made inside stars out into space, where they could form into new stars, planets, and living things. Scientists emphasize that everything we see around us, and we ourselves, are quite literally made of stardust.[31]

The process of the formation of atomic elements began with the formation of the nuclei of these elements, each of which is made up of one or many neutrons and protons. The simplest and earliest nucleus was that of the most basic form of hydrogen (hydrogen 1), which has a single proton as its nucleus. Then pairs of particles fused to make a two-particle nucleus—hydrogen 2. (This element is also called *deuterium*, from the Greek word *deuteros*, which means "second," because it is the second kind of nucleus.) The process of "fusion," by which smaller nuclei combine to make larger ones, continued until all of the elements were made. These fusion processes release energy and are what power the sun and other stars—and thus they are the energy source, ultimately, for life on earth.

The attractive force that causes protons and neutrons to stick together to form nuclei is called the *strong nuclear force*. Scientists discovered that the strength of this force is "fine tuned" in such a way as to make life possible.

What interests us is the attractive force that causes protons and neutrons to stick together to form nuclei, which is called the *strong nuclear force*. Scientists discovered that the strength of this force is also "fine tuned" in such a way as to make life possible. If it were only a few percent weaker, then protons and neutrons could not stick together; if it were only a few percent stronger, then the fusion processes in stars would be able to happen in a completely different way that would allow them to burn hundreds of times faster than they do. In the first case, the building blocks of life would never have formed; in the second, the sun (and other stars) would have burned out so quickly that there would not have been time for living organisms to evolve.[32] This force *in* us seems to be *for* us.

3. Cosmic Convergence and the Chemistry of Life

WITH OUR THIRD ANTHROPIC COINCIDENCE, we move from the inorganic world of gravity and subatomic particles to the chemical foundations of the *biosphere*, the global system of living beings and their relationships, and the issue of biological evolution. In the last thirty years increasing attention has been paid by evolutionary biologists to the phenomenon called *evolutionary convergence*, "whereby unrelated [species] evolve nearly identical biological traits."[33] A classic example is the camera-type eye that has evolved independently in both humans and octopuses. Both the human eye and the octopus eye have an iris, a circular lens, pigment cells, and photoreceptor cells, even though the evolutionary lineages of mammals and mollusks diverged before eyes evolved in either lineage.[34] Marsupial mammals in Australia and placental mammals in the Americas provide another example. These separated from some common ancestor more than 100 million years ago. Despite this massive separation of space and time, we find that on these two continents there has been the independent evolution of species with similar ways of life, with similarities in shape, feeding, and locomotive patterns: marsupial mice and placental mice, marsupial wolves and placental wolves, etc.[35] The variation between these convergent species is minor compared to the striking similarities that they share.

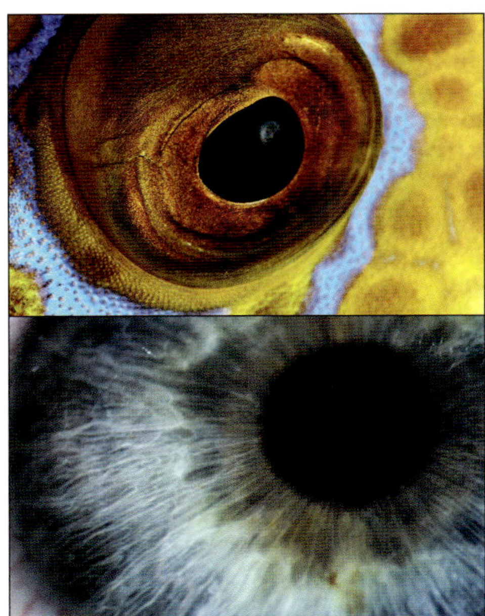
A classic example of *evolutionary convergence* is the camera-type eye present in both humans and octopuses that evolved in separate yet nearly identical ways.

In a series of important books, most recently his 2015 book *The Runes of Evolution*, the Cambridge paleontologist **Simon Conway Morris** has followed this trail of convergences to a remarkable conclusion: The general forms that life can develop and adapt are not haphazard but follow definite genetic and environmental pathways that were largely "predetermined from the Big Bang."[36] In other words, there is a deeper structure that makes the adventure of biological life not utterly random but orderly, somewhat like jazz music in which basic tunes (such as "When the Saints Go Marching In") are recognizable when played but are always played with innovation and creativity so that they are also a little different each time. *The Runes of Evolution* offers hundred of examples of convergence. For example, aquatic creatures developed the ability to breathe air at least thirty-eight separate times in the history of evolution, following separate paths but converging upon the capacity for acquiring oxygen from the air. Also, all of the major steps in the evolution of human beings—multicellularity, tissues, sensory systems, immune systems, eyes, limbs, and brains—are convergent.[37]

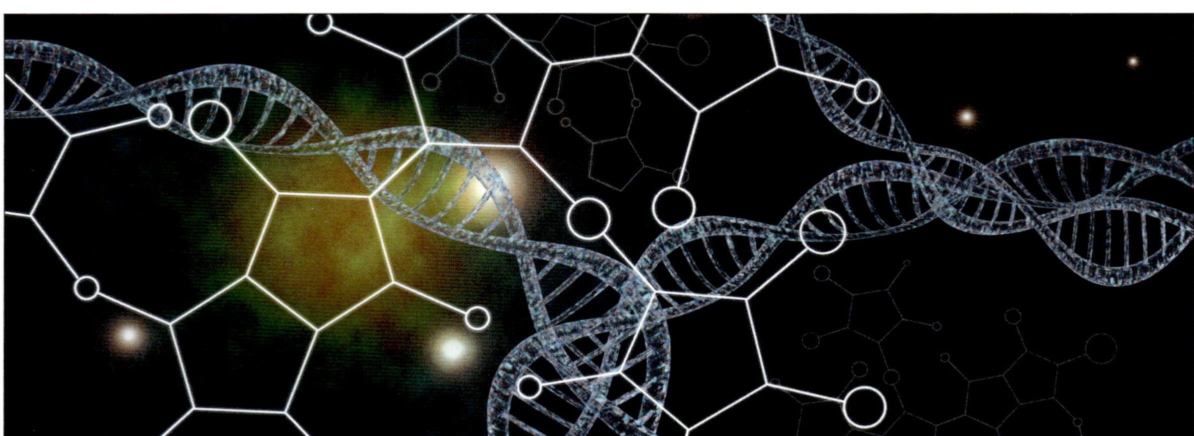
The genetic code that all organisms use to construct proteins from the sequences of DNA is amazingly optimized.

Let us focus on one such chemical convergence that makes life possible. The genetic code that all organisms use to construct proteins from the sequences of DNA is amazingly optimized. With "eerie perfection," evolution has converged upon an extremely efficient code given all the possible codes that exist. According to Morris, "Perhaps the genetic code... is an inevitable outcome. And if so, than what else might be inevitable, both here on Earth and elsewhere?".[38]

Morris compares the surprising precision by which these chemicals converged in just the right way to the discovery of Easter Island, the most remote speck of land on earth in the earth's vastest ocean, by Polynesian seafarers 1500 years ago. Superficially, one might guess this to have been an accident, a vessel blown off course and randomly drifting, but, as anthropologist **Geoffrey Irwin** has demonstrated, this view is incorrect. The clever Polynesian seafarers had developed superb navigation techniques and had discovered a way to quarter the ocean, century by century, widening their net of exploration until they covered it all and came upon Easter Island. In a similar way, the nucleotides somehow "navigated" over a vast "ocean" of chemical possibilities until they converged upon the fantastically complex genetic code that all life shares. In Morris's own words:

> **As with the audacious and intelligent Polynesians, so life shows a kind of homing instinct. Its central paradox revolves around the fact that despite its [abundance] and... richness life is also strongly constrained. The net result is a genuine creation, almost unimaginably rich and beautiful, but one also with an underlying structure in which, given enough time, the inevitable must happen.**[39]

The laws of physics and chemistry, therefore, seem not only fine tuned to make life possible, but even fine tuned to produce life. The universe, like the ancient Polynesian mariners, seems to have a kind of homing instinct for life's chemistry that is "built into" its chemical laws.

4. Anthropic Coincidences and God the Creator

WE HAVE LOOKED AT THREE EXAMPLES OF ANTHROPIC COINCIDENCES, but physicists and cosmologists have discussed many more. These coincidences have to do with strengths, ranges, and characteristics of the basic forces of nature; the masses, electric charges, and other properties of the particles that exist; the properties of space and time (for example, that time is an "arrow," and that space has three dimensions); and various other features of the laws of physics and the structure of the universe. Numerous factors have to balance just right and be in just the correct relationships to each other for the universe to produce life and human beings.[40]

Could all these anthropic coincidences really *just* be coincidences? Most people who have looked into the matter find that impossible to believe. Let us go back to the oven analogy, except now let us imagine the laws of physics are like a device with a large number of switches, knobs, and dials that control various features of the universe. One switch would turn on and off the force of electromagnetism; one dial would set the strength of that force, another dial would control the mass of the electron, and so forth. If all those switches and dials have to be set to just the right positions—some of them to fantastic accuracy—in order for life to appear, and we indeed find them set that way, is that not pretty strong evidence for a Creator who had the intention of creating a world with life in it? So it has seemed to many people, even many who did not start off believing in God. Even the famous astrophysicist **Fred Hoyle** (1915-2001), an atheist who came up with the term "Big Bang" as an insult to the theory and who died without ever accepting it, remarked that the universe looks like a "put-up job," i.e., something carefully arranged.

If you are unsure, consider this quote from **Roger Penrose**, a famous English mathematical physicist and Oxford scholar. He is describing the size of the number that represents the odds *against* the emergence of human life:

> **This is an extraordinary figure. One could not possibly even write the number down in full in the ordinary . . . notation: it would be 1 followed by 10^123 successive 0's. *Even if we were to write a 0 on each separate proton and on each separate neutron in the entire universe*—and we could throw in all the other particles for good measure—we should fall far short of writing down the figure needed.[41]**

Do the anthropic coincidences "scientifically prove" that God exists and so designed the laws of the universe that life and human beings would emerge? As we learned in regard to the Big Bang Theory, that would be saying too much. In fact, some scientists have already proposed a way to explain some of the anthropic coincidences without invoking God. It is called the "multiverse" hypothesis.

The lesson of the anthropic coincidences is that a universe that can give rise to life probably has to be very special indeed.

The multiverse idea can be explained with the same control-panel analogy we used before. Suppose that all those "switches" and "dials" are not set to the same positions everywhere in the universe but, instead, vary randomly from place to place. For example, the strength of the strong nuclear force might be different here and in parts of the universe very far away. (They would have to be *very* far away indeed, since there is conclusive evidence that in all the places we can see with telescopes the "dial settings" are the same as here.) If so, then in most places in the universe the dial settings would be wrong for life, but if the universe were big enough, then there might be some places where the dial settings were just right for life to be possible. In other words, if you buy enough lottery tickets, one is bound to be the "lucky ticket."

The multiverse idea is interesting, but it is not yet a testable scientific theory, and it is hard to see at present how it could ever become one. However, even if it turned out to be true, then it would not really explain away the anthropic coincidences. The point is that a "multiverse", i.e., a universe some of whose "switches" and "dials" were set differently in different places, is a very strange kind of universe and probably could not arise unless some *other* switches and dials were set to special values. The lesson of the anthropic coincidences is that a universe that can give rise to life probably has to be very special indeed.

The seeming fact that the universe had to be extremely precise, fine tuned "just so" for human beings to exist, seems suspiciously like a plan. The anthropic coincidences leave one with the overwhelming impression that, contrary to scientific atheism, the universe's fine-tuning was built in by a "Fine Tuner"—God the Creator, who made the universe for the sake of life and humanity. In this regard, we must recall that such "fine tuning" should not be understood as God violating the integrity of nature by constantly intervening through miracles; rather, God upholds in existence a universe that naturally fulfills his will. In the words of the International Theological Commission, "God's action does not displace or supplant the activity of creaturely causes, but enables them to act according to their natures and, nonetheless, to bring about the ends he intends."[42] God does not need to tinker with the universe that he wills into existence; rather, he wills a universe into existence that is what he desires it to be, a wisely ordered universe that is capable of producing and sustaining life. In the words of Nobel Prize-winning physiologist **George Wald**:

> **...mind, rather than emerging as a late outgrowth in the evolution of life, has existed always, as the matrix, the source and condition of physical reality—that the stuff of which physical reality is composed is mind-stuff. It is mind that has composed a physical Universe that breeds life, and so eventually evolved creatures that know and create: science-, art-, and technology-making animals.**[43]

Or, as **St. Paul** says of Christ in his Letter to the Colossians (1:16), "In him all things were created, in heaven and on earth, visible and invisible...—all things were created through him and for him." The anthropic coincidences, when considered with the eyes of faith, are reflective of the divine mind, the Son-*Logos* through whom the universe is created and sustained in its existence. This brings us to the final "twist" in the tale of modern science.

The anthropic coincidences leave one with the overwhelming impression that, contrary to scientific atheism, the universe's "fine tuning" was built in by a "Fine Tuner"—God the Creator, who made the universe for the sake of life and humanity.

E. Beauty Beyond Description: Symmetry, Modern Physics, and the Argument from Design

IN CHAPTER THIRTEEN OF THE BOOK OF WISDOM, written just 50 to 100 years before the Birth of Jesus, the Sacred Author condemns nature worship, the pagan practice of worshiping natural forces as if they were divine beings. He then goes on to suggest a proper way in which beauty in the natural world can lead us to worship the one true God:

1 All men who were ignorant of God were foolish by nature; and they were unable from the good things that are seen to know him who exists, nor did they recognize the craftsman while paying heed to his works;

2 but they supposed that either fire or wind or swift air, or the circle of the stars, or turbulent water, or the luminaries of heaven were the gods that rule the world.

3 If through delight in the beauty of these things men assumed them to be gods, let them know how much better than these is their Lord, for the author of beauty created them.

4 And if men were amazed at their power and working, let them perceive from them how much more powerful is he who formed them.

5 For from the greatness and beauty of created things comes a corresponding perception of their Creator.

"Their Lord...the author of beauty created them" (Wis 13:3).

What is meant here by the "beauty" of created things? The ancients defined *beauty* as the proper relationship between the parts of something and the whole. Beauty is the splendor we discover when we see order and harmony in things. Think of a beautiful face, or a beautiful piece of music, and you get the idea. As the author observes in verse three, such beauty causes delight. God is seen by analogy in the beauty and greatness of created things.

In our own day, scientific atheists would disagree. They see the world as governed not by a loving, personal God but by blind and impersonal forces, mechanisms, and processes. Everything, they believe, can be explained by a combination of mathematical laws and pure chance. An ordinary person might point to some beautiful natural phenomenon—a gemstone, a rainbow, an *aurora borealis*, the harmonious movements of the planets—and say, along with the Book of Wisdom, "Here, clearly, is evidence of the divine Artist at work." Scientific atheists, while not denying the beauty of these things, would answer, "We do not need to invoke any Artist, because we know exactly how these things arise. We understand the forces and principles that cause those gemstones and rainbows to form, and we know that those forces and principles are merely natural, the products of blind chance." The scientific atheist does not deny that there are elegant patterns, harmonious structures, beautiful forms, and remarkable examples of order to be found in nature. He or she thinks, however, that they can all be explained, ultimately and exhaustively, by the laws of physics.

This is where the next plot twist comes in. In the twentieth century one discovery after another revealed that the very laws of physics *themselves* exhibit patterns even more elegant, structures even more harmonious, forms even more beautiful, and order far more remarkable than those that they were invoked to explain. It turned out that, in discovering the laws of physics, scientists did not "explain away" the beauty and order that was visible in nature, but they instead uncovered a beauty within the depths of nature much greater than that which is visible on its surface.

Let us look at one example. Consider the harmonious movements of the planets. At the beginning of the seventeenth century, **Johannes Kepler** (1571-1630) unlocked the secrets of these movements and published his three great Laws of Planetary Motion. (One of these was that the planets went around the sun in elliptical orbits, with the sun at the "focus" of the ellipse. The second was that in its course around the sun a planet always "sweeps out equal areas in equal times." The third was a precise algebraic relationship between the time it takes a planet to orbit the sun and its distance from the sun.) Kepler himself saw these as magnificent examples of divine artistry. He exclaimed in his great treatise entitled *Harmonices Mundi* (The Harmonies of the World), "I thank thee, Lord God our Creator, that thou allowest me to see the beauty in thy work of creation."

Consider the harmonious movements of the planets. Johannes Kepler saw the three great Laws of Planetary Motion as magnificent examples of divine artistry.

More than eighty years later, **Isaac Newton** articulated his Universal Laws of Motion and the Law of Gravitation. These explained all three of the laws of Kepler and much else about the movements of the heavenly bodies. But, in fact, the laws Newton discovered were far more majestic and mathematically elegant than even the laws that Kepler had discovered and which had made Kepler cry out in praise of his Creator.

And this is only the beginning of the story. For, as we have seen, more than two centuries later Einstein found that Newton's laws did not exhaust the richness of the phenomenon of gravity. He showed that Newton's law of gravity was just an approximation to a much more beautiful and profound theory of gravity in which gravity was caused by the curvature of spacetime described by Einstein's Equations. Since then, evidence has begun to emerge in recent decades that Einstein's theory is itself but a piece of some even deeper and more remarkable mathematical structure. This newer theory (which is still untested) is so mathematically rich that one of the leading theorists, **Edward Witten**, proclaimed its "wonder, incredible consistency, remarkable elegance, and beauty."[44]

This is the third twist in the plot: The deeper into nature that science has penetrated, the *more* beauty it has uncovered. This is why, as the twentieth century unfolded, fundamental physicists began to be guided in their search for deeper laws more and more by the criterion of beauty. **Stephen Barr** describes how one of the greatest discoveries of twentieth-century physics, the Dirac Equation, was found:

> **The physicist *Paul Dirac* [1902-1984] was seeking an equation to describe electrons in a way that would be consistent with the principles of relativity theory. In this search he was guided primarily by mathematical beauty: "A great deal of my work is just playing with equations and seeing what they give," he said. In this case, as he was playing with some equations he found something "pretty." "[It]**

> **was a pretty mathematical result. I was quite excited over it. It seemed that it must be [of] some importance."** ***Notice that it was the "prettiness" of the mathematics that convinced him he was on the right track*** **[italics mine]. Soon after, he found the great equation...**[45]

Physicist Paul Dirac (1902-1984)
"God is a mathematician of a very high order, and He used very advanced mathematics in constructing the universe."
(*The Evolution of the Physicist's Picture of Nature*, 1963)

In fact, Dirac famously remarked that it was more important to have "beauty in one's equations" than to have them fit one's experiments. **Werner Heisenberg** (1901-1976), one of the founders of quantum mechanics, also stressed the importance of the criterion of beauty in physics. He wrote, "In exact science, no less than in the arts, beauty is the most important source of illumination and clarity."

Some people have argued that the beauty referred to by physicists like Dirac is a purely subjective judgment, one based on personal taste. Maybe scientists come to think that their theories are beautiful just because they discovered them, that is, out of some kind of vanity. But there is a powerful argument against this: Dirac did not see the beauty *after* he discovered the equation, it was the beauty that *led* him to the equation.

In fact, this has happened many times accidentally. Again and again throughout history, mathematicians have come up with mathematical ideas and developed branches of mathematics purely for the sake of their "mathematical beauty" without ever dreaming that they had any relevance to the physical world, only to have it discovered much later that these mathematical formulations were needed to express fundamental laws of physics. For example, the idea of "complex numbers" was invented and thoroughly investigated by the early 1800s, at which time they seemed to have no relevance to physical reality at all. However, in the 1920s it was discovered that they were needed to write the equations of quantum mechanics.

In 1852, a system of numbers called quaternions were invented by the mathematician **William Rowan Hamilton** (1805-1865). Quaternions seemed to be a very elegant, but scientifically useless, piece of mathematics, until it was found that quaternions were needed to describe the way electrons and similar particles "spin," as well as other properties of subatomic particles. These and many other examples reveal that the beauty found in the laws of physics, the artistic perfection of their design, is so perfect that it seems to be accessible in some cases simply through mathematical creativity.

Hermann Weyl (1885-1955), one of the great mathematicians of the twentieth century, who also played a leading role in theoretical physics, once said the following in a lecture in 1931:

> **Many people think that modern science is far removed from God. I find on the contrary, that it is much more difficult today for the knowing person to approach God from history, from the spiritual side of the world, and from morals; for there we encounter the suffering and evil in the world, which it is difficult to bring into harmony with an all-merciful and all-mighty God. In this domain we have evidently not yet succeeded in raising the veil with which our human nature covers the essence of things. But in our knowledge of physical nature we have penetrated so far that we can obtain a vision of the flawless harmony which is in conformity with sublime reason.**[46]

What Hermann Weyl is saying here, and what Kepler was saying in his book *Harmonices Mundi*, is that the beauty, harmony, and order in the world are a sign of its creation by a Mind, by "sublime reason." This is a very ancient argument for the existence of God, sometimes called the "Argument from Design." It can be found in Sacred Scripture, particularly in Proverbs 8:22-31, Jeremiah 33:25-26, and Wisdom 11:20. We saw it clearly presupposed in the First Creation Account, where God's designing intelligence and awesome power is described as bringing the world and its creatures into existence—as we saw in Chapter Four, even the shape of the story, its symbolic structure, reveals God's design. This idea is also found in many places in the writings of early Christians. For example, at the beginning of the third century AD, the Catholic theologian **Minucius Felix** (died ca. AD 250) wrote:

> **If upon entering a home you saw that everything there was well-tended, neat, and decorative, you would believe that some master was in charge of it, and that he was himself much superior to those good things. So too in the home of this world, when you see providence, order, and law in the heavens and on earth, believe that there is a Lord and Author of the universe, more beautiful than the stars themselves and the various parts of the whole world.**[47]

As found in Sacred Scripture and in early Christian writings, the argument is primarily based on the fact that the universe as a whole is orderly, lawful, harmonious, and beautiful.

William Paley (1743-1805) compared the complexity found in living things to the complexity of a pocket watch.

In the eighteenth and early nineteenth centuries, however, some Anglican theologians and philosophers began to make the argument in a narrower and more questionable way. They pointed to specific *things*—especially living things—as evidence that God had directly *intervened* in nature in a supernatural way to produce them. The argument was that these things were too complex to have been the products of natural processes. The Anglican theologian **William Paley** (1743-1805) gave one of the most famous examples of such reasoning. In his book *Natural Theology* he compared the complexity found in living things to the complexity of a pocket watch one might find lying in a field where it had been lost. No one, Paley argued, would conclude that it, unlike a stone in the field, was made by natural forces acting at random: "There must have existed, at some time, and at some place or other, an artificer or artificers, who formed [the watch] for the purpose which we find it actually to answer; who comprehended its construction, and designed its use..." In other words, living things are too complex to have emerged naturally; God must have made them directly. (Often, when people think of the Argument from Design, they have Paley's ideas in mind.)

We have already seen in Chapter Five that this runs contrary to the Catholic approach, which has always upheld the integrity of nature. The trouble with Paley's argument is that it pits "design" *against* "nature" and "law"—it assumes that nature is chaotic and that, when we find complex and beautiful things in it, they stand out as proof that a Designer exists. Yet this is not what **Minucius Felix** meant in his quote above, which points to nature itself as designed and lawful. It was precisely this natural "order and law in the heavens and on earth" that points to God for the Catholic tradition.

Paley's narrowing and distorting of the emphasis of the "Argument from Design" had very unfortunate consequences, which we shall see in more detail in the next chapter on God and evolution. When **Charles Darwin** showed how the structures of living things might be explained naturally (just as others had shown that structures found in the inanimate world, such as the solar system, could be), it led him and others to think that the Design Argument for God had been refuted. The only thing that had been refuted was Paley's version of the design argument. The irony is that twentieth-century discoveries in physics and cosmology have actually given splendid examples of the older and deeper version of the design argument. For they have shown that the "order and law in the heavens and on earth" is much more profound and impressive than anyone had ever imagined. Indeed, as **Hermann Weyl** said, the laws of physics give us "a vision of the flawless harmony which is in conformity with sublime reason."

The physicist **Stephen Barr** uses a single term to sum up this great beauty uncovered by twentieth-century physics—*symmetry*, a word that means "equal measure" in Greek. All order that we see, including the beautiful complexity of living creatures, comes from and is founded upon the greater order of the universe's fundamental symmetry, the symmetry of the laws of nature.[48] In his words, "we do not live in a universe with a great deal of order. We live in a universe whose order is *perfect*, or nearly so..." As we continue, we will reencounter the concept of symmetry, which is very helpful for seeing how science and faith, nature and spirit, creation and redemption fit each other with "equal measure." Symmetry and beauty are crucial to rediscovering faith on the frontiers of science.

All order that we see, including the beautiful complexity of living creatures, comes from and is founded upon the greater order of the universe's fundamental symmetry.

Here is Barr's recapitulation of the Argument from Design, based on the latest and the best science:

> **At the roots of the physical world, therefore, one does not find mere...slime or dust but instead a richness and perfection of form based on profound, subtle, and beautiful mathematical *ideas*. This is what the famous astrophysicist Sir James Jeans meant when he said many decades ago that "the universe begins to look more like a great thought than a great machine." [Pope] Benedict XVI expressed the same basic insight when in his Regensburg lecture he referred to "the mathematical structure of matter, its intrinsic rationality."...**
>
> **It is true that the cosmos was at one point a swirling mass of gas and dust out of which has come the extraordinary complexity of life as we experience it. Yet, at every moment in this process of development, a greater and more impressive order operates within—an order that did not develop but was there from the beginning. In the upper world, mind, thought, and ideas make their appearance as fruit on the topmost branches of an evolutionary tree. Below the surface, we see the taproots of reality, the fundamental laws of physics that shimmer with ideas of profound simplicity....And we begin to discover that matter, although mindless itself, is the product of a Mind of infinite profundity and infinite simplicity.[49]**

The Creator is the Mind behind the universe, not merely an all-powerful mechanic. And his "thoughts" as Creator are discovered in the beauty of nature's laws, which are a dim reflection of the perfect beauty of the Son-*Logos*, God's eternal Word.

As we continue, we will reencounter the concept of symmetry, which is very helpful for seeing how science and faith, nature and spirit, creation and redemption, fit each other with "equal measure."

F. Conclusion: From the Universe to the Biosphere

IN THIS CHAPTER we have seen how the journey of two small bands of scientists at the end of World War I moved human thought in directions that no one anticipated. Scientists began to ask the ultimate scientific questions about the nature of space and time, the earliest state of the universe, and the deep mathematical structure of its laws. Far from making theological and philosophical reflection irrelevant, these discoveries suggested new applications and clarifications of classical philosophy and theology. The Big Bang stimulated theologians to clarify the difference between the beginning of time and the ultimate origin of the universe; the anthropic coincidences and the beauty of the universe's laws provided opportunities to see the hand of the Creator, who works through his creatures to bring about his will; the profound beauty found in the mathematical structure of the universe gave evidence of divine beauty in ways previously unknown. Scientific atheism, which seemed to many to be compelled by the discoveries of nineteenth-century science, turned out to be a superficial reaction in the light of twentieth-century physics.

Physics, however, is not the only science in which the existence of God and the truth of the Christian faith has falsely seemed to be in danger of being swept away by the currents of progress. This is even more so in biology. The greatest controversy in the relationship between faith and science centers around the theory of biological evolution. For over a century, American society has been the site of a great culture war, fought in print, from pulpits, in legal courts, and even in politics regarding the compatibility of evolution and the Christian faith, a war that still rages today. Is evolution the final nail in the coffin of Christian belief? Or is evolution another example of God's wisdom, love, and power—the "disguised friend of faith," as Christian theologian and biochemist **Arthur Peacocke** once called it? In the next chapter, we will address this crucial issue.

VOCABULARY

Define the following terms (or identify the person's significance):

1. General Theory of Relativity
2. Cosmological Constant
3. Edwin Powell Hubble
4. Georges Lemaître
5. Big Bang Theory
6. Spacetime
7. *Ab Initio Temporis*
8. Arno Penzias and Robert Wilson
9. Time
10. Anthropic Coincidences
11. *Anthrōpos*
12. Supernovas (atom formation)
13. Deuterium
14. Strong Nuclear Force
15. Evolutionary Convergence
16. Simon Conway Morris
17. DNA
18. Nucleotides
19. Multiverse Hypothesis
20. Book of Wisdom
21. Beauty
22. Johannes Kepler (*Harmonices Mundi*)
23. Paul Dirac (Dirac Equation)
24. Werner Heisenberg
25. William Rowan Hamilton (Quaternions)
26. Hermann Weyl
27. Argument from Design
28. Minucius Felix (Argument from Design)
29. William Paley
30. Stephen Barr (Symmetry)

Werner Heisenberg (1901-1976)
"In exact science, no less than in the arts, beauty is the most important source of illumination and clarity."

William Rowan Hamilton (1805-1865)
His work was of major importance to physics, particularly his reformulation of Newtonian mechanics, now called Hamiltonian mechanics.

STUDY QUESTIONS

Section A

1. What major changes occurred in science in the twentieth century? Why are they significant for the relationship between faith and science?

Section B

2. Why did the discovery of the laws of the conservation of matter and energy lead many nineteenth-century scientists to assert that the universe had no beginning?

3. Is the idea of a perpetual universe necessarily atheistic? If not, how can it be reconciled with belief in God?

4. How is the idea of a perpetual universe an obstacle to belief in the authority of Scripture and the Church?

5. What kind of causality leads logically to the conclusion that there must be an Uncaused Cause? How is this related to the issue of whether or not the universe has a beginning?

Section C

6. How did the Big Bang Theory originate?

7. Describe the major features of the Big Bang Theory regarding space and time.

8. Describe St. Augustine's explanation of time as it relates to the Big Bang Theory.

9. How was the Big Bang Theory finally confirmed?

10. Why did it take so long for the Big Bang Theory to gain acceptance? What does this reveal about the blind "faith" inherent in materialism and scientific atheism?

11. Why is the Big Bang Theory a major crack in the materialist worldview?

12. Does the Big Bang Theory prove the existence of God? Why or why not?

13. Does the Big Bang Theory prove that the universe had a first moment in time? Why or why not?

14. List three ways in which the Big Bang Theory is important for rediscovering faith on the frontiers of science.

Section D

15. In what new direction did the Big Bang Theory send physics?

16. Why is the role of gravity in the Big Bang considered an anthropic coincidence?

17. Why is the strong nuclear force considered an anthropic coincidence?

18. Describe how the chemistry of life can be understood as an anthropic coincidence.

19. Using the device analogy, explain why it is unlikely that the anthropic coincidences are really just coincidences.

20. Do the anthropic coincidences scientifically prove the existence of God? Why or why not?

21. In the light of faith, how can the anthropic coincidences be interpreted as reflective of divine wisdom and of the Son-*Logos*?

STUDY QUESTIONS Continued

Section E

22. Summarize Wisdom 13:1-5 and its message about the beauty of nature as leading to God.

23. How do scientific atheists explain the phenomenon of beauty in the universe?

24. What has modern science revealed about beauty in the universe? What does this fact imply?

25. Describe the processes of discovery in science and mathematics with respect to beauty in the universe. Why does this process reinforce that the discovery of beauty is not simply a matter of purely personal taste?

26. What mistake was made in the eighteenth and nineteenth centuries by philosophers and theologians (e.g., William Paley) regarding the Argument from Design? What did this mistake fail to recognize?

27. Where does the beauty that we see around us come from, according to modern physics?

28. Restate the Argument from Design, using a) the notion of symmetry and b) the discovery of beauty and order in the laws governing the universe.

PRACTICAL EXERCISE

1. Rampant materialism created blinders for the scientific community that kept many from accepting the Big Bang. What other natural truths about the universe might be inaccessible to materialists? (Note: list only philosophical and scientific truths.)

Hermann Weyl (1885-1955)
"Symmetry is a vast subject, significant in art and nature. Mathematics lies at its root." (*Symmetry,* 1952)

William Paley (1743-1805)
He made use of the watchmaker analogy for God in a way that incorrectly recast the theological Argument from Design.

Endnotes – Chapter Seven

1. These two principles are now recognized by scientists to be the same principle.
2. St. Thomas Aquinas, *Summa Theologiae* I.46.2 resp.
3. W. Norris Clarke, *The One and the Many*, 216.
4. Stephen M. Barr, *Modern Physics and Ancient Faith*, 258-259.
5. Clarke, 216.
6. Barr, *Modern Physics*, 261.
7. Koltermann, *Grundzuege der modernen Naturphilosophie. Ein kritischer Gesamtentwurf* (Frankfurt, 1994), 134, as quoted by Christoph Cardinal Schönborn, "He upholds the universe by his word and power," *www.stephanscom.at/edw/katechesen/articles/2006/02/15/a10185/.*
8. Barr, *Modern Physics*, 259; cf. St. Thomas Aquinas, *Summa contra Gentiles*, II.38 ad 5.
9. George Gamow, *My World Line* (English: Viking, 1970), 44. There are many historical ironies in this story. Theorists since Einstein's day have considered that Einstein's equations make more sense *with* the cosmological constant. And the term may indeed be needed to explain a discovery made in 1998. So even some of Einstein's blunders were pretty smart.
10. Barr, *Modern Physics*, 38-39.
11. Georges Lemaître, "The Beginning of the World from the Point of View of Quantum Theory," *Nature* 127 (1931): 706, as quoted in Stacy Trasancos, *Particles of Faith: A Catholic Guide to Navigating Science* (Notre Dame, IN: Ave Maria Press, 2016), 63.
12. Barr, *Modern Physics*, 43.
13. For example, see Steven Weinberg, "The cosmological constant problem," *Reviews of Modern Physics* 61 (1989): 15, n.13.
14. Bertrand Russell, *History of Western Philosophy* (London: Allen and Unwin, 1946), 373.
15. St. Augustine, *Confessions*, XI.13, as quoted by Stephen Barr, *Modern Physics*, 48.
16. Dominique Lambert, "Einstein and Lemaître: two friends, two cosmologies . . . ," *inters.org/einstein-Lemaître*.
17. Barr, *Modern Physics*, 44-45.
18. Ibid., 46.
19. Francis Collins, *The Language of God: A Scientist Presents Evidence for Belief* (New York: Free Press, 2007), 64-65.
20. Robert Jastrow, *God and the Astronomers* (New York: W.W. Norton, 1992): 207.
21. Barr, *Modern Physics*, 35.
22. Jastrow, 14.
23. St. John Paul II, Message to the Reverend George V. Coyne, S.J., Director of the Vatican Observatory, June 1, 1988.
24. St. John Paul II, General Audience, July 10, 1985, *inters.org/John-Paul-II-Science-Proofs-God.*
25. Stacy Trasancos, *Particles of Faith: A Catholic Guide to Navigating Science*, 64-65.
26. Stephen M. Barr, *The Believing Scientist*, 128.
27. Paul Haffner, *Mystery of Creation*, 170.
28. St. John Paul II, "Address of October 3, 1981 to the Pontifical Academy of Sciences," *www.casinapioiv.va/content/accademia/en/magisterium/johnpaulii/3october1981.html.*
29. Barr, *Modern Physics*, 25. I have modified Stephen Barr's definition slightly for clarification.
30. Owen Gingerich, *God's Universe* (Cambridge: Harvard University Press, 2006), 49.
31. Barr, *Modern Physics*, 119.
32. Ibid., 119-121.
33. Conor Cunningham, *Darwin's Pious Idea: Why the Ultra-Darwinists and Creationists Both Get It Wrong* (Grand Rapids: Eerdmans, 2010), 144.
34. Ibid., 147.
35. "Convergence: Marsupials and Placentals," *www-tc.pbs.org/wgbh/evolution/library/01/4/pdf/l_014_02.pdf.*
36. Simon Conway Morris, *Life's Solution: Inevitable Humans in a Lonely Universe* (Cambridge: Cambridge University Press, 2003), 310.
37. Ian Curran, "Headed Toward Christ: The Grand Narrative of Evolution," review of Simon Conway Morris, *The Runes of Evolution: How the Universe Became Self-Aware* (West Conshohocken, PA: Templeton Press, 2015); March 17, 2016, *The Christian Century*.
38. Morris, *Life's Solution*, 13-19.
39. Ibid., 20.
40. Collins, 74.
41. Roger Penrose, *The Emperor's New Mind*, rev. ed., (Oxford: Oxford University Press, 1989), 445-446.
42. International Theological Commission, C&S, 68.
43. George Wald, "Life and Mind in the Universe," *International Journal of Quantum Chemistry Biology Symposium* 11 (1984): 1-2.
44. Quoted in John Horgan, *The End of Science* (New York: Addison-Wesley, 1996), 69.
45. Barr, *Modern Physics*, 23.
46. Herman Weyl, *The Open World: Three Lectures on the Metaphysical Implications of Science* (New Haven, CT: Yale University Press, 1986), 28-29.
47. Minucius Felix, *Octavius* 18.4 as quoted in Stephen Barr, *Modern Physics*, 68-69.
48. Barr, *Modern Physics*, 80-81.
49. Barr, *The Believing Scientist*, 166-167.

Chapter Eight
Going "Deeper than Darwin"[1]: God and Biological Evolution

What is evolution? Are evolution and the Catholic faith in conflict?

How does the Church approach the theory of evolution?

Can evolution provide opportunities for reflecting on the mystery of God?

> What response shall we make to [evolution]? It is the affair of the natural sciences to explain how the tree of life in particular continues to grow, and how new branches shoot out from it. This is not a matter for faith.... More reflective spirits have long been aware that there is no either-or here. We cannot say: "creation or evolution", inasmuch as these two things respond to two different realities.
>
> —Pope Benedict XVI, *In the Beginning...*

A. Strange Signs and Deceptive Discoveries

In Chapter One we made a distinction between "how" and "why" explanations. Just as in the case of the music festival example, it is possible to get caught up in the amazing scientific details of the universe and to fail to see beyond them to their deepest meaning. When we only have a grasp of the "how" and no notion of the "why," reality ceases to be seen for what it truly is, and life's beauty and complexity loses its deepest "level." The history of the universe comes to be seen only as a sequence of events, not as the creation of our loving God who is, to all things, the source and summit of their beauty, goodness, and truth. Sometimes this happens because of our own failure to look closely enough. But, when it comes to biological evolution, for many it is more of a failure in understanding what they see. The details are surprising, not exactly what one might expect.

The Silver Chair is the fourth book of the *Chronicles of Narnia*, C.S. Lewis's famous children's series about a world that has mysterious connections to our own. In the story, an English schoolgirl named Jill enters Narnia and is given a challenging quest—to rescue a prince who is being held captive by a magical and

"Remember the Signs and believe the Signs."
—Aslan, *The Silver Chair*

wicked enemy. To fulfill her quest she must recognize four signs that she will find in her adventure. Once each sign is encountered, she and her companions must faithfully perform certain actions.

As she stands on a mountain, looking down into Narnia, she is warned by Aslan, the loving creator and redeemer of Narnia, that the signs will not always be as obvious as they might seem. She is made to recite them, over and over, before she begins her quest. Then, once they are memorized, Aslan gives her the following counsel:

> **Here...I have spoken to you clearly: I will not often do so down in Narnia. Here on the mountain, the air is clear and your mind is clear; as you drop down into Narnia, the air will thicken. Take great care that it does not confuse your mind.**

Aslan completes his counsel with a warning:

> **And the Signs which you have learned here will not look at all as you expect them to look, when you meet them there. That is why it is so important to know them by heart and to pay no attention to appearances. *Remember the Signs and believe the Signs.***[2]

Jill begins her quest looking for the Signs but never with the care and attention they deserve. In fact, she and her friends either overlook or misinterpret the first three, and each time the quest suffers and almost fails. Only after repeated misadventures caused by misinterpretations of the Signs do she and her friends learn how to see them for what they are and not for what they expect them to be. They learn, through costly mistakes, to keep their eyes and their minds open. Slowly but surely they begin to understand the Signs, even while they overcome the hardships and dangers their mistakes had brought upon them. When they reach the final Sign, their learning experiences make it possible for them to finally overcome their obstacles and succeed at their attempt to rescue the captive prince.

The Silver Chair has an important moral for us and for everyone who wishes to understand the relationship between faith and science when it comes to the scientific consensus that all living things came into existence through biological evolution. In a real sense, many scientists and believers today are very much like Jill and her companions. We have been given very clear indications by God in Sacred Scripture and Catholic doctrine that he is the Creator of all things, including living things. Those living things, he tells us, are his creatures, willed by him and created by him. And yet, as in Jill's case, the fact that the signs of God's creative activity do not appear as they were expected to appear prior to the discovery of evolution has created a challenge. We remember the Signs, but do we still believe them? Or, have we disbelieved or become confused because they now appear to us in ways that are different than we expected? To answer these questions, let us look more closely at biological evolution and at the life of the man whose discovery of it forever changed the way human beings understand themselves and the universe.

B. Darwin's Theory of Evolution

UP UNTIL THE MID-NINETEENTH CENTURY it was commonly assumed that all of the different kinds of living things on our planet were brought into being by *special creation*. That is, it was thought that the first plants and animals of each kind were directly formed by God from inorganic (i.e., nonliving) matter by miraculous intervention. The idea was that if one could trace back through the ancestry of elephants, eventually one would come to the first group of elephants, who had no ancestors, but were directly made by God. The reason for this assumption was not that people back then preferred supernatural explanations to natural ones. They assumed it because no good natural explanation had ever been discovered. There was no plausible explanation of how things as intricate as plants and animals could have arisen by natural processes. So the creation accounts in Sacred Scripture were often taken as offering not only symbolic images of deeper, great truths, but also factual accounts.

As we saw in Chapter Seven, for theologians like **William Paley**, the lack of a natural explanation for living things seemed in itself to be a powerful argument for the existence of God. What else, it was asked, except a direct miraculous intervention by God could explain the complexity and brilliant beauty of all these living creatures? And so some theologians in the eighteenth and nineteenth centuries began to lean very heavily on this biological version of the Argument from Design. This turned out to be a mistake because not long afterwards someone finally did come along with a brilliant idea for explaining how the various kinds of living things could have arisen naturally. That someone was the English aristocrat and naturalist **Charles Darwin** (1809-1882).

Charles Darwin (1809-1882)
The way in which Darwin came first to be convinced of the reality of evolution is one of the most wonderful stories in the history of science.

In 1859, Darwin published a book entitled *On the Origin of Species*, one of the epoch-making works in the history of science. Darwin proposed that all living species in the world descended from a small number of common ancestors, possibly even only one, which lived a long time ago. In other words, originally there was perhaps just one type of living thing, which gradually evolved over great stretches of time into the many forms of life we see today. Therefore, all the extremely diverse forms of life, including trees, fish, bacteria, frogs, and even higher mammals like deer and apes, are related to each other in a vast and very ancient "tree of life." In 1871, in his book *The Descent of Man*, Darwin proposed that humanity itself was the product of evolutionary processes and was part of this tree.

This is the idea of *biological evolution*, which can be summarily defined as the change in populations of living things through genetic inheritance. Some distinguish macroevolution, the emergence of new species, from microevolution, the minor incremental changes that occur within a species. Ultimately, as Darwin realized, these are the same kinds of changes, and so it is preferable to refer to *speciation*, the divergence of living populations into separate species, as one result of evolution, but not the only one. The *idea* of evolution was not completely new; Darwin's own grandfather, **Erasmus Darwin** (1731-1802), among others, had speculated that all living things were related to one first living thing. What was new was Darwin's theory of how this evolution happened, i.e., the natural mechanisms he proposed for explaining evolution.

The way in which Darwin came first to be convinced of the reality of evolution is one of the most wonderful stories in the history of science. After being educated in medicine and then theology, including Paley's biological version of the Argument from Design, Darwin spent five years (1831-1836) traveling the world on the *HMS Beagle*, a survey vessel that mapped the entire coast of South America and sailed to Australia and Africa before returning to England. During his journey Darwin observed many different land and marine organisms, taking copious notes and collecting specimens. He was puzzled by certain strange dichotomies that one would not expect were God to have populated the earth through special creation. For example, Darwin's England was the perfect environment for rabbits, which were plentiful there. And yet his visit to Australia introduced him to a very similar environment but one with *no* rabbits. This puzzled Darwin; if special creation were true, then why would God not have placed rabbits in both environments?

The Galapagos Islands, part of the Republic of Ecuador, are an archipelago of volcanic islands distributed on either side of the equator in the Pacific Ocean west of continental Ecuador. The islands are known for their large number of endemic species and were studied by Charles Darwin during the second voyage of the HMS Beagle.

Above all, his experience in the *Galapagos Islands*, a string of volcanic islands off the coast of Ecuador, convinced him that evolution, not special creation, was the right account of biodiversity. There he collected bird specimens, which turned out to contain nine different species of finches. Darwin realized that these very different species, with their distinct characteristics, had probably evolved from one common ancestor species but had changed according to the different environments on the various islands where he discovered them. In 1845, Darwin summed up his view, "Seeing this gradation and diversity of structure in one small, intimately related group of birds, one might really fancy that from an original paucity of birds in this archipelago, one species had been taken and modified for different ends."[3]

While on the voyage Darwin also read the first volume of *Principles of Geology*, a book by the geologist **Charles Lyell** (1797-1875), which was given to him by the captain of the *Beagle*. In this book Darwin encountered Lyell's argument that the planet earth is indefinitely old. If that is true, speculated Darwin, perhaps the history of life on the planet is also extremely long, and life forms have been gradually evolving over that long history. Lyell's geology provided the framework of an ancient planet that Darwin needed to plausibly theorize about the evolution of life. The evolution of so many vastly different life forms would take an incredibly long time, which is precisely what Lyell's geology predicted.

Just as it was birds, the Galapagos finches, that "led" Darwin to see the reality of evolution, it was a popular English hobby involving another bird, the breeding of domestic pigeons, which helped him explain how it works. Breeders of pigeons and other animals take advantage of naturally occurring variations among members of a species. Even in the same litter of puppies, for example, there are variations in size, color, and behavioral traits. In each generation, a breeder selects those animals or plants that possess the traits that he wants and then allows only those to reproduce. Since traits tend to get passed on, gradually over many generations a new "breed" appears. In this way, for instance, domestic breeds of cattle and dogs were produced that were strikingly different from the wild varieties from

Darwin's Finches
"Seeing this gradation and diversity of structure in one small, intimately related group of birds, one might really fancy that from an original paucity of birds in this archipelago, one species had been taken and modified for different ends." (*The Voyage of the Beagle*, Darwin, 1839)

which they originally descended. The effectiveness of breeding is obvious when one compares poodles and dachshunds to wolves—all three species are members of the same genus, *Canis*, and yet their characteristics are drastically different.

Darwin realized that, in any domestic breeding process, there are two elements: *naturally occurring variation* within a species and *selection*. His breakthrough was his suggestion that selection does not require the artificial conditions of a farm or laboratory or the decisions of a plant or animal breeder. It can happen naturally (although more slowly) in the wild; hence, the name of the mechanism he proposed for evolution: *natural selection*.

Lonesome George, a tortoise discovered on the Galapagos Island Pinta in 1971, was the lone survivor of his species living on the island. When he died in 2012, he was over 100 years old, and his tortoise species then became extinct. The islands were once home to over 250,000 tortoises, which fell to just 3000, having been consumed by sailors from many countries over the centuries. Before conservation efforts, three species of the original fifteen were extinct.

Darwin pointed out that in the wild some naturally-occurring variations would make members of a species better adapted to the challenges and opportunities of their environment. The organisms that inherited such advantageous variations would tend to thrive and have more offspring than other members of the same species. Thus, the advantageous variations would spread through the population as generations passed; while, on the other hand, disadvantageous variations would tend to die out, since their inheritors would be at a disadvantage and have fewer offspring on average. The accumulation of small changes over many generations could produce new kinds of plants and animals. Some species would change more rapidly than others. Some would divide into two or more species, and some would die out altogether.[4] In every case it would depend on the complicated interactions of natural variation and the environment. Ultimately, Darwin argued, the world as we know it now, a world teeming with a multiplicity of species, would be the result. Natural selection, then, is "a process by which organisms better fitted to their environment [leave] more [offspring] with their characteristics to the next generation than less well adapted organisms."[5] The theory that species originate through an evolutionary process driven by natural selection acting on natural variation is called *Darwinian evolution* or *Darwinism*.

A Galapagos marine iguana with blue-footed boobies on the Galapagos Island Isabela. The Galapagos marine iguana is the only iguana species with the ability to forage in the sea.

Darwin's theory raised questions that could not be answered in his day. For example, why did not interbreeding among members of the same species blend their characteristics and over time eliminate all the "variations"? (For example, why did plant specimens with red flowers and specimens with white flowers in the same species not interbreed to produce eventually only pink flowers?) Another problem was that evolution required advantageous variations to get passed on with little or no change to the next generation, so that they would not be lost. But there also had to be something that *did* cause changes from one generation to the next, or else there would not be any way for "variations" to arise in the first place. Problems such as these could not be resolved until **Gregor Mendel**, an Augustinian monk, discovered the basic principles of heredity and thus inaugurated the science of genetics, a breakthrough that was not appreciated until a decade or so after his death. In the 1930's, Darwinian evolution and *Mendelian genetics* were combined into a more rigorous theory of evolution called *neo-Darwinism*. This "neo-Darwinian synthesis" is the basis of the modern understanding of the origin of species and is accepted by virtually all biologists today. According to the modern neo-Darwinian theory of evolution, the "variations" on which natural selection acts are *genetic variations* that arise by chance, for example, through mutations—or, as it is often put, "random genetic mutation." (Those little words "random" and "chance" have led to much misunderstanding and needless trouble, as we shall see.)

1. Evolution: Theory or Fact?

WHAT IS THE EVIDENCE FOR EVOLUTION? It comes from many directions. One source of evidence is the *fossil record*—the remains of long-dead organisms found by digging deep into the layers of rock and sediment under the earth's surface. As we saw in Chapter Five, **Blessed Nicholas Steno** showed that the deeper layers of sedimentary rock were deposited earlier, so that the fossil record gives us a "timeline" for the appearance of various kinds of plants and animals on earth. A second source is *comparative anatomy*, which studies the similarities and differences between species. A third is *biogeography*, which studies the geographical distribution of different plants and animals over time. A fourth, which has undergone the most explosive growth over the last forty years, is *genetics*. *Genes* are the blueprints for the construction of living bodies through the assembly of protein molecules, the "workhorses of life's processes," which are necessary for all the processes of physical life.[6] By comparing the "gene sequences" of different species, biologists can see deep relationships between them that are not apparent just by studying the creatures themselves. Furthermore, because scientists know something about how fast genetic mutations take place, they are able to work out genetic "timelines"; these coincide with timelines established from fossil records. There is now a huge amount of interlocking and mutually supporting evidence that confirms that all living things on earth, including human beings, are indeed related to each other in a giant "web" of life.

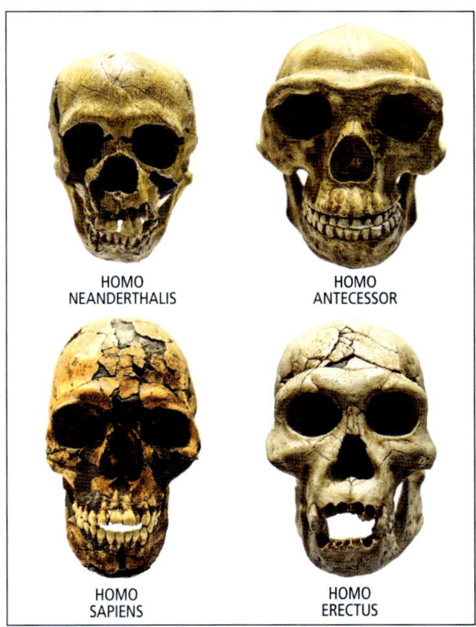

Fossil skulls of *Homo Neanderthalis, Homo Antecessor, Homo sapiens,* and *Homo Erectus*. The fossil record gives us a "timeline" for the appearance of various kinds of plants and animals on earth.

So, is evolution a "theory," or is it a fact? This question is misleading. In everyday speech the words "theory" and "fact" are sometimes used in contrast to each other: A theory is something uncertain and not yet proved, while a fact is something directly observed and accepted as true. From this, some people argue that the "theory of evolution," since it is still called a theory, is not yet regarded as well-established. For example while he was still a congressman from Indiana in 2002, future U.S. Vice President Mike Pence referred to the theory of evolution as unproven, and he urged American educators to consider teaching "other theories of the origins of species."[7]

However, this way of dismissing or casting doubt upon evolution is based on a misunderstanding of the way scientists use the word "theory." In science, a precise and coherent set of ideas for explaining some set of phenomena is called "a theory" of those phenomena. After it is rigorously tested and then generally accepted, it is often referred to as "*the* theory" of those phenomena. So, "the theory of relativity," "the BCS theory of superconductivity," and "the Big Bang Theory" are all regarded by scientists as very solidly established. The same is true of Darwin's theory of evolution.

In 1973, the geneticist **Theodosius Dobzhansky** (1900-1975) published a now famous article entitled "Nothing in Biology Makes Sense except in the Light of Evolution" that helps explain what a theory actually is. He quotes a Muslim sheik who, in 1966, asked the King of Saudi Arabia to suppress a "heresy" spreading through the land that the earth revolves around the sun. Dobzhansky quipped, "The good sheik evidently holds the Copernican theory to be a 'mere theory,' not a 'fact.'" He then explained that scientists accept the Copernican theory as true because "it makes sense of a multitude of facts" which have been directly observed.[8] In other words, a theory is how large groups of known facts are explained. He concludes by quoting the Jesuit priest and scientist **Teilhard de Chardin**: "Evolution is a light which illuminates all facts, a trajectory which all lines of thought must follow—this is what evolution is."[9]

Biological evolution has become the universally accepted theory for explaining the diversity of the world's living creatures. Humans and dandelions share 25% of the same genetic code.

So, is the theory of evolution factual? The answer is "yes" because it gives the best explanation for the facts, much like the theory of gravity gives the best explanation for the fact that, when I let go of an object, it drops to the earth at a particular velocity. Biological evolution has become the universally accepted theory for explaining the diversity of the world's living creatures, the gradation in life forms discovered in the fossil record, the discovery that humans and dandelions share 25% of the same genetic code, and countless other observed facts. The theory results from the evolutionary convergence of a number of indisputable facts and, for this reason, it shares in the certainty of the many facts upon which it depends and which it was formulated to explain.

2. Darwin's Faith, Darwin's Doubt

It is likely that Darwin ended his life as an agnostic.

MUCH SPECULATION HAS BEEN DEVOTED to Darwin's religious beliefs and whether he remained a faithful Christian to the end of his life. We know that he was baptized in the Church of England and was raised in a household in which prayer was an important component of family life. He also retained traditional Christian beliefs well into his young adulthood; he even earned a Bachelor's degree in Theology from Cambridge University. Yet, in his later years he expressed many doubts about the Christian faith. There is no evidence that Darwin ever became an atheist. In fact, at the end of his life he wrote that "in my most extreme fluctuations, I have never been an Atheist in the sense of denying the existence of a God..."[10] But, it is likely that he ended his life as an *agnostic*, a person who refrains from any judgment about God's existence.

Why did Darwin have doubts? In large part it was the result of his theological interpretation of what evolution tells us about reality and his inability to overcome the simplistic theological conceptions he had inherited from his upbringing and education that caused him to doubt the truth of Christianity. In his younger years he had been deeply impressed by Paley's biological version of the Argument from Design, an idea that no longer made sense in light of his theory (and, as we have seen, is really *not* the traditional Christian version of the argument). In his own words:

> **The old argument of design in nature, as given by Paley, which formerly seemed to me so conclusive, fails, now that the law of natural selection has been discovered. We can no longer argue that, for instance, the beautiful hinge of a bivalve shell [such as those of clams and oysters] must have been made by an intelligent being, like the hinge of a door by a man.**[11]

In this comparison of God to a carpenter designing and making a door hinge, we see a recurrence of the univocal conception of God, God as a mechanic or engineer, that also plagued **Sir Isaac Newton** (see Chapter Three). Darwin seems to have assumed that such a simplistic conception was the truly Christian conception, and so he concluded that the Christian faith itself was no longer believable in light of his discovery. Others, such as the Anglican priest and theologian **A.L. Moore**, recognized that Darwin's doubts arose not from his theory, which many saw as compatible with faith in a Creator, an opportunity to renew the Christian appreciation of divine wisdom, but from his flawed philosophical assumptions.[12] Darwin had shown that God is not a "how" explanation for living things, which is precisely correct from the Catholic point of view. But he had no other way of thinking about God's relationship to the universe to replace that conception.

"There is grandeur in this view of life, with its several powers, having been originally breathed by the Creator."
(*On the Origin of Species*, Darwin, 1860)

It seems that for a while Darwin resorted to deism to keep God in the picture, putting him at the beginning of life to perform a miracle to get it started. In the very last paragraph of *On the Origin of Species*, Darwin attributed all living things that we see now to evolution, but the very first being(s) to special creation:

> **It is interesting to contemplate a tangled bank, clothed with many plants of many kinds, with birds singing on the bushes, with various insects flitting about, and with worms crawling through the damp earth, and to reflect that these elaborately constructed forms, so different from each other, and dependent upon each other in so complex a manner, have all been produced by [evolutionary] laws acting around us.... There is grandeur in this view of life, with its several powers, having been originally breathed by the Creator into a few forms or into one; and that, whilst this planet has gone circling on according to the fixed law of gravity, from so simple a beginning endless forms most beautiful and most wonderful have been, and are being evolved.**[13]

In this poetic passage we see the sad contradiction of Darwin's theology. There is a deep respect and reverence for the integrity and beauty of nature ("endless forms most beautiful"), but there is also a deistic reference to God's activity at the historical beginning of life ("originally breathed by the Creator..."). He was unable to see that not just the first living thing, but indeed all things, are creatures of God, who causes them both to be (creation *ex nihilo*) and also to be causes of each other. Here we can recall what we learned in Chapter Three from **St. Thomas Aquinas**, that God is "the Cause hidden from every human being." God is not merely the cause of the first life form but of "the all," establishing the universe as a vast system of real causes and effects, all with their own integrity.

Darwin, much like Jill and her companions in *The Silver Chair*, failed to correctly interpret the signs he was given. The signs of God's creative activity in the beautiful, endless forms of life produced through evolution became a stumbling block, rather than a stepping-stone.

In summary, Darwin, much like Jill and her companions in *The Silver Chair*, failed to correctly interpret the signs he was given. Therefore, the signs of God's creative activity in the beautiful, endless forms of life produced through evolution became a stumbling block, rather than a stepping-stone, for this great scientist.

Darwin's doubt was and is still reflected by the fierce controversy among those who, like him, are incapable of thinking beyond the "how" to the "why." While many religious people accepted Darwin's theory of evolution, there were also many who did not. Indeed, there are many Christians today who bitterly oppose Darwinian evolution. As we have seen, some of them think it is contrary to the teaching of the Book of Genesis; others have theological or philosophical objections to it. (We shall look at some of these objections and the answers to them more closely later in this chapter.) On the other side, many scientific atheists have interpreted Darwinian evolution in reductionist and materialist ways. They have argued that Darwinian evolution has unavoidable atheistic implications and have used it as the basis of a militant antireligious ideology, sometimes called "evolutionism." (One could call this ideology "atheist Darwinism," "reductionist Darwinism," or "materialist Darwinism.")

Evolution has frequently been used to attack religion ever since Darwin's day, and this has frightened many religious believers into thinking that evolution is indeed incompatible with Christianity. Their misguided counterattacks are taken by atheists as evidence that Christians are opposed to science. In other words, believing opponents of evolution and evolutionist opponents of faith have tended to feed off of each other and to provoke each other to more and more extreme positions. Ironically, as we will see in a later section, they have something important in common—they suffer from the same misunderstandings of the Christian faith.

C. The Catholic Church, the Theory of Evolution, and the Human Soul

HOW HAS THE CATHOLIC CHURCH RESPONDED to the theory of evolution? The "short answer" is that the Church has never condemned either the idea of evolution or the Darwinian theory of it, and Catholics have always been free either to accept or reject it. The "long answer" requires that we make some distinctions. The first distinction is between "evolution" and "evolutionism," i.e., between the actual *science* of evolution and the radically reductionist and materialist *philosophy* or *ideology* that some people base upon it. Unfortunately, since several leading evolutionary biologists have promoted such views in their own writings, some people find it hard to see the difference between the actual science and the "spin" that atheists put on it. In spite of that, we must always be careful, along with the Catholic Church herself, to make that distinction. Occasionally one will hear Catholic theologians criticize "Darwinism"; however, in those cases, they are usually using the term to mean atheistic evolutionism, not the scientific theory of evolution. Unfortunately, the use of the same term by different people to mean different things has caused many misunderstandings.

A second distinction must be made between the various parts of the theory of evolution. There are three: (a) the idea that living species evolved from other, earlier species, (b) the Darwinian or neo-Darwinian mechanism of evolution (i.e., natural selection), and (c) the idea that humanity itself is the product of evolution.

The Church has never seen any objection, difficulty, or problem, from the point of view of Catholic doctrine, with either (a) or (b). The basic reality of evolution and the mechanism of natural selection are, theologically, not controversial for Catholics. However, the evolution of the human race (c) does raise significant theological and philosophical questions, for it touches on deep questions about the nature of human beings. It is a dogma of the Catholic faith that man is both physical and spiritual and that the spiritual is not "reducible" to matter. One cannot, therefore, ever hope to completely explain a human being just from the point of view of physics, chemistry, or biology. We are biological organisms, to be sure, but we are also something more. The Church, as well as many philosophers and theologians, have always insisted that the human "spiritual soul," not being merely physical, cannot possibly arise as the result of physical processes alone. Even in procreation, the spiritual soul of the child is not produced by a simple rearrangement of atoms, as happens when sperm and ovum combine. In the same way, the spiritual souls of the first human beings were not the result of a merely biological process. In other words, *the human spiritual soul did not evolve.*

Pope Ven. Pius XII (1876-1958) taught in 1950 that the evolution of the human body was an allowable scientific hypothesis.

This leaves the question of whether the human body evolved. From the time of Darwin, Catholic theologians saw this as an "open question," about which no definite conclusion could be drawn from Catholic doctrine. So, when it comes to evolution as a matter of biology, Catholics have never had a quarrel with it. This is why the Church never attempted to prevent evolution from being taught in Catholic schools. There was never a Catholic equivalent to the famous Scopes Trial of 1925, in which a science teacher was brought to trial for teaching about evolution.

1. Church Pronouncements on Evolution

THERE WAS NO OFFICIAL CATHOLIC TEACHING at all on evolution for almost a hundred years after Darwin published his theory. The first official statement by the Church that touched on evolutionary questions was the encyclical letter *Humani Generis* of Venerable Pius XII, written in 1950. So, from 1859 to 1950, one has to talk about the opinions of theologians, rather than explicit Church doctrine, when it comes to the Catholic reception of evolutionary theory. During this period there are many examples of openness, even at the level of general religious instruction (i.e., catechesis).

Fr. Erich Wasmann (1859-1931)
"It [evolution] is in perfect agreement with the Christian conception of the universe."

For example, the 1907 version of the famous *Catholic Encyclopedia*, in its article "Evolution" by the Austrian entomologist and Catholic priest, **Fr. Erich Wasmann** (1859-1931), summarized the theory of evolution as it stood at that time, and then said, "This is the gist of the theory of evolution as a scientific hypothesis. It is in perfect agreement with the Christian conception of the universe."[14] A very popular book was published in the 1920s called *The Question Box*, which explained Catholic beliefs in a question and answer format. It was written by a priest and carried an *Imprimatur* and *Nihil Obstat*, which are formal acknowledgments by the Church that a book contains nothing contrary to Catholic doctrine. In answer to the question "May a Catholic believe in evolution?" the book said, "As the Church has made no pronouncement upon evolution, Catholics are perfectly free to accept evolution, either as a scientific hypothesis or as a philosophical speculation."[15] This has consistently been the attitude of the Church from the first decades of the twentieth century down to our own day.

In 1950, **Venerable Pius XII** (1876-1958) taught in *Humani Generis* that the evolution of the human spiritual soul was incompatible with Catholic doctrine but that the evolution of the human body was an allowable scientific hypothesis. In 1986, **St. John Paul II** reaffirmed Ven. Pius XII's openness in an even more positive way. While Ven. Pius XII had not forbidden research and discussions regarding evolution, St. John Paul II went further by declaring: "There are no difficulties, from the viewpoint of the doctrine of the faith, in explaining the origin of man in regard to the body by means of the theory of evolution." Like Ven. Pius XII, he affirmed that the human spiritual soul is not the result of physical processes alone: "The doctrine of faith affirms that man's spiritual soul is created directly by God.... The human soul, on which man's humanity definitively depends, cannot emerge from matter, since the soul is of a spiritual nature."[16]

In 1996, St. John Paul II addressed the Pontifical Academy of Sciences regarding evolution. Looking back to Ven. Pius XII's statement in 1950, the Pope declared that the increasing probability of biological evolution revealed through new findings "lead us toward recognition of evolution as more than a hypothesis." This increase in certainty about evolution was the result of "different scholarly disciplines" all converging in their discoveries on the conclusion that evolution is the best explanation for the history of life. The strength of the theory had been bolstered by various researchers in different fields all discovering independently of one another the same phenomena which point to the truth of evolution.[17]

St. John Paul II also commented on the atheistic interpretations of the theory of evolution. Some of these are "materialist and reductionist" ideas that are not compatible with the truth about God

The Olduvai Gorge in Tanzania is one of the most important paleoanthropological sites in the world. The fossil remains of *Paranthropus boisei* (once classified as *Australopithicus boisei*) was first discovered here by anthropologist Mary Leakey in 1959. The well-preserved cranium was dated to 1.75 million years ago. *Paranthropus boisei* proved to be a scientific treasure, especially when Richard Leakey suggested it was the first hominin species to use stone tools.

and the human person revealed in the Christian faith.[18] The Pope rejected certain ideologies that make man's spiritual reality nothing more than the product of physical forces or which describe the human soul as epiphenomenal. *Epiphenomenalism* is the idea that spirit exists along with the body, is dependent upon matter, and ceases to exist when the body ceases to exist. These theories, and others, do not do justice to the truth about human beings as the image and likeness of God.[19]

At this point, St. John Paul II offered a crucial insight regarding the human person: "With man, we find ourselves facing a different *ontological* order—an *ontological* leap." "Ontological" refers to existence, and "ontological order" is another way of saying "level of existence." The Pope is saying that the "leap" to rationality and spirituality that occurred at the origins of our species puts us on a fundamentally higher level of existence than other animals. In other words, human origins involved a leap to a higher level, in which the animal world was brought up to a qualitatively new way of existing. We will explore this in more detail in the next few chapters.

More recently, **Pope Benedict XVI** reaffirmed St. John Paul II's teaching in a question-and-answer session with priests on July 24, 2007. He specifically rejected the opinion that "whoever believes in the Creator cannot think about evolution and whoever affirms evolution must exclude God." Calling this position "absurd," he remarked as follows: "There is a great deal of scientific proof in favor of evolution, which appears as a reality that we must see and that enriches our knowledge of life and of being as such." He also critiqued scientism, which embraces biological evolution but rejects complementary philosophical and theological explanations:

> **The doctrine of evolution does not answer everything and does not answer the great philosophical question: Where does everything come from? And how does everything take a path that ultimately leads to the person? It seems to me that it is very important that reason opens up even more, that it sees this information [about evolution], but that it also sees that this information is not enough to explain all of reality.[20]**

Now that we have reviewed the theory of evolution and the Church's teaching about it, let us consider some misinterpretations of the theory.

D. Philosophical and Theological Misunderstandings and Misinterpretations of Evolution

THERE ARE MANY PEOPLE WHO HAVE NO TROUBLE accepting the idea of evolution or Darwin's theory of natural selection, but they find it hard to accept the idea that human beings are the product of evolution. The evolution of human beings does indeed raise special questions because of our spiritual nature. However, there are many people who see an incompatibility between Christianity and Darwin's theory *even as an account of the origin of nonhuman species.* We will see that there are two basic reasons. The first involves misunderstandings of Christian theology—misunderstandings sadly embraced by many Christians. The second involves assumptions about the implications of Darwin's theory.

The most obvious theological mistake concerns the way the Book of Genesis should be understood. We have already seen in Chapter Four why it is an error to read Genesis as if it were a science textbook. It is wrong to read it that way because that is not how it was intended either by its human authors or by its divine Author. As **Pope Leo XIII** said in his 1893 encyclical *Providentissimus Deus*: "The sacred writers did not intend to teach men . . . the essential nature of the things of the visible universe."[21] Nevertheless, many non-Catholic Christians do read the Book of Genesis in this "literalistic" way, and this is one of the primary reasons why they reject evolution. We will come back yet again to the Book of Genesis later in this chapter to discuss how it should be read, and also in the next chapter, when we consider the Second Creation Account. In doing so, we will see that there is nothing in either that excludes the possibility of evolution.

Pope Leo XIII (1810-1903)
Providentissimus Deus is an encyclical letter issued by Pope Leo XIII on November 18, 1893. In it, he reviewed the history of the study of the Bible from the time of the Church Fathers to 1893. He also addressed the issues of apparent contradictions between the Bible and physical science and how such apparent contradictions could be resolved.

The second theological mistake is more subtle, and usually involves three mistaken assumptions: (1) that chance is incompatible with divine Providence, (2) that natural selection is incompatible with Divine Design and Purpose, and (3) that natural explanations eliminate the possibility of the creative activity of God in the universe. Let us consider each of these in turn.

1. Chance *Versus* Divine Providence

CHANCE PLAYS AN IMPORTANT ROLE in Darwinian theory. *Chance* is the intersection of two or more lines of causality that are independent of each other, in a way that is accidental and unintended by the agents involved.[22] Species evolve because of "genetic variations" and the effects of "natural selection." Biologists explain genetic variations as "random" occurrences, or as a matter of chance. Those genetic variations produce variations in the organisms themselves and affect the way they interact with their environments. Those environments, being very complicated, also involve chance in many ways. This is why the process of evolution is often presented as a blind, blundering, trial-and-error process *and, on the level of natural causes, that is not an incorrect way to think about it*. The question arises whether this somehow contradicts the teaching that an all-knowing God is governing the universe and that all things in it are part of a "divine plan," which is called divine Providence. In other words, if we agree with evolutionary biologists that "chance" plays a large role in evolution and that genetic mutations are "random," are we denying the doctrine of God's governance of all creatures?

The simplest way to answer this is to quote **St. Thomas Aquinas**. In his long treatise *Summa Contra Gentiles*, there is a chapter (Book III, chapter 74) with the title "That divine Providence does not exclude fortune and chance," in which the great theologian argues exactly that. **St. Augustine** writes in his book, *The City of God*, that no one can in this life "escape being tossed about by chance and accident."[23] Scripture itself speaks of the role of chance in the world. In a very famous passage, the Book of Ecclesiastes says, "I saw that under the sun the race is not to the swift, nor the battle to the strong, nor bread to the wise, nor riches to the intelligent, nor favor to the men of skill; but time and chance happens to them all" (Eccl 9:11).

Of course, all these texts were written many centuries before Darwin's theory came along. But that is precisely the point: It did not take Darwin's theory to show people that many things in this world depend on chance. Anyone who reads history knows this. Indeed, anyone who has lived knows this. So, really, "random genetic variation" does not raise any new theological questions on this point that had not been previously known and addressed. It is the same question that St. Thomas Aquinas analyzed in his treatise more than 700 years ago. Nevertheless, new or not, it is an important question. What is the answer?

Accepting the presence of chance or random events in evolution, as well as in human life, is not a denial of God's Providence. Even in the "accidental" elements involved in life, God is still the Lord of both history and the universe.

The first step is to recognize that chance is to some extent in the eye of the beholder. If someone deals a poker hand from a deck of cards, it is a matter of chance which cards will turn up. One might even calculate the "odds" of getting certain hands. But, to someone who knows exactly the order of cards in the deck, the outcome of the deal is not at all uncertain or a matter of chance. He knows exactly what hand will be dealt. So what is chance for one person need not be chance for another. For God, who knows everything, nothing is a matter of chance. That is why the Book of Proverbs says, "The lot is cast into the lap, but the decision is wholly from the LORD" (Prv 16:33).

In summary, accepting the presence of chance or random events in evolution, as well as in human life, is not a denial of God's Providence. Even in the "accidental" elements involved in life, God is still the Lord of both history and the universe.

2. Natural Selection *Versus* Divine Purpose

BEFORE DARWIN, WHEN PEOPLE ASSUMED that each type of plant and animal had been directly crafted by the hand of God through "special creation," it was easier to say that living things, including ourselves, were "designed." Moreover, since God presumably had a reason for making each creature and for making it exactly the way it is, one could also say that each living thing had a "purpose." Darwin's theory seemed to undercut that way of thinking. Rather than being crafted directly by the hand of God, species were crafted by the blind and impersonal forces of random genetic mutations and natural selection. Both design and purpose seemed to go out the window.

The fact that something involved natural processes that have random outcomes in no way implies that it has no purpose. There are countless examples in nature whereby nature accomplishes its purposes by "playing the odds."

The fact that a process involves natural processes that involve random outcomes in no way implies that it has no purpose. To help us understand this point, the philosopher **Dennis Bonnette** invites us to envision a roulette game.[24] The game of roulette depends on it being impossible for the players to predict exactly where the ball will land on any given spin of the roulette wheel. But this is not because the process, which involves chance, is without plan or purpose. In fact, everything is carefully orchestrated. The ball is given a round shape to allow it to bounce around the table. The wheel is carefully crafted so as to facilitate the bouncing of the ball at the beginning of the spin when the speed of the turning of the wheel is strongest and to facilitate the landing of the ball in a numbered slot when the speed slows to a certain point. The whole set-up is designed to operate in a precise way, in accordance with the laws of physics. Not only would a physicist be able to explain in general terms how the roulette wheel functions, but he or she also would be able to tell you exactly where a particular ball would land given the exact force of the spin, the exact dimensions of the ball, the diameter and shape of the wheel, etc.

We see, then, a situation that involves at the same time both chance and purpose, and where in fact chance is involved in that purpose. The *purpose* is that of a certain kind of game. That game cannot be played unless *chance* is a part of it. (It is a "game of chance.") In order for the roulette wheel to produce the required "chance" or "random" events, it has to be *designed* in a certain way.

There are a countless number of similar examples in nature, where nature accomplishes its purpose by "playing the odds." Many insects produce large numbers of larvae, and most will be eaten by fish, birds, or other predators. Whether a particular larva gets eaten is a matter of chance, and the chances of any one's survival is very small. However, the small chance of survival of the individual larvae is compensated for by their large numbers. And the large numbers of larvae are not an accident. That is part of the "survival strategy" (an unconscious one, to be sure) of the species. In human procreation, many sperm are produced; the chance of any one sperm fertilizing an ovum is extremely small. In each of these examples, there is an evident "natural purpose," namely, reproduction. Now, if nature can so arrange things that many sperm are sent in search of an ovum, in order that one of them might "win through" and produce an offspring, why should not God will that many genetic mutations occur in nature, so that a few of them might "win through" to make a new and interesting species? If we can see "purpose" in one case, then why not in the other?

Sometimes, then, chance or randomness do not reflect a lack of order, design, or guiding purpose, but is a part of a larger overarching order, design, and purpose. Unfortunately, many people have jumped from the mere fact that chance plays an important role in the world—which, of course, everyone has always known—to the idea that the world is entirely a matter of chance, that there is no ultimate meaning or purpose to anything, and that the universe is "unguided" and "unplanned."

Let us ask, then, why God might have decided to create a world in which "chance" plays a role in his plan. Professor **Michael Tkacz** of Gonzaga University noted, "One of the reasons Thomas Aquinas thought it was necessary to acknowledge the chance element in nature is that it is the way that novelty is introduced into nature."[25] Think again of human procreation. Because we reproduce sexually, so that genes from two people are combined to produce each offspring, there is a constant "reshuffling" of the genetic deck. This means that new and interesting individuals are constantly being produced. No two people are exactly alike. So the chance that is built into the system of human procreation has the effect of drawing forth ever new possibilities and thus helping to realize the rich possibilities of the human species. In the same way, the system of evolution is constantly producing new kinds of creatures, thus realizing the wonderful possibilities of the material world. This conception of chance and contingency drawing forth novel forms is certainly consistent with the role of chance in neo-Darwinian evolutionary theory.

The chance that is built into the system of human procreation has the effect of drawing forth ever new possibilities and thus helping to realize the rich possibilities of the human species.

Another reason emerges if we ask ourselves what a world without chance would be like. It would be a world in which everything would happen in simple and predictable ways. One of the reasons that "chance" events arise is that the world is a complicated place in which many things are going on that have nothing directly to do with each other. For example, my life follows a certain pattern, and your life follows a certain pattern. But, my life and yours are only loosely connected with each other. So, when these two patterns intersect—for example, if I run into you on the street—it appears as a "chance event." It is not an event that could have been predicted by just knowing the pattern of my activities. In order for there to be no chance events, everything would have to be closely related to everything else in a highly organized way. That is, the world would have to have just a *single pattern*. That would translate into a world in which we could not choose to impose our own patterns on things. It would be a world without freedom. It would be a completely regimented world in which we could not have any meaningful activity of our own. Our God is consistent; he made the world for the sake of free human beings, and so he made a world that supports freedom—an evolving world.

3. Natural Explanations *Versus* Divine Creation

SOME PEOPLE WHO ATTACK EVOLUTION do so because it is *naturalistic*. Naturalism in its extreme form says that *only* natural explanations are valid. In other words, it denies any supernatural reality, which is wrong. But some people who oppose extreme naturalism go too far in the other direction. They think any attempt to find natural explanations is an attack on God. They think that the more we can explain "naturally," the less there is for God to do, thus the less there is for which to praise God. For example, if it is said that an insect species arose by the natural processes of evolution, such people see this as a rival explanation to saying that God is the Creator of the world and everything in it. They imagine that we must then subtract the insect from the list of things that God created.

God's use of natural causes, including "chance," reveals his power, intelligence, and skill in an even greater way than if he directly caused all things. The greater the powers and potentialities that God has implanted in nature, the more it shows forth his power and greatness.

In other words, such people see nature and God as being in competition with each other. The more nature does, the less God is doing. As was explained in Chapter Three, this mistake is based on a failure to understand the principle of double agency and the fundamentally important notions of primary and secondary causality. If we say that a character in a play kills another character to get revenge, this does not take anything away from the author of the play as an explanation of the events in the play. In fact, the more we understand what the characters are doing on their own terms, at the level of cause and effect *within* the play, the *more* we understand the mind of the playwright, and the more we know what he or she was up to in writing the play. The primary cause (the author) creates his or her story *through* the actions of the secondary causes (the characters). That is why it would obviously make no sense to ask, "Does Voldemort try to kill Harry Potter for revenge, or because J.K. Rowling wrote the book that way?" The answer is "*Both*." And, in fact, the first is only true because the second is true. In the same way, it is simply incorrect to ask, "Does this insect species exist because it evolved, or because God created the universe that way?" Again, the answer is "*Both*."

Of course, God can act directly without making use of secondary causes. He could create an insect species out of thin air, rather than have it evolve by natural processes. However, God's use of natural causes, including "chance," reveals his power, intelligence, and skill in an even greater way than if he intervened miraculously. The *Catholic Encyclopedia* article on evolution mentioned above put it this way:

> **If God produced the universe by a single creative act of his will, then its natural development by laws implanted in it by its Creator is to the greater glory of**

> **his divine power and wisdom.... St. Thomas says, "the potency of the cause is greater the more remote the effects to which it extends"; and Suarez [says], "God does not interfere directly with the natural order where secondary causes suffice to produce the intended effect."[26]**

The Church has always taught that there is a natural order that comes from God, and the *greater* the powers and potentialities that God has implanted in nature, the *more* it shows forth his power and greatness.

E. Remembering the Signs: The First Creation Account and Biological Evolution

GOD'S TRUTH IS CERTAIN BEYOND AND BEFORE ALL OTHER TRUTHS and is the very certainty on which our life is based. As we have seen, rather than holding fast to God's Word given in Sacred Scripture and Sacred Tradition as transmitted by the Church, Darwin experienced a crisis of faith because the signs of God's loving, creative activity did not appear as he expected. In our own quest to rediscover faith on the frontiers of science, let us also look at the testimony of Sacred Scripture. But, unlike Darwin, let us approach the Book of Genesis for what it is, not a scientific account but a symbolic, theological account. From this perspective, evolutionary science can help us better appreciate the theological picture of creation given in Genesis.

1. Divine Openness and Evolution: The Spirit of God, the Giver of Life (Genesis 1:1-3)

HOW DOES GOD BRING ABOUT HIS CREATION? Many atheists and even many Christians seem able to envision only one way in which the production of living creatures could be the work of God—by special creation, like Geppetto building Pinocchio on his woodworking table.[27] Confronted with the evidence that living creatures did not arise in that way, some turn against religion and some turn against the scientific evidence. But, when we turn to Sacred Scripture, we find that it offers us a much more subtle account of creation.

We should attribute to the Holy Spirit the openness of the universe to new, unexpected things.

The beginning of the First Creation Account gives us the first clue in our quest to rescue Darwin's biology from his flawed philosophy. In its first verse it declares, *"In the beginning God created the heavens and the earth . . . the Spirit of God was moving over the face of the waters. And God said . . ."* The "Spirit of God," later to be revealed not simply as God's power but as a true divine Person, the Third Person of the Blessed Trinity, is portrayed here as the agent of God's activity in creation. Before God speaks any command, the Spirit of God is ready to act.

As we saw in Chapter One, we should attribute to the Holy Spirit the openness of the universe to new, unexpected things, to a free flourishing of God's creatures. As **St. Paul** says, "Where the Spirit of the Lord is, there is *freedom*" (2 Cor 3:17). The new level of complexity that comes about when inanimate matter transitions to become life, in its first form and in all those forms that gradually arise from it, is a free unfolding, full of surprises and unexpected directions. In the words of biologist **Darrel Falk**:

> **Just as God built freedom into the nation of Israel, and just as God [builds] freedom into our lives today, so freedom may well be a central component of God's biological world as well.... God's Spirit guides the progression of life. His presence is never far from creation, just as it is never far from the events of my life. Nonetheless, God respects my freedom and (I suspect) values freedom in the rest of creation as well.[28]**

American biologist Darrel R. Falk (1946-)
"God's Spirit guides the progression of life."

Falk uses the word "freedom" in this passage, but, when referring to the freedom of the "biological world," he does not mean it in the sense of free will, a capacity that only our species has. Instead, he is using the word to describe the reality of secondary causality: God grants every created nature the ability to have its own proper way of moving and its own proper effect on the surrounding world.

It is interesting to think about *abiogenesis*—the origin of the first living thing(s)—from the perspective of the Holy Spirit, the Gift-Love of God, enabling creation to reach newer levels: first self-replicating life, then multicellularity, then organisms with body plans, then vertebrates, then those with complex brains and nervous systems with the ability to learn and remember, and, finally, human beings. The issue of life's origin is actually not a question of biology alone but also of chemistry, of the right chemical processes and environmental conditions needed for life to emerge. Most scientists think that a convergence of natural causes somehow resulted in the first living cell (or cells) from which all living species eventually evolved, though how this happened is not yet fully understood.

Scientists have known since the 1950s that certain kinds of nonliving molecules can spontaneously combine, under the right conditions, to produce important "biological building blocks" that are required for living cells, such as amino acids.[29] This discovery encouraged the hope that abiogenesis would soon be understood. However, it has turned out to be a much harder problem than people had thought.[30] Many even hypothesize that life had to emerge elsewhere in the universe and travel to earth inside comets or asteroids in order to allow enough time for this process to occur naturally. The first evidence of cellular life on earth is found in rocks almost exactly as old as the planet itself, which presents a rather unclear picture as to how the highly improbable prospects of the development of life could have occurred so quickly, if at all. Of course, scientists may someday find a mechanism that shows the probabilities to be much higher than they now appear. But let us suppose that they do not.

The seeming impossibility of abiogenesis ceases to be a problem if we keep in mind that the Spirit's loving presence to creation empowers, but does not replace, natural causes. Even extremely small chances that are effectively zero can work out through divine Providence.[31] God, who not only causes all things to be but also to act as true causes,[32] can determine that a "vanishingly small" possibility such as life emerging *will* happen—not through a miracle, but through the natural order he gave to his creation to bring it about. Faith in the Holy Spirit, "the Lord and Giver of Life," therefore, gives a compelling theological perspective on the origin of life.

2. Divine Order and Evolution: The Son-*Logos*, the Word

THE FIRST VERSE OF GENESIS does not only mention the Spirit of God. In a subtle way it indicates another divine Person when it refers to God speaking: *"And God said..."* The Word of God, his Son-*Logos*, is the Father's perfect "utterance," and so can be understood as the divine wisdom involved in creation, the one who gives the process of evolution its fundamental order, its patterns.

The Word of God, his Son-*Logos*, is the Father's perfect "utterance," and so can be understood as the divine wisdom involved in creation.

Perhaps the best evidence of divine wisdom in biological evolution can be found in the rather recent discovery of RNA, DNA, and the genetic code present in all living things. RNA and DNA offer compelling evidence of divine order. Modern science has revealed that the presence of RNA and/or DNA in living things acts as the blueprint for their biological structures and characteristic activities. In the development of any living being, the formation of each and every cell is subject to the transmission of a code—the genetic code. The genetic code in DNA is duplicated and then copied from DNA to RNA. Then the code is conveyed to the amino acids that are assembled into proteins.

What is often overlooked is the fact that *the genetic code is an intelligible code* in which information is coordinated in a way much like human writing, substituting the pen, paper, and alphabet with amino acids, proteins, and DNA. According to **Antony Flew**, a very famous twentieth-century atheist who ultimately came to believe in a creator, the origins of the genetic code, which is nothing less than "a system of coded chemistry," cannot be explained without reference to an intelligent source.[33] Meaningful information that emerges from collections of mindless molecules gives us a glimpse into the presence of divine rationality, the Son-*Logos*, in creation. In the words of **Francis Collins**, the former director of the Human Genome Project, the genetic code is "the language of God," a set of intelligent commands from the Creator. Without the genetic code, evolution would be impossible.

The Son-*Logos* is "the word through whom God made the universe." Divine Revelation reveals that from all eternity the Son is God's perfect wisdom, and so we find that life is the result of an intelligible "message," that it follows a pattern. Genomes are like words uttered by the Word of God, the Son, who became flesh in Jesus Christ and who in his Incarnation shared in the human genome that modern science has discovered. The presence of the Trinity to creation, making it capable of his purposes for it, gives us the framework for understanding the compatibility of the scientific theory of evolution and the Christian, biblical doctrine of creation.

3. Evolutionary Biology as the Great "Amen"

THE FATHER'S OVERSHADOWING LOVE; the Holy Spirit; and the Father's perfect utterance, the Son, indicated within the first few verses of the First Creation Account, give us strong reasons for expecting something like evolution within God's creation, in which freedom and order go hand in hand. But, when we read further, we see an even more direct indication. We learn that the various living species are commanded by God to be real causes, *collaborating* with him because of the power he gives them to act. In the poetic, prescientific language of the First Creation Account, God *speaks*, but it is his creation that *acts*.

On the third day of creation, God commands the earth to act, saying "Let the earth put forth vegetation" (Gn 1:11). On the fifth day (Gn 1:20-23), God does not act; he commands the water to act, saying "Let the waters bring forth swarms of living creatures." On the sixth day (Gn 1:24-31), God commands the earth to act again, saying, "Let the earth bring forth living creatures according to their kinds." What we see, therefore, is God working *through* his creation. Thanks to his commands, the earth is active in the production of living creatures, in which water and earth are active agents. In the Genesis account, water and earth produce living creatures, which is very hospitable to Darwin's idea that the environment provides the context and the stimulating force for the production of changes in living creatures and the proliferation of numerous species. Such a scenario does not imply the absence of God; it reveals a world actively responding to God's command and God's active presence.

Creation of the Animals (detail) by Tintoretto.

God creates by commanding the world. The world acts in creation by unfolding the potential with which God suffuses it. What is produced is a *cooperation* in creation, in which creatures, even "the most elementary particles of matter," participate in God's power and purpose. God makes creatures his collaborators "by giving them the laws, the powers and the capacity for acting on their own."[34]

Our Christian faith offers us a word that captures this relationship between God and creatures, a word used throughout the Christian liturgy and in personal prayer. It is the Hebrew word AMEN, a word that means "let it be," or "so be it." As the *Catechism of the Catholic Church* teaches, "*Amen* expresses solidity, trustworthiness, faithfulness..." It goes on to declare that it expresses "*both* God's faithfulness towards us *and* our trust in him."[35] The "amen," the "let it be," of believers is the expression of their willingness and openness to participate in God's plan.

Reading the First Creation Account in light of evolution reveals that it is as if even unconscious matter and nonrational, living creatures display a kind of "amen" in their acting according to their natures and capacities. Only when God says his own "Let there be," as he is portrayed doing throughout the First Creation Account, can creatures respond with the "So be it!" of their participation in God's plan. The greatness of the biblical account of creation is that, long before Darwin, it sees the both/and of an originating, empowering, "Amen" of God and the responding, empowered, participating "amen" of the universe, its elements, and each level of creaturely existence.

Some atheists have seen the long length of the universe's existence without life as a sign that there is no divine craftsman behind it. When we remember the signs, we can see that this long period is something very different and much more amazing—it is a long chorus of response, a growing sustained and magnificent "amen" offered by the universe in response to God's powerful Word and omnipresent Spirit. The billions and billions of years of cosmic history simply reveal that it takes finite creatures a very long time to pronounce their "amen," while God's "Amen" is perfect and eternal, taking no time at all.

F. Believing the Signs: The Christian Faith and the Origins of Living Things

1. Evolution and the Example of Great Believers

DARWIN DESERVES CREDIT for being a pioneer of the scientific theory of evolution as we know it today. But long before Darwin, as well as after him, many Christian thinkers have understood the creation of living things as being the result not of "special creation" but of the unfolding of what God has implanted in matter, i.e., by God's acting through secondary causes that cooperate with and bring to completion his plan of creation.

The great bishop and theologian **St. Gregory of Nyssa** wrote a dialogue AD 380 entitled *On the Soul and Resurrection* in which he envisions a discussion between himself and his older sister **Macrina**, who is on her deathbed and to whom he refers with great love and respect as "the Teacher." He is puzzled by the many different qualities and powers human beings have and whether they should be considered as evidence of many different human souls, rather than just one. Referring to the First Creation Account, Macrina offers this interpretation:

> **Scripture informs us that the Deity proceeded by a sort of graduated and ordered advance to the creation of man. After the foundations of the universe were laid, as the history records, man did not appear on the earth at once; but the creation of the animals preceded his, and the plants preceded them.... [Therefore man] took up into himself every single form of life, both that of plants and that which is seen in animals.... But his faculty of thought and reason is incommunicable, and is a peculiar gift in our nature, to be considered by itself.[36]**

Many historians today consider St. Augustine to be the real father of the idea of evolution.

Of course, this is a simplistic account; it offers no explanation for *how* human beings "took up" all these powers. But, the fact remains that some unity between all life forms and human beings at their origins was envisioned by this great Catholic thinker.

As we saw briefly in Chapter Five, **St. Augustine** (AD 354-430), the greatest theologian of the early Church, went even further. He held that all things were produced by God in a single instant, taking the form of "rational seeds" that matured over time into actual living creatures.[37] Many historians today consider St. Augustine to be the real father of the *idea* of evolution, as distinct from the scientific theory. **St. Thomas Aquinas** (AD 1225-1274), the greatest theologian of the Middle Ages, acknowledged that, on the surface, the notion of special (successive) creation seemed to be more in accord with what the Book of Genesis says. However, he concluded that St. Augustine's explanation was more in accord with reason and was preferable as an explanation of the meaning of Genesis.[38]

Theodosius Dobzhansky (1900-1975)
"It is a blunder to mistake the Holy Scriptures for elementary textbooks of astronomy, geology, biology, and anthropology."

In modern times, great and influential Catholic thinkers such as **St. John Henry Newman** (1801-1890) and **G.K. Chesterton** (1874-1936) have been able to see the signs of God's creative activity in the evolutionary hypothesis. Newman taught that God lets his creative action develop through secondary causes. God imparted, said Newman, "certain laws to matter millions of ages ago, which have surely and precisely worked out... those effects which he... proposed." He concluded that "Mr. Darwin's theory need not be atheistic, be it true or not; it may simply be suggesting a large idea of divine... skill."[39] For his part, Chesterton noted that "if evolution simply means that a positive thing called an ape turned very slowly into a positive thing called a man, then it is stingless;... for a personal God might just as well do things slowly as quickly, especially if, like the Christian God, he were outside time."[40] We will see in the next chapter that we now know that we share a common ancestor with apes and did not evolve from them; however, the basic point remains valid.

One important example of a believing scientist who embraced the notion of an evolutionary origin for living creatures is **Theodosius Dobzhansky** (1900-1975), a Russian Orthodox Christian who was hailed by **Stephen Jay Gould** as one of the greatest evolutionary geneticists of his generation. As we saw above, Dobzhansky is famous for declaring that "nothing in biology makes sense except in the light of evolution." But he also saw nothing in the theory to be contrary to creation as it is portrayed in the Bible: "Does the evolutionary doctrine clash with religious faith? It does not. It is a blunder to mistake the Holy Scriptures for elementary textbooks of astronomy, geology, biology, and anthropology. Only if symbols are construed to mean what they are not intended to mean can there arise imaginary, insoluble [unsolvable] conflicts."[41]

While not proving evolutionary biology to be true, these great witnesses reveal that is in no way contrary to Christianity. Indeed, God's perfect Wisdom can be glorified through an evolutionary perspective.

2. Believing the Signs: The Church and the Biosphere

THE FACT THAT MANY GREAT BELIEVERS have speculated something like evolutionary theory is compelling evidence that Darwin's biology does not require Darwin's agnosticism. But perhaps an even more compelling example of the harmony between faith and evolutionary biology is the symmetry it reveals between the first creation and the New Creation, between the order of nature brought about through God's creative activity and the order of grace and the supernatural brought about through our redemption in Jesus Christ. The created world is a preparation for a New Creation that elevates, heals, and fulfills the physical universe. In the first creation, God causes the universe to exist. In the New Creation, he causes the Church to exist as the beginning and the "initial budding forth" of the Kingdom of God.[42] Therefore, we should expect symmetry between the universe and the Church—in some mysterious way they have a corresponding pattern. Evolution may be key to seeing that symmetry.

For example, in each creation there is a long period of preparation. Before the first human beings ("Adam") could emerge, eons passed, during which the way was prepared for him: by the formation of the elements, of the sun and earth, of the first living thing, and then through stage after stage of evolutionary development. So, too, the coming of Christ, the "second Adam," required that a "way be prepared for him." From the calling of Abraham, Isaac, and Jacob, and the forming of the Jewish people, many centuries had to pass, and stage after stage of the unfolding of God's Revelation, so that "when the time had fully come" Christ appeared (Gal 4:4). Furthermore, Christ's Body, the Church, continues to undergo growth as members are added to her and until it achieves its "stature of the fullness" of Christ (Eph 4:13), i.e., until all the faithful perfectly radiate the life of Christ and have perfect unity with him. In both natural and salvation history, small and unforeseen events occurred that had momentous consequences. The "randomness" of history, even the tragedy of human evil and sin, played a role in the unfolding of the divine plan.

Each creation, the first and the New, involves an environment that is essential to its development. In the first creation, God establishes an environment that ultimately evolves creatures capable of being his image and likeness. In the New Creation, the Son of God takes up natural elements and makes them into a new environment, the *liturgy of the Church*, that makes human creatures capable of the Kingdom of God. In creation, elements such as earth and water constitute the stuff out of which life emerges. In the liturgy, natural realities such as water, bread, wine, and oil are "supernaturalized" to form a new environment, and, in interaction with this new environment, eternal life emerges in all those who believe as we "become partakers of the divine nature" (2 Pt 1:4) through grace.

We "become partakers of the divine nature" (2 Pt 1:4) through grace.

Each creation also begins with a single form of life. The world of living creatures begins with one organism that, containing all future life within itself, so to speak, diffused that life to all organisms in the long history of evolutionary development. In the liturgy the one man, Jesus Christ, contains all of eternal life in himself and diffuses that life to all who believe and are reborn in him.

Each creation involves a progress from uniformity to greater complexity and diversity. In evolution, inorganic matter becomes simple, single-celled organisms, which ultimately evolve into more diverse forms of life, many of which are more complex. In the New Creation, the Church progresses to a deeper and deeper understanding of God's truth, to more diverse forms of the Christian life (such as the various religious orders), including within herself an ever-increasing variety of human races, languages, peoples, and cultures.

But the New Creation experienced in the Church and the liturgy also seems to develop in a contrasting way to the first creation, though maintaining the symmetry that exists between them. It is almost as if the first creation is the mirror image of the second. In evolution, the one form of life becomes many, but, in the liturgy, the many forms of human life become one in the one Body of Christ. In evolution, simplicity yields to a diversity that divides living populations;

but, in the liturgy, the divided are reunited while retaining their diversity. In evolution, the one organism possessing life succeeds in passing on that life by surviving. But, in the liturgy, the One who bears the fullness of eternal life succeeds in passing that life along by dying and by making himself our food in the Eucharist in order to strengthen us for eternal life.

Of course, there are many differences between biological evolution and the emergence of the New Creation. Our adaptation to eternal life is something that we must freely and consciously choose, unlike the adaptations that occur through genetic mutation. But, when seen as the work of God, evolution displays a beautiful symmetry between the world and the Church, the first creation and the New Creation. It reveals the Church to be the fulfillment of the natural world, and helps to explain the ancient Christian declaration that "the world was created for the sake of the Church."[43]

But a sobering spiritual truth is also revealed in this comparison. As Darwin recognized, some creatures do not adapt well to their environment and so perish. Here we see why the Church, our Mother and Teacher, challenges us with the requirement of Mass attendance on Sundays and Holy Days of Obligation and encourages us frequently to receive the Sacraments, especially the Sacraments of Penance (also called Reconciliation or Confession) and the Eucharist in Holy Communion. She remembers the sobering words of Our Lord about the heavenly environment to which we are destined: "Many, I tell you, will seek to enter and will not be able" (Lk 13:24). The liturgy adapts us to a new habitat, the Kingdom of God, for which our biological inheritance alone cannot prepare us.

G. Looking Forward: The Missing Amen

Our adaptation to eternal life is something that we must freely and consciously choose. The liturgy adapts us to a new habitat, the Kingdom of God.

IN SUMMARY, IT IS SAFE TO SAY that, on the basis of history, Church teaching, philosophy, the example of great Christians, and our own theological reflection, faith can be found on the frontiers of evolutionary biology. Darwin's theory is in "perfect agreement" with the Christian conception of the universe, but the harmony between them can only be fully understood when approached through the eyes of faith.

Earlier, we noted that evolution can be understood as the "amen" of creatures responding to the "Amen" of God. But as we imagined that chorus of creatures participating in God's creative activity, we might have noticed a unique set of voices.

Only one of the many creatures we encounter throughout life's history on our planet can say "amen" to God in the way God says "Amen" to creation. Only one of the creatures able to be studied by science can say "amen" to God with reason and freedom. The "amen" of creation would be missing its most perfect expression without the one creature that can express the "amen" offered by creation to God in the same "melody" with which God says it to the universe. That creature is the human person, created in the image of God. Our journey to the frontiers of science now brings us to those sciences that study the origins of our own species.

VOCABULARY

Define the following terms (or identify the person's significance):

1. Special Creation
2. Charles Darwin
3. *On the Origin of Species*
4. *The Descent of Man*
5. Biological Evolution
6. Speciation
7. *HMS Beagle*
8. Galapagos Islands
9. *Principles of Geology*
10. Natural Selection
11. Darwinism
12. Gregor Mendel
13. Neo-Darwinism
14. Fossil Record
15. Comparative Anatomy
16. Biogeography
17. Genetics
18. Genes
19. Scientific Theory
20. Agnostic
21. Evolutionism
22. Theory
23. Venerable Pius XII (*Humani Generis*)
24. St. John Paul II (Evolution)
25. Benedict XVI (Evolution)
26. Chance
27. Divine Providence
28. Naturalism
29. Abiogenesis
30. Amen
31. St. Gregory of Nyssa (Unity of Life)
32. St. Thomas Aquinas (Creation)
33. St. John Henry Newman (Creation and Evolution)
34. G.K. Chesterton (Creation and Evolution)
35. Theodosius Dobzhansky (Creation and Evolution)

St. Gregory of Nyssa (ca. 335-ca. 395)
Some unity between all life forms and human beings at their origins was envisioned by this great Catholic thinker.

STUDY QUESTIONS

Section A

1. What lesson does C.S. Lewis's *The Silver Chair* have for those approaching the issue of biological evolution in the light of faith?

Section B

2. How did Darwin arrive at his theory of evolution?

3. Explain the concept of natural selection by reference to animal breeding.

4. What did genetics contribute to Darwin's theory of evolution after his death?

5. What is a scientific theory, and why is it correct to refer to evolution as a theory?

6. How is Darwin's agnosticism related to a false understanding of God's relationship to the universe and life?

7. Distinguish the theory of evolution from evolutionism.

8. Where has the Catholic Church historically stood on the question of evolution?

9. Where does the Church stand now on the theory of evolution?

10. What distinction does the Church make regarding the evolution of human beings? Does this make the Church antiscientific in any way?

Section C

11. Is the reality of chance in the universe and in evolution a denial of divine Providence? Explain.

12. Does the fact that a process makes use of chance necessarily imply that it is not designed or that it is without purpose? Explain.

13. Give an example in which a person designs and brings about an outcome through the use of chance. How does this apply to the question of God in relation to evolution?

14. According to St. Thomas Aquinas, why did God introduce the element of chance into nature?

15. What would a world without chance be like?

Section D

16. Relate abiogenesis to the Holy Spirit, the "Giver of Life."

17. Relate the genetic code to the Son-*Logos*.

18. Explain the significance of the biblical word "Amen" to the issue of the compatibility of biological evolution and the Christian faith.

19. How does the biblical word "Amen" reveal the origin and development of living species to be both God's work and the work of God's creatures?

Section E

20. Explain the potential symmetry between an evolutionary view of the origin and development of living things and the redemption in Christ of all things.

21. Might evolution be the key for understanding the mystery of symmetry between the natural universe and man's supernatural destiny, between the old creation and the New Creation? If so, give some examples.

PRACTICAL EXERCISES

1. Watch the video "Biological Evolution and the Kinship of All Life" (8 minutes, 24 seconds, *mtfresources.org/videos*). Discuss some of the issues found therein as they relate to the misunderstandings some believers have of evolution.

2. Watch the video "A Closer Look: What Makes Evolution a Theory?" (2 minutes, 29 seconds, *mtfresources.org/videos*). How would you explain the relationship between a scientific theory and observable facts?

3. Imagine that you have a time machine and that you travel back in time and become a friend of the young Charles Darwin. How might you explain to him the difference between God as First Cause, understood in a deistic sense, and the Christian notion of God as Uncaused Cause? How might your explanation impact his thinking about the universe and evolution?

The HMS Beagle at Tierra del Fuego by Conrad Martens, who became the ship's artist in 1833.
The second survey expedition of the HMS Beagle was from December 27, 1831 to October 2, 1836, under Captain Robert FitzRoy. FitzRoy sought a gentleman naturalist, Darwin, to accompany them as a supernumerary. Darwin spent most of his time exploring on land: three years and three months on land, eighteen months at sea. At Punta Alta in Argentina he made a major find of gigantic fossils of extinct mammals, then known from only a few specimens. He collected the fossils and made detailed observations of plants and animals with results that shook his belief that species were fixed and ultimately led to his theory of evolution by natural selection.

Endnotes – Chapter Eight

1. The title of this chapter is inspired by John Haught, *Deeper than Darwin: The Prospect for Religion in the Age of Evolution* (Boulder: Westview Press, 2003).
2. C.S. Lewis, *The Silver Chair*: Book 4 in *The Chronicles of Narnia* series (New York: Scholastic, 1987), 21.
3. Charles Darwin, as quoted in "Happy 200th, Darwin!" February 2009, *evolution.berkeley.edu/evolibrary/news/090201_darwinday.*
4. Paulinus Forsthoefel, *Religious Faith Meets Modern Science* (New York: Alba House, 1994), 67-70.
5. Ibid., 142.
6. Darrel Falk, *Coming to Peace with Science: Bridging the Worlds Between Faith and Biology* (Downers Grove: Intervarsity Press, 2004), 171.
7. Sarah Kaplan, "Trump and Pence on science, in their own words," *The Washington Post*, November 10, 2016, *www.washingtonpost.com/news/speaking-of-science/wp/2016/11/10/trump-and-pence-on-science-in-their-own-words/.*
8. Theodosius Dobzhansky, "Nothing in Biology Makes Sense except in the Light of Evolution," in *The American Biology Teacher* 35:3 (March 1973), 125.
9. Ibid., 129.
10. Charles Darwin, Letter to J. Fordyce, May 7, 1879, as quoted in Józef Życiński, *God and Evolutionism: Fundamental Questions of Christian Evolutionism*, trans. by Kenneth W. Kemp and Zuzanna Maślanka (Washington, D.C.: Catholic University of America Press, 2006), 21.
11. Charles Darwin, *The Life and Letters of Charles Darwin, Including an Autobiographical Chapter*, Ed. by Francis Darwin (London: John Murray, Ablemarle Street, 1887), 309.
12. Józef Życiński, *God and Evolution: Fundamental Questions of Christian Evolutionism* (Washington, D.C.: Catholic University of America Press, 2006), 26-28.
13. Charles Darwin, *On the Origin of Species by means of Natural Selection; or, the Preservation of Favoured Races in the Struggle for Life* (London: John Murray, Albemarle Street, 1860), 490.
14. E. Wasmann, "Evolution," in *The Catholic Encyclopedia*, Vol. V (New York: The Gilmary Society, 1909), 654.
15. Bertrand L. Conway, *The Question Box*, 2nd ed. (New York: Paulist Press, 1929), 8-9.
16. St. John Paul II, "Humans are Spiritual and Corporeal Beings," April 16, 1986, *inters.org/John-Paul-II-Catechesis-Spiritual-Corporeal.*
17. St. John Paul II, "Magisterium is Concerned with the Question of Evolution for It Involves the Conception of Man," Message to the Pontifical Academy of Sciences (October 22, 1996), 4, *inters.org/John-Paul-II-Academy-Sciences-October-1996*.
18. Ibid., 4.
19. Ibid., 5.
20. Benedict XVI, Meeting with the clergy of the Dioceses of Belluno-Feltre and Treviso in Auronzo di Cadore (July 24, 2007), *w2.vatican.va/content/benedict-xvi/en/speeches/2007/july/documents/hf_ben-xvi_spe_20070724_clero-cadore.html.*
21. Leo XIII, *Providentissimus Deus*, no. 18.
22. W. Norris Clarke, *The One and the Many*, 207-209.
23. St. Augustine, *City of God*, 19, 4.
24. Dennis Bonnette, *Origin of the Human Species*, 2nd ed. (Ypsilanti, MI.: Sapientia Press, 2003), 55.
25. Michael Tkacz, "A Designer Universe: Chance, Design, and Cosmic Order," a presentation given at the "Physics and the God of Abraham" Conference, Gonzaga University (April 2004), 8 (unpublished).
26. E. Wasmann, "Evolution," in *The Catholic Encyclopedia*, Vol. V (New York: The Gilmary Society, 1909), 654. Francisco Suárez (1548-1617) was a Jesuit theologian and philosopher.
27. Falk, 101.
28. Ibid., 102-103.
29. Francis Collins, *The Language of God*, 90-91.
30. Bernard Lovell, *In the Center of Immensities* (New York: Harper and Row, 1978), 63.
31. Bonnette, 117-118.
32. International Theological Commission, C&S, 68.
33. Antony Flew, with Roy Abraham Varghese, *There is a God: How the World's Most Notorious Atheist Changed His Mind* (New York: HarperCollins, 2007), 127.
34. Ibid.
35. CCC 1062.
36. St. Gregory of Nyssa, *On the Soul and Resurrection*, in Philip Schaff and Henry Wace, eds., *Nicene and Post Nicene Fathers*, Vol. 5 (Edinburgh: T&T Clark), 440.
37. St. Augustine, *De Genesi ad litteram*, VI.18.
38. St. Thomas Aquinas, *In II Sent.* 12.3.1, as quoted in Barr, *Modern Physics*, 6.
39. St. John Henry Newman, "Letter to Pusey," as quoted in Hodgson, 54.
40. G.K. Chesterton, *Orthodoxy*, 56.
41. Theodosius Dobzhansky, "Nothing in Biology Makes Sense except in the Light of Evolution," 129.
42. Vatican II, Dogmatic Constitution on the Church *Lumen Gentium* (hereafter abbreviated *LG*), no. 5.
43. *The Shepherd of Hermas*, Visio II.4.2.

Chapter Nine
The Emergence of the Image: God and the Sciences of Human Origins

What can modern science tell us about the evolution of human beings?

What were our evolutionary ancestors like?

When and where did our species emerge?

How are we like our evolutionary relatives? How are we different?

What has God revealed about human origins? How does this relate to the picture provided by the science of human origins?

What is the human rational soul? How do we receive our souls from God?

> **[B]iological evolution has transcended itself in the human "revolution." A new level or dimension has been reached. The light of the human spirit has begun to shine.... [This] does not mean that a new force or energy has arrived from nowhere; it does mean that a new form of unity has come into existence...**
>
> **—Theodosius Dobzhansky, *The Biology of Ultimate Concern***

In December 2000, in a remote part of Africa north of the Ethiopian badlands, a team of scientists came face to face with an amazing glimpse into the past. While fossil hunting, they spotted a small skull peering down a slope. Years of painstaking excavation revealed other bones as well: a torso, a foot, a kneecap, and tiny finger bones. The skull even contained teeth, which further examination revealed to be baby teeth. Ultimately, scientists identified the bones to be those of a baby, probably a female of about three years of age at the time of her death, the cause of which is still unknown. But the date of that death is just as important—using sophisticated methods of dating, scientists estimate the age of the bones to be 3.3 million years old, making it the world's oldest fossil of its kind.[1]

Baby Selam (paleoartist's reconstruction). Quite likely our evolutionary ancestor.

This fossil, initially nicknamed the *Dikika Baby* after the place where it was found, but later named *Selam* ("peace"), is tremendously important for understanding the biological beginnings of our species. Accord-

Baby Selam in the hands of her discoverer. "It took me, and I underline, *5 years*. It was thousands and thousands of hours cleaning, preparing, and describing this fossil since it was discovered in 2000." —Dr. Zeresenay Alemseged, Max Planck Institute

ing to the majority of experts, Selam is a member of the species *Australopithecus afarensis*, a long-extinct hominin species, quite likely an evolutionary ancestor of all members of the genus *Homo*. Selam had a lower skeleton much like a human child's and an upper skeleton and skull with ape-like features, including shoulder blades that would be useful for climbing. These suggest a creature that could walk on two feet but also climb and spend time in trees.[2] Selam is a member of the biological family *Homininae* that includes our species *Homo sapiens* and other extinct species of primates closely related to us.

As we complete our consideration of modern scientific discoveries and their theological significance, Baby Selam points to a key issue: How can we relate what we know from faith to what we know from science about human origins? For example, how can one say that man is made in the image of God and also that he shares a common ancestor with chimpanzees and gorillas?

"The LORD sees not as man sees; man looks on the outward appearance, but the LORD looks on the heart" (1 Sm 16:7). These words from the Old Testament remind us that appearances can be deceiving. Could Selam be a stepping stone, rather than a stumbling block, on the path to a greater understanding of God and his divinely revealed truth? Perhaps this little hominin can lead us to a deeper appreciation of God's magnificent wisdom, love, and power—a wisdom, love, and power that links her to all humans living today. To make this connection requires that we first explore the amazing, yet still fragmentary, story of human evolution that has been pieced together by modern science. To do so requires that we consider the findings of three sciences: *paleoanthropology*, the study of fossil evidence of human evolutionary history; *paleoarchaeology*, the study of artifacts left behind by our evolutionary ancestors; and *evolutionary psychology*, the study of mental traits such as memory, perception, and language as they developed at various moments in the long process of hominin evolution.

As we follow the fossil trail that leads to our own species, and consider the features of hominin life as they grew in sophistication, becoming more and more like our own, we will encounter a paradox regarding the nature of humanity, no less a paradox than the mystery of light discussed in Chapter One. On the one hand, the origin of our species is a natural process, with the same mechanisms and processes involved in the evolution of any mammal. And yet evolutionary biology can only take us as far as its own method will allow, a method that strictly focuses on natural causes. At the advent of the specific kind of life we call human, we will see nature reach a terrain that requires perspectives that the science of biology cannot provide, the wider wisdom of philosophy and theology.

Paleoanthropology attempts to show evolutionary relationships between our species and those that went before us.

American paleoanthropologist Donald Johnson with "Lucy," a female *Australopithecus afarensis* he discovered in the Afar Triangle region of Hadar, Ethiopia, in 1974.

A. Out of Africa: Hominin Evolution

1. Defining "Human"

THE WHOLE SCIENCE OF HUMAN ORIGINS revolves around the meaning of the word "human." Confusion often arises from the different ways in which various disciplines define the term. In Catholic theology, as well as in the Western philosophical tradition, the term is used to refer to one species, *Homo sapiens*, and to those capacities that make our species different from all other species alive today: the closely related capacities of reason and free will. In the words of St. Thomas Aquinas, man is a *rational animal*, an animal that has the capacity for reason and, therefore, a unique kind of freedom. The *Catechism of the Catholic Church*, following the Second Vatican Council, declares that our capacity for self-knowledge (reason, rationality) and self-possession (free will) makes our species to be "in the image of God."[3] We will explore the "human difference," which is at the heart of the philosophical/theological use of the term, later in this chapter and in more detail in Chapters Ten and Eleven. In Chapter Twelve, we will learn yet another, and more essential, way in which the term "human" is used theologically.

Of course, the theological and philosophical definition of "human" developed long before anyone was aware that our species was connected to the rest of the natural world via evolution. Based on the discovery of many fossils that share very similar characteristics to our own, paleoanthropologists use the term *human* (or the genus *Homo* in Latin) to refer not only to members of our own species but also to a wide range of close relatives of our species—now all extinct—that have dwelt on the planet.[4] They make this classification based upon bodily characteristics and toolmaking abilities. The list of *Homo* species is incomplete and is growing; in the decade between 2003-2013, fossils of three previously unknown *Homo* species were discovered: *Homo floresiensis* in 2003, the Denisova hominins in 2008, and *Homo naledi* in 2013. It seems that there were many relatives of our species, and some may have shared the same habitats with *Homo sapiens* as recently as 18,000 years ago (hereafter abbreviated YA).

In this text, in which we are considering philosophical/theological insights as well as scientific ones, we will use the term *hominin* to refer to species closely related to our own, and will reserve the word *human* for our own species.

2. Evolutionary Developments Among Hominins

PALEOANTHROPOLOGY IS A FASCINATING FIELD, and it has largely been driven by the attempt to show evolutionary relationships between our species and those that went before us. The popular term "missing link" points to the desire many have to discover our whole biological lineage in exact detail. But it is not possible to draw a straight line between any hominin species that came before us to our own. The fossil record is far too fragmentary, both for our species and for many others, to conclude that any one of the earlier hominin species is our direct ancestor, especially the further back in time they lived. So it is best to focus on evolutionary developments that occurred throughout the 7 million year history of hominin evolution, identifying certain traits that we also possess today.

Chimps have the ability to infer emotions and desires in others of their species. They are highly social and engage in play.

Our tour of hominin evolution begins by noting traits and abilities we find in our living primate relatives, the chimpanzees, with whom we share a common ancestor that lived approximately 7 million YA. Chimps have five-fingered hands, toolmaking abilities, and the same spectrum of color vision that we have.[5] They also have the ability to infer emotions and desires in others of their species.[6] They communicate using vocalizations, gestures, body postures, and facial expressions that can be classified into greetings, expressions of displeasure or fear, and delight or familiarity. They have even been taught how to use sign language by researchers to indicate their desires for food and to express emotions. They are highly social and engage in play. Since these are all traits and behaviors that we share with them, it is safe to assume that extinct hominins possessed them as well. But hominins also exhibited traits and behaviors that great apes do not.

Dated to 3.6 million years ago, the Laetoli fossil footprints demonstrate that these hominins habitually walked upright as there are no knuckle impressions. The feet do not have the mobile big toe of apes. Instead, they have an arch, the bending of the sole of the foot, similar to modern humans.

Upright Walking: A good way to visualize hominin evolution is to do so starting from the bottom up, from the legs upward to the skull, for it is the lower body where we see the oldest difference between hominins and other primates. All hominins have straight legs that are capable of upright walking on two feet, called *bipedalism*, as contrasted with the knuckle-walking behavior of modern apes, who go from place to place using their hands to bear their upper body weight. Early on, upright walking was not the only way of getting around for hominins; climbing remained vital to food gathering and protection from predators. In the Great Rift Valley of Africa, a vast valley created by massive subterranean forces about 20 million YA, the combination of scattered valleys and open spaces created a situation favorable to the development of bipedalism, although it may have also evolved elsewhere in other hominin lineages. There, 4 to 5 million YA, some of the earliest hominins originated, the *Australopithecines*, the species of Baby Selam, as well as the famous 3.2 million-year-old *Lucy* fossil discovered in 1974, the most complete *Australopithecus* fossil ever discovered. In 1976, in Laetoli, Tanzania, 3.6 million-year-old fossilized footprints were discovered that had been made by a group of three australopiths who traveled across open land through volcanic ash between one wooded area to another. The footprints indicate that their feet and walking patterns were remarkably similar to our own. Such footprints are precious and rare glimpses into the past because they are "fossilized behaviors," "an arrow-straight double trail of prints some eighty feet long, more or less like anyone might leave walking along a wet beach."[7]

Over time, climate change created a situation in which the continent of Africa became hotter and drier. As wooded habitats shrunk, some of these small primates moved out into the open plains, teeming though they were with large predators, relying more on two feet than on their strong climbing abilities. Bipedalism became more important than climbing, freeing hands that, after much more evolution, ultimately could make and use tools.[8] This brings us to two other closely related activities that emerged as early as 2.5 million YA and which became characteristic of future hominins.

Members of *Homo habilis* had a much larger brain than the *Australopithicenes* and the ability to use their hands to make things and modify objects. The tools made by *Homo habilis* indicate that they were omnivorous.

Toolmaking/Omnivorous Diet: In the 1960's, in sediments dating back 2 to 2.5 million YA, ancient stone tools were discovered in close proximity to fossils that were dubbed *Homo habilis*. Members of *Homo habilis* had a much larger brain than the *Australopithicenes*, as well as a significant level of *manual dexterity*, the ability to use their hands to make things and modify objects. The tools they made were crude, consisting of pebbles chipped down to their cores and the flakes that had come off of those pebbles. These remnants have a random appearance, "as if the maker was not holding any design in mind and was content to accept whatever shape of stone nature might produce."[9] Although molecular analysis of australopith teeth show that they were largely herbivorous, the tools made by *Homo habilis* indicate that they were *omnivorous*, regularly eating meat as well as plants. Meat made up a significant part of their diet; the sharp rock flakes they made have been shown to be very effective at butchering large animals, even elephants.[10]

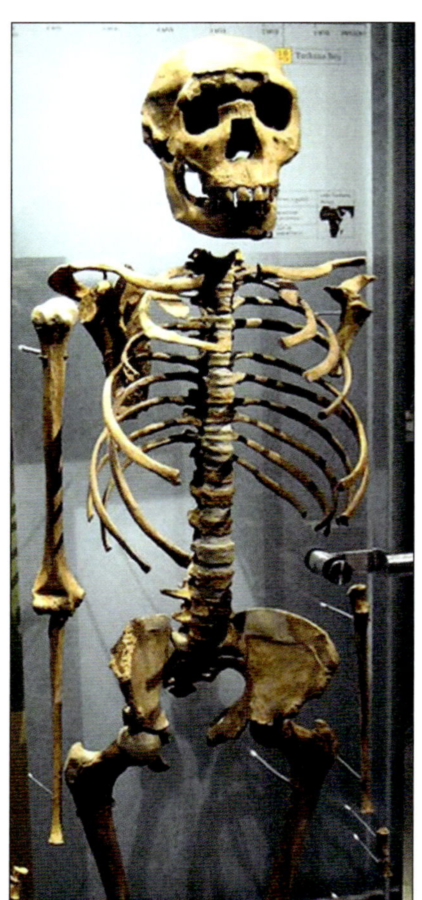
Turkana Boy, an almost complete, 1.6 million-year-old *Homo ergaster* skeleton of a male adolescent.

Much more striking in terms of sophistication are the hand axes associated with another species, *Homo ergaster*, which originated around 1.9 million YA. These large, tear-drop-shaped axes were carefully worked on both sides to produce a specific shape; the oldest such axe is 1.76 million years old and was found near Lake Turkana in northwest Kenya. This is also the region in which the *Turkana Boy* fossil was found, an almost complete, 1.6 million-year-old *Homo ergaster* skeleton of a male adolescent. Turkana Boy was radically different than Lucy and the Dikika Baby; at a height of 5 feet, 3 inches, with an upright, slender body shape and with a much larger brain (more than half the size of our own), he was clearly adapted to a new way of life on the open savannah.[11] From this point forward, increased brain size and brain complexity become defining features of hominin evolution, as does more and more sophisticated toolmaking.

A hand axe known as an Acheulean tool. The tool found in Kenya was dated to about 1.76 million years ago, making it the oldest known hand axe in the world.

Prosociality and Migration: The evidence of large game hunting says much more about *Homo ergaster* than just a change in diet and brain size; it also indicates an incredible amount of cooperation among their kind. All primates, especially the great apes such as chimpanzees and gorillas, are highly social animals, with intricate social networks and forms of communication and cooperation. But working together on a hunt for large game using hand axes is far beyond anything seen among apes. The amount of coordination and planning required for such hunting is unknown among any modern primates except humans. This may be evidence for a level of social sophistication heretofore unseen in hominin life.

As hominin evolution continued, the increasing complexity of their social life took an interesting turn. In the ruins of the medieval town Dmanisi, in the Republic of Georgia, archaeological digs unearthed artifacts and fossils of *Homo erectus*, a hominin species which originated around 1.89 million YA and went extinct as recently as only 40,000 YA. One skull, dated to approximately 1.8 million YA, belonged to an aged male whose tooth sockets had shriveled and who had been toothless (except for one tooth) for many years before he died. This is powerful evidence of a high degree of *prosociality*, a general concern for others that is found in some mammals. Prosocial behaviors usually require investments of time, energy, and sacrifice. For the elderly *Homo erectus* to have survived without teeth for so many years would have required care on the part of his relatives, in which soft foods were chosen, reserved, and probably even chewed for him.[12] This capacity and natural impulse to care for one's own in fairly regular and complex ways, as well as an increasing reliance of one member of a group on the others, comes to be an even more pronounced and widespread feature in later hominins.

The fact that these fossils were discovered over 4,200 miles from Lake Turkana points to another development—the tendency of some hominins to migrate far and wide. By 1 million years ago,

Homo erectus was on the island of Java and ultimately migrated as far east as China and as far west as Spain, not to mention all over the continent of Africa where they originated.[13] The various developments noted above—bigger, more complex brains, upright walking, tool-making, a varied diet, cohesive and cooperative lifestyle—made it possible for them to thrive in a wide range of environments, wet and dry, warm and cold. No other hominin species would rival this range of migration until our own.

There is evidence for the controlled use of fire by *Homo erectus*, beginning some 1 million years ago. Cooking requires a great deal of cooperation among individuals and families.

Home and Hearth: As brain complexity increased, so did hominin sophistication. In southern France, at a site called *Terra Amata*, the traces of the first artificial shelters, dating back 400,000 years, were discovered in 1966. The dwellings were oval-shaped and fashioned out of saplings and rings of stone. In one of them a shallow area filled with blackened stones and burnt bones, undoubtedly a primitive cooking hearth, was discovered. Hominins had been using fire for at least 300,000 years before this, but this site showed that by this time the domestic use of fire for cooking had developed.

The hominins of this region were also advancing in their toolmaking. Between 1994 and 1998 at Schöningen, Germany, eight remarkably well-fashioned wooden spears of about the same age were discovered, preserved in a peat bog. These were carefully whittled out of spruce and pine branches to put the weight at the sharpened front part of the spear so that they could be used as projectile hunting weapons to bring down large game.[14] Such spear making required a high level of intelligence and manual dexterity, and spear hunting for large game requires an incredible amount of group cooperation and coordination. Both sites have been associated with fossils of *Homo heidelbergensis*, which originated in Africa around 600,000 YA and spread into Europe and Asia. In the words of paleoanthropologist Ian Tattersall, "Altogether, they lived more complex lives than any hominins had ever done before them."[15]

Homo heidelbergensis originated in Africa and migrated into Asia and Europe. "They lived more complex lives than any hominins had ever done before them."

The innovation of controlling fire and cooking food, which may have occurred as early as 1.6 to 1.8 million YA, the time of *Homo erectus*, had become an essential feature of hominin life by this point.[16] Cooked food is softer and much denser in calories than raw food, which larger-brained hominins need in order to support their brain development and activity; our own brains use about 25% of our daily available energy! Cooking also requires a great deal of cooperation among individuals and families—some must hunt and gather, others must cook, and food must be shared. Dwellings naturally follow as centers of these activities. The deep prehistory of domestic and family life as we know it now was beginning to emerge, a situation in which social bonds became increasingly important between group members and in which even more varied and deeper prosocial behaviors could develop.

Our hominin "cousin," *Homo neanderthalensis*. Human beings alive today carry anywhere from 1.5 to 2.1% of genes inherited from our Neanderthal ancestors.

The Neanderthals: The various adaptations above can be seen at a very advanced stage in our hominin "cousin," *Homo neanderthalensis*. When trying to understand our own species, both in what makes us unique and in what we share with all hominins, they are the very best "mirror" available to us.[17] In regard to the features we share with all later hominins, such as diet, toolmaking, and cooking, Neanderthals are the closest to us in terms of sophistication, and they had certain traits they may have shared only with us. In fact, DNA analysis has shown that, with the exception of native Africans, all human beings alive today carry anywhere from 1.5 to 2.1% of genes inherited from the interbreeding of our ancestors with Neanderthals at some time between 60,000 and 40,000 YA.[18]

The first distinctively Neanderthal fossils are found in sediments dating to around 250,000 to 300,000 YA. They originated in Europe and inhabited Europe and western Asia until as recently as 35,000 YA. At *Cueva del Sidrón* (a.k.a. El Sidrón Cave), a 50,000-year-old Neanderthal site, the fossil remains of twelve Neanderthals—three male adults, three female adults, three adolescent boys, two children, and one infant—were discovered in 1994. This is about the size of groups found in *small-band hunter-gatherer (SBHG) societies* of our own species, universally until around 11,000 YA and even today among SBHG groups such as the *Khoe-San* in Africa.[19] DNA analysis revealed that the adult males were siblings and that the females had each belonged to different families.[20]

Moreover, Neanderthals seem to have been the first hominins to intentionally bury their dead. In 1908 two priests who were also archaeologists, **Jean and Amedee Bouyssonie**, discovered a complete 50,000-year-old adult Neanderthal skeleton inside a cave located near *La Chapelle-aux-Saints* in central France. A pit had been carved out of a natural depression in the cave, and the body had been positioned to fit the pit and then covered. The priests immediately speculated that the skeleton had been buried, but at the time their hypothesis was ignored. However, in 2014 a more detailed analysis confirmed their suspicion.[21] Another Neanderthal burial at *Shanidar Cave* in northern Iraq is of an aged male with a withered arm that was probably the result of a congenital birth defect.[22] Taken together, the sites offer evidence of compassion for the living and of mourning for the dead among this species.

Finally, there is evidence that Neanderthals created geometric structures and markings within some of the caves in which they dwelled. At *Bruniquel Cave* in southwestern France, a 176,000-year-old Neanderthal settlement was discovered containing circular arrangements of broken stalagmites that were used to contain fires—soot and burnt bone were found within the circles.[23] And in 2018, a ladder-like drawing was found on a cave wall on the coast of southeastern Spain and was tentatively dated to 65,000 YA, a time that is well before the estimates of the arrival of our own species in Europe.[24]

Broken aligned stalagmite circles discovered in the Bruniquel Cave, France.

In summary, Neanderthals seem to match us in our own behaviors and abilities to a very high degree. Therefore, it has become more and more common for paleoanthropologists to assume that they were like us in every way; or, as one recent study puts it, that they were "cognitively indistinguishable" from our own species.[25] But is this the case? As we conclude our consideration of hominin evolution, consider the judgment of paleoanthropologist Ian Tattersall:

> **We find nothing in the technological record of the Neanderthals to suggest that they were symbolic thinkers. Skillful, yes; complex, certainly. But not in the way we are. As a species, *Homo neanderthalensis* seems to have fully participated in the hominin trend over time toward more challenging behaviors, and toward more subtle and intricate relationships with the environment. It certainly participated in the hominin trend toward bigger brains, and possibly taking this tendency to its most extreme expression. But behaviorally there was *no qualitative break with the past*; the Neanderthals were simply doing what their predecessors had done, if apparently better. In other words, they were like their ancestors, only more so. *We are not. We are symbolic.*[26]**

Neanderthals seem to match us in our own behaviors and abilities in incredible ways.
But we possess reason, a wholly different kind of intelligence.

Tattersall's claim is that *symbolic thought* is what sets us apart from Neanderthals and all other animals, which he defines as the ability to organize the world around us mentally by generating a vast array of mental, verbal, and physical symbols. The word *symbol* comes from the Greek verb *symballein*, which means "to put together." A symbol is a sign, sound, or object that allows the sign, sound, or object to represent something other than itself. While studies have shown that some animals can be taught to use rudimentary signs, they do not engage in symbolic behaviors in the thorough way that we use symbols to represent the world in our minds. Human language, which we will further investigate in the next section, is the height of symbolism, in which sounds and written words are put together with real things to represent them.

This ability to not only use symbols but to mentally generate them, in fact to engage in the kind of thinking that symbolism makes possible, is a hallmark of our species alone. It is at the heart of the difference between animal communication and human language, between skillful problem solving and reflection upon the intrinsic nature of things, between personal ornamentation and artistic expression, between intelligence and reason. In symbolic thought, we have reached the edge of the "human difference" that distinguishes us from the other animals. As far as we can tell, the Neanderthals had all of the animal intelligence that we have, and more than most other hominins. They were capable of a high degree of empathy for those in their social groups. They may have even developed a preference for symmetry and a way of signaling difference or relatedness via personal ornamentation. We do such things, too, but we are not merely beings possessing more brainpower. We possess a wholly different kind of intelligence. They had reasons for acting, even if they could not deliberately conceive and articulate them, but we have the power of reason.

This difference between animal intelligence and human reason was well known to St. Thomas Aquinas, who ascribed to many animals a very high degree of cognitive ability, what we might call intelligence or brain power. Nonhuman animals, he observed, have the ability to learn from past experience. They are capable of judging situations correctly and can learn to solve problems; St. Thomas called this "natural judgment." But the power of reason allows our species alone to make judgments about our judgments, to hold real things in our minds mentally, and to come to understand them not only for how they concern us and how we might use them, but for what they are. Animals can make natural judgments, St. Thomas acknowledges, but he also adds, "To pass judgments on one's own judgments belongs only to reason."[27] We shall explore the human capacity for reason in more detail later in this chapter and again in Chapter Ten.

3. *Homo Sapiens*: Something Old, Something New

The Lion-man is an ivory sculpture discovered in a German cave in 1939. The lion-headed figurine carved out of mammoth ivory with a flint stone knife is the oldest-known example of figurative art at 35,000 to 40,000 years old.

WHEN WE ARRIVE AT OUR OWN SPECIES, we discover an interesting puzzle. There is no doubt among experts that we originated in Africa; the earliest plausibly human fossils are found there, and numerous DNA comparisons of modern humans all show a common African ancestry.[28] Fossils that bear our own skeletal characteristics have been discovered in North Africa and dated to as far back as 300,000 YA.[29] Yet up until 120,000 to 60,000 YA, these remains are found accompanied by artifacts that do not differ in any significant way from our Neanderthal cousins, who themselves were not much more advanced than *Homo Heidelbergensis*. It seems that our modern human skeletal structure, including our large skull cases and brains, were around for a long time before any robust evidence of human uniqueness "arrived." When it did, as recently as 60,000 YA, but perhaps as far back as 120,000 YA, the picture changed dramatically. In the words of Nicholas Wade:

> **There is a new set of stone tools, more carefully crafted to attain specific shapes. There are complex tools made of bone, antler, and ivory. The bringers of the new culture... played bird-bone flutes. Their missile technology was much improved.... They buried their dead with rituals. They could support denser populations. They developed trade networks through which they obtained distant materials.**[30]

Sculptures and cave paintings followed. For reasons that shall become clear, these new behaviors demonstrate "self-consciousness, self-determination, and therefore freedom," including an understanding of time and an orientation toward the future.[31]

Wall art from the Lascaux Cave in France. Over 600 parietal wall paintings cover the interior walls and ceilings of the cave dated Upper Paleolithic, 12,000 to 17,000 years old.

How did this change occur? In their book, *Why Only Us: Language and Evolution*, **Robert Berwick** and **Noam Chomsky** focus on the difference between animal communication and human language to answer this question. Nonhuman animal communication involves linear order between sounds or signs, i.e., the sounds or gestures must follow each other in exact patterns. For example, when chimps are taught sign language, they never get beyond two-word combinations. By contrast, human language is structured hierarchically, which means that we can relate words in sentences according to rules that transcend the mere proximity of words to each other. Even more, we can combine words into new units of meaning, then relate them to other words, and so on, so that the possibilities of language are infinite. The ability to do this, called "Merge" by Berwick and Chomsky, is simple enough neurologically that a slight rewiring of the brain through a few genetic mutations could have given our species the type of brains capable of Merge.[32]

They also speculate that, when this change occurred, it acted not first as a tool for communication but for thought, for thinking first and only after for speaking. They suggest that this change probably occurred in one early *Homo sapiens* more than 60,000 YA and that, as it spread through the *Homo sapiens* population, it triggered explosive progress in technology and art, a "Great Leap Forward" that ushered in the fully symbolic, human way of life that we live now.[33]

According to most experts, the fully developed form of the human being bearing all the characteristics described above emerged in one population of *Homo sapiens* in Africa before we began to spread out of Africa and across the globe, around 120,000 to 70,000 YA. Genetic studies have revealed that the original ancestral population from whom all today's human beings are descended seems to have numbered only a few thousand, maybe even a few hundred, individuals.[34] In fact, geneticists have even discovered that all human beings alive today can be traced back to a single male and a single female. These two individuals are often referred to as "mitochondrial Eve" and "Y chromosomal Adam," and all modern humans share a common ancestry with these two individuals. However, this does not mean that these two mated and were the first parents of our species, nor that they even lived at the same time, nor does this indicate they were the only members of an ancestral population. But it does reinforce the genetic relatedness of all humankind.[35] The proliferation and migration of *Homo sapiens* was explosive—by 60,000 YA they were in Europe and Asia; by 50,000 YA, they had reached Australia. The foundations of human history and modern human societies were in place, although recorded history would not begin until around 3000 to 3500 BC (5000 to 5500 YA).

All human beings alive today can be traced back to a single male and a single female. These two individuals are often referred to as "mitochondrial Eve" and "Y chromosomal Adam."

B. The Human Difference

IN OUR TOUR OF HOMININ EVOLUTION, we have identified symbolic thought and language as key indicators of what we are calling the human difference, that which sets us apart from all other hominins. Over and above those qualities already explained, two additional human qualities that are unique to us help us to better appreciate the rationality of our species: self-reflection and an appreciation of the beautiful.[36] In order to better grasp these essentially human qualities, we can now return to our hominin cousins.

What separates you and me from the other hominins? We have seen many ways in which they were very much like us, but were they like us in the most essential ways? The evidence is too scanty to make a solid judgment either way. However, based on the evidence we do have, at present it seems unlikely that the other hominins, including the Neanderthals, were rational animals as we are. A closer look at these two qualities reveals the difference between the human and the hominin.

1. Self-Reflection

ALL ANIMALS WITH NERVOUS SYSTEMS have some kind of self-perception that can be generally called self-awareness; the very ability to feel external objects involves recognition by an organism of the difference between the organism and things outside itself. Higher animals, such as dolphins and chimpanzees, exhibit high degrees of self-perception that allows them to relate themselves to their environment, to other animals and especially to other members of their species. There is no doubt that, in their highly organized form of life, Neanderthals exhibited this kind of self-awareness. And yet human self-awareness extends to the ability to see one's own self almost as another self, to reflect on one's self, and to correct and deepen one's self-understanding. This is more than self-awareness; it is *self-reflection*.

A paleoartist's reconstruction of a Stone Age teen from the Sunghir grave site in Russia. The burial rituals indicated belief in life after death or a meaning to death.

Consider a humorous but helpful indicator of this difference given by **Walker Percy** (1916-1990), the Louisiana novelist and Catholic philosopher. Considering the many scientists who have devoted themselves to proving that human intelligence is simply an advanced form of animal intelligence, he observed that human beings are constantly trying to prove that they are no different from the rest of the animals, and by doing so prove their uniqueness; no other species tries to prove that it is not unique![37] Ironically, human efforts to disprove human uniqueness testify most eloquently to it, for only humans are capable of proving or disproving anything. "Only man knows that he knows"—only a human can think about his or her self, origins, destiny, behavior, death, and the possibility of life after death.

From what is known currently about the other hominins, there is no evidence that they were capable of self-reflection. One important indicator is the difference between Neanderthal burials and the burial practices of early humans. For example, neither the grave at La Chapelle-aux-Saints nor any other Neanderthal burial site currently known shows undisputed evidence of rituals that indicate belief in life after death or attribute meaning to death.[38] But in the 34,000-year-old graves found at Sunghir in modern Russia, the ancient humans who lived there

A 34,000-year-old grave found at Sunghir in modern Russia. This adult male was buried with 3000 mammoth ivory beads, pierced fox canines, and ivory armbands, carefully arranged around his body.

buried their dead with specially crafted "grave goods," the archaeological term for items deliberately buried with the dead. One adult male was buried with thousands of ivory beads, which were carefully arranged around the body, and two children, buried side-by-side, with weapons and other symbolic objects.[39] In the latter case, we see self-reflection mirrored in the way other humans are adorned, in which their importance to their relatives is reflected in a symbolic way. Also, the cave art left behind by humans as far back as 40,000 YA include hand stencils, which we recognize today as a way of indicating a sense of self, the artistic equivalent of a personal "signature."

2. Appreciation of Beauty

AMONG THE HOMININS, NEANDERTHALS might stand alone as having a preference for symmetry (as we saw in the case of the stalagmite circles in Bruniquel Cave), and they may have even ornamented themselves, although the latter claim is heavily disputed. They were gifted at toolmaking, even attaching stone points to wood, and showed a preference for the best materials as they crafted them. However, their tools show a strict practicality, which one paleoanthropologist has gone so far as to call "practical monotony."[40] Even crows make practical tools, sharpening sticks with their beaks to get at food, and have even been observed inserting such sticks into objects that are too big to fit into their beaks but which they want to carry.[41] But the tools left behind by our human ancestors are not just usable or even symmetrical; they are quite often decorated with designs. In other words, they were crafted to be visually pleasing, to be beautiful, and in this way there can be no doubt that they are human tools—tools that reveal an appreciation for beauty in their design.

What is beauty? It has been described as the coming together of three characteristics in a being or beings. The first characteristic is *unity*—in order to be beautiful, a thing must have a wholeness, a completeness. The ancients referred to this as *integrity*. Second, to be beautiful, a thing must have *harmony*, a "fitting together" of everything integral to it. In physical beings, this is called proportion or symmetry. The ancients referred to this quality as *consonance*. Finally, to be beautiful, a thing must have *splendor*. This splendor, which comes from harmony and integrity, is what evokes feelings of delight, wonder, awe, and respect from those who perceive it.[42]

Discovered in 1994, Chauvet Cave in France is considered one of the most significant prehistoric art sites in the world. Over 420 paintings have been documented in the cave, including thirteen species of animals (some extinct), human handprints, and abstract dot paintings. UNESCO granted it World Heritage status on June 22, 2014.

The greatest evidence of the human appreciation for beauty is the breathtaking cave art dated to 30,000 to 40,000 YA, to which nothing the Neanderthals ever produced can compare. In places as distant as southern France and Indonesia, common artistic conventions had developed among our ancestors: hand stenciling, the depiction of animals and human beings, and even the use of abstract shapes. In the *Chauvet Cave* in France, 32,000-year-old paintings of animals, including extinct species such as cave bears and cave lions, woolly rhinoceroses, and woolly mammoths, cover the cave walls. Some of the animals were depicted with many legs so as to give the impression of movement by firelight. The place was obviously special, perhaps even sacred, to these ancient artists and their companions because they did not live in the caves. The caves were places set apart.[43] Other artifacts from the period include the Vogelherd Horse, crafted out of the ivory of a wooly mammoth (35,000 YA), a flute made of a vulture bone (40,000 YA) and a female figurine, the Venus of Hohle Fels, also crafted out of mammoth ivory to be worn as an amulet. The *human aesthetic capacity* revealed in these examples, the human desire for and appreciation of beauty, are a key part of the human difference.

In summary, the gap between spiritual human rationality and the animal intelligence of Neanderthals seems to have been more than a matter of mere brain size or advanced brain structure. Like the Neanderthals, humans are also animals—we depend on our bodies and especially our brains in order to think. But we can transform purely instinctive patterns and brain activity, which we share with animals, into something much more. We can also fail to do so and not rise above the level of behavior that we share with the animals. Indeed, we can choose to become far more depraved than any other animal could ever become, as we will explore in Chapter Eleven, by using our advanced rational capacities for maleficent ends in ways that other creatures are not capable.

Now that we have a better idea of the human difference, we can begin to reflect theologically upon human evolution and origins. We begin with the picture offered us in the Second Creation Account, which is found in Genesis 2, which in one verse captures the deepest mystery of human origins and of every human life.

C. The Divine Perspective: The Book of Genesis and the Human Soul

THE SECOND CREATION ACCOUNT narrates the creation of human beings in one verse, Genesis 2:7: "The LORD God formed man (Hebrew: *āḏām*) of dust from the ground (Hebrew: *āḏāmah*), and breathed into his nostrils the breath of life, and man became a living being." The connection between the word for "ground" (*āḏāmah*) and the word for "human being" (*āḏām*) shows that humans are naturally made of physical elements. It is a humbling image, and one that is "wide" enough to include the discovery of a long natural evolution from earlier living creatures in which matter, the stuff of the ground, is ultimately fashioned into humanity, the image of God. Based on this theological truth, which harmonizes so beautifully with the truth about human origins, no one of us can say, "I, or my race, is somehow better than all others." In the words of Pope Benedict XVI, "Despite every distinction that culture and history have brought about, it is still true that we are, in the last resort, the same... earth, formed from dust, and destined to return to it.... The Bible says a decisive 'No' to all racism and to every human division."[44]

Just as the First Creation Account was responding to and correcting the violent, dehumanizing worldview of the Babylonian myth *Enûma Eliš*, Genesis 2 responds to yet another Ancient Near Eastern myth, the *Atrahasis* (named after its main character), which was first written down sometime around 1700 BC. In this myth humanity is created by Enki, the god of wisdom, to be the slaves of the gods. Clay and the blood of a slain god are mixed together, and all the gods spit upon the mixture. After ten months seven male and seven female human beings are produced, beginning the human race.

Genesis 2:7 shares obvious commonalities with this pagan myth. For example, divine activity is depicted in a very anthropomorphic way. *Anthropomorphic* in this context refers to the description of divine creation as if it were a human activity—in Genesis 2:7 God "forms" as if he had fingers and "breathes" as if he had lungs. Just as in the *Atrahasis*, humans are made out of clay. But unlike the *Atrahasis*, God breathes into the human being his own "breath." Recognizing the symbolic nature of the account, it is clear that this second element is precisely what sets humans

In Genesis 2:7 God "forms" as if he had fingers and "breathes" as if he had lungs.
Recognizing the symbolic nature of the account (God breathing into the human being his own "breath"),
it is clear that this second element is precisely what sets humans apart from the other animals.

From the theological perspective, the "human difference" is located in the fact that the soul is spiritual and directly created by God; it is not merely the result of a biological process.

apart from the other animals, who also have the breath of life (see Gn 6:17), but not as breathed directly from God. The picture, then, is of an animal that has a life more like God's than the rest of the animals, an animal who is not simply one of God's creatures but who becomes a "living being" precisely because of a special relationship to him. The Hebrew word for "being" in Genesis 2:7 is *nephesh*, a word that can be translated as "soul" or "life principle." Thanks to God's mysterious action, a living human being exists.

As we have seen in Chapter Eight, the issue of the origin of the human soul is the one issue about which the Church has qualified her openness to what science has revealed about our evolutionary origins. To quote **St. John Paul II** again, "The doctrine of faith affirms that man's spiritual soul is created directly by God.... The human soul, on which man's humanity definitively depends, cannot emerge from matter, since the soul is of a spiritual nature." So from the theological perspective, the "human difference" is located in the fact that the soul is spiritual and directly created by God; it is not merely the result of a biological process. In fact, this is the case for every human being; whenever a new human being is conceived, it must involve the direct creation of the soul of that human being. This is directly related to the special powers of the human soul, rationality and free will, that we will explore in Chapter Ten.

How does God "directly create" a human soul? In our ordinary way of thinking, it is easy to imagine that whenever a human body is "made," God makes a soul for this body, "attaching" the two. Many mistakenly think of themselves as *two* things, a living body and a mysterious ghost that is the real self. This, however, is to misunderstand the nature of the soul, which is not a separate thing that God makes but, along with the matter from which our body is made, is one of two principles that make a human being a living being. In the words of the Fifth Lateran Council, an Ecumenical Council of the Church, the human soul is the "substantial form" of the human body. No part of us is simply soul, no part of us is merely body. In fact, a body without a soul is not a body at all. As the soul is the very life principle of a living body, a body without a soul is only a corpse.

At the beginning of our species, and indeed at the beginning of every human life, we have a paradox. From one perspective, human beings are the natural product of primate evolution, the product of a meandering process that involved trends we see in other hominins: bigger brains, more sophisticated tools and social organization, etc. From the other perspective, each human being is a rational and spiritual being, the product of God's loving initiative that engages each of us in a special relationship with our Creator. The International Theological Commission (ITC) expresses the mystery of the *direct* (also called *special*) *creation* of the human soul in a way that sheds light on this paradox: God can "bring about effects that transcend the capacity of created causes acting according to their natures" in which God directly causes the soul in a "non-disruptive" way.[45] Human souls, then, do come from parents; through the fertilization of the female ovum by the male sperm, human parents are the created causes acting according to their sexual natures. What makes human reproduction different is not that God disrupts this process, but rather causes it to produce a life principle that transcends that of the other animals.

Therefore, the direct creation of the human soul is not to be understood as a miracle, at least not in the strict theological sense that we explored in Chapter Six. Miracles are singular, one-time events, and the direct creation of the human soul happens whenever human sexual reproduction is successful in the normal course of nature. Yet it is more like a miracle than other natural events because, as in the case of miracles, natural causes are empowered to produce something beyond their capacity. In the words of **Pope Benedict XVI**:

> **If creation means dependence of being, then special creation is nothing other than special dependence of being. The statement that man is created in a more specific, more direct way by God than other things in nature, when expressed somewhat less metaphorically, means simply this: that man is willed by God in a specific way, not merely as a being that "is there", but as a being that knows him; not only as a construct that he thought up, but as an existence that can think about him in return. We call the fact that man is specifically willed and known by God his special creation.**
>
> **The clay became man at that moment in which a being for the first time was capable of forming, however dimly, the thought "God." ... For it is not the use of weapons or fire, not new methods of cruelty or of useful activity that constitute man, but rather his ability to be immediately in relation to God.... The theory of evolution does not invalidate faith, nor does it corroborate it. But it does challenge faith to understand itself more profoundly and thus to help man to understand himself and to become increasingly what he is: the being who is supposed to say "thou" to God in eternity.[46]**

"The human soul...cannot emerge from matter, since the soul is of a spiritual nature."
—St. John Paul II

In summary: the human soul, the very life-principle that makes a human body to be a living body of a specific kind, is not a thing God makes separately. Rather, due to the free unfolding of a universe that he sustains in being precisely for this purpose, a body of the human kind is, of its essence, a body that must have a spiritual soul to be the kind of creature that it is, a body that, in the words of the seventeenth-century Catholic philosopher **John of St. Thomas**, "calls out to God out of justice for a soul." The spiritual soul is the principle that, with the body, makes a human being this kind of living being. Evolution, according to the God-given laws of the universe and due to the activity of creatures over millions of years, has yielded a situation where in our universe there is now a material creature for whom to be spiritual is its natural state, whose origins implicate God and require his direct involvement.

This wonderful mystery reveals a truth that science could never discover but which faith and reason together can discern—that *Homo sapiens* is the ultimate reason why the universe exists, the point of God's creative activity. From all eternity God did not merely will to share his goodness with creatures, but he willed for there to be a creature that could receive the gift of the created universe and, ultimately, the gift of his own divine life. In the words of **St. John Paul II**:

> **Creation is a gift because man appears in it, who, as an "image of God," is able to understand the very meaning of the gift in God's call from nothing to existence.... Man appears in creation as the one who received the world as a gift, and vice versa, one can also say that the world has received man as a gift.**[47]

The created universe could not be a gift unless there was a creature who, being capable of understanding, could wonder at its beauty, respond to it with delight, and begin to comprehend its patterns and laws. The human difference, and the paradox of special creation, lies precisely in this uniquely human capacity, which places us in an intimate relationship with the Trinity, who calls us into being out of nothingness and then calls out to us in love.[48]

D. From the Dikika Baby to the Christ Child: The Theological Implications of Human Evolution

THE GREAT CHRISTIAN AUTHOR **C.S. LEWIS** offers a beautiful summary of the picture that faith and science combine to give us of the dawn of humanity. We will quote it here in full:

> **For long centuries, God perfected the animal form which was to become the vehicle of humanity and the image of Himself. He gave it hands whose thumb could be applied to each of the fingers, and jaws and teeth and throat capable of articulation, and a brain sufficiently complex to execute all of the material motions whereby rational thought is incarnated. The creature may have existed in this state for ages before it became man: it may even have been clever enough to make things which a modern archaeologist would accept as proof of its humanity. But it was only an animal because all its physical and psychical processes were directed to purely material and natural ends. Then, in the fullness of time, God caused to descend upon this organism, both on its psychology and physiology, a new kind of consciousness which could say "I" and "me," which could look upon itself as an object, which knew God, which could make judgments of truth, beauty and goodness, and which was so far above time that it could perceive time flowing past...**[49]

Are there any important benefits offered by seeing the divine act of creating humanity through the lens of paleoanthropology? Here are two that come to mind:

1. The Loving Patience of God

The Transfiguration by Raphael

GOD'S PREPARATION OF THE HUMAN BODY took millions of years; in fact, it took billions of years of cosmic history for just the first life form to evolve on earth. It involved the slow process of primate and hominin evolution, a process that unfolded with fits and starts, with detours and many side-roads. But the delay came not on the part of God but on the part of creation itself, which took time to realize its potential to produce a being capable of being the image of God. Matter had to "mature," starting all the way back at the Big Bang, to the point where its organization had been realized just so. At that moment, when evolution had produced a brain capable of the processes of language and symbolization, we now no longer speak of hominins but of humans in the fullest sense, rational animals in whom the life pattern of hominins is taken up as the foundation of a new and greater way of being and acting.

What this reveals is the loving patience of God, who sustains creation while it freely develops. As the product of the Son-*Logos*, the Mind through whom the universe is made, there are trajectories toward life, and ultimately toward rational life, that are built into the very structure of matter, as we saw when we discussed the anthropic coincidences in Chapter Seven. As the product of the Holy Spirit, the Gift-Love of God, creatures are allowed to freely develop. The human person is both the summit and surprise of evolution, not only of the evolution of life but of the entire universe.

2. The Unity of Creation

THE PROSPECT THAT WE EVOLVED from earlier living creatures infuriates some Christians who fear that it is an attack on human uniqueness and dignity, as if to be biological relatives of chimpanzees means that we are nothing more than naked apes. But what it actually reveals is a marvelous truth—that all of creation is intimately related. From nonliving matter evolved the simplest living organisms, from the simplest life eventually came animals, from the animals came man, in whom the animal is united to spirit so as to bring together the two vast realms of reality—spirit and matter, heaven and earth—which neither nonhuman animals nor angels are capable of realizing on their own. And finally, in the fullness of time, "the Word became flesh and dwelt among us" (Jn 1:14). The coming of God in the flesh in Jesus completes the process God created and guided to unite all things to each other and to himself. In the Incarnation of the Son-*Logos*, God unites to himself a human nature and, therefore, the whole universe! Now we await the final moment—"When all things are subjected to him, then the Son himself will also be subjected to him who put all things under him, that God may be everything to every one" (1 Cor 15:28).

E. Conclusion

AS WE END OUR TOUR OF HOMININ EVOLUTION and our investigation of the human difference, we must humbly recognize that our understanding of human prehistory is fragmentary. The sciences of human origins deal with a radically incomplete fossil and artifact record, and important discoveries may be just around the corner. Perhaps we will one day discover that, at some point, Neanderthals also began to exhibit the human difference. It is not out of the question, for science or for faith, that we will one day discover remains that would reveal that they, or perhaps some previously undiscovered hominin species, also crossed the threshold from hominin to human. If so, we could happily add them to our account as yet another example of the human difference. The same would be true of any bodily creatures in our universe that, like us, are also rational animals. If "E.T." is out there, then nothing within our Christian faith would prohibit us from recognizing him as a "brother," not biologically but spiritually, in his capacity for truth and freedom. **Br. Guy Consolmagno S.J.**, the current Director of the Vatican Observatory, was once asked, "Would you baptize an extraterrestrial?" His response was, "Only if she asked me to!" The special dependence upon God, and the intimacy with God it makes possible, need not be exclusive to *Homo sapiens*.

As we begin Part III, which is devoted entirely to the human species, we will begin by reflecting upon the theological understanding of the human person, a "brief" on the essential truths about being human, exploring the meaning of being human in the light of faith, as a being created in the image of God. **Pope Benedict XVI**, whose openness to evolutionary science we discussed in Chapter Eight, had this deeper truth about the human person in mind when in his inaugural homily as Pope he said, "We are not some casual and meaningless product of evolution. Each of us is the result of a thought of God. Each of us is willed, each of us is loved, each of us is necessary."[50] This will pave the way for considering the tragic side of human existence, as well as the possibility of human redemption and fulfillment.

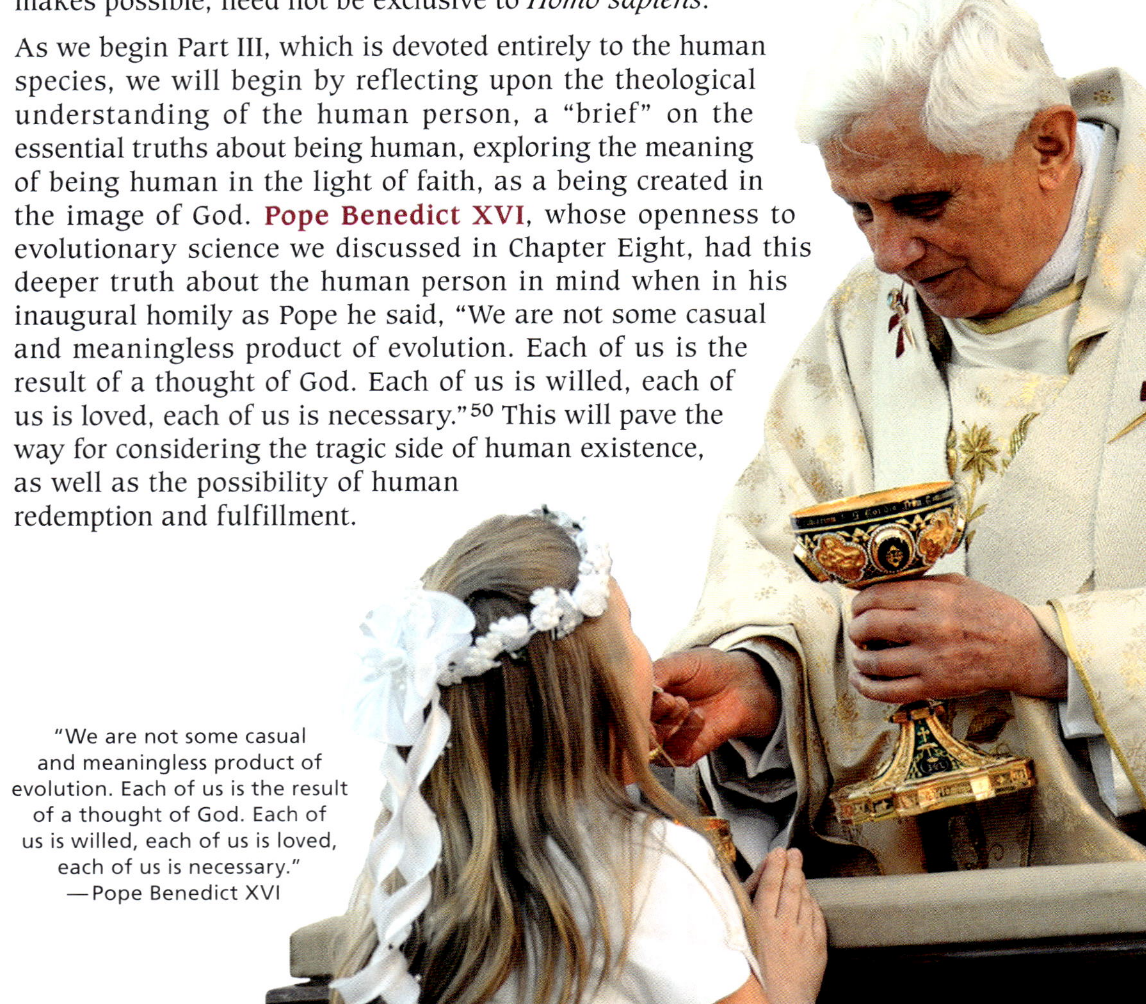

"We are not some casual and meaningless product of evolution. Each of us is the result of a thought of God. Each of us is willed, each of us is loved, each of us is necessary."
—Pope Benedict XVI

VOCABULARY

Define the following terms (or identify the person's significance):

1. Dikika Baby/Selam
2. *Homininae*
3. Paleoanthropology
4. Paleoarchaeology
5. Evolutionary Psychology
6. Hominin (Scientific)
7. Human (Scientific)
8. Human (Philosophical/Theological)
9. Rational Animal
10. Bipedalism
11. Manual Dexterity
12. Omnivorous Diet
13. Prosociality
14. *Terra Amata*
15. *Homo neanderthalensis* (Neanderthals)
16. *Cueva del Sidrón*
17. Small-band hunter-gatherers
18. Jean and Amedee Bouyssonie
19. La Chapelle-aux-Saints Cave
20. Shanidar Cave
21. Bruniquel Cave
22. Symbolism (Symbolic Thought)
23. Merge
24. Human Difference
25. Self-reflection
26. Beauty
27. Chauvet Cave
28. Genesis 2:7
29. *ădāmah* (Hebrew)
30. *ādām* (Hebrew)
31. Atrahasis
32. *nephesh* (Hebrew)
33. Direct (Special) Creation of the Human Soul

Self-reflection: cave wall hand stencils, the artistic equivalent of a personal "signature."

Cueva de las Manos (Spanish for "Cave of Hands") is famous for multiple stencils of hands. The art in the cave dates from 13,000 to 9,000 years ago. Several waves of people occupied the cave, and early artwork has been carbon-dated to ca. 7300 BC. The age of the paintings was calculated from the remains of bone blow-pipes used for spraying the paint on the wall to create the stencils of hands.

STUDY QUESTIONS

Section A

1. How does the different uses of the term "human" by paleoanthropologists and philosophers/theologians reveal the distinction between the different perspectives provided by these disciplines?

2. Why is it not possible to have an exact picture of hominin evolution and the evolutionary relationship between our species and other hominins?

3. Briefly describe the historical panorama offered by science regarding human origins. What physiological and behavioral changes seem important to understanding our own species? Which environmental factors played important roles?

4. Why is the capacity for symbolic thought important for understanding the difference between *Homo sapiens* and other hominins?

5. What is the difference between animal intelligence and human reason, according to St. Thomas Aquinas?

6. What is the difference between animal communication and human language, according to Berwick and Chomsky?

7. Who are "mitochondrial Eve" and "Y chromosomal Adam"? What do they tell us about our origins? What misinterpretation is possible?

Section B

8. How does self-reflection figure into the difference between humans and other animals? What evidence of self-reflection do we have from the paleoarchaeological record?

9. How is the capacity for beauty involved in the difference between humans and other animals? What evidence of the human aesthetic capacity do we have from the paleoarchaeological record?

Section C

10. What does the relationship between the Hebrew words *ăḏāmah* and *āḏām* tell us about the harmony between faith and science? What do they indicate about the nature of human beings?

11. What is the symbolic significance of God breathing his "breath" into human beings?

12. What is the human soul? Does its direct creation by God involve the human parents as well? Explain.

13. What is meant by the direct or special creation of the human soul according to the International Theological Commission?

14. How did Pope Benedict XVI interpret the doctrine of the special creation of the human soul?

15. How is the special creation of the human soul like a miracle? Despite the similarity, why is it not considered miraculous?

16. How are human beings the goal of the creation of the universe? Is this a scientific truth or a theological one?

Section D

17. What theological insights can be gained from seeing human evolution and origins in the light of faith?

PRACTICAL EXERCISES

1. Watch the video "To Be Human" (9 minutes, 8 seconds, *mtfresources.org/videos*). Relate the video to the picture of human origins given in Genesis 2:7.

2. One topic in this chapter stands out as an issue of massive importance for bioethics and medical interventions in human reproduction, namely, the issue of the special creation of the human soul. Discuss the following questions: When does human life occur? Does the special creation of the human soul cancel out biological parenthood as true parenthood? Why or why not? What important implications does the special creation of the human soul at the moment of conception have for medical research that involves the creation of human embryos in a laboratory for the purposes of scientific experimentation and research?

3. Watch the full-length documentary *Cave of Forgotten Dreams* (1 hour, 30 minutes, 7 seconds, *mtfresources.org/videos*) by Werner Herzog (Barcelona: Cameo, 2010). Consider the question, "How are the human symbolic imagination and the human capacity for beauty connected?"

The Chauvet Cave is named after its discoverer, Jean-Marie Chauvet. The soft, clay-like floor of the cave retains the paw prints of cave bears. Fossilized bones are abundant and include the skulls of cave bears and the horned skull of an ibex. A set of foot prints of a young child and a wolf or dog walking along side was also found, suggesting the origin of the domestic dog could date to before the last ice age.

Endnotes – Chapter Nine

1. Christopher P. Sloan, "Dikika Baby," *National Geographic* (11/2006).
2. Ibid.
3. CCC 357.
4. Ian Tattersall, *Masters of the Planet: The Search for Our Human Origins* (New York: Palgrave-MacMillan, 2012), 81-82.
5. Matt J. Rossano, *Supernatural Selection: How Religion Evolved* (Oxford: Oxford University Press, 2010), 62-63.
6. Matt Rossano and Benjamin Vandewalle, "Belief, Ritual and the Evolution of Religion" in James R. Liddle and Todd K. Schakelford, ed., *The Oxford Handbook of Evolutionary Psychology and Religion* (Oxford Handbooks Online, 2016), 2, *www.oxfordhandbooks.com/view/10.1093/oxfordhb/9780199397747.001.0001/oxfordhb-9780199397747-e-8.*
7. Tattersall, *Masters*, 33.
8. Ian Tattersall, *Paleontology: A Brief History of Life, Templeton Science and Religion Series* (West Conshohocken, PA: Templeton Press, 2010), 149-177; see 176, Figure 9.3.
9. Nicholas Wade, *Before the Dawn: Recovering the Lost History of Our Ancestors* (London: Penguin Books, 2007), 19.
10. Tattersall, *Paleontology*, 170.
11. Tattersall, *Masters*, 129-134.
12. Ibid., 113-114, 122-124.
13. Joseph Castro, "Homo Erectus: Facts About the 'Upright Man'," LiveScience, June 22, 2015, *www.livescience.com/41048-facts-about-homo-erectus.html.*
14. Tattersall, *Paleontology*, 178-180.
15. Tattersall, *Masters*, 142.
16. Richard Wrangham, *Catching Fire: How Cooking Made Us Human* (New York: Basic Books, 2009), 98-99.
17. Tattersall, *Paleontology*, 188.
18. Ian Tattersall, *The Strange Case of the Rickety Cossack: and Other Cautionary Tales from Human Evolution* (New York: St. Martin's Press, 2015), 197.
19. Darcia Narvaez, *Neurobiology and the Development of Human Morality* (New York: Norton, 2014), 7.
20. Tattersall, *Masters*, 172-175.
21. William Rendu, et al., "Evidence supporting an intentional Neandertal burial at La Chapelle-aux-Saints," *PNAS* 111:1 (January 2014): 81-86.
22. Tattersall, *Paleontology*, 185.
23. Taylor Kubota, "Neanderthals Likely Built These 176,000-Year-Old Underground Ring Structures," *Live Science*, *www.livescience.com/54906-neanderthals-built-bizarre-underground-ring-structures.html.*
24. Lorraine Boissoneault, "Were Neanderthals the Earliest Cave Artists? New Research in Spain Points to the Possibility," Smithsonian.com, February 22, 2018, *www.smithsonianmag.com/science-nature/were-neanderthals-earliest-cave-artists-new-research-spain-points-possibility-180968236/.*
25. Andrew Masterson, "Neanderthals and Early Modern Humans Were Cognitively Indistinguishable," Cosmos, February 22, 2018, *cosmosmagazine.com/archaeology/neanderthals-and-early-modern-humans-were-cognitively-indistinguishable.*
26. Tattersall, *Masters*, 177.
27. Alasdair MacIntyre, *Dependent Rational Animals: Why Human Beings Need the Virtues*, Paul Carus Lecture Series 20. (Chicago: Open Court, 1999), 53-55. Cf. St. Thomas Aquinas, *De Veritate* 24.2; *Summa Theologiae* I.84.1.
28. Tattersall, *Masters*, 185.
29. Ann Gibbons, "World's Oldest Homo Sapiens Fossils Found in Morocco," Science | AAAS, July 26, 2017, *www.sciencemag.org/news/2017/06/world-s-oldest-homo-sapiens-fossils-found-morocco.*
30. Wade, 30.
31. Fiorenzo Facchini, "Man, Origin and Nature," *inters.org/origin-nature-of-man.*
32. Stephen M. Barr, "First Words | Stephen M. Barr," *First Things*, April 01, 2017, *www.firstthings.com/article/2017/04/first-words*.
33. Nicanor Austriaco, Review of *Why Only Us: Language and Evolution*, by Robert Berwick and Noam Chomsky, Thomist 81 (October 2017): 619.
34. Ian Tattersall, *The World from Beginnings to 4000 BCE* (Oxford: Oxford University Press, 2008), 89.
35. Dennis R. Venema and Scot McKnight, *Adam and the Genome: Reading Scripture After Genetic Science* (Grand Rapids, MI: Brazos Press, 2017), 62-65.
36. Paulinus Forsthoefel, *Religious Faith Meets Modern Science* (New York: Alba House, 1994), 92-95.
37. Walker Percy, *Lost in the Cosmos: The Last Self-Help Book* (New York: Farrar, Straus and Giroux, 1983), 254.
38. Paul Mellars, "Neanderthal symbolism and ornament manufacture: The bursting of a bubble?" *PNAS* 107:47 (2010): 20147–20148.
39. Lea Surugue, "Why This Paleolithic Burial Site Is So Strange (and so Important)," *SAPIENS*, March 5, 2018, *www.sapiens.org/archaeology/paleolithic-burial-sunghir/.*
40. Tattersall, *Paleontology*, 183.
41. Agata Blaszczak-Boxe, "Crows Are First Animals Spotted Using Tools to Carry Objects," New Scientist, July 28, 2016, *www.newscientist.com/article/2099246-crows-are-first-animals-spotted-using-tools-to-carry-objects/.*
42. W. Norris Clarke, *The One and the Many*, 298-302.
43. For a thorough examination of Chauvet Cave and its significance, see *Cave of Forgotten Dreams*, dir. Werner Herzog (Barcelona: Cameo, 2010).
44. Joseph Ratzinger, *In the Beginning*, 43-44.
45. International Theological Commission, C&S, 70.
46. Joseph Ratzinger, *Dogma and Preaching: Applying Christian Doctrine to Daily Life*, 2nd ed. (San Francisco: Ignatius Press, 2017), 141-142.
47. St. John Paul II, General Audience, January 2, 1980, *www.ewtn.com/catholicism/library/creation-as-a-fundamental-and-original-gift-8469.*
48. International Theological Commission, C&S, no. 66.
49. C.S. Lewis, *The Problem of Pain* (New York: Simon and Schuster, 1996), 68-71.
50. Benedict XVI, Inaugural Homily, April 24, 2005, *w2.vatican.va/content/benedict-xvi/en/homilies/2005/documents/hf_ben-xvi_hom_20050424_inizio-pontificato.html.*

Part III

In His Image: Human Personhood, Human History, and Modern Science

Chapter Ten
In His Image: The Human Person from the Divine Perspective

What does it mean for humans to be the image of God?

How does the truth about the human person revealed by God complete the picture offered by modern science?

What is human reason and human freedom, and how do they relate us to God, to other humans, and to creation?

Indeed, to the question as to what distinguishes the human being from an animal...the answer has to be that they are the beings that God made capable of thinking and praying. They are most profoundly themselves when they discover their relation to their Creator...the image of God means that human beings are beings of word and of love...

—Pope Benedict XVI, *In the Beginning*...

At the end of Chapter Eight, we made a crucial transition—from animal evolution to human origins. There we observed that only one creature is capable of saying, "let it be," *amen*, to God in the same way that God says, "let there be," *Amen*, to creatures. All creatures participate in God's act of creation as secondary causes, but as far as we know only one kind of creature (other than the angels, which we will bracket out for this chapter) can offer itself knowingly, freely, and lovingly to this great partnership. That creature is the human person. ***The Great Amen is ourselves.***

The *Catechism of the Catholic Church* proclaims this unique and central role of humanity in God's plan of creation and redemption. It begins by quoting the First Creation Account: "God created man in his own image, in the image of God he created him; male and female he created them" (Gn 1:27). Man is this image because "of all visible creatures only man is 'able to know and love his creator.' He is 'the only creature on earth that God has willed for its own sake,' and he alone is called to share, by knowledge and love, in God's own life."[1] In this chapter, we will focus primarily on what God has revealed about the deepest meaning of being human, which consists in being the embodied image of God.

"God created man in his own image, in the image of God he created him; male and female he created them."

A. Reason and Freedom: The Foundations of the Divine Image

1. The ABC's of Imaging God

THE GREAT THEME OF THE CHRISTIAN FAITH regarding the human person is that all human beings are created in the image of God (Latin: *imago Dei*). In Sacred Scripture, "image of God" is the central definition of being human, which reveals that "the mystery of man cannot be grasped apart from the mystery of God."[2] The key Old Testament text is Genesis 1:26-28:

> 26 Then God said, "Let us make man (*āḏām*) in our image (*tzelem enu*), after our likeness; and let them have dominion over the fish of the sea, and over the birds of the air, and over the cattle, and over all the earth, and over every creeping thing that creeps upon the earth."
>
> 27 So God created man in his own image, in the image of God (*tzelem Elohim*) he created him; male and female he created them.
>
> 28 And God blessed them, and God said to them, "Be fruitful and multiply, and fill the earth and subdue it; and have dominion over the fish of the sea and over the birds of the air and over every living thing that moves upon the earth."

The great theme of the Christian faith regarding the human person is that all human beings are created in the image of God.

First, let us notice the difference between how the creative action of God is depicted here in contrast to the creation of light or the other animals. Unlike in the other acts of creation, God is depicted as deliberating when he makes humanity ("let us make *āḏām*..." [Gn 2:7]), symbolizing the special status of human beings among all creatures. In the words of **St. Gregory of Nyssa** (334-395):

> **What a marvel!...only to the making of man does the Maker of all draw near with careful thought, so as to prepare beforehand for him material for his formation, and to liken his form to an archetypal beauty, and, setting before him a mark for which he is to come into being, to make for him a nature appropriate and allied to the operations, and suitable for the object in hand.**[3]

The whole human person is seen as created in the image of God.

In this passage upon which St. Gregory is commenting, God almost seems to be reflecting on his own nature as he prepares to make his image. The Hebrew term *tzelem* reflects the ancient Near Eastern idea that the king is the image of God on earth; notice that immediately after God creates them he gives them dominion over the earth (see verse 28). But here, it is not just the king that is the image of God; every human being shares in a kind of royal dignity. Notice also that what God is making is not merely bodies or souls but whole human beings, body and soul, male and female. The whole human person is seen as created in the image of God. Therefore the *imago Dei* is not restricted to one or another aspect of human nature such as upright stature, sexuality, or even intellect.[4]

Besides its royal connotations, what does it mean for something to be an image? **St. Thomas Aquinas** developed an excellent way of understanding the uniqueness of an image: by contrasting *images* with *vestiges*. Some things that are made are simply vestiges (traces) of their maker, as when a paleoarchaeologist finds stone tools made by early humans. Some information about the maker can be gathered through such vestiges, such as that the maker had opposable thumbs or that he or she was an intelligent creature. Vestiges of the Trinity can be found in all creatures.[5] An image, however, expresses the thing it images directly, such as in a self-portrait. As St. Thomas Aquinas says, "An image represents a thing in a better defined manner according to all its parts and the arrangement of its parts."[6] In other words, an image is a precise representation of something. An image, unlike a vestige, is an image because of its likeness to what it resembles.

2. God Is Truth and Love

SINCE GOD IS PURE SPIRIT, the foundations of our imaging of God are not "located" in some part of us; rather, they are to be found in our unique spiritual capacities as human creatures. The Bible and the Christian faith tell us that God is Truth. We have already seen that God is the unlimited, infinite source of all perfections in creation, including the orderliness and knowability of all things. This is what Jesus meant when he said, "I am the Light of the world" (Jn 8:12): he is God himself, the Son-*Logos*, the perfect source of the truth of all things.

Scripture also tells us that God is Love—"He who does not love does not know God; for God is Love" (1 Jn 4:8). *Love* in the fullest Christian meaning of the term refers to the giving of one's self for the good of another, to the willing of the good of the other for his or her own sake. As the *Catechism* explains, "God's very being is love. By sending his only Son and the Spirit of Love in the fullness of time, God has revealed his innermost secret: God himself is an eternal exchange of love, Father, Son and Holy Spirit."[7] God's "family structure" is the perfect expression of the meaning of the word "love" in its purest sense.

If "God's very being is Truth and Love,"[8] then being God's image must somehow involve these two attributes, too. Humans cannot be the image of God, who is Truth and Love, unless they have a unique capacity for truth and love. *Reason*, which is the ability to know truth, and *free will*, which is the ability to love and to determine one's self and one's actions, are the twin foundations of man's imaging of God.

In summary: God is Truth and Love, and the human person is the image of God because he or she can know truth and love freely. Understanding these two human attributes reveals the image of God within every one of us.

Let us first look at the human ability to know truth.

God's "family structure" is the perfect expression of the meaning of the word "love" in its purest sense.

3. Human Reason: The First Foundation of Imaging God

OF ALL VISIBLE CREATURES, only human beings are able to know and to pursue truth, a capacity called *reason*. What does this capacity entail? **Cardinal Christoph Schönborn** offers us one key aspect of human reason—man has a *capacity for objectivity*. The capacity for objectivity is man's "ability to go beyond his immediate interests and needs and to perceive himself and others as the beings they are in their own right." He continues:

Cardinal Christoph Schönborn

I do not just feel, I can also examine my feelings, approach them "objectively," interpret them. I am not completely immersed in my world, I can look at it, can change it, compare it with other things, and can stand over against it with a critical spirit. I can think about it as well as myself.[9]

This objectivity is also the power to transcend mere appearances and to get at how things are in themselves.

As a helpful thought experiment in seeing the way reason works, consider an indigenous woman, a dog, and a New Yorker making a hike together across the Australian Outback. The indigenous woman is carefully guiding the New Yorker to safety by teaching her to understand the hazards and opportunities of the environment, including the various plants and animals they encounter along the way. The dog is also actively investigating the environment, sniffing plants, growling at kangaroos, and running from saltwater crocodiles. But there the similarities cease. The dog, which does not possess reason, perceives the similarities between each experience and acts according to its instincts (running, hiding, growling, etc.). The New Yorker does not know the natures of the various things she encounters, but she is quickly coming to understand them through the expert guidance she is receiving. She might make mistakes about the various things she encounters. But the indigenous woman, whose people have lived in the Outback for centuries, deeply understands the natures of the animals and plants they encounter.

In time and with some explanation, the New Yorker would come to the indigenous woman's understanding of the terrain, whereas the dog would not. The difference between the dog and the two humans is that the dog's perception is only *sensory*, while the perception of the humans on the hike is both sensory and rational (they are interested in what things are, their truth).[10]

Human rationality, therefore, involves the ability to transcend the senses and to understand the meaning of *abstract concepts*. Abstract concepts are also called *universals*—ideas that do not refer to this or that object but to all possible objects of a certain kind. Some examples of abstract concepts are "justice," "visibility," and "beauty." For instance, consider one such abstract concept—*circularity*. It applies to all circles and circular objects "of any size, position, and orientation." In fact, circularity is not a physical object, although it can be correctly attributed to all physical objects which are circular. Its universality has an "unlimited reach" to all possible circular things: It is infinite in scope.[11]

Another element of human reason is that it involves the ability to judge the truth and falsehood of propositions (i.e., statements proposed to be true). For instance, we can think about "$2 + 2 = 4$" and come to the conclusion that it is a correct or true mathematical equation. A computer can also distinguish between true and false propositions, but it can do this only when a human with understanding builds it and programs it to carry out such steps in an automatic way. Unlike a computer, we can reason correctly about true or false propositions even when we have not been programmed to do so, that is, even when we have never been given a precise set of instructions telling us exactly what to do.[12]

Human beings not only can judge truth and falsehood, but they are also capable of certitude that some truths are necessarily true.

Even more fascinating is that human beings not only can judge truth and falsehood, but they are also capable of certitude that some truths are necessarily true. For instance, take the mathematical equation "$1 \neq 0$." Once we understand the concepts involved, namely, "1," "0," and "inequality," and the idea "$1 \neq 0$" is grasped, we also can see with certainty the impossibility that "$1 = 0$." In the words of physicist **Stephen Barr**, humans can know with certainty that necessary truths like $1 \neq 0$ are "true here and now, true a billion years ago and true a billion years hence, true in galaxies too remote to be seen with a telescope, even true in any other possible universe." To be human, therefore, is to know truth in itself and even to recognize the utter necessity of some truths. Indeed, we can even know that some truths remain true in an infinite number of cases, such as "$a \times b = b \times a$, for all numbers a and b."[13]

4. The Rational Soul and Existence Beyond Death

THE REMARKABLE HUMAN CAPACITY to know truth is clearly essential to human uniqueness and dignity. But it also reveals that the soul is *immaterial* (not made of matter) and, therefore, *immortal* (enduring in existence even after the cessation of biological life).

How can such a claim be justified? If the human ability to know truth is such that it can get beyond how things appear to the bodily senses and know them as they really are; can know things (like circularity and beauty) in the abstract, independent of their concrete existence in the physical world; and can know that some truths are true in all cases, even in infinite cases, then the human ability to know truth transcends the capacity of any merely physical thing, including the brain. The human faculty of reason reveals that the soul is not intrinsically dependent upon matter, since any purely material entity would be incapable of knowing or generating immaterial ideas and truths. Although it may rely upon the senses and upon matter in various ways, human reason *in itself* is something intrinsically spiritual. It is a power of the human spiritual soul.

Assumption of the Virgin
The immateriality and immortality of the soul is yet another paradox at the heart of being human.

If this is the case, then the soul can be neither physically destroyed nor be subjected to material decay. To destroy something is to divide it into separate parts, to break it up. But only something that is material can be divided or decomposed.[14] Philosophical analysis, therefore, indicates what God also reveals, namely, that the soul "does not perish when it separates from the body at death."[15]

The immateriality and immortality of the soul is yet another paradox at the heart of being human. As we observed in Chapter Nine, the human soul is the form of the human body, not a separate thing God makes independently of it. Along with the physical stuff of which our bodies are made, it is one of two principles that makes a human being a living being. The same could be said of all living things, which are all constituted by matter and a life principle. And yet, unlike the souls of any other animals, the human soul can and does endure beyond the death of the body, it does not cease to be when the body ceases to be a living body.

As human technology advances, a common trend both in philosophy and in entertainment is to compare artificial intelligence and human intelligence. Computers have become more and more powerful over time, and have been made capable of vastly more efficient and complex activities. A question that has been around for as long as computers, but is taken with increasing seriousness, is whether computers will ultimately be capable of thought at the human level. The reverse question also arises: Is the human mind nothing more than a "wet computer" or "a machine made out of meat"? According to the materialist/reductionist mindset, the human mind is nothing more than the brain, which, with its sophisticated neural circuitry, certainly has a great deal in common with computers.

But as we can see above, reason is not a higher level of intelligence; it is a power that transcends intelligence or brainpower. A computer is trapped in its own rules. A human being, by contrast, can think about the rules themselves: understanding why they have the structure they do and what their limitations are. For example, we can use mathematical insights to discover new rules that are consistent with old ones but also go beyond them. We can discover new ways of proving things. A human being can think about any and all propositions and can even reason about the process of reasoning. And so, human beings can do something that the most advanced computer cannot and could not.

A computer can use numbers, but a child can grasp the concept of *number*.

A computer can use numbers, but a child can grasp the concept of *number*, a concept that embraces the entire series of numbers, which is infinite. The human mind does not simply compute, it *comprehends*, which literally means "holds together," a vast, even infinite multiplicity of things in a single, simple insight.[16] Here we see another way in which the capacity for reason is at the foundation of our imaging of God. God is a simple and indivisible unity, an infinite act of understanding that grasps all of reality in a single thought. God is the Infinite Mind; man, by reflection, is the finite mind,[17] a reality which no computer, no machine however sophisticated, can begin to match.

Now let us investigate the second power that is foundational to human beings as the image of God and that stems from human reason: free will.

5. Free Will: Imaging the God Who Is Love

THE HUMAN CAPACITY FOR KNOWING TRUTH, as we have seen, means that humans can know things in themselves, in their essences. But because of this ability, human beings are also capable of knowing things in relationship to *goodness*. Goodness refers to that which contributes to the perfection of a being. For example, in a plant or animal health is "a good," and in a rational being wisdom and friendship are "goods." We can also say that food is good for an animal because it contributes to its having the good of health, and a book may be good for a human being because it contributes to his or her having the good of knowledge or enjoyment. The goodness of some goal we seek or some action we perform refers to its ability to meet some need we have or to actualize some potential that we possess. For instance, we can comprehend that shopping online can meet a need we have for a new pair of shoes or a new jacket. We can also comprehend that we might also spend that time enjoying a comedy, actualizing our capacity for

In the fully human sense, *love* is the free choice to will the true good of another.

laughter. In both cases we use our ability to know things as they are in themselves and in their relation to goodness, to consider actions we may perform, and then perform them or avoid performing them based on rational deliberation.[18]

Parable of the Man Who Hoards (Lk 12:16-21)
Animals are moved by appetites and instincts, humans can either be moved by those same appetites and instincts *or* they can move themselves by free will in opposition to these inclinations.

This ability to act or to not act on the basis of reason is called *freedom*, "the power, rooted in reason and will, to act or not to act, to do this or that, and so to perform deliberate actions on one's own responsibility."[19] Based on reason, human beings are capable of consciously choosing or avoiding this or that action. Unlike the other animals, which are moved by appetites and instincts, humans are capable of directing their appetites and instincts through reason. Whereas the other animals are moved by appetites and instincts, humans can either be moved by those same appetites or instincts *or* they can move themselves freely in opposition to these inclinations. This freedom includes "the possibility of choosing between good and evil, and thus of growing in perfection or of failing and sinning."[20] It is by our wills that we enact freedom, and our free wills are in turn grounded in our reason, our ability to know the truth. This is what **St. Thomas Aquinas** meant when he referred to the uniquely human ability to make judgments about our own judgments. Only a creature that can make such judgments freely is a truly moral being.

Consequently, human beings are capable of love. There are many dimensions or levels to love. The first is one we share with the animals—the inclination to act due to being attracted by a good. In human beings this attraction "causes a desire for the absent good and the hope of attaining it; [it] finds completion in the pleasure and joy of the good possessed."[21] Thus, our natural love of self leads us to pursue goods that fulfill us and give us joy. We also share the tendency among many animals toward prosociality or prosocial behavior, as we saw in the case of *Homo erectus* and the Neanderthals. Such instinctive tendencies toward our own good and also the good of others are part of the animal natures that are part of our evolutionary inheritance. They provide reasons for acting that are naturally good.

Christianity, when considered with respect to our own self, is often mischaracterized as an abusive hatred of self, or at least indifference toward one's self, as if following natural tendencies to care for ourselves is intrinsically evil. But, as St. Thomas Aquinas observed, quite the opposite is the case. *Self-love*, in the sense of desiring physical goods like food and drink, physical well-being, knowledge of the truth, and moral goodness, is the natural source of all other free acts for human beings. This becomes the basis for knowing what is good for others and learning how to best provide it for them. In this way, self-love is not the opposite of the love of others; it actually makes that love possible.[22]

Such tendencies, good and necessary as they are, however, do not entirely capture the human ability to love. In the fully human sense, *love* is the free choice to will the true good of another.[23] Through knowing ourselves and also being able to understand reality objectively, humans are capable of knowing the true good of another person and of freely choosing to act for the sake

Animals are capable of something like love; they are attracted to goodness as well. But this attraction is one that *possesses the animal.*

of that good. In this way human beings can love in the way that God loves, not just for the good someone brings me but for the sake of their own good. We see, then, that fully human love is not a mere "feeling" or emotion; it is an act of the will. To love someone is to will and act for what is good for that person—and in the case of proper self-love it is willing what is genuinely good for oneself, i.e., what helps to perfect oneself.

As mentioned above, animals are capable of something like love; they are attracted to goodness as well. *But this attraction is one that possesses the animal, even when it acts altruistically, and is not possessed by it.* Humans on the other hand, are capable, by reason and will, of *self-possession*. Therefore, we are capable of making our lives a gift and blessing for others and, above all, of giving ourselves in love to God.

Of course, we do not find it easy to choose the good for ourselves and others; in fact, we find ourselves often inclined toward moral evil. We experience great conflict within ourselves, and human history is saturated with tragedy because of this, as we discussed in Chapter Six when we considered the problem of evil. The dark riddle at the heart of human existence revolves around the divorce between our desires and our reason, between our best tendencies toward knowing the truth and loving what is good and our common struggle to overcome evil tendencies and habits within ourselves. We will explore this universal human experience in the next chapter.

B. The Divine Image in Three Dimensions: Holism, Sexuality, and Personhood

WE HAVE GONE A LONG WAY toward understanding why human beings, out of all the visible creatures on the planet, can alone be called the image of God. Now that we have seen the foundations of this unique status, let us consider the specific ways in which reason and freedom are realized.

To be a human being is to be able to know and love, but human knowledge and love are expressed in very particular ways. What makes human love different from angelic love and divine love is that human love is twofold: 1) humans love in their unique status as a union of body and soul, and 2) human love is expressed in the equality and complementarity of masculinity and femininity, of being male and female.

Finally, human beings love as *persons*, and this is something that they share in common with angels and with God. All of these dimensions add more detail to our understanding of the human being as the image of God.

Romeo and Juliet
Human beings love as *persons*, and this is something that they share in common with angels and with God.

1. "Body and Soul But Truly One"[24]

IT IS CLEARLY TRUE THAT SOMETHING OF MAN is immaterial, which is why humans can exercise the faculties of reason and free will, as we saw above. But, as we also saw in Genesis 2:7, the Lord God made man from "dust." In other words, the human person is a being that is both bodily and spiritual simultaneously.[25] To be human is to be a hybrid, a creature that has one foot in the world of nonrational animals and another in the world of the angels, although he or she is neither. In other words, a human being is not two things but one, a single substance made up of two distinct principles. These principles are a material body and an immaterial soul, and this union of body and soul is not like the union of two parts.[26] In the words of **St. Thomas Aquinas**, "The soul... is not an entire man, and I am not my soul."[27] St. Thomas will not even call a soul without a body a *person* in the proper sense, for to be a living human person is to be both body and soul.

The theological doctrine of the resurrection of the body is crucially important for Christians. Between the time of his Crucifixion and Resurrection, Christ brought salvation to all of the righteous who had died since the beginning of the world.

This means that bodiliness is essential to being human. The Christian faith rejects all forms of *dualism* (i.e., theories that assert that the body and soul are separate substances, different things). This is what is meant by the Church teaching that the intellectual (rational) soul is the form of the human body, a teaching first declared at the *Council of Vienne* in 1311-1312 (and later at Lateran V in 1513).[28]

The body is so essential to being human that even our spiritual powers of reason and freedom are dependent upon our bodiliness. Catholic thought has long recognized that the body is necessary for all acts of reason and will in this life;[29] the discoveries of neuroscience about brain activity involved in human thought are not in conflict with Christian theology. However, the Christian faith also declares what is attested to by our own experience and philosophical reflection, that the brain is not sufficient by itself for acts of reason and will. Because of the close dependence of body and spirit upon one another, man is the image of God as a body-soul composite.[30] Our imaging of God is not reducible to our body or our soul in isolation from one another; it is the whole human being in his or her integrity that is the image of God.

The intrinsic unity of body and soul is in no way compromised by the fact that the immaterial soul survives the death of the body. Even though a soul sees the vision of God in heaven, this is not a proper situation for the soul. This is the reason why the theological doctrine of the resurrection of the body is so crucially important for Christians, that all the dead will be reunited with their bodies in a new and permanent way that cannot be imagined. Our souls need our bodies to be fully human, to be fully the image of God.

As we have already seen, the fact that human beings are a union of matter and spirit means that the biological production of human beings through the sexual act, *procreation*, involves God in a very special way. A bodily process cannot of itself produce a spiritual soul, nor can a perishable body produce an immortal reality. The Church therefore teaches that every human soul is created immediately by God. This does not mean that the body is produced by the parents and the soul by God, separately. Rather, God causes human procreation to produce an effect that transcends its biological capacity.[31] When the material that makes up the human body is organized sufficiently for human life, so that a living human being is produced, then that human being has a soul, not because of the mere powers of biology but because of the power of God.[32] This is true even when human life is created in ways contradictory to God's plan and to human dignity; even a human created through cloning would have an immortal soul.

Why did God create humanity as a hybrid of body and spirit? Perhaps it is because of his love for unity. God, as we know, is three divine Persons who are so intimately united that the real distinction between Father, Son, and Holy Spirit coincides with the perfect unity of the divine nature. God's creation, then, should also be a unity in some way. But, in order for there to be such a unity, a creature that possesses both body and spirit unites the physical universe with the realm of the spirit. Humanity is the link between the world of atoms and the world of angels, while nonetheless being something quite different than an angel.

The human person, the image of God, is a unity of body and soul that brings about the unity that God intended for the entire realms of matter and spirit. Beyond this awesome cosmic unity, God also intended another unity within humanity itself: the unity of man and woman.

2. Man and Woman: "A Unity in Two"

IN THE WORDS OF the *Catechism of the Catholic Church*, "God created man and woman *together* and willed each *for* the other."[33] Therefore, the difference between man and woman and the relationship that this difference makes possible are essential elements in their imaging of God.[34]

We have already noted that, due to the union of body and soul, bodiliness has a part to play in a person's acts of reason and will. Therefore, all human actions, including spiritual acts, are also conditioned by the unique bodiliness manifested in maleness and femaleness, masculinity and femininity: "Each [sex] possesses a way of being in the world, to see, to think, to feel, to engage in mutual exchange with other persons who are also defined by their sexual identity."[35] It is important to note here that the Church recognizes that sex and gender inform each other; sexual identity is not chosen but is gifted to us from the moment of conception.[36]

"God created man and woman *together* and willed each *for* the other."

In their imaging of God, man and woman are *equal*, *different*, and *complementary*. First, the Christian faith teaches that man and woman are equally created in God's image. Both have reason and freedom, and neither sex possesses a greater dignity than the other. Second, it also affirms that man and woman are different—they exercise reason and freedom in a way "proper and [unique] to their sexual identity."[37]

The third characteristic is just as crucial: "Man and woman were made 'for each other'"; that is, they are reciprocal (mutually supportive) and complementary (mutually enriching). In marriage, they become "one flesh" and have the potential of uniting "their bodies and spirits in an attitude of total openness and self giving." When they do so, "they form a new image of God," who is a perfect communion of persons. The image of God that is found in each and every human person is fulfilled in a special way in this union of man and woman.[38]

3. Personhood and Communion

THE SPIRITUAL POWERS OF REASON AND FREE WILL, made manifest and expressed visibly in the human body united to the human soul and gloriously revealed in marital love, point to the fact that the human being, out of all the visible creatures on this planet, is a *personal being*, a subject (one who possesses himself or herself) and not simply an object. A *person* is a being capable of knowledge and love; a human person is a person who, due to knowledge and love, exists bodily in the world as a relational and social being, the embodied image of God.[39] Because a human person can reason and freely determine him- or herself, he or she has a level of uniqueness that is much more radical than simply being an individual member of a species. An individual is a unique *what*, but a *person* is also a *who* with a unique *personality*.

A human community of 83,000 attended Mass celebrated by St. John Paul II in 1995 at Giants Stadium. Personhood and community are essential dimensions of the image of God that is humanity.

Because of this self-possession, which reveals a deep interior life, the human person is capable of having the closest contacts with the things and beings of the world, especially with other persons. That contact begins on the natural bodily level by virtue of the senses, but it also blossoms into an interpersonal contact, a contact that is interior as well as exterior.[40] Because of reason and free will, human persons are capable of *communion*—a commitment of self to other persons in which mutual self-giving forms a spiritual unity. Personhood is the basis of the human ability to form communities, such as families, friendships, local, state, and national societies, teams, and the Church, which is the Body of Christ.[41] In the Trinity, there is a perfect communion of Persons who share a single divine life. In human communities, even though humans have been wounded by sin, the human race reveals the image of God once again. Personhood and community are essential dimensions of the image of God that is humanity.

The highest form of communion that human persons can have is their relationship with God, expressed and realized especially in receiving the Sacrament of the Eucharist, which we appropriately call Holy Communion, because in it Christ gives himself to us—Body, Blood, Soul, and Divinity—and we give ourselves to him in return.

Because a human being is a person, he or she is the subject of special rights. No good, even if it seems to be that of society as a whole, is sufficient grounds for the violation of a human person. **St. John Paul II** said that, when it comes to persons, only one rule applies. Positively expressed, this rule is the obligation to love: "Thou shalt love!" Negatively, this rule is expressed as a prohibition: "Thou shalt not use!"[42] The message is clear: *A person is not an object to be exploited but a subject to be loved.* Only by loving others, and never using them in an exploitative fashion, can we respect the absolute integrity and dignity of human beings.

C. The Natural Virtues: The Art of Being Human

THE FACT THAT HUMANS HAVE REASON AND FREEDOM means that our lives have ceased to simply be the outcome of our evolutionary instincts and tendencies and have become something that can be, and are, deeply shaped by both our capacity for reason and our free choices. In this regard we can recall the First Creation Account, wherein God makes human beings but never pronounces that they are morally good, only that his entire creation has become very good now that his image dwells within it. With the emergence of the image of God, the world has become not only a stage for love and moral goodness but also the setting for the whole range of moral evils.

The Beatitudes given to us by Jesus Christ in the Sermon on the Mount help us develop the cardinal virtues of prudence, justice, courage, and temperance. It is by these virtues that the divine image of the human person is brought to its natural fulfillment.

In light of this Revelation from God, we can know in faith that every human being, knowingly or not, receives his or her being from God as not only a gift but a task, a crucial project. The moral, virtuous life is not so much about what we ought to do; instead, it is about who we ought to be.[43] The real task of human life is to strengthen our natural tendencies toward goodness and to correct, purify, and master those tendencies we have toward evil. When we are successful, we develop *virtues*, habits of goodness that are the greatest realization of what a human life can be according to its God-given nature apart from supernatural grace. The art of being human consists precisely in the cultivation of these possibilities, all of which build upon important elements of our human nature as a union of body and soul.

The first natural virtue, *prudence*, is based upon and perfects our capacity for knowing the truth. The prudent person is one who sees things as they really are and understands how to best choose what is right and good in the light of the whole truth about God, the world, his or her self, and others. Christian tradition has sometimes depicted the virtue of prudence as a human being with two faces: One face is of an old, wise man that looks backward to the past. The other is a beautiful, young woman that faces the present and the future with eyes that reveal that she is engaged in careful thought. To be prudent is to move with careful deliberation into the future while being informed by the wisdom of past experience. Prudence is the opposite of *moralism*, which is an approach to moral decisions that is focused on moral rules without understanding the reasons for them. Moralism makes moral decision-making rigid, uncreative, and unspontaneous. Prudence makes us authentically and creatively good, able to light the way for others because we understand the rules, why rules are necessary, and also the limitation of rules. All of the other natural virtues depend upon prudence; she has often been called the "mother" of the other virtues.

The second natural virtue is *justice*, the habit of giving to others what is due to them. Justice directs us in our relationships with others, and in justice we really conceive of other people as entirely distinct from ourselves, worthy of their own lives and happiness, and act accordingly. The third is *courage*, which is the habit of choosing what is right regardless of the consequences, the willingness to even endure suffering rather than betray what is right. One subvirtue of courage is patience because when we are patient we endure the delay of the good we desire rather than act selfishly and immediately. The fourth is *temperance* or moderation, by virtue of which we master our animal instincts, our natural desires for physical goods, and pursue those goods in ways that truly serve our growth and happiness.

St. Agnes of Rome
"Probably the most revered female martyr of the early Church."—Mike Aquilina, Catholic author and lecturer.
Together the natural virtues produce human beings that are more able to not only receive divine grace but to also cooperate with it.

It is by these virtues that the divine image of the human person is brought to its natural fulfillment through the right exercise of our God-given reason and free will. Together they produce human beings that are more able to not only receive divine grace but to also cooperate with it. Through our free cooperation with divine grace we are invited to participate in the very life of God. *Grace* is "the free and undeserved help that God gives us to respond to his call to become children of God, adoptive sons, partakers of the divine nature and of eternal life."[44] Through this special help, we become capable of new virtues—faith, hope, and charity—which fulfill the art of being fully human, raising our natural virtues to the level of the supernatural. Living in God's grace means to participate in the life of God, imperfectly in this life but perfectly in the life to come. Divine creation makes humans the image of God; through grace we become more like God, radiating his truth, goodness, and love to one another. We will revisit this in Chapter Twelve.

D. Conclusion: The Human Person, Stewardship, and Science

AS THE IMAGE OF GOD, HUMAN BEINGS share the world with other creatures but are distinguished from them by reason and freedom. Therefore, we have a special relationship with the rest of visible creation; as far as we know, only human beings are capable of enjoying the privilege of sharing in God's own governance of the universe. In fact, this vocation is given by God himself. In the First Creation Account, we read that God blessed the man and woman, saying, "Be fruitful and multiply, and fill the earth and subdue it" (Gn 1:28). Human beings do not replace God, but they do act as his stewards of the universe and its goods. *Stewardship* is a participation in the ownership of something whose primary ownership belongs to another.[45]

In stewardship over creation, humans are called to rule over it much as someone might act as the master of someone else's household, such as the servants in the parable Jesus tells of the man who gives his servants money to invest and then to return to him with interest (Lk 19:12-27). Man is master of creation but not in a way in which he can abuse the world. In fact, his dominion over the world involves a responsibility and service that he owes to God;[46] our care for the earth and its creatures is an act of justice by which we give to God the Creator what he is due. Careful stewardship of the earth is an act of justice, both to God who creates it and by extension to the creatures who share the planet with us.

This important truth was affirmed by **Pope Francis** in *Laudato Si'*, his 2015 encyclical letter subtitled "On Care for Our Common Home." Pointing to pollution, climate change, the scarcity of clean water, and the loss of biodiversity, which are the direct effects of human overconsumption, the Pope observed that, in the biblical creation accounts, to be human means to be grounded not only in relationships with God and others but also with the earth itself.[47] Noting **St. Francis of Assisi's** joyous recognition of the earth as "our sister," the Pope declared:

"Our Common Home—Our Sister." The beautiful "Blue Marble" photograph taken from space by the crew of Apollo 17 in 1972.

> **This sister now cries out to us because of the harm we have inflicted on her by our irresponsible use and abuse of the goods with which God has endowed her. We have come to see ourselves as her lords and masters, entitled to plunder her at will. The violence present in our hearts, wounded by sin, is also reflected in the symptoms of sickness evident in the soil, in the water, in the air and in all forms of life. This is why the earth herself, burdened and laid waste, is among the most abandoned and maltreated of our poor; she "groans in travail" (Rom 8:22). We have forgotten that we ourselves are dust of the earth (cf. Gn 2:7); our very bodies are made up of her elements, we breathe her air and we receive life and refreshment from her waters.[48]**

Rather than acting as stewards of the rest of creation, human beings have too often ravaged it out of greed and indifference. **Pope Benedict XVI** referred to our current environmental crisis as evidence that humans have lost their way, like sheep lost in the desert:

> **And there are so many kinds of desert. There is the desert of poverty, the desert of hunger and thirst, the desert of abandonment, of loneliness, of destroyed love. There is the desert of God's darkness, the emptiness of souls no longer aware of their dignity or the goal of human life. The external deserts in the world are growing, because the internal deserts have become so vast. Therefore the earth's treasures no longer serve to build God's garden for all to live in, but they have been made to serve the powers of exploitation and destruction. The Church as a whole and all her Pastors, like Christ, must set out to lead people out of the desert, towards the place of life, towards friendship with the Son of God, towards the One who gives us life, and life in abundance.[49]**

The human capacity for truth and goodness has been deeply wounded, as we see in our growing environmental crisis and in so many dark places within human life and history, and the destruction of our common home is an outward sign of this interior darkness. Our consideration of the image of God, therefore, now leads us to consider the sad reality of sin, in which the image of God in us is broken and disfigured.

VOCABULARY

Define the following terms (or identify the person's significance):

1. ***Imago Dei*** **(Latin)**
2. ***Tzelem*** **(Hebrew)**
3. **Image (St. Thomas Aquinas)**
4. **Reason**
5. **Freedom**
6. **Capacity for Objectivity**
7. **Sensory**
8. **Universals (abstract concepts)**
9. **Immaterial (immateriality)**
10. **Immortality**
11. **Goodness**
12. **Freedom (free will)**
13. **Love (desire)**
14. **Self-love (animals and humans)**
15. **Love (self-gift)**
16. **Self-possession**
17. **Dualism**
18. **Council of Vienne**
19. **Man and Woman**
20. **Person**
21. **Human Person**
22. **Communion**
23. **Virtues**
24. **Prudence**
25. **Moralism**
26. **Justice**
27. **Courage**
28. **Stewardship**

Plastic pollution on a beach in Ghana.
Careful stewardship of the earth is an act of *justice,* both to God who creates it and by extension to the creatures who share the planet with us.

STUDY QUESTIONS

Section A

1. Briefly recount the symbolism of Genesis 1:26-28. What do these symbols tell us about human beings?

2. Using St. Thomas Aquinas's definition of an image, apply it to the human being as the image of God.

3. Why must man's imaging of God involve truth and love? How does it involve these two crucial elements?

4. What three abilities characterize rationality?

5. Justify the assertion that human rationality reveals the human soul to be immaterial and immortal.

6. What is the difference between artificial intelligence and human reason? What is an example of something that human beings are capable of reasoning about which extends beyond the capabilities of artificial intelligence?

7. Why is reason absolutely essential to free will?

8. Why is free will absolutely essential to love?

Section B

9. What elements of human knowing and loving are unique to humans? What elements do humans share in common with angels and with God?

10. Is the human body part of man's imaging of God? Why or why not?

11. Why is it fitting for God to create each human as a unity of body and soul?

12. What three things characterize the relationship between man and woman as willed by God?

13. What is the relationship between personhood and communion?

14. Explain the special rule of St. John Paul II that applies to all persons, expressed both negatively and positively. Does this rule have consequences for society? Explain.

Section C

15. What role do the natural virtues play in human life?

16. How does grace transform human life?

Section D

17. According to divine revelation, what is the relationship between humans and the earth? How is it both a privilege and a responsibility?

18. How is science involved in the human stewardship of creation?

The image of God is fulfilled in a special way in the union of man and woman.

PRACTICAL EXERCISE

1. Imagine that you are an astronaut who discovers life on another planet. How would you be able to identify whether a life form is a creature in the image of God or just simply a creature of God? Make a list of behaviors that would reveal the life form to be rational, free, and personal.

2. Make two lists of human behaviors. The first list should only include characteristics of personhood, those that are exclusive to humans. The second should only include characteristics that humans share with animals. Discuss how the behaviors of the second list sometimes influence the behaviors of the first list.

3. St. John Paul II once said, "A person is not an object to be used, but a subject to be loved." Make a mental examination of the actions and words you observed in the past week on social media. Which were actions or words of use? Which were actions or words of love?

"What a marvel!" —St. Gregory of Nyssa

"The image of God means that human beings are beings of word and of love."
—Pope Benedict XVI

Endnotes – Chapter Ten

1. CCC 356.
2. International Theological Commission, C&S, 7.
3. St. Gregory of Nyssa, *De hominis opificio*, III.2.
4. International Theological Commission, C&S, 8-9.
5. Aidan Nichols, *Discovering Aquinas* (Grand Rapids: Eerdmans, 2002), 75.
6. Thomas Aquinas, *In I Sent.* 3.3.1.
7. CCC 221.
8. Ibid., 231.
9. Cardinal Christoph Schönborn, "What is Man that Thou art Mindful of Him? Is Man Really the Crown of Creation?", *stephanscom.at/edw/katechesen/articles/2006/07/17/a11155.*
10. Bonnette, *Origin of the Human Species*, 101. Grateful acknowledgment to Willis McCarthy for this analogy.
11. Barr, *Modern Physics*, 191.
12. Ibid., 197-198.
13. Ibid., 199-204.
14. F.C. Copleston, *Aquinas* (Baltimore: Penguin, 1955), 161.
15. CCC 366.
16. Barr, *Modern Physics*, 221-224.
17. Ibid., 225.
18. Copleston, *Aquinas*, 179-180.
19. CCC 1731.
20. Ibid., 1732.
21. Ibid., 1765.
22. David M. Gallagher, "Thomas Aquinas on Self-Love as the Basis for Love of Others," in *Acta Philosophica* 8:1 (1999): 25-30. Cf. St. Thomas Aquinas, *ST* II-II.25.4; *ScG* III.153; *In III Sent.* 29.3 *ad* 3.
23. CCC 1765.
24. Cf. Ibid., 362-368.
25. Ibid., 362.
26. Ibid., 365.
27. St. Thomas Aquinas, In 1 Cor 15.2 no. 924.
28. Haffner, *Mystery of Creation*, 78.
29. Barr, *Modern Physics*, 173.
30. International Theological Commission, C&S, 31.
31. CCC 366.
32. Haffner, *Mystery of Creation*, 74.
33. CCC 371.
34. ITC, *Communion and Stewardship*, no. 33.
35. Ibid., no. 33.
36. Cf. Congregation for Catholic Education, *Towards a Path of Dialogue on the Question of Gender Theory in Education* (June 10, 2019), 24.
37. International Theological Commission, C&S, 36.
38. Ibid., no. 38.
39. Ibid., no. 40.
40. Karol Wojtyla, *Love and Responsibility* (San Francisco: Ignatius Press, 1993), 23.
41. International Theological Commission, C&S, 42-43.
42. Ibid., 40-43
43. Josef Pieper, *The Christian Idea of Man* (South Bend: St. Augustine's Press, 2011), 4.
44. CCC 1996.
45. International Theological Commission, C&S, 57.
46. Ibid., no. 58-59.
47. Francis, *Laudato Si*, no. 66.
48. Ibid., no. 2
49. Pope Benedict XVI, Inaugural Homily (April 24, 2005), *w2.vatican.va/content/benedict-xvi/en/homilies/2005/documents/hf_ben-xvi_hom_20050424_inizio-pontificato.html*

Chapter Eleven
Human Sin and Modern Science: The Tragic History of the Image of God

If God created us to be good, why do human beings seem to tend toward moral evil?

How is the evolutionary history of the human brain involved in the tragedy of sin?

What does the Christian faith reveal about the relationship between God and humanity at its origins?

What is Original Sin? Who are Adam and Eve?

How does the love of Christ and Christian holiness overcome the human tendency toward moral evil?

If only there were evil people somewhere insidiously committing evil deeds, and it were necessary only to separate them from the rest of us and destroy them. But the line dividing good and evil cuts through the heart of every human being. And who is willing to destroy a piece of his own heart?

—Alexander Solzhenitsyn, *Gulag Archipelago* (1973)

With these sobering words a former Russian political prisoner and Nobel Prize-winning author reflects upon two tragic facts—that every human being is capable of evil and that very often our outrage at the crimes of others hides from us our own capacity for crimes against goodness. For all its potential, human life is shadowed by acts of ignorance and violence, pettiness and hatred, greed and lust. Even when we choose what is good, we often fail at realizing our best intentions, at making good choices and living virtuous lives. **St. Paul** captured this tragic paradox perfectly as he lamented his own life experience in his Letter to the Romans: "I do not understand my own actions. For I do not do what I want, but I do the very thing I hate.... I can will what is right, but I cannot do it. For I do not do the good I want, but the evil I do not want is what I do" (Rom 7:15-19). The greatness of the image of God that we have celebrated thus far is not the entire picture of what it means to be human from the perspective of faith. In the words of the theologian **David Bentley Hart**, "The Christian view of the human person is wise precisely because it is so very extreme: It sees humanity, at once, as an image of the divine, fashioned for infinite love and imperishable glory, and as an almost inexhaustible wellspring of vindictiveness, cupidity and brutality."[1]

In this chapter we will investigate the ways in which science, philosophy, and faith can together deepen our understanding of this tragic element of human nature and history, the pervasiveness of sin and moral evil. Using the examples of blind ideology and racism, we will explore how so many of the worst human tendencies have been illuminated by modern cognitive science, which shows that the animal nature we inherit from hominin evolution has some degree of influence over our tendencies toward both moral goodness and moral evil. With **St. Thomas Aquinas** as our guide, we will explore how the Christian tradition has recognized this and what it tells us about God's original plan for humanity, which was postponed—but not terminated—by sin. Finally, we will consider the Church's teaching on Original Sin and the entrance of moral evil into human life at the dawn of human history. Sinfulness is often wrongly considered to be what Christianity is all about, as if our salvation is primarily about blame or condemnation. On the contrary, the center of the Gospel is God's love for humanity made flesh in Jesus Christ; the topic of sin merely shows us our need for redemption so that we might fully receive that love.

To begin, let us explore two examples that highlight the dilemma of being human.

A. Blind Ideology and Racism

IN HUMAN HISTORY GREAT IDEAS have often mutated into poisonous and even murderous ideologies in which a partial explanation is taken as the *only* explanation for just about everything. In the early twentieth century, as Darwin's brilliant discovery of natural selection began to be more fully appreciated, it just as quickly began to be wrongly applied to human life and society. In this misinterpretation of Darwin's theory, called *social Darwinism*, it became the responsibility of governments to play the role of the environment, to "aid" natural selection by controlling breeding (called *eugenics*) and even sterilizing those considered physically or mentally deficient. In *Buck v. Bell*, a 1927 U.S. Supreme Court ruling, the door was opened nationally for compulsory sterilization of the unfit, including the mentally handicapped, "for the protection and health of the state," which was an attempt to improve the human race by eliminating "defectives" from the gene pool. In the *Immigration Act of 1924*, the U.S. Congress passed a law that restricted immigration to favored races and nationalities in order to maintain the racial heritage of the nation, completely excluding immigrants from Asia.[2] Across the Atlantic, in Nazi Germany, social Darwinism was behind one of the most horrific events in human history—the unspeakable evil of the Holocaust.

Carrie Buck and her mother Emma. After the eight to one decision by the U.S. Supreme Court against her, Carrie was sterilized by surgeon John H. Bell on October 19, 1927. Justice Holmes wrote: "Three generations of imbeciles are enough."

Social Darwinism fueled movements of white supremacy and gave them a pseudo-scientific justification. It legitimized various expressions of *racism*, which has been condemned by the Church as "a violation of human dignity and a sin against justice."[3] In the words of Vatican II, "Every form of social or cultural discrimination in fundamental personal rights on the grounds

An exhausted and desperate Rwandan woman collapses with her baby on her back on a road to a refugee camp. During the Rwandan genocide of 1994, an estimated 1 million members of the minority Tutsi tribe were slaughtered by members of the majority Hutu tribe over a period of 100 days. This constituted roughly 70% of the entire Tutsi population. The conflict produced 2 million refugees.

of sex, race, color, social conditions, language, or religion must be curbed and eradicated as incompatible with God's design."[4] In the name of the pseudo-science of social Darwinism, the racist lies of white superiority, and even of a "master race," flourished and found expression in widespread violence and discrimination.

The great irony is that any seemingly scientific basis for racism has been largely undermined by modern genetics. It turns out that all human beings are 99.9% genetically the same and that the differences between races and ethnicities are vanishingly tiny. A study conducted in the early part of the last decade tested the DNA of 1056 people from fifty-two populations in five major geographic regions of the world: Africa, Eurasia (Europe, the Middle East, Central and South Asia), East Asia, Oceania, and the Americas. Of the tiny 0.1% difference, 94% is among individuals of the same populations, and only 6% between individuals from different populations.[5] By comparison, a single population of chimpanzees in West Africa is said to have more diversity in its DNA than the entire human population has today![6] Skin color—which has been and remains a source of social division and an ocean of misery, violence, and misunderstanding throughout history—turns out to be a micro-adaptation to various climates that has actually been independently acquired numerous times by human populations living in various regions of the world.

Racism, then, has no foundation, scientific or otherwise. And yet, its dark legacy continues. It is only one example of the numerous ways in which fear, discrimination, and even murderous violence against those considered different and inferior have cast shadows over virtually every human society. In the Middle Ages, murderous attacks on European Jews were spontaneously undertaken by mobs of Christians, who saw the call to liberate the Holy Land as requiring that non-Christians in their own societies be slaughtered, despite condemnations by Church leaders. In 1992, ethnic cleansing in Bosnia-Herzegovina after the fall of the Soviet Union brought the murder of over 25,000 Muslim civilians. In 1994, an estimated 1 million members of the Tutsi tribe were slaughtered by members of the Hutu tribe, led by the Hutu majority government of the African nation of Rwanda, over a period of 100 days. Innocent blood spilt over differences of skin color, culture, and religion runs like a river through human history.

From where do such evils come? Placing the poisonous ideology of social Darwinism and violence against those different from us side-by-side highlights an important fact about our human nature: We have inherited certain instinctive inclinations which seem to leave us prone to the acceptance of both of these insidious realities. With respect to blind ideologies like social Darwinism, it seems that the repetition of false claims, even claims that are known to be false, have the effect of making them seem more truthful to those who encounter them.[7] The human brain favors statements that have already been processed, which can create a situation in which groups large and small become blinded by falsehoods. Such "thinking shortcuts," also known as *cognitive biases*, tend to limit our openness to new ways of thinking, even when our standard ways of thinking are absurd.[8] And yet, this very tendency is one that also makes us capable of trusting all kinds of genuine sources of knowledge, upon whom we rely for 99% of the information that we have and the truths that we know. What can lead in some cases to the spread of ideologies like social Darwinism is also essential to knowing the truth and living in society.

We have an innate tendency to favor members of the "ingroup" and to be less inclined toward trusting members of "outgroups."

Moving to the evil of racial and ethnic discrimination, other research shows that we have a natural tendency "to make distinctions between 'us' and 'them.'" As social animals who live in groups, we have an innate tendency to favor members of the "ingroup" and to be less inclined toward trusting members of "outgroups." Similar behaviors have been detected in other primates, which indicates that the roots of *outgroup bias* reach far back into our evolutionary history. And yet, the same tendency is also behind our inclination to bond into groups and to offer mutual support to each other within them.[9]

Paleoanthropologist Ian Tattersall. "The rational and the irrational constantly jostle in our heads."

Do trust and ideology, group bonding and racism, and good and evil go hand in hand? How do we explain the "dividing line" between them that runs through our hearts? The paleoanthropologist **Ian Tattersall** suggests that this "dividing line" is probably due to our rapid and very recent emergence as a species and the stunning cognitive revolution it involved. We arrived in an evolutionary blink of an eye—if the history of the universe was put in the time scale of one year, *Homo sapiens* appeared three minutes before the fireworks on New Year's Eve, at 11:57 pm. As we have seen, through the past several million years the hominin brain was growing in size and complexity, and hominins had been making more and more amazing tools, becoming more socially organized and cohesive. But with the advent of symbolic thought and of language, our thinking processes shifted into a radically new mode, "unpredicted by anything that had gone before." We did not evolve this capacity gradually, and, unlike all prior evolutionary adaptations, this one placed us in an entirely new situation:

> **This messy process explains our apparently contradictory cognitive condition. It explains why we have such brilliant rational abilities yet so often behave irrationally. It shows us why we so frequently use the unprecedented communicative potential of language to obfuscate and tell lies. It explains why we sometimes cannot justify our actions even to ourselves... and why we reason so powerfully, yet make so many dreadful decisions. All this, and much more, occurs because the rational and the irrational constantly jostle in our heads, combining to make us the simultaneously creative yet reflexive creatures that we are...[10]**

Because the human brain is the product of evolution, it has been compared to a building that was built with one story first, but to which new levels were added with little or no modification of the earlier levels. In the 1960s the neuroscientist **Paul MacLean** identified three levels: the hindbrain, which is the oldest "floor" and controls our basic biological functions like breathing and coordination; the limbic system, which is the next level and governs "emotions, instincts, sexual behavior, and feelings of well-being"; and the forebrain, the most recent "floor," which handles language, choices, and thinking. In the words of cell biologist **Kenneth Miller**, this is an oversimplification but is basically accurate: "The circuitry of the brain is in fact a poorly integrated mixture of the truly ancient, the very old, and the relatively new all working side-by-side."[11]

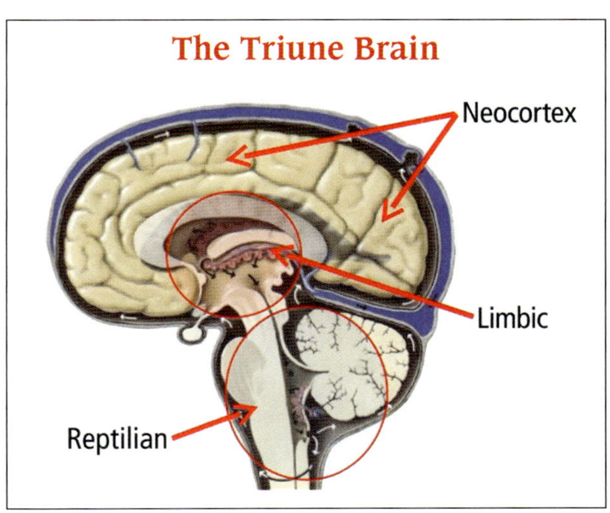

Neuroscientist Paul MacLean's "Triune Brain Theory" proposed that the human brain is in reality three brains in one—structures sequentially added to the brain in the course of evolution: the reptilian complex or hindbrain, the limbic system, and the neocortex or forebrain.

In summary, despite being one of the great wonders that evolution produced, our biological and neurological inheritance has its shortcomings. This fact explains a great deal about why humans act irrationally and contrary to goodness, why racism and other forms of bias seem to crop up throughout society and history, why male human beings find it so hard to treat women as equals and not as objects, and why wars and the killing of the innocent are constants in human history. There is nothing from the scientific perspective that should make us surprised by this. Yet what makes sense from the "how" perspective of human evolutionary science falls short of the "why" perspective of theology, which looks at human life from the perspective of human happiness and God's intentions for the human family. We yearn for better than what evolution could give us, and thanks to the Christian faith we know that what evolution produced was not the finished product.

Thanks to the Christian faith we know that what evolution produced was not the finished product.

B. Physical Evil and Preternatural Gifts: Animal Imperfection and Human Nature

1. St. Thomas Aquinas and Our Animal Nature

We have been made for perpetual, everlasting happiness, something we are capable of thanks to being created in the divine image.

IN CHAPTER THREE, WE ENCOUNTERED the problem of evil. There we noted that evil is the absence of a good that ought to be present. We also observed that in the physical world, it seems that most physical evils occur as a matter of course because of physical good. "The life of the spider is the death of the fly"; physical evil is so deeply intertwined with physical good that they are impossible to separate. At the same time, we know that, even though we are rational, we are also animals whose brains are physical organs that are necessary for our exercise of reason in this life. So our brains share the same ambiguity as the rest of physical reality. We have instincts and inclinations that can be interpreted as evil from one angle, but never from *every* angle. In fact, it is possible for human beings to come to understand their instincts and inclinations and to consciously choose between them; to treat those different than us as if they were beloved blood relatives, to confront with logic and truth the false ideologies that threaten to sway our minds toward darkness, and to discipline urges that are contrary to goodness. To quote Miller once more: "Evolutionary history may dictate the pleasures, anxieties and prejudices of our minds, but we, distinct from other creatures, have discovered that history."[12]

The insight that our physical bodies, including our brains, bear the same ambiguities as all of physical reality is not new. While writing his greatest theological work, the *Summa Theologiæ*, **St. Thomas Aquinas** puzzled over this strange paradox. On the one hand, he observed, we have been made for perpetual, everlasting happiness, something we are capable of thanks to being created in the divine image, endowed with reason and freedom. In thinking of human fulfillment and happiness, St. Thomas had in mind the great mysteries of our salvation—the resurrection of the body and the eternal joy of communion with God discussed in Chapter Six, which we will revisit in Chapter Twelve. On the other hand, when he considered our nature from the perspective of our biological makeup, he observed that the human body is not perfectly adapted to our spiritual capacities. Nature, he speculated, gave the best it was capable of, producing a body with features that are useful for rational animals (like sense and touch). But much like a blacksmith might choose iron to make a knife for one set of reasons (iron is hard, for example, and can be made very sharp), he might also regret that same material for other reasons, such as the tendency of iron to rust easily. "For we may note a twofold condition in any matter, one which the agent chooses, and another which is not chosen by the agent, and is a natural condition of matter."[13]

And, as it is with the blacksmith's use of iron to make a knife, so it is with human beings, creatures made in the image of God who are also the products of evolution. We have the proper kind of biological makeup for a rational animal, but due to the very limitations of the material world, this makeup cannot in itself provide us with everything needed to be the perfect embodied image of God. God is eternal and the source of perfect life, but given our fallen nature, our bodies are corruptible; they are subject to sickness, aging, and ultimately death. Also, our reason and freedom are constantly interacting with our animal instincts and inclinations, and these are not always easy to harmonize with knowing the truth and loving freely. Thanks to the gift of reason, we are capable of understanding what intellectual, moral, and physical excellence entails, but we so often cannot be our "best selves," choosing rather to do what we know we ought not to do.

It is utterly incorrect, however, to conclude that what we received from evolution has made us intrinsically evil. It has made us only what any biological process can produce: a creature that pursues survival, physical health, sensual pleasure, and other goods. We share these tendencies with animals, while we strive for what is good according to our human nature. As St. Thomas also knew, God made us capable of knowing the difference, of being able to "make judgments about our judgments." In addition, the Christian perspective of God's intention for humanity offered St. Thomas an insight that science and philosophy, left to themselves, could not provide.

In summary, we receive ambiguous inclinations from our evolutionary inheritance that are not yet moral or immoral, but can become so through our own free choices. The very things that lead us toward bonding and generosity, or toward self-defense and the defense of the innocent, can also tempt us to mistrust, suspicion, and even unjust acts of violence. Those who claim that such ambiguous inclinations show that human nature is intrinsically evil simply do not understand that no inclination can be understood without reference to the end or purpose to which it inclines us. We find the pursuit of bodily pleasures, aggression, killing, and death among animals for hundreds of millions of years before humans came along. But when we find these inclinations in humans, we do not know whether or not they are sinful until we ask, "To what kind of free choice—expressed in thought, word, or deed—is this inclination leading me?" As long as they are oriented toward choosing what is truly good, then they are good; the same inclinations that are involved in adultery and murder are also involved in true sexual love and in daring acts of heroism, respectively. And yet, these ambiguous inclinations also reveal that our evolutionary inheritance *alone* is not sufficient for us to be the virtuous, loving, and sinless human beings God created us to be. As our Catholic tradition tells us, God had more to provide for us.

2. Original Integrity and the Preternatural Gifts

IN KEEPING WITH BOTH SACRED TRADITION and the divine purpose of moral perfection and perfect happiness for which God created human beings, St. Thomas concluded that God not only created us in a special dependence upon him, but that he also endowed our first parents with special gifts that go beyond what they could have received from the material world and our animal nature. Through a supernatural grace given to the soul, and as long as humans did not separate themselves from God through sin, the body would have been preserved from all corruption and from death,[14] their bodily desires and emotions would have been wholly subject to reason,[15] and a life lived in untainted goodness and happiness, in unbroken communion with God, would have been the result. These special endowments, called the *preternatural gifts*, were graces given to perfect our natural state, making it correspond to God's ultimate intentions for us. Reason and freedom made humans capable of communion with God but not yet capable of living out that communion. These gifts were added to human nature so that God's loving desire for our unending happiness would be realized.

Along with the gift of immortality (to overcome our natural biological end, which is death) and infused knowledge (to overcome our natural lack of knowledge), St. Thomas speaks of the gift of *original integrity* as that by which God assisted our first parents to overcome their tendency toward a conflict between knowing, choosing, and desiring, what Ian Tattersall calls our "apparently contradictory cognitive condition." Assumed here by St. Thomas is that our animal nature is not well integrated, or at least not integrated well enough. As animals, we are not able to easily integrate our reason and freedom with our desires; as composite beings, we tend over time toward physical disintegration, not integration. Taken together, the supernatural grace with which God endowed our first parents empowered them to readily realize the best possibilities provided to them by the "human difference."

When trying to conceive of what preternatural existence would have been like, with original integrity and freedom from suffering and death, our imaginations can tend to run away with us. Some think of the first humans living in an earthly paradise in which our planet, or at least some region of it, was radically different than it is, a place where nothing ever died and in which no physical evils were present. Others assume that freedom from death would have meant a perpetual lifetime for humans on earth. However, many important theologians, including **St. Augustine**, thought that eventually our first parents and their sinless descendants would have entered into a glorified state comparable to the risen Christ, or to the Blessed Virgin Mary after she was assumed body and soul into heaven. The *Catechism of the Catholic Church* teaches that from the beginning "man was destined to be fully 'divinized' by God in glory."[16] Still others assume that freedom from suffering would have meant freedom from any pain whatsoever and a situation in which humans would not need to strive or mature in wisdom and virtue. But this has never been the teaching of the Catholic Church.[17]

We do not know how long the first humans remained in a preternatural, sinless state. **St. Maximus the Confessor**, the last of the great Church Fathers, was of the opinion that this state was lost at the very instant of the creation of the first human beings: "At the instant he was created, the first man, by use of his senses, squandered this spiritual capacity—the natural desire of the mind for God—on sensible things."[18] However long it may have lasted, the period of human sinlessness, of original integrity and original holiness, was an imperceptible glimmer that happened tens of thousands of years ago. Original integrity and holiness may very well have been lost as quickly as they were received, or perhaps they remained for a day, a week, or a year. Regardless of how long such gifts were retained, such a short span of time would quickly perish from human memory, especially considering that human life became inundated by sinful tendencies, separation from God, suffering, and death.

3. The Broken Image

REGARDLESS OF HOW LONG OUR ANCESTORS possessed the preternatural gifts, humans no longer have them now. What we are left with, according to St. Thomas, is a fourfold wound: the wound of ignorance in which human reason is deprived of its path toward truth; the wound of malice, an inclination toward moral evil in which the human will is deprived of its path toward goodness; the wound of weakness in which the *irascible appetite*, our ability to strive for goodness, is deprived of its tendency toward persevering in the face of difficulty; and the wound of concupiscence in which our *concupiscible appetite*, our capacity to approach our sensible desires with our true good always in mind, is wounded in its tendency to rejoice in true sensible goods *versus* merely apparent ones.[19] St. Thomas notes that we are not entirely deprived of reason, good will, strength, etc., but that we are deeply wounded in these capacities.

St. Thomas calls this loss of preternatural gifts a "wounding of *nature*." When we define human nature only by virtue of our physical and biological heritage, then it makes no sense to call the loss of gifts that go beyond that heritage a "wounding." If man is defined simply as a particular primate species, then what St. Thomas calls wounds are not wounds at all; the good or bad to which our instincts incline us are, from the biological perspective, simply an expression of our nature.

When the Holy Spirit dwells in us, we are made capable of communion with God and of participation in his life.

St. Thomas, however, is not thinking of human nature only as a matter of our biological heritage. He is thinking of human nature in regard to what God ultimately intends us to be, what the second-century bishop, **St. Irenæus of Lyons**, meant when he said that man is properly composed of "body, soul and the Holy Spirit."[20] Just as this kind of body cries to God out of justice for a rational soul, so a living man or woman, body and soul, cries out for the ability to be everything he or she is capable of being, and, thanks to understanding and freedom, we are capable of so much more than what our biological heritage offers us. When the Holy Spirit dwells in us, we are made capable of communion with God and of participation in his life. Since God created us with the intention of giving us this perfect mode of being, then St. Thomas's idea of the fourfold wound makes sense.

In other words, man, the rational animal, is not all he can be, nor is he all that he is meant to be. But without our dependence upon God and the bestowal of his supernatural gifts, what we are now is, in fact, all we can ever be. The one who, in the words of Genesis, breathed into our nostrils the breath of life wished to complete our formation, to give us the ability to be fully integrated rational animals well situated to receive the fullness of his sanctifying grace in communion with himself and with one another. The doctrine of the preternatural gifts tells us that even this rational animal is not yet what God fully intended when he said, "Let us make man in our image." The next part of Genesis 1:26, "after our likeness," is just as crucial. Evolution and divine creation gave us the ability to be the image of God, but not yet the ability to be like God fully. God has gifts for us beyond what biological evolution and even the powers of reason and free will could provide.

St. Thomas Aquinas directly confirms this when he asserts that, after the Fall of humanity, the first humans simply reverted to their biological heritage: "When man turned his back on God, he fell under the influence of his sensual [bodily] impulses.... [After the Fall] he is likened to beasts that are led by the impulse of sensuality...a deviation from the law of reason."[21] Here St. Thomas—who knows nothing of evolution, genetics, paleoanthropology, or evolutionary psychology—sees that what we are by nature is "the rational and the irrational constantly" jostling, to paraphrase Tattersall. Reflecting upon this quote from St. Thomas, the theologian **Henri Rondet** helps us see how the evil tendencies we find in ourselves are observable from the scientific perspective and yet part of our *wounded* nature from the divine perspective:

> **Man has been left to his nature; but it is precisely this that is the paradox and stumbling block. Death, suffering, ignorance, the revolt of the senses—all this is in fact natural, since man is made of flesh and spirit. *But what is natural to an animal organism becomes unnatural for a soul made in the image of God.***[22]

In light of this, the wound caused by Original Sin, our fallen state, is best understood as a supernatural spark that was snuffed out by sin, a higher way of life that was lost—thanks to sin, the human person was left unfinished. God had more gifts to give, but he did not get to bestow them—he was stopped, and, like the wise and loving father in the Parable of the Prodigal Son (Lk 15:11-32), he respected the freedom of his children and permitted them to go away. With this in mind, we can now approach the doctrine of Original Sin.

C. The Tragedy of Original Sin

"Man, tempted by the devil, let his trust in his Creator die in his heart and, abusing his freedom, disobeyed God's command." (CCC 396)

ORIGINAL INTEGRITY WAS LOST precisely when the disobedience of sin entered the world, an event which is called *the Fall*:

> **Man, tempted by the devil, let his trust in his Creator die in his heart and, abusing his freedom, disobeyed God's command. This is what man's first sin consisted of. All subsequent sin would be disobedience toward God and lack of trust in his goodness. In that sin man *preferred* himself to God and by that very act scorned him. He chose himself over and against God, against the requirements of his creaturely status and therefore against his own good.**[23]

This sin, freely committed by our first parents, resulted in the loss of the preternatural gifts and of sanctifying grace: of original holiness and original justice, of interior harmony, the loss of the harmony between man and woman, and between humanity and the rest of creation. Death, the natural end of all biological life, made its entrance into *human* history.[24] But, worst of all, our friendship with God was broken. As a consequence, human history became "inundated by sin."[25] The state of separation from God caused by the Fall, called *Original Sin*, is passed down to all generations. In the words of the *Catechism*, "Original sin is a sin 'contracted' and 'not committed'"—a state and not an act. Human nature has been wounded by Original Sin, but not totally corrupted; the image of God has been disfigured and stained but still remains.[26]

Return of the Prodigal Son

Once again, with Original Sin we come upon a doctrine that is easily misunderstood. Original Sin is misunderstood as something that is passed on like an infectious disease. St. Thomas Aquinas, however, rejects this idea, although he affirms that it is passed on by sexual generation, "transmitted with human nature," in the words of **St. Paul VI** (1897-1978). He asserts that we should think of all human beings as if they were one man, "Adam," like the members of a single bodily organism. The first sin changed what it means to be human for all of us, although we are not all guilty of the actual sin that caused our downfall as a human family. In his words, "The disorder which is in [this or that] man born of Adam, is voluntary, not by his will, but by the will of his first parent, who, by the movement of generation, moves all who originate from him."[27]

Pope Benedict XVI approached the mystery of Original Sin from the perspective of human personhood and relationships. As we saw in Chapter Ten, the fact that we are created "in the image of God" means that we are persons who are capable of communion, of bonding in close relationships, and whose lives make no sense without being in loving relationships with each other. Sin is the disturbance of relationships; whenever I sin, I make myself the center of the universe, rejecting God and others. Therefore, the first sin damaged the network of relationships at the very beginning of human history. The world of human community we all enter at the beginning of our existence "is marked by relational damage":

> **At the very moment that a person enters human existence, which is a good, he or she is confronted by a sin-damaged world. Each of us enters into a situation in which relationality has been hurt. Consequently each person is, from the very start, damaged in relationships and does not engage in them as he or she ought. Sin pursues the human being, and he or she capitulates to it.[28]**

Decades later, Pope Benedict XVI would complete this insight with a beautiful contrast: between the nature of human sinfulness as slavery *versus* the sinless freedom of the Blessed Virgin Mary, who was preserved from all stain of sin from the moment of her conception. We all carry the "drop of poison" of thinking that, standing all alone, raising ourselves to God's level, we will fulfill ourselves, finding real happiness. "We call this drop of poison 'Original Sin.'" In sinning every human being "sets his sights on power, with which he desires to take his own life autonomously in hand. And in doing so, he trusts in deceit rather than in truth and thereby sinks with his life into emptiness, into death."

But God's love and the love of others are gifts; trying to sinfully stand on our own is to enslave ourselves, for the freedom we have must be lived "with one another, and for one another" in order for it to be realized. Mary, on the other hand, shows us what freedom truly means.

> **The person who abandons himself totally in God's hands does not become God's puppet, a boring "yes man"; he does not lose his freedom. Only the person who entrusts himself totally to God finds true freedom, the great, creative immensity of the freedom of good.**
>
> **The person who turns to God does not become smaller but greater, for through God and with God he becomes great, he becomes divine, he becomes truly himself. The person who puts himself in God's hands does not distance himself from others, withdrawing into his private salvation; on the contrary, it is only then that his heart truly awakens and he becomes a sensitive, hence, benevolent and open person.**

The closer a person is to God, the closer he is to people. We see this in Mary. The fact that she is totally with God is the reason why she is so close to human beings.[29]

Mary is our sign of hope that the cycle of sin can be broken and our humanity made complete. She is the object of our hope only as one who points to her Son, who is the perfect answer to the dilemma of our sinfulness and the tendencies toward it we have by nature. In his life, Death, and Resurrection, Jesus moved the dividing line between good and evil out of the human heart, leaving only the good. We will focus on this shortly, but first we must tackle a dilemma that modern science seems to create for the idea of a sin committed by our "first parents." The story of Adam and Eve and their disobedience is one that is often assumed by believers to be a factual account. Who are Adam and Eve, and what role do they play in the tragic history of humanity? Were they the only first humans? If not, then in what way can we understand the biblical account of human origins such that its deepest and most fundamental truth remains and shines forth?

1. The Theology of Human Origins

THE BIBLICAL STORY THAT COMPLETES the Second Creation Account, Genesis 3, tells of a man and a woman, the first humans and parents of all human beings to come, being tempted by a serpent to eat fruit from a tree which God had forbidden them to eat after creating them. Their disobedience changes their perspective of themselves and each other; they realize their nakedness, and hide their bodies from each other with leaves. They also try to elude God when he walks through the garden, hiding themselves "among the trees." God punishes them for their rebellion; it results in their being expelled from the garden. Henceforth, they both will be subject to death, the man to fruitless and wearying toil, the woman to agony in childbirth.

Modern literary analysis identifies this story as a symbolic narrative, more about the meaning of life than the beginning of human history. As **St. John Paul II** once noted, Genesis 2–3 uses "mythical language" to express a "deeper content."[30] However, **St. Augustine** believed this account to be actual history.[31] Following him, much of the western Christian tradition assumed the same: human history began with only one man and one woman, who both sinned.[32] *Monogenism* is the theological idea that "the whole human race is descended from Adam and Eve."[33] For centuries monogenism, based upon a particular interpretation of Genesis 3, was assumed to accurately describe the beginning of human history. It now seems quite unlikely, perhaps genetically impossible, that monogenism is an accurate account. Evolution works through changes within populations, not through the sudden appearance of two individuals. Also, the genetic diversity that we encounter today among modern humans, despite our very close genetic unity, seems to require thousands of human beings at the beginning of human history, a doctrine theologians refer to as *polygenism*.

So where does that leave Adam and Eve? In 1950 **Venerable Pius XII**, responding to the evolutionary science of his day, warned the faithful against embracing polygenism in his encyclical *Humani Generis*. He was very careful in his wording. He said that it "is not apparent" how polygenism can be squared with the doctrine of Original Sin.[34] He could have said, "It cannot be reconciled" with definitive Catholic teaching, but he did not. He was clearly being cautious and leaving the door open for possible scientific discoveries that might generate some theory of polygenism that could be harmonized with what we know by faith: that Original Sin is passed on to all human beings due to a real human sin committed at the dawn of human history.

Since that time, the paradigm of human origins has shifted significantly. The prevailing hypothesis in 1950 was the *Multi-Regional Model*. According to this model, the various ethnic groups had all evolved independently of each other: "Native Africans evolved from archaic non-humans in Africa, native Europeans evolved from archaic non-humans in Europe, native Asians evolved from archaic non-humans in Asia," etc. Each race had its own distinct origin.[35] To Ven. Pius XII, who had opened his pontificate in 1939 with an encyclical denouncing "the forgetfulness of that law of human solidarity and charity which is dictated and imposed by our common origin and by the equality of rational nature in all men,"[36] the Multi-Regional Model would have seemed a step backwards toward the diabolical ideas that had fueled the murderous Nazi regime. For, if there is no unity to the human family, then it can also be argued that some people only *seem* human or have an inferior form of humanity and are, thus, not equal in dignity and rights.

The magisterium of the Church has not given any specific guidance on the monogenism/polygenism issue since the rapid advances in our understanding of human origins from the last several decades. Furthermore, it is noteworthy that Ven. Pius XII's warning about embracing polygenism has not been repeated by any Pope since the 1980s. In 2004, the International Theological Commission left the issue open. In *Communion and Stewardship*, the ITC recognized that the scientific evidence points to a population, not to two individuals, and refers to the emergence of the first humans as involving either "individuals" or "populations."[37] Here we see the principle of "faith and science together" discussed in Chapter Five; the Church allows science to inform its understanding of what God has revealed and remains open to new scientific discoveries.

Blombos Cave in South Africa has yielded the oldest artifacts that give evidence of symbolic thought, datable to around 75,000 YA.

Thanks to modern genetics we now know that the Multi-Regional Model is incorrect, having been replaced by the *Out of Africa Model*. As discussed in Chapter Nine, there is firm evidence that anatomically modern humans evolved in Africa around 300,000 YA and migrated out of Africa around 60,000 YA. Genetic studies indicate that there were about 10,000 breeding individuals at the time of our anatomical origins, although the number of behaviorally modern humans, truly rational animals, may have been quite smaller and certainly emerged much later. Blombos Cave in South Africa has yielded the oldest artifacts that give evidence of symbolic thought, datable to around 75,000 YA. However, such artifacts have only been found there and at another nearby site with artifacts datable to about the same time.[38] So the current evidence seems to indicate that the human difference may have come about within a few groups at a specific time and place, over 200,000 years after our modern anatomical features evolved.

It is interesting to reconsider polygenism in light of the Out of Africa Model. It does not seem to be a wild leap, in light of the most recent discoveries, to consider Adam and Eve as symbolic of a community, the first community to make the breakthrough to rationality and freedom. Perhaps the genetic and neurological changes that made us capable of being rational animals remained latent for some time, spreading through the population before these uniquely human powers were actualized. Perhaps the first of our kind to make the breakthrough from potential to actual symbolic thought, language, and reason also turned quickly away from the goodness being offered by God, in a manner similar to that which was envisioned by **St. Maximus the Confessor**, and then drew the others into a way of being human marked by "relational damage," into a community characterized by sin.

Of course this all remains at the level of speculation, but speculation is essential to all human thought. Much like scientists, theologians oftentimes find themselves having to go back to the data and challenge their assumptions. This is not a threat to faith, in which we entrust ourselves to God despite the limits of our understanding. In fact, it refines and purifies faith to find itself faced with new questions, and it is through such faithful theological reflection that our understanding of divine truth moves forward.[39] The Blessed Virgin Mary, who asked the angel Gabriel, "How shall this be, since I have no husband?" regarding his announcement that she would "conceive . . . and bear a son" (Lk 1:28-35), is the model for all theological speculation. Questions are not bad; faith is not blind.

The Blessed Virgin Mary asked the angel Gabriel, "How shall this be, since I have no husband?" (Lk 1:34).

It is, furthermore, worth noting that what is being reconsidered here is not the question of *whether* an Original Sin occurred and fundamentally altered the manner in which all human beings henceforth live and experience their humanity, finding themselves in need of a divine savior and redeemer. Rather, what is being reconsidered here in light of the progress of modern science is how we ought to interpret *the context in which* this Original Sin took place. The substance of the faith itself is not what is at issue, only our understanding of how we ought to best understand and articulate it in a reasonable and responsible manner.

In the end, however sin entered the world and however many first parents were involved, there can be no doubt that it affected humanity in a universal way. **Br. Guy Consolmagno, S.J.**, recognizing the new frontier that evolutionary science has opened for theological reflection, points to the reality of Original Sin as it touches the universal experience of humanity:

> **There can be no doubt that the source of human evil, the urge that people have to choose to do things they know are wrong, has been a part of our human experience since before the beginning of recorded history. Original sin is a fact. But explaining it in light of what we now know of human origins is going to be a lot trickier than the theologians would have guessed a hundred years ago.**
>
> **And that's OK. More power to them.**
>
> **Meanwhile . . . I don't need to know the instant or the process when human beings first became capable of making free choices. It's enough for me, today, to know that I do have the power (and responsibility) to make free choices myself and that for whatever historical reasons, I can't depend on my own power to make the**

> **right choice every time. In a practical sense that's what the doctrine of Original Sin is all about. And that's true, regardless of how it came to be.**[40]

More important than how sin entered the world and how many humans were involved is how its destructive power is overcome. As noted above, Jesus Christ has pushed the line dividing between good and evil out of the human heart. And it is to his Heart that we now turn.

D. The Sacred Heart of Jesus

IN ITS CONSTITUTION ON THE CHURCH IN THE MODERN WORLD, the Second Vatican Council identified Christ as the "final Adam," the one who "fully reveals man to himself and makes his supreme calling clear." Continuing this line of thought, it points to Christ as the perfect human:

> **He Who is "the image of the invisible God" (Col 1:15), is Himself the perfect man. To the sons of Adam He restores the divine likeness which had been disfigured from the first sin onward.... For by His incarnation the Son of God has united Himself in some fashion with *every human being*. He worked with human hands, He thought with a human mind, acted by human choice and *loved with a human heart*. Born of the Virgin Mary, He has truly been made one of us, like us in all things except sin.**[41]

Jesus Christ, the final Adam.
In the Revelation of Jesus Christ, sin and moral evil are met with mercy and a loving power that draws good out of evil.

In this short summary of the mystery of the Incarnation, we see the solution to the dark riddle of human existence when it is only considered from the biological and philosophical perspectives. Christ answers the ambiguity of our moral fragility and inclinations toward evil with perfect love, living out an ordinary human existence in an extraordinary way. He did not take up human nature as it existed before sin damaged human life, endowed with preternatural gifts. Instead, he assumed our *fallen* human nature in order to redeem it, purifying it through the abundance of his love and his perfect obedience to the will of the Father.

The key phrase in this important text from Vatican II is its assertion that Jesus "loved with a human heart." In biblical symbolism, the heart represents the center of thinking, willing, and acting. With this in mind, the Church celebrates the Feast of the Sacred Heart of Jesus as a reminder of the pure love with which Jesus loved all human beings and united himself to us totally and irrevocably. The Son-*Logos*, the Mind through whom the universe was made, has now become the Savior through whom it has been redeemed. In Chapter Three we recognized that the love by which God creates the universe is a love springing from mercy, which causes goodness where goodness is absent. In the Revelation of Jesus Christ, the Word made flesh, even the "holes in being" created by sin and moral evil are met with mercy and a loving power that draws good out of evil.

The author of the Letter to the Hebrews captures this beautifully. Christ, he tells us, has become our "merciful and faithful high priest" precisely by loving us in the midst of his own human suffering and temptations: "Because he himself has suffered and been tempted, he is able to help those who are tempted" (Heb 2:18). Recognizing that Jesus faced the same struggles that we face, he also tells us that this was necessary for our sake: "We have not a high priest who is unable to sympathize with our weaknesses, but one who in every respect has been tempted as we are, *yet without sin*. Let us then with confidence draw near to the throne of grace, that we may receive mercy and find grace to help in time of need" (Heb 4:15-16). Jesus reversed the disobedience of sin by persevering through his suffering and temptations in obedience to his Father and so became "the source of eternal salvation to all who obey him" (Heb 5:9).

The Temptation of Christ by the Devil. The perfect divine Son grappled with and mastered our imperfect nature, making himself subject to its weakness but yet never being overcome by it, so that he could bring us into a new kind of life.

St. Paul expressed this mystery of our salvation in a single verse of his Second Letter to the Corinthians: "Though he was rich, yet for your sake he became poor, so that by his poverty you might become rich" (2 Cor 8:9). This "marvelous exchange" was frequently celebrated and proclaimed by the Fathers of the Church: the perfect divine Son grappling with and mastering our nature, making himself subject to its weakness but yet never being overcome by it, so that he could bring us into a new kind of life. Echoing the Letter to the Hebrews, the fourth-century bishop and theologian, **St. Gregory of Nazianzus**, depicts this mystery as God coming to know by direct experience the suffering caused by temptation and weakness:

> **In the form of a slave, he the Word descends to his fellow slaves...and takes upon himself an alien form, bearing me and all mine in himself, so that in himself he may consume the bad, as fire consumes the wax, or as the sun the mists of the earth, and that I may partake of his [divine] nature....Thus he honors obedience by his action and experiences it by his passion....He probes our obedience and, through his inventive love, he measures everything by his own sufferings. Thus he can learn from his experience what we experience, how much is demanded from us and how much we are excused. He weighs our weakness according to what he suffered.[42]**

The process of salvation, by which we slowly begin to regather the riches lost through sin, begins when we enter into the mystical Body of Christ, the Church, through *the Sacrament of Baptism*. In Baptism, the tragic alienation of "the sin of Adam" is replaced by a redemptive unity in Christ, the final Adam, who has broken the chains of sin and death. As the *Catechism* states, "Baptism not only purifies from all sins, but also makes the [baptized] 'a new creature,' an adopted son of God, who has become a 'partaker of the divine nature,' member of Christ and co-heir with him, and a temple of the Holy Spirit."[43] The reception of this Sacrament does not annihilate or replace our biological human nature—we remain fundamentally the same human being after being baptized as before. And yet, through this and the other Sacraments, through a life of prayer and of communion with fellow Christians, through sacrifice, care for others, and the practice of virtue, the translation of our humanity into this new way of life in Christ is not only possible, but it also has the guarantee of a divine promise. As we pray in the Preface of the Mass that opens the Eucharistic Prayer, "In goodness you created man and, when he was justly condemned, in mercy you redeemed him, through Christ our Lord."[44]

E. Slave of the Slaves: From Outgroup Bias to Universal Love

THE LOVE AND HOLINESS DESCRIBED ABOVE is not something seen only in Christ and the Blessed Virgin Mary. It is a theme that runs throughout the lives of all holy men and women, the great Communion of Saints whom the Church holds up for us as examples and as our powerful intercessors. We began this chapter by honestly facing the human inclination toward outgroup bias which, when unchecked, turns into nightmarish forms of violence against "outsiders." Let us now look at what happens when the light of Christ shines upon the human heart.

St. Peter Claver never missed the arrival of a slave ship. He would carry gifts of food and would care for the sick.

One of the most horrific embodiments of violence in human history is racial slavery; the capture, bondage, and forced labor of Africans is a dark phase in the history of the colonization of the Americas. For two and one-half centuries, until 1852, the slave trade was active, and it is estimated that about 125,000 Africans entered the port city of Cartagena, Columbia, in chains between 1595 and 1640. Each ship would carry 400-500 slaves, and it was not uncommon for one-third of them to die on the two-month voyage. It would have been a hopeless situation were it not for heroic Christians like **St. Peter Claver**.

Claver was born to a wealthy family in Catalonia, Spain, the son of the mayor of his town. During his university studies he encountered the Society of Jesus (the Jesuits) and joined them, and shortly thereafter encountered a lay brother who helped him realize a call from the Lord to go to the New World. In 1611, he arrived in Cartagena and was ordained a priest in 1616. There he became an assistant to **Fr. Alonso de Sandoval**, who first began the outreach to African slaves. Then he began his own work, becoming a "slave to the slaves." Over the span of thirty-five years, he never missed the arrival of a ship. He would board the ships, bathe the slaves in perfumed water, and give them clean water to drink. He would carry gifts of food and would care for the sick. Over the years he would travel widely to visit those whom he had once cared for on the ships and continued his ministry to them. By virtue

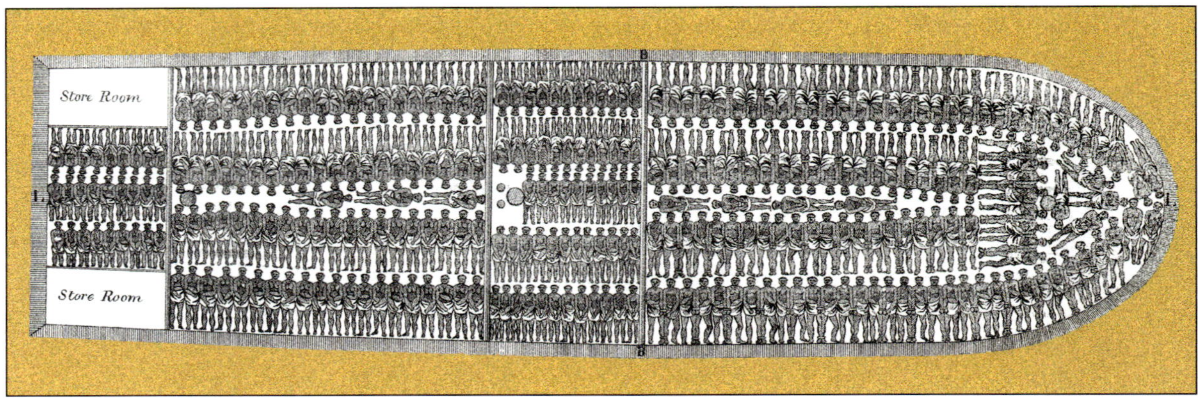

Plan of the lower deck of a British slave ship showing the stowage of 292 slaves.

of his witness of faith and his selfless acts of love, over 300,000 slaves would be baptized by his hands.

The lengths to which St. Peter Claver went to care for these slaves showed a depth of love that was truly supernatural, far surpassing any kind of natural empathy or compassion:

> **Claver would wipe the sweat from the faces of the slaves with his own handkerchief. Moreover, he would often clothe the sick and diseased in his own cloak. As some of his interpreters witnessed, the cloak had to be washed up to seven times a day from the stink and filth which it had accumulated. It was routine for Claver to console his fellow man by joyfully undertaking practices which were considered extremely repugnant to most. As one eye-witness notes, "Most admirable was that he not only cleansed these plague-ridden ulcers with the two handkerchiefs he kept for that, but did not hesitate to press his lips to them." He plainly saw Christ "in the least of these brethren."[45]**

St. Peter Claver ministering to slaves in Cartagena. "No life, except the life of Christ, has moved me so deeply as that of Peter Claver." —Pope Leo XIII

It may be a natural inclination for human beings to fear and distrust those who are different; when hardened into evil choices and habits, whole cultures have been corrupted. What we see in St. Peter Claver is the "new" natural—the recognition of all human beings as brothers, made possible by the grace of God given to us in Christ. As the words of **St. Paul** reveal, this "new natural" involves replacing bias with belonging: "There is neither Jew nor Greek, there is neither slave nor free, there is neither male nor female; for you are all one in Christ Jesus" (Gal 3:28).

This perspective is not unique to St. Peter Claver and St. Paul; it is at the heart of the new reality of human life that radiates from the Sacred Heart of Jesus Christ. From the beginning of Christianity, we see a new standard dawning in the world: the conviction that ethnicity, culture, and color do not make anyone inferior or worthy of maltreatment, slavery, or death, and that love must extend beyond the boundaries created by "family and tribe." In the words of sociologist **Rodney Stark** in his study of the rise of Christianity from its origins as a tiny movement in Palestine to becoming the majority religion of the Roman Empire, "what Christianity gave to its converts was nothing less than their humanity. In this sense virtue *was* its own reward."[46]

The work of God in fashioning his image, postponed by sin, has been definitively accomplished by Christ, who invites all human beings to freely join him in this new way of being human. As we will see in the next chapter, this fantastic mystery has remade the universe and the human race. In fact, it has revealed where the true origin of humanity is to be discovered: neither in the relics of prehistory nor in the advent of language and symbolism, but in the man who showed us what it means to be truly human, Jesus, the "final Adam."

The Transfiguration by Francesco Zuccarelli.

VOCABULARY

Define the following terms (or identify the person's significance):

1. Social Darwinism
2. Eugenics
3. Buck v. Bell
4. Immigration Act of 1924
5. Racism
6. Cognitive Bias
7. Outgroup Bias
8. Preternatural Gifts
9. Original Integrity
10. Irascible Appetite
11. Concupiscible Appetite
12. Human Nature (scientific definition)
13. Human Nature (theological definition)
14. The Fall of Humanity
15. Original Sin
16. Monogenism
17. Polygenism
18. *Humani Generis*
19. Multi-Regional Model of Human Origins
20. Out of Africa Model of Human Origins
21. Sacred Heart of Jesus
22. Baptism
23. St. Peter Claver

"Am I Not a Man and a Brother?"
Official Medallion of the British Anti-Slavery Society, 1787.

STUDY QUESTIONS

Section A

1. How are social Darwinism and racism related? What does the Church teach about racism?

2. Are ideological thinking and outgroup bias "natural" ways of thinking and acting for human beings? Explain with reference to cognitive psychology.

3. How do Ian Tattersall and other evolutionary biologists interpret the ambiguity in our natural inclinations from an evolutionary perspective?

Section B

4. What is the relationship between our cognitive inclinations toward evil and the larger reality of physical evil?

5. How did St. Thomas Aquinas explain the ambiguities involved in our biological makeup?

6. Is it correct or incorrect to conclude that humans are intrinsically evil based upon the real tendencies we have toward certain immoral forms of behavior? If not, then how should such tendencies be understood?

7. Explain what the preternatural gifts are and the original integrity that they produced in light of the ambiguities discussed in the previous questions.

8. What is the fourfold wound that results from Original Sin, according to St. Thomas Aquinas? Is it proper to call the loss of preternatural existence through sin a wounding from every perspective? Explain.

Section C

9. What is Original Sin, and how is it transmitted, according to St. Thomas Aquinas?

10. What is Original Sin, and how is it transmitted, according to Pope Benedict XVI? What contrast does he make between human sinfulness and the sinlessness of the Blessed Virgin Mary?

11. How did Ven. Pius XII approach the question of polygenism? To which model of human origins was he responding in 1950, and why is this significant today?

12. Interpret the figures of Adam and Eve, as well as the Fall of humanity, from the perspective of the Out of Africa Model of human origins.

Section D

13. How does Christ redeem our fallen human nature? Why is the symbolism of the Sacred Heart of Jesus so helpful for understanding the way in which Christ reverses the tragedy of sin?

14. Explain the theology of Christ's weakness and temptation as expressed by the Letter to the Hebrews.

15. Explain the theology of the marvelous exchange by reference to St. Paul and St. Gregory of Nazianzus.

Section E

16. What does the life of St. Peter Claver reveal about our redemption as it relates to the ambiguities in our biological instincts and inclinations?

Endnotes – Chapter Eleven

1. David Bentley Hart, *Atheist Delusions: The Christian Revolution and Its Fashionable Enemies* (New Haven, CT: Yale University Press, 2010), 17-18.
2. Conor Cunningham, *Darwin's Pious Idea*, 187.
3. CCC "Glossary"; cf. CCC 1935.
4. Vatican II, *GS*, 29.
5. Mark Schwartz, "People from Distant Lands Have Strikingly Similar Genetic Traits, Study Reveals," *Stanford Report*, January 8, 2003, *news.stanford.edu/news/2003/january8/genetics-18.html*.
6. Ian Tattersall, *Masters of the Planet*, 194.
7. Lisa K. Fazio, et al., "Knowledge Does Not Protect Against Illusory Truth," *Journal of Experimental Psychology* 144:5 (2015): 993-1002.
8. Emanuel Maidenberg, "Why We Believe What We're Told," *Psychology Today*, June 27, 2017, *www.psychologytoday.com/us/blog/belief-and-the-brain/201706/why-we-believe-what-we-re-told.*
9. Elizabeth Culotta, "Roots of Racism," *Science*, May 18, 2012, *science.sciencemag.org/content/336/6083/825.full.*
10. Ian Tattersall, *The Strange Case of the Rickety Cossa*, 219.
11. Kenneth R. Miller, *The Human Instinct: How We Evolved to Have Reason, Consciousness and Free Will* (New York: Simon & Schuster, 2018), 130-131.
12. Ibid., 145.
13. St. Thomas Aquinas, *Summa Theologiæ* (*ST*) I-II.85.6.
14. Ibid., I.97.1.
15. Ibid., I.95.2.
16. CCC 398.
17. Nicholas Lombardo, "Original Sin, Evolution and Death" (paper presented at the Academy of Catholic Theology Annual Conference, Washington Retreat Center, Washington, D.C., May 20, 2014).
18. St. Maximus the Confessor, *Ad Thalassium* 61, in *On the Cosmic Mystery of Jesus Christ*, trans. by Paul M. Blowers and Robert Louis Wilken (Crestwood, NY: St. Vladimir's Seminary Press, 2003), 131.
19. St. Thomas Aquinas, *ST* I-II.85.3 resp.
20. St. Irenæus, *Against Heresies*, V.6.1.
21. St. Thomas Aquinas, *ST* I-II.91.6 resp.
22. Henri Rondet, *Original Sin: The Patristic and Theological Background* (New York: Alba House, 1972), 166-167.
23. CCC 396.
24. Ibid., 400.
25. Ibid., 401.
26. Ibid., 404-405.
27. St. Thomas Aquinas, *ST* I-II.81.1, resp.
28. Joseph Ratzinger, *In the Beginning*, 73.
29. Pope Benedict XVI, Homily on the Feast of the Immaculate Conception (December 8, 2005), *w2.vatican.va/content/benedict-xvi/en/homilies/2005/documents/hf_ben-xvi_hom_20051208_anniv-vat-council.html.*
30. St. John Paul II, General Audience of November 7, 1979: 2, *www.ewtn.com/library/PAPALDOC/jp2tb8.htm.* The Pope offers further explanation in the footnotes to this audience, especially footnotes 2-4.
31. Ernan McMullin, "Darwin and the Other Christian Tradition," *Zygon* 46:2 (June 2011): 296.
32. David Bentley Hart, *The Story of Christianity: A History of 2,000 Years of the Christian Faith* (New York: Quercus, 2009), 99, 163.
33. Paul Haffner, *Mystery of Creation*, 71.
34. Ven. Pius XII, *Humani Generis*, no. 37.
35. Nicanor Austriaco, et al., *Thomistic Evolution*, 230.
36. Ven. Pius XII, *Summi Pontificatus*, no. 35-36.
37. International Theological Commission, C&S, 63, 70.
38. Austriaco, et al., *Thomistic Evolution*, 232-235.
39. *Dei Verbum*, no. 8.
40. Guy Consolmagno, *God's Mechanics: How Scientists and Engineers Make Sense of Religion* (San Francisco: Jossey-Bass, 2008), 219.
41. *Gaudium et Spes*, no. 22.
42. St. Gregory of Nazianzus, *Theological Orations* IV.6, as quoted in Roch Kereszty, *Jesus Christ: Fundamentals of Christology*, rev. and updated edition (New York: Alba House, 2002), 205.
43. CCC 365.
44. *Roman Missal*, Third Edition. The Order of Mass: Common Preface II, no. 73.
45. Joseph F.X. Sladky, "St. Peter Claver: Slave of the Slaves Forever," Crisis Magazine, September 8, 2014, *www.crisismagazine.com/2014/st-peter-claver-slave-slaves-forever.*
46. Rodney Stark, *The Rise of Christianity: How the Obscure, Marginal Jesus Movement Became the Dominant Religious Force in the Western World in a Few Centuries* (New York: HarperOne, 1996), 215.

Chapter Twelve
From Evolution to Resurrection: Jesus Christ, the True Origin of Humanity

**How is Jesus Christ the true origin of humanity?
How is this related to human evolution?**

**How should we understand the Resurrection of Christ
in light of modern science?**

**How does the Eucharist complete our picture
of the unity of faith and science?**

In reality it is only in the mystery of the Word made flesh that the mystery of man truly becomes clear. For Adam, the first man, was a type of him who was to come, Christ the Lord. Christ the new Adam, in the very revelation of the mystery of the Father and of his love, fully reveals man to himself and brings to light his most high calling.

—Vatican II, *Gaudium et Spes*

In the last chapter, we considered human moral imperfections and tendencies toward evil. Focusing on our instinctive inclinations toward out-group and cognitive biases, we connected these to our biological heritage, our nature as animals. This led us to contemplate the mystery of Original Sin, shrouded by our fragmentary knowledge of human origins but evident within every aspect of human life as we experience it now. Finally, we turned to the heart of the Christian message and to the Sacred Heart of Jesus, who purifies humanity from sin not through erasing our fallen human nature but by actually redeeming it from within, in solidarity with us but without sin. Through his perfect love, expressed above all in his Death on the Cross, Jesus has recreated humanity and has given to human history a new start and a new direction. With this in mind, let us consider the process of "becoming human" from the perspective of that love.

Christ Crucified by Diego Velazquez

A. Becoming Human: An Image in Stone

The Formation of Adam, central bay, north porch, Chartres Cathedral, ca. 1220.

THE CATHEDRAL OF CHARTRES IN FRANCE is considered by many to be one of the most beautiful buildings in the world; it is doubtless the greatest architectural accomplishment of the Catholic culture of the Middle Ages. It was built to be a complete account of the history of salvation, and it includes creation as one of its artistic themes. One example is found on the exterior, among the exquisitely carved images found on the north porch of the cathedral. There we find an image depicting the formation of Adam, based on a verse from Genesis with which we are already familiar: "Then the LORD God formed man of dust from the ground, and breathed into his nostrils the breath of life; and man became a living being" (Gn 2:7). The medieval artist might have appreciated the irony that he was sculpting God as a sculptor, and crafting an image of God forming his own image. It would not be surprising if an educated modern viewer looked at the work and thought back to a beginning completely unknown to the medieval artist, when in a "Great Leap Forward" hominin life became rational. The master of stone, however, had a different and much more important idea in mind as he chipped and chiseled.

In this sculpture a sleeping human being, Adam, clings to the divine sculptor's knee, his head reclined almost on his lap. His lower body is only partially formed out of the clay lump that rests to the lower right side of the image. The divine sculptor is moving his hands gently and skillfully under and above Adam's head, with each hand actively sculpting him. But when we look to the face of the divine sculptor, with its careful attention to the human being he is forming, we find a surprise; the face is not that of an elderly man by which medieval art often represented God the Father, "the Ancient of Days" (Dn 7:9-10). The face is the face of Christ—he is the divine sculptor who is forming Adam.

We have already seen that the divine Son is the one through whom God creates the universe, the *Logos* who gives to all things their orderliness and intelligibility. This sculpture, however, adds another dimension to the consideration of human life—we are the image of God by being formed by Christ, the *Logos*-made-flesh, into the image of his perfect humanity. In the words of the International Theological Commission:

> **The origins of man are to be found in Christ: for he is created "through him and in him" (Col 1:16), "the Word [who is] the life... and the light of every man who is coming into the world" (Jn 1:3-4, 9). While it is true that man is created *ex nihilo*, it can also be said that he is created from the fullness (*ex plenitudine*) of Christ himself who is at once the creator, the mediator and the end of man.[1]**

In this chapter, we will consider the reality of being human from the perspective of Christ as the last Adam and the true human being, the one who brings the creation of humanity to its completion. We will see that the first "Adam," the first human being or beings, was simply a preparation for the real goal of the creation of humanity, in which Christ fulfills what began long ago. If we define ourselves by the first Adam, we fail to discover and realize the fullness of our humanity as intended and willed by God.

From this perspective we will also consider Christ's Resurrection as the central point of human history, as a new kind of evolution in which biology ceases to be the foundation of rationality and freedom, but in which human beings are brought into unending life that is freed from its limitations. Finally, we will conclude with the way in which we begin to enter into that life by receiving Christ, crucified and risen, in the Eucharist, which Vatican II called "the source and summit of the Christian life."[2]

B. Jesus Christ, the New and Final Adam

1. Completing the Creation: The Baptism and Death of Jesus

IN CHAPTER FOUR WE NOTED AN INTERESTING DETAIL of the First Creation Account, the omission of a declaration of goodness when God created human beings. In other cases, God beholds what he has made, affirms its goodness, and then that "day" of creation ends—"evening came, and morning followed." The First Creation Account leaves no doubt that humans are the summit of God's creation and are certainly good according to their being creatures of God, who only produces good things. In fact, only when human beings are in the world does God behold everything he has made and declares it "very good." But human moral goodness is never declared at the end of the sixth day, nor does God "behold" (in Hebrew, *yar*) what he has made when he makes human beings. This could indicate that the Lord is not finished with the formation of his image; he is awaiting the human response. In other words, God's "human project" is incomplete at the end of Genesis 1. In fact, even the words "and it was so," which follow the other acts of creation, are mysteriously absent.[3] Equally curious is the omission of any declaration of an end to the seventh day, the final day of creation.

When we come to the New Testament, however, these seeming omissions are finally resolved. The undeclared goodness of humanity is finally pro-

The presence of God the Father at the baptism of Jesus indicates that in Jesus the goodness he intended for humanity has been finally and fully achieved.

claimed near the beginning of the Gospel of Matthew, when Jesus submits himself to the baptism of John the Baptist "in order to fulfill all righteousness" (Mt 3:15). As soon as he receives baptism, the voice of God is heard:

> 16 And when Jesus was baptized, he went up immediately from the water, and behold, the heavens were opened and he saw the Spirit of God descending like a dove, and alighting on him;
>
> 17 and lo, a voice from heaven, saying, "This is my beloved Son, with whom I am well pleased."

In this event (which is also recounted in the Gospels of Mark and Luke) in which Jesus humbly submits himself publicly to the Father's will, God's declaration of pleasure indicates that in Jesus the goodness he intended for humanity has been finally and fully achieved—a human has arrived who pleases him in every way, who is perfectly good. The disobedience with which human history began, which postponed the completion of humanity, has now been overcome.

Ecce Homo! by Mihaly Munkacsy.
"Idou ho anthrōpos!" (Jn 19:5) can be translated into English as, "Behold the human!"

In the Gospel of John we discover the divine "behold" in reference to human beings. After Pontius Pilate has Jesus scourged, he has him brought before the crowd and declares, *"Idou ho anthrōpos!"* (Jn 19:5) which can be translated into English as, "Behold the human!" The missing "behold!" which we expect to come in Genesis at the creation of human beings, appears where we least expect it, on the lips of Jesus' cynical, unbelieving judge. In other words, through Jesus' unjust judge God gives us a "behold!" signaling that in Christ's loving Sacrifice, in his obedience to God, and in his love for us, we finally see what God intended for us to be. Only in his loving Sacrifice is the making of humanity completed.

"It is finished!"
With the completion of Jesus' Sacrifice,
God's greatest project, the human person, is also complete.

As Jesus breathes his dying breath, he says, "It is finished" (Jn 19:30).[4] Jesus' words offer the missing "end" to the seventh "day" of the First Creation Account. With the completion of his Sacrifice, God's greatest project, the human person, is also complete. Christ "gives over the Spirit," the Gift-Love of God, to the rest of humanity, so that we can find the completion of our own humanity in union with him.

2. The Last Adam

AT THE HEART OF THE NEW TESTAMENT MESSAGE, then, is the proclamation that Jesus Christ is the true human in every respect, the new and final Adam. While St. Matthew and St. John present this to us symbolically, **St. Paul** is more direct in the fifteenth chapter of his First Letter to the Corinthians:

> 45 Thus it is written, "The first man Adam became a living being"; the last Adam became a life-giving spirit.
>
> 46 But it is not the spiritual which is first but the physical, and then the spiritual.
>
> 47 The first man was from the earth, a man of dust; the second man is from heaven.
>
> 48 As was the man of dust, so are those who are of the dust; and as is the man of heaven, so are those who are of heaven.
>
> 49 Just as we have borne the image of the man of dust, we shall also bear the image of the man of heaven.

In theology, a *type* is something or someone that prefigures a new and greater reality called its *antitype*. The Crossing of the Red Sea (type) points to Christian Baptism (antitype), in which humans are freed from the slavery of sin.

Here, we have St. Paul extending the concept of humanity beyond that which we are given in Genesis. As the opening quote of this chapter from Vatican II tells us, quoting St. Paul's Letter to the Romans (Rom 5:14), the first Adam is a *type* of the final Adam: "Adam, the first man, was a type of him who was to come." In theology, a type is something or someone that prefigures a new and greater reality called its *antitype*. For example, the Crossing of the Red Sea (type) points to Christian Baptism (antitype), in which humans are freed from the slavery of sin, a much greater liberation than the deliverance of the Israelites from slavery in Egypt. In a type-antitype relationship, also known as a *typological relationship*, the antitype is everything that the type was but in a new and greater way.

To declare Jesus to be the last Adam, and to identify Adam as a type of Christ, is to place the beginning of human history, and in some way all human beings, in a new light. In Genesis 2:7, we hear of the formation of the human being as a living being, but the human formed there is not the last Adam to be formed; a new and greater Adam, for whom the first Adam is only a sketch, is still to come.

St. Paul's designation of Christ as the last Adam is rooted in the language of his Jewish background. For the ancient Hebrew mind, temporal order (first, last) is a way of indicating permanent, everlasting principles. To refer to someone or something as "last" is to identity them as the fulfillment and completion. When St. Paul calls Christ the last Adam, he does not mean to say that he is the last human being to be born, as if no other human beings would ever be born after him. Instead, he means that Christ is the exemplary human, the one who takes humanity to its fulfillment. He means that Christ is the one who finishes what God began when he formed man from the clay of the ground and gave him the breath of life, what we now see as the process of human evolution. He is the last Adam because, once he is present in the world, God has no more "work" to do to realize the fullness of human existence; his masterpiece is complete. By saying that Christ is the last Adam, the last human, he is saying that Christ is the perfect human, exhibiting the kind of humanity God intends for all people to live. Therefore, we have to say that, theologically speaking, it is not in the mists of prehistory, in Blombos Cave, or some as-yet undiscovered place, but only in the manger in Bethlehem, and even more so on Calvary, that humanity discovers its origin. Becoming human began far in the past, but its true "beginning" was revealed and reached its completion in Christ thousands of years later.

Crucifixion with Mary and St. Dominic

What is it about Christ that makes him the last Adam, the true man? According to **Pope Benedict XVI**, it is his radical dependence upon God and his openness to us. Jesus knows being fully human means being entirely for God and for others. He knows that the human creature only realizes his or her fullest potential by moving beyond the self, by finding oneself insufficient when he or she is not in communion with others, living only for the self. As Jesus tells us in Luke 9:24: "Whoever would save his life will lose it; and whoever loses his life for my sake, he will save it." Only through others, through being with and for others, does *Homo sapiens* come to be fully human—the other above all being God. In Christ the image of God becomes pure openness to God, which is what man was made to be.

In his 1967 masterpiece, *Introduction to Christianity*, Ratzinger made this point in cosmic and evolutionary terms. Referring to the moment in which we became rational animals as a first step, he points to the Incarnation, when God became man, as the completion of *hominization*, of "becoming human":

> **The Rubicon of becoming man . . . was first crossed by the step from animal to *logos*, from mere life to mind. Man came into existence out of the "clay" at the moment when a creature was no longer merely "there" but, over and above just being there and filling his needs, was aware of the whole. But this step, to which *logos*, understanding, mind, first came into this world, is only completed when the *Logos* itself, the whole creative meaning, and man merge into each other. Man's full hominization presupposes God's becoming man; only by this event is the Rubicon dividing animal from [human] finally crossed forever. . . . For . . . that man is most man, indeed the true man, who is most unlimited, who not only has contact with the infinite . . . but is one with him: Jesus Christ. In him hominization has truly reached its goal.**[5]

The fact that Jesus Christ is the "last Adam," the true man, means that his existence concerns all that are called "*āḏām*," all human beings. He is not some unrealizable ideal that stands above us, showing us how incomplete and broken we are so that we can despair of ever achieving true fulfillment and everlasting happiness. To call him the last Adam is to say that it is in him that all humanity is to be gathered into completion. This is the meaning of the opening of his Body on the Cross—for John's Gospel this moment is the climax of the whole Passion narrative: "But when they came to Jesus and saw that he was already dead, they did not break his legs. But one of the soldiers pierced his side with a spear, and at once there came out blood and water" (Jn 19:33-34). The opening of his side is symbolic of his interior openness to include us within his life. Now, from his pierced side, a new humanity can be formed, as prefigured in the symbolic image of the creation of Eve from the side of the sleeping Adam in the Second Creation Account (Gn 2:20-25). He lets the walls of his existence be broken down, and, rather than this ending his existence, his unbounded life flows out and carries all human beings who believe in him back into it. The redeemed human beings, who are saved by the Blood and water that flow out of the last Adam, we call the Body of Christ, the Church.

The Martyrdom of St. Ignatius of Antioch.
St. Ignatius of Antioch saw in his own martyrdom a chance to perfect both his love and his humanity.

3. Becoming Fully Human

IT IS NOT SURPRISING, THEN, to discover that the earliest Christians considered their union with Christ, and their imitation of him, to be an essential part of the process of becoming human. In the first decade of the second century of the Christian era, around AD 110, a bishop from the Holy Land, **St. Ignatius of Antioch**, made his way to Rome under escort of Roman soldiers as a prisoner on his way to martyrdom. Along the way he wrote letters to the various Christian communities in the places along his route: Smyrna, Philadelphia, Ephesus, and others. He also wrote ahead to the Church in Rome, and he made an urgent appeal to the Christians there not to attempt to avert his execution:

> **I am God's wheat and shall be ground by the teeth of wild animals. I am writing to all the churches to let it be known that I will gladly die for God if only you do not stand in my way. I plead with you: show me no untimely kindness. Let me be food for the wild beasts, for they are my way to God...**

And then he closes with this request:

> **The time for my birth is close at hand. Forgive me, my brothers. Do not stand in the way of my birth to real life; do not wish me stillborn. My desire is to belong to God.... *Only on my arrival there can I be fully a human being.*[6]**

Full humanity, therefore, comes from living and loving as Christ did. The man who shows us the real meaning of life and the path to unending happiness is not the one at the beginning of Scripture but the one who appears at the end.

It is easy to misunderstand this important Christian truth, especially because it comes in the context of Jesus' painful Death. What makes Christ the fulfillment of our humanity, the true Adam, is not the grisliness of his Death but the perfection of his love. This love is what makes his Sacrifice to God perfect and complete. As **St. Augustine** once observed, a true sacrifice is an "act done for the purpose of clinging to God in a holy fellowship... directed to that final Good which makes possible our true happiness."[7] St. Ignatius of Antioch saw in his own martyrdom a chance to perfect both his love and his humanity. But it is in the Christian life, which always involves clinging to God and loving one's neighbor, that the process of becoming "fully a human being" is possible for all of us. The Christian life is the adventure in which the image of God is completed in all who believe by being refashioned into the very image of Christ, the *imago Christi.*

What makes Christ the fulfillment of our humanity, the true Adam, is not the grisliness of his Death but the perfection of his love.

To become fully human, then, to repent of sin and believe in the Gospel, the Good News of Jesus Christ, means finally to open ourselves to the man who is fully God. Ultimately, every human being draws near to him whenever they forget themselves and love selflessly and in truth, and the Church teaches us to hope that there are and have been non-Christians who have come very close to him without even knowing him explicitly, as "[God] desires all men to be saved and to come to the knowledge of the truth" (1 Tm 2:4).[8] The Christian life is the explicit awareness and full acceptance of the real meaning of being human—to be like Christ, to be fully and entirely with and for others. Christian formation, which is also called discipleship, is not simply a lifestyle choice, nor is it "the result of an ethical choice or a lofty idea,"[9] as Pope Benedict XVI once wrote, but from the divine perspective it is nothing less than an encounter with the Person and event of Jesus Christ and the completion of what hominin evolution began. It is a completion that leads to a life that never ends.

C. The Resurrection as the Final Stage of Human Evolution

JESUS DID NOT ONLY DIE; we believe that he rose to an entirely new and indestructible kind of life, a life that is beyond the biological kind that we have by nature and that he had by virtue of the Incarnation—a life sustained by oxygen, nutrients, etc. His Resurrection was a real historical event that shattered the dimensions of history and transcended it. As we draw our consideration of the human person and science to a close, the Resurrection brings us to a new horizon in which matter, space, and time are enveloped by divine love and power.

1. The Event of the Resurrection

WITHOUT THE RESURRECTION OF JESUS, Christianity is absurd and its promises are false. **St. Paul** openly declared this when he said, "If Christ has not been raised, then our preaching is in vain and your faith is in vain" (1 Cor 15:14). If Jesus is merely dead, then death, the natural biological end of all life, is all that awaits each of us. The problem of physical and moral evil overshadows any hope we might have for everlasting happiness. What God has revealed in the Resurrection of Christ is that his eternal decision to create the world is simply one glimmer of the immense love he has for humanity. So it is all-important that we understand what the word *resurrection* means. As **Pope Benedict XVI** explains:

> **Jesus' Resurrection was about breaking out into an entirely new form of life, into a life that is no longer subject to the law of dying and becoming, but lies beyond it—a life that opens up a new dimension of human existence. Therefore the Resurrection of Jesus is not an isolated event, that we could set aside as something limited to the past, but it constitutes an "evolutionary leap." . . . In Jesus's Resurrection a new possibility of human existence is obtained that affects everyone and that opens up a future, a new kind of future, for mankind.**
>
> **So Paul was absolutely right to link the resurrection of Christians and the Resurrection of Jesus inseparably together: "If the dead are not raised, then Christ has not been raised. . . . But in fact Christ has been raised from the dead, the first fruits of those who have fallen asleep" (1 Cor 15:16, 20). Christ's Resurrection is either a universal event, or it is nothing, Paul tells us. And only if we understand it as a universal event, as the opening up of a new dimension of human existence, are we on the way toward any kind of correct understanding of the New Testament Resurrection testimony.[10]**

As Pope Benedict XVI points out, resurrection is not something that only concerns Jesus but, rather, all of us. It is not simply the return to a normal human life by a resuscitated corpse, but it is a "leap" to a whole new kind of life, which Jesus makes first but which is also promised to all humanity. This is what is meant when in the Creed we profess to "believe in . . . the resurrection of the body, and life everlasting." As the *Catechism* states, "Who will rise? All the dead will rise, 'those who have done good, to the resurrection of life, and those who have done evil, to the resurrection of judgment.'"[11]

Noli me tangere
"Do not hold me" (Jn 20:17) is the phrase spoken by Jesus to Mary Magdalene when she recognized him after his Resurrection.

What makes the accounts of Jesus' Resurrection so unlike mythical stories that involve resurrections is that there is no fanfare. It is revealed to only a handful of witnesses to whom Jesus personally appeared. And in his appearances, the risen Lord acts normally; he speaks to his disciples, cooks for them, asks for a piece of fish so that he can eat it and show that his body is real; he is not a ghost. "His presence is entirely physical, yet he is not bound by physical laws": despite his bodily presence, his disciples often do not recognize him; he suddenly appears and then just as suddenly is removed from their sight. Within this strange combination of the familiar and unfamiliar, the message is clear: This man is the same Jesus with the same body, but he has transitioned to a new way of existing.[12]

2. The Miracle of the Resurrection and Science

The Risen Christ by Salvator Rosa.

CONSIDERING THE RESURRECTION OF CHRIST with modern science as a backdrop helps us look upon the mystery of the Resurrection with fresh eyes. From the perspective of physics, the Resurrection is the elevation of matter to a new way of existing beyond what is possible in the normal state of the universe. From the perspective of biology, the man Jesus, belongs totally to the sphere of the divine and eternal. Now "in" God there is a place for bodiliness, which means that human beings now have a "place" in God's life.

This also means that our universe is subject to renewal and redemption. As we have learned from modern science, humanity and the world are not easily separable quantities, with the world existing as a container that just happens to hold all kinds of living creatures that could just as well have been placed in a different box. The cosmos and its evolution form the prehistory of the human spirit, of the human mind; The animals all participate, insofar as their natures allow them, in the building blocks that would become intelligence, self-reflection, reason, and free will in humans. In the first human, mind and personhood appeared at a particular point in hominin evolution thanks to the special dependence of man upon God for his being and spiritual faculties. In the Resurrection, the last Adam, Jesus Christ the true man "doubles back" and draws up into himself what came before him.

It is in light of the Resurrection that we best see the difference between the "how" explanations of science and the "why" explanations of faith. **St. Paul** himself saw the folly of trying to ask how the dead will be brought to new life in the General Resurrection, which is the term that refers to the resurrection of all people to unending life when Christ will come again. In chapter fifteen of his First Letter to the Corinthians, he used what he knew of natural bodies as an analogy that shows, dimly but beautifully, the fittingness of the resurrection of the dead:

35 But some one will ask, "How are the dead raised? With what kind of body do they come?"

36 You foolish man! What you sow does not come to life unless it dies.

37 And what you sow is not the body which is to be, but a bare kernel, perhaps of wheat or of some other grain.

38 But God gives it a body as he has chosen, and to each kind of seed its own body.

39 For not all flesh is alike, but there is one kind for men, another for animals, another for birds, and another for fish.

40 There are celestial bodies and there are terrestrial bodies; but the glory of the celestial is one, and the glory of the terrestrial is another.

41 There is one glory of the sun, and another glory of the moon, and another glory of the stars; for star differs from star in glory.

42 So is it with the resurrection of the dead. What is sown is perishable, what is raised is imperishable.

43 It is sown in dishonor, it is raised in glory. It is sown in weakness, it is raised in power.

44 It is sown a physical body, it is raised a spiritual body. If there is a physical body, there is also a spiritual body.

Does St. Paul's analogy, and our faith in the Resurrection of Jesus, contradict reason and a proper respect for the integrity of nature? As we saw in Chapter Six, this would be the case only if we turned bodily resurrection into a function of nature, or if we saw it as the violation of nature by divine power. But resurrection is about the ultimate destiny of God's creation, the "new heavens and the new earth," which God intends. If science is done with the unprovable assumption that the material universe in its current state is all that does exist and can exist, then not only will the skeptic find the Resurrection to be absurd, but he will ultimately be unable to make sense of the objectivity and wonder that makes human beings uniquely capable of investigating the world scientifically and coming to understand it as it truly is. If science is polluted by an unjustified commitment to reductionism, then not only will life after death seem absurd but so will life *before* death, because the living things we see are only collections of parts, acting as the sum of those parts.[13]

"If there really is a God, is he not able to create a new dimension of human existence, a new dimension of reality altogether?"
—Pope Benedict XVI

Pope Benedict XVI asked the question: "Does the Resurrection contradict science?" Applying principles that we have already encountered, he combines a thorough respect for faith and reason together and the integrity of nature, while also bidding us to posit the possibility of something beyond our experience:

> **Naturally, there can be no contradiction of clear scientific data. The Resurrection accounts certainly speak of something outside the world of our experience. They speak of something new, something unprecedented—a new dimension of reality that is revealed. What already exists is not called into question. Rather we are told that there is a further dimension, beyond what was previously known. Does that contradict science? Can there really only ever be what there has always been? Can there not be something unexpected, something unimaginable, something new? If there really is a God, is he not able to create a new dimension of human existence, a new dimension of reality altogether? Is not creation actually waiting for this last and highest evolutionary leap, for the union of the finite with the infinite, for the union of man and God, for the conquest of death?[14]**

With this in mind, the Resurrection does not require that we deny what we see in history and the universe, but that we see them against the backdrop of God's love. As we learned in Chapter Three from the English mystic **Julian of Norwich**, all things have existence from the love of God; he is to all things the Source of being. And so, the Source of the universe and all its creatures has the power to beckon us beyond the limits of biological life.

In the Resurrection of Christ, the realm of biological evolution has been left behind and in Christ humanity has leapt to a quite different plane.

3. The Last Shall Be First: From *Bios* to *Zoē*

AS WE HAVE SEEN, THE KEY TO UNDERSTANDING the Resurrection is the reality of love. In the Resurrection, we see that the final stage of human evolution reverses the paradigm of existence. In the first phase of human existence, biological life is necessary in order to love. In his sacrificial Death, Jesus, as we have seen, valued love more highly than the biological life that made it possible. His Resurrection tells us that, although in this existence one must first have biological life in order to love, the power of love is greater than the power of the merely biological. In the Resurrection, biology is encompassed by and incorporated into the power of love. And so love makes it possible for us to transcend the limits of biological existence.

After his Resurrection, Christ did not go back to his previous earthly life as did Lazarus, whom he raised from the dead (Jn 11:1-44). He rose to a definitive new life no longer governed by the chemical and biological laws that govern our lives now. In this new reality love is the foundation of life, and, therefore, in love life becomes indestructible. He who loved us to the end has founded our immortality on that love. This is why Scripture says that Christ is our life—"When Christ who is our life appears, then you also will appear with him in glory" (Col 3:4). If he has risen, then we will, too, for in his risen humanity he loves us now and always; if he is not risen, then we will not either, for then the situation is that death still has the last word, nothing else. Our own love, left to itself, cannot overcome death; taken in itself, our own love would have to remain a feeble unanswered cry for resurrection and eternal life. But when his love envelops our love, then our own immortality has a foundation that can be neither shaken nor removed.

Thus, a new kind of life has dawned in the world through the new Adam. In the Resurrection of Christ, the realm of biological evolution has been left behind and in Christ humanity has leapt, so to speak, to a quite different plane, in which love is no longer subject to biology but now supports it. As Jesus himself once said to his disciples, the last has become the first (cf. Mt 10:16). The final stage of evolution, therefore, is no longer a biological stage; the dominion of biology has ended. Since biology always involves death, the sovereignty of death has ended as well. Christ has opened up the realm that the Bible calls, in the original Greek, *zoē*, that is, definitive life unqualified or restricted by biology, life that has left behind the rule of death. The last stage of evolution needed by the world to reach its goal has been achieved within the realm of biology by Jesus, who brings humanity past the purely biological realm.

Of course, our faith tells us that the mode of our immortality will depend upon our mode of living. If we place biological life above love, or self-interest above other selves, then we begin hell right now on earth. The Resurrection of Christ reveals the tragic dimension of sin even more deeply. St. Augustine's definition of sin is for one to be *incurvatus in se*, "caved in on oneself"—the exact opposite of Christ's openness to God and neighbor. **Bishop Robert Barron** shows us the absurdity of sin: "The powers of the human soul, which are meant to orient us to nature and other human beings and the cosmos and finally the infinite mystery of God, are focused on the tiny and infinitely uninteresting ego [self]. Like a black hole, the sinful soul draws all the light and energy around it into itself."[15]

From this we can learn a great deal from the tapeworm. The tapeworm has evolved from a much more complex organism to the form it has now. In its evolution it adopted a "less is more" approach to parasitism, losing its nervous system, its digestive system, leaving nothing but the ability to latch onto its prey and reproduce. Similarly, humans in hell would be those who cling to a lower form of existence and have rejected the possibility of opening themselves up to the adventure of a new kind of life, losing their capacity for anything beyond themselves. As Jesus teaches, "Whoever would save his life will lose it, and whoever loses his life for my sake will find it" (Mt 16:25).

In other words, the prospect of eternal damnation is not one that comes from Christ but, rather, from us. As **Joseph Ratzinger** recognized, "Christ inflicts [damnation] on no one. In himself he is sheer salvation. Anyone who is with him has entered the space of deliverance and salvation. Perdition is not imposed by him, but comes to be wherever a person distances himself from Christ. It comes about whenever someone remains enclosed within himself."[16] The Christian life is the highest risk, but it ultimately offers the highest kind of fitness—if we live for love in Jesus Christ, then we open ourselves to a life that never ends.

The prospect of eternal damnation is not one that comes from Christ but, rather, from us.

D. The Eucharist: The Source of Our New Life

JESUS, THE LAST ADAM, the perfect man, has given himself to us in the humblest of forms, the form of bread and wine, the form of food. In the Holy Sacrifice of the Mass, Christ crucified and risen feeds us in a way unlike any other. Whatever else we eat must die and be assimilated to ourselves through digestion before it can nourish us. Christ, who died and now lives eternally, perfect God and perfect man, is not assimilated to us when we receive the Eucharist. Instead, we are assimilated into him, into his Body. And so, through the grace of receiving him into ourselves, we receive the grace to enter into the eternal happiness of heaven, the Communion of Saints where God will wipe away the tears from every eye.

In the consecrated Host, the believer encounters God the Creator, the Son-*Logos*, really and truly, though in the humblest of forms.

The miracle of Jesus Christ "really, truly and substantially contained"[17] in the Eucharist brings our study of faith and science to a close. We now see science, the study of the physical universe, as the study of a stage that exists to focus our attention on the actors and on the Author whose loving hand and creative mind unfolds its story. With all its beauty and grandeur, it is given to us to foreshadow the coming of a greater reality that awaits us. Therefore, of all the acts of faith that God offers to us, one of them is most fitting to the believer who also wishes to be a scientist. That act of faith is Eucharistic Adoration. In the Adoration of the Eucharist, we do in prayer what all scientists, knowingly or unknowingly, are doing in their research—gazing upon a reality whose appearance veils a reality much deeper and more amazing than appears at first glance. In the consecrated Host, the believer encounters God the Creator, the Son-*Logos*, really and truly, though in the humblest of forms. In the microscope and the telescope, in the laboratory and in the field, the believing scientist encounters God through the order, harmony, and intelligibility that nature, simply by virtue of its existence as a creation of God, manifests. In both cases, one must look beyond the surface to see the deeper truth; in both cases, awe and wonder beckon us, and paradoxes await us.

As we conclude, let us heed the words and receive the blessing that **St. John Paul II** gave to the young scientists of the world:

> **To you young scientists belongs the future of the dialogue between faith and science: I urge you to carry it forward with sincerity and humility. Strive for excellence in your scientific endeavors, and keep your minds and hearts ever open to the different channels which lead us to a better understanding of ourselves and the universe in which we live. May God, whose infinite love and wisdom fashioned the heavens and established the moon and stars, ever guide you into his grace and peace.**[18]

Amen!

VOCABULARY

Define the following terms (or identify the person's significance):

1. Cathedral of Chartres
2. *Yar*
3. *Idou ho anthrōpos*
4. Type
5. Antitype
6. Typological Relationship
7. Hominization
8. St. Ignatius of Antioch
9. Sacrifice
10. *Imago Christi*
11. Resurrection of Christ
12. Resurrection of the Body
13. *Bios*
14. *Zoē*
15. *Incurvatus in se*
16. Eucharist

Cathedral of Our Lady of Chartres was constructed between 1194 and 1220.
It is built in both the Gothic and Romanesque styles and attracts large numbers of Christian pilgrims, many of whom come to venerate its famous relic, the *Sancta Camisa*, said to be the tunic worn by the Virgin Mary at Christ's Birth.

STUDY QUESTIONS

Section A

1. What does the image of the formation of Adam in Chartres Cathedral symbolize about the real meaning of being fully human?

Section B

2. What missing element of the First Creation Account is provided in the account of Jesus' baptism in the Gospel of Matthew (3:15-17)? What does this reveal about Jesus?

3. What missing element of the First Creation Account is provided in the account of Jesus' Passion in the Gospel of John (19:5)? What does this reveal about Jesus?

4. What missing element of the First Creation Account is provided in the account of Jesus' final words in the Gospel of John (19:30)? What does this reveal about Jesus?

5. How does St. Paul use the term "the last Adam" in reference to Jesus? Why is Christ the last Adam, according to Pope Benedict XVI?

6. How does St. Ignatius of Antioch confirm that only in Christ is the full realization of our humanity possible?

7. Is a violent death the only way to conform ourselves to Christ? Explain, using St. Augustine's notion of sacrifice.

Section C

8. How is resurrection different than resuscitation?

9. Why does Jesus' Resurrection affect all of us, according to Pope Benedict XVI?

10. Explain the Resurrection in the context of physics, biology, and cosmic evolution. Be sure to make reference to *bios* and *zoē*.

11. How does St. Paul use the science of his day analogically to help us better understand the Resurrection?

12. Does the idea of the Resurrection violate the principle of upholding the integrity of nature? Explain.

13. What is sin? What is eternal damnation? Does Christ inflict damnation on sinners? Explain.

Section D

14. How does the Eucharist bring about our incorporation into Christ?

15. Reflect upon the Catholic practice of Eucharistic Adoration and relate it to the daily activity of the Catholic scientist and his or her faith-filled gaze upon the created order. What do they have in common? How do they differ?

The Person who shows us the real meaning of life and the path to unending happiness is not the one at the beginning of Scripture but the one who appears at the end.

Endnotes – Chapter Twelve

1. International Theological Commission, *Communion and Stewardship*, no. 53.
2. Vatican II, *LG*, 11.
3. John Behr, *Becoming Human: Meditations on Christian Anthropology in Word and Image* (Crestwood, NY: St. Vladimir's Seminary Press, 2013), 34.
4. Ibid., 35.
5. Joseph Ratzinger, *Introduction to Christianity*, 173.
6. St. Ignatius of Antioch, "Letter to the Romans," IV.
7. St. Augustine, *De civitate Dei* 10.6, as quoted in Kereszty, Jesus Christ, 212.
8. Cf. *Lumen Gentium* no. 14-16.
9. Pope Benedict XVI, Deus Caritas Est, no. 1, *w2.vatican.va/content/benedict-xvi/en/encyclicals/documents/hf_ben-xvi_enc_20051225_deus-caritas-est.html.*
10. Pope Benedict XVI, *Jesus of Nazareth: Holy Week: From the Entrance into Jerusalem to the Resurrection* (San Francisco: Ignatius Press, 2011), 244.
11. CCC 998; Cf. Jn 5:29; Dn 12:2.
12. Pope Benedict XVI, *Jesus of Nazareth: Holy Week*, 265-266.
13. Conor Cunningham, "Why Study Life Before Death with Conor Cunningham," YouTube, September 26, 2016, *www.youtube.com/watch?v=McZMBqw8bb8.*
14. Pope Benedict XVI, *Jesus of Nazareth: Holy Week*, 246-247.
15. Robert Barron, *The Strangest Way: Walking the Christian Path* (Maryknoll, NY: Orbis Books, 2002), 75.
16. Joseph Ratzinger, *Eschatology: Death and Eternal Life*, 2nd edition (Washington, D.C.: The Catholic University of America Press, 1988), 205.
17. CCC 1374.
18. St. John Paul II, "Address to Participants in the Fifth Summer School in Astrophysics," Vatican Observatory, July 7, 1995, *w2.vatican.va/content/john-paul-ii/en/speeches/1995/july/documents/hf_jp-ii_spe_19950707_astrofisica.html.*

Appendix
More Catholic Scientists Throughout the Ages

The following list is a continuation of the list provided in Chapter 5, Section B, "Catholic Scientists Throughout the Ages" (pp. 108 ff.). Even taken together, these two lists are very incomplete, but they do provide a helpful, short tour of the remarkable scientific achievements of Catholics over the last 1500 years.

Sylvester II (Pope: Mathematics, Astronomy, ca. 946-1003) also known as Gerbert of Aurillac, introduced Arabic numerals, the abacus (an ancient computing device), and other scientific methods and devices into the Western world. During three years in a Spanish monastery, he studied the writings of Muslim scholars in the monastic library and discovered numerous innovations unknown in Europe. At that time people were still using Roman numerals for calculation. Sylvester II realized that Arabic numerals, with their inclusion of the number zero, were much easier to use in math than the cumbersome, often lengthy Roman numerals. In astronomy he reintroduced the *armillary sphere*, a model of objects in space centered on the earth (depicted as a globe) and showing their movements in relation to the earth; in fact, he constructed one with such precision that it was amazingly accurate for its day. He even invented and built a hydraulic-powered musical organ.

St. Hildegard of Bingen (Nun, Abbess, Naturalist: Botany, Zoology, Medicine, 1098-1179) was a German Benedictine mystic, abbess, playwright, composer, and philosopher of nature who wrote texts on botany and medicine, a genius who even constructed an alternative alphabet and language. Her book entitled *Physica* is an encyclopedia of information on plants, trees, animals, stones, metals, and elements. She also composed a book on diseases and their causes, although in this regard her insights were limited by a lack of information about microscopic organisms that no one possessed at the time. Hildegard may have been the first woman to produce such works, and so is considered one of, if not the, first female scientist in Western civilization. She was declared a Doctor of the Church in 2012 by Pope Benedict XVI, who also officially added her to the list of the Church's saints due to her eminent holiness.

Robert Grosseteste (Bishop: Physics, 1168-1253) used both mathematical analysis and experimentation in the study of the behavior of light (the branch of science called *optics*). These were vitally important steps in the development of truly empirical science. Grosseteste formulated a geometric law for the refraction of light that was qualitatively correct, and used it to explain (correctly) how lenses magnify images.

Thomas Bradwardine (Priest, Archbishop: Physics 1290-1349) analyzed Aristotle's ideas on motion and showed that they were mathematically inconsistent. He then attempted to develop a mathematical law that related the force acting on a body, the body's resistance to force, and the resulting velocity of the body. Even though Bradwardine's law was not correct, it was the first attempt to formulate a mathematical law of motion. And it illustrates both the creativity of medieval scientists and their willingness to criticize the mistakes of the science that they inherited from the ancient world.

Nicholas of Cusa (Priest, Bishop, Cardinal: Cosmology, 1401-1464) was an important figure in medieval philosophy. In fact, he was really more of a theologian and philosopher than a scientist. For theological and philosophical reasons, Cusa suggested that the universe is infinitely large and has no center and that all bodies in the universe, including both the earth and the sun, are in motion in infinite space. He also theorized favorably about the existence of intelligent life on other planets, which he thought was probable due to God's perfect wisdom and creativity.

José de Acosta (Jesuit Priest, Naturalist: Geography, Botany, Zoology, 1539-1600) entered the Jesuits at age 15 and later became a missionary to South America, serving for fourteen years in Peru and then three years in Mexico. While there he began compiling what would become the *Historia natural y moral de las Indias*, a work which catalogued the constellations, elements, metals, plants, and animals of that part of the New World, and offered accounts of Incan and Aztec cultures and languages. Acosta theorized that the native peoples he encountered in South America had migrated from Asia via a land bridge or narrow strait located to the north, a hypothesis about human migration that is now widely accepted and has recently been boosted through genetic analysis of the remains of an Alaskan infant who died over 11,000 years ago.[1]

Christoph Scheiner (Jesuit Priest, Astronomy, 1573-1650) was one of five people who discovered sunspots independently of each other, and practically at the same time. (The others were Thomas Herriot, Johannes and David Fabricius, and Galileo.) To be more precise, these men were the first to discover them *with telescopes*. It was Galileo who first figured out what sunspots were, but it was Scheiner who made the most sustained and systematic observations of them, published in his massive treatise, *Rosa Ursina*, in 1640. Scheiner tracked sunspots as they moved across the face of the sun, and showed from this data that the sun was rotating on an axis that is tilted with respect to the earth's orbit.

Benedetto Castelli (Benedictine Priest: Founder of Hydraulics, 1578-1643) was a student of none other than Galileo himself. Castelli defended Galileo and Copernicanism throughout Galileo's troubles. At a critical moment in these troubles, when Galileo decided to defend himself publicly against some of his accusers, he chose to do so by means of an open letter addressed to Castelli.

At Galileo's recommendation, Castelli was made professor of mathematics at the University of Pisa in 1613. There he began to study water in motion. In 1628, he published his magnum opus, *On the Measurement of Water Currents*, which is considered the beginning of modern hydraulics.

Niccolò Zucchi (Jesuit Priest, Astronomy, 1586-1670) made no great discovery. However, he was the first person to build a reflecting telescope (i.e., telescopes which use mirrors to gather light, rather than lenses). Today the reflecting telescope is still the most advanced nonelectric apparatus for observing planets and other bodies in space. Zucchi constructed his telescope in 1616, or perhaps even earlier—more than 50 years before Isaac Newton, who is often credited with building the first reflecting telescope. Zucchi used his telescope to make accurate observations of spots on the surface of Mars in 1640, and his data contributed to the discovery in 1666 that Mars rotates on its axis.

Giambattista Riccioli (Jesuit Priest, Astronomy, 1598-1671) has the distinction of being the first person to observe a binary star. We now know that most stars are not single stars like the sun, but orbit around other stars in binary systems. Riccioli also perfected the pendulum as an instrument to measure time precisely, which was important for later scientific research. With his fellow Jesuit, Francesco Grimaldi, he mapped the surface of the moon. A copy of their map stands at the entrance to the lunar exhibit at the Smithsonian Museum in Washington, D.C.

Thirty-five of the moon's craters are named after Jesuit astronomers, including several of the largest craters. For example, a crater 250 miles in diameter is named after Grimaldi.

Francesco Grimaldi (Jesuit Priest, Astronomy, 1618-1663), who helped Riccioli map the surface of the moon, made his greatest discovery in physics, not astronomy. It is one of the truly great discoveries in the history of science. He discovered (and named) the very important phenomenon of the "diffraction of light." Grimaldi studied the shadows cast on a screen by objects of various shapes illuminated by a thin beam of sunlight that he allowed to enter a darkened room through a small aperture in the wall. He discovered that, within the shadow region on the screen, there were faint fringes of light, and in the illuminated region there were faint fringes of shadow. Grimaldi not only discovered these "diffraction fringes," he made very careful observations of their number, intensity, and coloration.

Grimaldi's pioneering work was known by later investigators, including Hooke and Newton. However, it was not until almost two centuries later that the significance of the diffraction effect was understood: It shows that light is a wave. In the twentieth century it was discovered that all matter is made up of waves, and consequently the phenomenon of diffraction is important in many branches of physics—entire chapters are devoted to it in college and graduate-level physics textbooks. A commonly seen diffraction effect is in CDs and DVDs: Those bands of light color appear because of diffracted light. So when you see those colors, think of Fr. Grimaldi.

Laura Bassi (Laywoman: Physics, 1711-1778) was only the second woman in history to receive a European university degree, and the very first woman ever to receive a chair at a European university, the University of Bologna. She spent her early career studying gravity, performing experiments based on the work of Sir Isaac Newton. In her later career she focused her experiments on electricity but managed to perform experiments in virtually every other area of physics known in her day.[2] While obviously opening doors for future female scientists, Bassi also raised eight children and maintained a close friendship with Pope Benedict XIV, who included her as the only woman in the *Benedettini*, an elite group of 25 scholars that he encouraged to promote theoretical physics and other sciences.

Lazzaro Spallanzani (Priest: Biology, 1729-1799) is regarded as one of the top biologists of the eighteenth century. He investigated digestion, the dynamics of blood circulation, regeneration of limbs in lower animals, fertilization, respiration in plants and animals, and the senses of bats. He disproved the idea of *spontaneous generation*, the ancient belief that some complex organisms, such as worms and flies, are generated from nonliving matter as opposed to biological reproduction. When Louis Pasteur sought to do the same thing 100 years later, he based his own experiments on those of Spallanzani.

Rene-Just Haüy (Priest: Founder of Crystallography, 1743-1822) is regarded as the founder of the science of crystallography and helped to establish the metric system. His name is inscribed on the southeast side of the Eiffel Tower.

Giuseppe Piazzi (Priest: Astronomy, 1746-1826) was the director of the Palermo Observatory. On January 1, 1801 (the first day of the nineteenth century), he discovered the first known—and also the largest—asteroid, which he named *Ceres*. In 2006 Ceres was reclassified as a dwarf planet, making Piazzi the first discoverer of a dwarf planet (Pluto would not be discovered until 1930). To honor him, a crater on the moon was named Piazzi in 1935 by the International Astronomical Union.

Henri Breuil (Priest: Paleoanthropology, 1877-1961) was for decades one of the leading paleoanthropologists in the world. In particular, he was considered the foremost authority on cave paintings and prehistoric art. In a humorous take on his religion, he is often called "the pope of prehistory."

Julius Nieuwland (Holy Cross Priest: Inventor, 1878-1936) was a professor of chemistry at the University of Notre Dame. His work led to the development of "neoprene," the first synthetic rubber.

Hilary Ross (Daughter of Charity: Biochemistry, 1894-1982) was not a trained scientist nor was she a cradle Catholic. Raised an Episcopalian in California, she frequently attended a Catholic Mass with a friend and converted at the age of 19. She entered the Daughters of Charity two years later and undertook their mission of nursing. Struck with facial paralysis after a botched surgery, she could no longer be a nurse, and so she became a pharmacist and was sent to Carville, Louisiana, to serve in that capacity at a leprosarium. It was there that she took up biochemistry and began publishing papers on the biochemistry of leprosy (also called Hansen's Disease), especially the changes it makes to human tissue. There was no laboratory when she first arrived, so she established one, and continued her study for 37 years. In 1958 she received the Damien-Dutton Award for her significant contributions toward the conquest of leprosy.[3]

Endnotes – Appendix

1. Michael Price, "Ancient Americans arrived in a single wave, Alaskan infant's genome suggests." Science | AAAS, January 3, 2018, *www.sciencemag.org/news/2018/01/ancient-americans-arrived-single-wave-alaskan-infants-genome-suggests.*
2. Ulrich Lehner, The Catholic Enlightenment: The Forgotten History of a Global Movement (Oxford: Oxford University Press, 2016), 78.
3. "Sister Hilary Ross," International Leprosy Association—History of Leprosy, *leprosyhistory.org/database/person41*; "Inventive, Even to the Point of Infinity: Sister Hilary Ross," Maria Climbs a Mountain, August 8, 2012, *www.mariasmountain.net/search/label/sr%20hilary%20ross.*

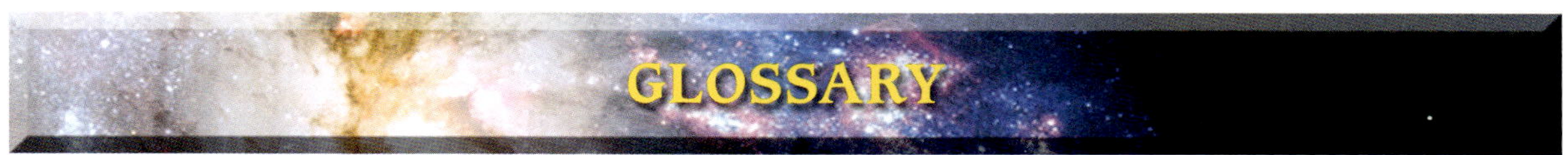

GLOSSARY

The number [in brackets] indicates the chapter in which the term is found.

A

Ab Initio Temporis [7] Latin for "from the beginning of time"; the revealed doctrine that God created the universe with an actual first moment.

Abiogenesis [8] The origin of the first living things from nonliving matter.

Academy of the Lynx-Eyed [5] A scientific association founded in 1603 by Roman Prince Federico Cesi to encourage research based on observation, experiment, and the inductive method.

***ādām* (Hebrew)** [9] "Human" or "humanity"; the name given to the first male human being in the Second Creation Account.

***ādāmah* (Hebrew)** [9] "Ground" or "earth," referred to in Genesis 2:7 as that out of which humanity is formed.

Affirmation [2] An assertion that something exists or that a proposition is true.

Agnostic [8] One who believes that the existence of God cannot be known or proven, often accompanied by the opinion that religious faith is irrational and that human reason must confine itself to those truths that are observable.

Albert the Great, St. [5] (1200-1280) A Dominican friar and bishop who emphasized the importance of an experimental approach to science; the teacher of St. Thomas Aquinas. The patron saint of science, whose Feast Day is November 15.

Amen [8] "Let it be," or "so be it." From the theological perspective, the cooperation of created things—in a special way human beings, who are the image of God—to bring about his ends.

Analogy (Analogous) [3] A limited comparison in which there are similarities but also differences.

Anthropic Coincidences [7] The features of the universe that are exactly "fine tuned" to what is needed for the existence of life, based on the proposition that the conditions that allow life can occur only when certain universal physical constants lie within a very narrow range of values.

Anthrōpos [7] The Greek word for "human being," applied to Jesus Christ by Pontius Pilate (cf. Jn 19:5).

Antitype [12] A person, event, or place that is everything that the type was or is but in a new and greater way; the fulfillment of a type.

Apsu [4] The sky god and father of the gods in ancient Babylonian mythology.

Aquinas *See* Thomas Aquinas.

Argument from Design (Biological) [7] An eighteenth- and nineteenth-century argument, foundational to the Anglican natural theology movement, that tried to argue from the complexity of living creatures to the existence of God; it was effectively demolished by Darwin's theory of evolution. A current version is Intelligent Design (ID) Theory.

GLOSSARY

Argument from Design (Cosmic) [7] An ancient proposition that the beauty, harmony, and order in the world are a sign of its creation by a Mind, by sublime reason.

Atrahasis [9] An Akkadian epic recorded in various versions on clay tablets that include both a creation myth and a flood account.

Autonomy of Science [5] The freedom of scientific inquiry to engage in discovery and speculation without artificial constraints, proclaimed by Vatican II.

B

Babylonian Exile [4] (587-539 BC) The forced migration of the Jews to Babylon following Nebuchadnezzar's capture of Jerusalem.

Baptism [11] The first of the Seven Sacraments, which gives access to the other Sacraments; the first and chief Sacrament of Forgiveness of Sins because the baptized Christian receives the remission of both personal and Original Sin, incorporating him or her into the Church, which is the Mystical Body of Christ.

Barberini, Maffeo *See* Urban VIII.

Barr, Stephen [7] An American theoretical physicist, Catholic author, and professor of physics and astronomy who founded the Society of Catholic Scientists.

Beagle *See* HMS Beagle.

Beauty [7, 9] A property or characteristic that provides a perceptual experience of pleasure or satisfaction, especially what the ancients defined as the proper relationship between the parts of something and the whole, having order and harmony. The coming together, in one being, of unity, harmony, and splendor.

Being Subsisting in Itself [3] God understood the infinite fullness of pure unlimited existence; the one ultimate Source of all being. God is Being subsisting in itself.

Ben Sira [3] The author of the Old Testament Book of Sirach in the second century BC.

Benedict XVI (Evolution) [8] (b. 1927) The Pope who reaffirmed St. John Paul II's teachings about scientific inquiry and discovery, cautioning that biological evolution cannot explain from where everything comes or how its path leads to the human person (creation of the soul).

Big Bang Theory [7] The prevailing cosmological model for the beginning of the observable universe, describing how the universe expanded from a high-density, high-temperature state billions of years ago.

Biogeography [8] The study of the geographical distribution of different plants and animals over time, which is one of the chief sources of evidence for the theory of evolution.

Biological Evolution [8] The change in the characteristics of biological populations over generations by the expressions of genes and genetic mutations that are passed on from parent to offspring.

GLOSSARY

Bios [12] The Greek word for biological life.

Bipedalism [9] A form of locomotion whereby an organism moves by means of its two rear limbs or legs, which evolved among primates about four million years ago.

Book of Wisdom [7] An Old Testament book written in Alexandria, Egypt, fifty to 100 years before the Birth of Jesus Christ. A book that urges the rulers of the earth to seek wisdom.

Bouyssonie, Jean and Amedee [9] Priests and archaeologists who led digs in La Chapelle-aux-Saints Cave from 1905 to 1908; first discoverers of a Neanderthal burial site.

Brahe, Tycho [5] (1546-1601) A Danish nobleman, astronomer, and writer known for his accurate and comprehensive astronomical and planetary observations.

Bruniquel Cave [9] An archeological site in southwestern France that has shed light on the complexity of early Neanderthal social organization and cognitive capacities.

Buck v. Bell [11] (1927) A United States Supreme Court decision that a state could require sterilization of some people, including the intellectually disabled, without violating the Due Process clause of the Fourteenth Amendment of the Constitution.

Buridan, Jean (Theory of Impetus) [5] (ca. 1300 - ca. 1358) An influential French philosopher who developed the concept of impetus, the first step toward the modern understanding of inertia.

C

Caccini, Tommaso [5] (1574-1648) A Dominican friar who criticized Copernicus and Galileo by name as teaching erroneous doctrine in a sermon preached in Santa Maria de Novella in Florence in 1614.

Calandrelli, Giuseppe [5] (1749-1827) A mathematician who measured the stellar parallax of a star, demonstrating that the earth orbits the sun. *See also* Stellar Parallax.

Capacity for Objectivity [10] The ability of human beings to go beyond immediate interests and needs and to perceive oneself and others as the beings that they are in their own right.

Castelli, Benedetto [5, Appendix] (1578-1643) A priest, mathematician, and Galileo's pupil who defended Galileo against claims that Galileo's writings contradicted Joshua 10:12-14.

Cathedral of Chartres [12] A Gothic French cathedral constructed from 1194 to 1220, a masterpiece of architecture.

Cesi, Federico [5] (1585-1630) A Roman prince who started the Academy of the Lynx-Eyed in 1603, the first scientific academy in the world.

Chance [8] The intersection of two or more lines of causality that are independent of each other in a way that is accidental and unintended by the agents involved.

Change [3] A process that involves going from one real state to another.

GLOSSARY

Charism of Infallibility [3] A special and unique grace that preserves the Pope and bishops of the Church from error in matters of faith and morals under well-defined circumstances.

Chauvet Cave [9] A cave in southern France that contains some of the best-preserved figurative cave paintings in the world, which date to 35,000-30,000 BC.

Chesterton, G.K. (Creation and Evolution) [8] (1874-1936) An English writer, poet, philosopher, journalist, theologian, biographer, and literary and art critic who noted in reference to Darwin's theory of evolution that God, who is outside time, is no more likely to create quickly than slowly.

Christian Faith [2] The truth that God has revealed in Sacred Scripture, Sacred Tradition, and the teaching of the Church.

Clavius, Christoph [5] (1538-1612) A Jesuit mathematician and astronomer who combined his astronomical observations and mathematical genius to develop the Gregorian calendar, which remains the calendar in use today throughout most of the world.

Clockmaker God [3] A weak analogy that describes God as an all-powerful engineer or mechanic, whose primary connection to created things was that of a craftsman who put parts together in ingenious designs.

Cognitive Bias [11] The tendency to favor, by the human mind, statements that have already been processed, which can lead people to exclude new, conflicting ideas and maintain a subjective perception of social reality that differs from objective reality.

Communion [10] The spiritual union with other persons that entails mutual self-giving, especially with God and other baptized Christians.

Comparative Anatomy [8] The study of similarities and differences in the anatomy of different species, which is one of the chief sources of evidence for the theory of evolution.

Complementarity (Science) [1] A principle that holds that objects have certain pairs of complementary properties which cannot all be observed or measured simultaneously. Formulated by Niels Bohr, a leading founder of quantum mechanics.

Concupiscible Appetite [11] The human capacity to approach sensible desires with true good always in mind, which because of wounded human nature, does not always rejoice in true sensible goods as opposed to merely apparent ones.

Concordism [4] A misguided attempt to harmonize scientific details regarding the origins of the universe and of life with biblical creation accounts.

Copernicus, Nicolaus [5] (1473-1543) A Polish priest and astronomer who speculated that the sun, not the earth, was at the center of the universe, and that the earth moves on its axis.

Corruption [6] Destruction. An example of physical evil that is often necessary for the good of biological life, such as the destruction of an ovum and sperm to form a new zygote or the destruction of a fly consumed by a spider.

Cosmogony [4] An account of the beginning and development of the universe.

GLOSSARY

Cosmological Constant [7] A concept introduced by Albert Einstein in 1917 that denotes the energy density of space, which could be included in his equations or left out.

Council of Florence (Evil) [6] (1431-1449) An Ecumenical Council of the Church that solemnly taught that evil has no nature because every nature, insofar as it is a nature, is good and willed by God.

Council of Vienne [10] (1311-1312) An Ecumenical Council of the Church that solemnly taught that the intellectual (rational) soul is the form of the human body.

Courage [10] One of the four cardinal virtues; a habit or disposition of the will that ensures firmness in difficulties and constancy in doing good.

Creation *cum Libertate* [3] The revealed doctrine proclaimed at the Fourth Lateran Council and Vatican I that God freely chose to create humans and the entire universe.

Creation *cum Tempore* [3] The revealed doctrine that every moment is the moment of creation, from the first moment of the universe's existence until now.

Creation *ex Nihilo* [3] The revealed doctrine that God created "from nothing," using no preexisting material to create the universe.

Creation *ex Trinitate* [3] The revealed doctrine that God the Father, Son, and Holy Spirit create together, taught at the Council of Florence.

Credibility [2] The quality of being believable or worthy of trust.

Cueva del Sidrón (El Sidrón Cave) [9] A cave system in northwestern Spain where Paleolithic rock art and the fossils of more than a dozen Neanderthals have been found.

D

Darwin, Charles [8] (1809-1882) An English naturalist, geologist, and biologist best known as the first proponent of the scientific theory of evolution: that all species of life have descended over time from common ancestors.

Darwinism [8] The theory of biological evolution developed by the English naturalist Charles Darwin and others. A term coined by biologist Thomas Henry Huxley.

***De Revolutionibus Orbium Cœlestium* ("On the Revolutions of the Heavenly Spheres")** [5] The great book by Nicolaus Copernicus that sparked the Scientific Revolution with its assertion that the sun, not the earth, was at the center of the universe.

Deism [3] A theology that understands God as a sort of architect or watchmaker who created and set up the universe with laws and guiding principles, limiting his present activities to legislating values and morality, rewarding the good, and punishing the evil.

Descent of Man, The [8] (1871) A book by Charles Darwin that presents evidence for human beings being the product of biological evolution.

Deuterium [7] Also known as hydrogen 2 or heavy hydrogen, one of two stable isotopes of hydrogen that, unlike hydrogen, has a two-particle nucleus.

GLOSSARY

Dialogue on the Two Chief World Systems, A [5] A dialogue published in 1632 by Galileo that defends heliocentrism, mocks the geocentric position, and occasioned the 1633 Trial of Galileo.

Dikika Baby/Selam [9] The hominin fossil specimen of the species *Australopithecus afarensis* found in the Dikika area of Ethiopia.

Dirac, Paul (Dirac Equation) [7] An English theoretical physicist and one of the most significant physicists of the twentieth century, he formulated the Dirac Equation describing the spin of particles and predicted the existence of antimatter. He wrote that it was more important to have "beauty in one's equations" than to have them fit one's experiments.

Divine Goodness (First Creation Account) [4] An attribute of God evidenced in the beauty of his creation, symbolized in the First Creation Account by the sevenfold declaration of the goodness of the world and of creatures.

Divine Inspiration [4] God's gift of grace to the human authors of the Bible, such that they communicate his saving truth through their writings.

Divine Providence [6, 8] God's governance of all creatures, providing what is needed for them, a task in which he invites our cooperation.

Divine Rationality (First Creation Account) [4] An attribute of God evidenced in the masterpiece of the design of the universe and in the structure of the First Creation Account.

Divine Unity (First Creation Account) [4] An attribute of God evidenced in the First Creation Account by the attribution of creation to only one God rather than many gods, as in most pagan creation accounts.

DNA [7] Abbreviation of deoxyribonucleic acid. A molecule carrying genetic instructions for the development, functioning, growth, and reproduction of all known organisms.

Dobzhansky, Theodosius (Creation and Evolution) [8] (1900-1975) A Ukrainian-American geneticist and evolutionary biologist who shaped the modern synthesis reconciling Charles Darwin's theory of biological evolution and Gregor Mendel's laws of heredity.

Dogma (Doctrine) [2] A complete, authoritative definition of a truth revealed by God in Christ; dogmas cannot be changed or challenged, but human understanding of them and their subsequent expression can progress.

Draper, John William [2] (1811-1882) A successful American chemist and early innovator of photography who wrote *History of the Conflict Between Religion and Science.*

Dualism (Anthropological) [10] A philosophical view that mental phenomena are nonphysical or that the mind and body are distinct and separable.

E

Ecumenical Council [3] An assembly of bishops from the whole world at which they come together to authoritatively teach regarding matters of faith and morals. There have been twenty-one Ecumenical Councils in Church history.

GLOSSARY

Emergence (Science) [1] A quality that occurs when a new entity is observed to have properties that its parts do not have on their own.

Enûma Eliš [4] The ancient Babylonian account of the creation of the world and of human beings.

Eternity (Divine) [3, 7] An attribute of the divine nature; due to divine perfection, God is not subject to change and therefore to time.

Eucharist [12] The ritual, sacramental action of thanksgiving to God which constitutes the principal Christian liturgical celebration of and communion in the paschal mystery of Christ. The liturgical action also called the Holy Sacrifice of the Mass. One of the Seven Sacraments of the Church.

Eugenics [11] A set of beliefs and practices that aim to improve the genetic quality of a human population by excluding certain genetic groups—those judged to be inferior—from reproducing and promoting the reproduction of genetic groups judged to be superior.

Evolutionary Convergence [7] A phenomenon whereby unrelated species evolve nearly identical or analogous biological traits.

Evolutionary Psychology [9] The branch of social and natural sciences that examines psychological structures from an evolutionary perspective.

Evolutionism [8] An interpretation of Darwinian evolution in a reductionist and materialist way, arguing that Darwinian evolution has unavoidable atheistic implications; also called "atheist Darwinism," "reductionist Darwinism," or "materialist Darwinism."

Existence [3] The ontological property of being, which is the most fundamental property of every being.

F

Faith [1] An act and disposition of the mind and will marked by the entrustment of one's whole self to God and the new path of knowing that it makes possible.

Fall of Humanity, The [11] The disobedience of the first human beings, causing a state of separation from God for all of humanity. *See also* Original Sin.

Foscarini, Paolo Antonio [5] (ca. 1565-1616) A Carmelite priest and scientist—as well as friend of Galileo—whose book on the mobility of the earth was condemned by the Roman Inquisition.

Fossil Record [8] The catalog of the remains, impression, and traces of once-living beings found in the layers of sediment that form the earth.

Free Will [10] The ability to love and to pursue the good and determine one's self and one's actions.

Freedom [10] The power to act or not to act based on reason, the ability to perform deliberate acts for which one is morally responsible.

GLOSSARY

Fullness of Time [6] The culmination of God the Father's preparation of his people to receive his Son, who was made man by the power of the Holy Spirit in the womb of the Virgin Mary.

G

Galapagos Islands [8] An archipelago of volcanic islands near the equator in the Pacific Ocean, west of Ecuador, which were studied by Charles Darwin during the second voyage of HMS Beagle.

Galileo Galilei [5] (1564-1642) An Italian astronomer, physicist, and engineer who is called the "father of observational astronomy" and the "father of the Scientific Method." He was tried and condemned by the Roman Inquisition in 1633 for his work on heliocentrism but was posthumously vindicated.

General Theory of Relativity [7] Theory of gravitation published by Albert Einstein in 1915 and the currently accepted theory of gravitation in modern physics.

Genes [8] Sequences of nucleotides in DNA that serve as blueprints for the construction of living bodies through the assembly of protein molecules.

Genesis 1:1–2:4a [4] The First Creation Account. A work of biblical literature that appears at the beginning of Sacred Scripture, describing the progressive creation of the universe from nothing to human beings through the symbolism of six days.

Genesis 2:4b-25 [4] The Second Creation Account. A work of biblical literature that describes the progressive creation of the world, beginning with the first man, the animals, and then the first woman.

Genesis 2:7 [9] "The LORD God formed man of dust from the ground, and breathed into his nostrils the breath of life; and man became a living being."

Genesis 2:19-20 [4] A passage in the Second Creation Account in which Adam names the animals, which God brings before him, portraying him as the first investigator of nature.

Genetics [8] The branch of biology founded by the Augustinian monk Gregor Mendel that deals with the heredity and variation of organisms, which is an important source of evidence for biological evolution.

Geocentrism [5] A model of the universe or solar system that has the earth at its center.

Geokineticism (Copernicanism) [5] A proposal that the earth moves around its own axis.

Gianna Beretta Molla, St. [6] (1922-1962) An Italian pediatrician who refused both an abortion and a hysterectomy while pregnant with her fourth child despite knowing that refusal could result in her own death.

"God of the Gaps" Error [5] The idea that God is constantly tinkering with, or "fixing," the universe through supernatural interventions.

Goodness [10] The quality of being morally good or virtuous; a condition shared by all creatures by virtue of their creation by God.

GLOSSARY

Gospel [1] The "Good News." The announcement of salvation through Jesus Christ's life, Death, and Resurrection.

Gould, Stephen Jay [2] (1941-2002) An American paleontologist, evolutionary biologist, and historian of science who wrote that science was about facts; religion was about "values and meaning."

Gregory of Nyssa, St. (Unity of Life) [8] (335-ca. 395) A bishop and Doctor of the Church who envisioned something like evolution in the creation of human beings.

Guglielmini, Giovanni [5] (1763-1817) An Italian priest and physicist who in 1792 showed that heavy objects dropped from a very tall tower actually deviate slightly to the east because of the rotation of the earth.

H

Hamilton, William Rowan (Quaternions) [7] An Irish mathematician who made important contributions to optics, mechanics, and algebra, inventing a system of numbers (Quaternions) that later were needed to describe the way electrons and similar particles "spin."

Hearing of 1615 (Galileo, Inquisition) [5] A voluntary hearing instigated by Galileo to uphold his reputation as a faithful Catholic against his detractors in Florence.

Heisenberg, Werner [7] A founder of quantum mechanics who is known for the Heisenberg Uncertainty Principle and stressing the importance of the criterion of beauty in physics: "In exact science, no less than in the arts, beauty is the most important source of illumination and clarity."

Heliocentrism (Copernicanism) [5] A model of the universe or solar system that has the sun at its center.

History of the Conflict Between Religion and Science [2] A book by John William Draper that falsely presents the history of science as a narrative of conflict between science and religion.

History of the Warfare of Science with Theology in Christendom [2] A book by Andrew Dickson White that falsely presents the history of science as a narrative of conflict between science and theology.

HMS Beagle [8] A British survey vessel that mapped the entire coast of South America and locations in the Pacific Ocean, on whose second voyage (1831) Charles Darwin kept a diary of his experiences.

Holistic Approach (Both/And) [4] A complete approach to understanding Sacred Scripture that respects the reality that Sacred Scripture is both fully divine and fully human.

Holy Spirit (Gift-Love) [1] The Third Person in the Trinity, who is associated with the new and surprising in God's work in creation and salvation.

Homininae [9] The taxonomic family that includes all *Homo* species, including human beings and many extinct species.

GLOSSARY

Hominin [9] A member the taxonomic family *Homininae*.

Hominization [12] The quality of becoming human, especially the evolutionary step when the first hominin(s) became human.

***Homo Neanderthalensis* (Neanderthals)** [9] An extinct subspecies of humans who lived within Eurasia from circa 400,000 to 40,000 years ago.

Hubble, Edwin Powell [7] An American astronomer—having helped to establish extragalactic astronomy and observational cosmology and one of the most important astronomers of all time—who discovered that other galaxies were moving away from our own at incredibly high speeds.

Human (Philosophical/Theological) [9] A rational animal, known to science as *Homo sapiens*.

Human (Scientific) [9] The taxonomic species *Homo sapiens*.

Human Beings (First Creation Account) [4] The pinnacle of God's creation. The only creatures to bear God's image and likeness, making them capable of reason.

Human Nature (Scientific) [11] The characteristic composition and behaviors of a primate species by virtue of physical and biological heritage.

Human Nature (Theological) [11] The characteristic composition and activities of human beings by virtue of a unique spiritual nature as well as physical and biological heritage.

Human Person [10] An individual substance of a rational nature that is complete in itself, is incommunicable, and possesses responsibilities and rights as well as the essential elements of distinctiveness, uniqueness, reason, and will.

Humani Generis [11] The encyclical by Venerable Pius XII that warned the faithful against embracing polygenism without sound evidence, saying that it "is not apparent" how polygenism can be compatible with the doctrine of Original Sin.

Hume, David [6] (1711-1776) A Scottish Enlightenment philosopher known for philosophical empiricism and skepticism who argued that if God is all-powerful, he could prevent all evil, and if he is all-good, he would do so.

Hypothesis (Science) [1] A proposition set forth as an explanation for the occurrence of some specified group of phenomena.

I

Idou ho anthrōpos [12] The Greek phrase for "Behold the man!" (Jn 19:5). The declaration of Pontius Pilate when he presented Jesus to the crowd after having had him scourged.

Ignatius of Antioch, St. [12] (ca. 50 - ca. 108) An early Christian bishop who—en route to Rome, where he met his martyrdom—wrote a series of letters foreseeing in his own martyrdom a chance to perfect both his love and his humanity.

GLOSSARY

Image (St. Thomas Aquinas) [10] That which "represents a thing in a better defined manner according to all its parts and the arrangement of its parts." A precise representation of something because of its likeness to what it resembles.

Imago Christi **(Latin)** [12] "Image of Christ"; the completion of human imaging of God by virtue of reason and will is to be transformed by grace into a representation of Christ's love.

Imago Dei **(Latin)** [10] "Image of God"; all human beings image God by virtue of their rationality and freedom.

Immaterial (Immateriality) [10] Not made of matter; having no mass and taking up no space, which is a quality of spiritual beings and of the human soul.

Immigration Act of 1924 [11] A United States federal law that prevented immigration from Asia, setting quotas on the number of immigrants from the eastern hemisphere.

Immortality [10] The quality of the spiritual human soul whereby it survives the death of the body and remains in existence without end, to be reunited with the body at the general resurrection.

Incarnation [6, 11, 12] The assuming of a human nature by the Son of God in order to accomplish our salvation in that same human nature, making him both fully God and fully man.

Incurvatus in se [12] A description of sin by St. Augustine: to be "caved in on oneself."

Independence Model [2] The belief that faith and science must tend to their own realms and not meddle in the affairs of each other because they have no points of contact.

Integrity of Nature [5] An idea that emphasizes the wisdom of God in establishing the universe in such a way that it could bring about the ends he intended for it according to its own secondary causality; an assumption of the scientific method.

Irascible Appetite [11] The human ability to strive for goodness, a tendency toward persevering in the face of difficulty.

J

John Henry Newman, St. (Creation and Evolution) [8] (1801-1890) A theologian, poet, priest, cardinal, and convert from Anglicanism who taught that Darwin's theory is not necessarily atheistic, seeing it as perfectly consonant with creation by a personal God.

John Paul II, St. (Evolution) [8] (1920-2005) The Pope who fully expressed the Church's openness to scientific inquiry and discovery, agreeing that biological evolution offered the best explanation for life on earth but cautioning that atheistic interpretations of this theory are not compatible with the Catholic faith.

GLOSSARY

Joshua 10:12-14 [5] A biblical passage at the center of the Galileo Affair that describes the sun standing still in the sky for a time "Spoke Joshua to the LORD in the day when the LORD gave the Amorites over to the men of Israel; and he said in the sight of Israel, 'Sun, stand thou still at Gibeon, and thou Moon in the valley of Aijalon.' And the sun stood still, and the moon stayed, until the nation took vengeance on their enemies. There has been no day like it before or since, when the LORD hearkened to the voice of a man; for the LORD fought for Israel."

Justice [3, 10] One of the four cardinal virtues; this refers to the steady and lasting willingness to give to God and to others what is due to them by right.

K

Kepler, Johannes (*Harmonices Mundi*) [5, 7] (1571-1630) A German astronomer, mathematician, astrologer, and key figure in the Scientific Revolution who is best known for his laws of planetary motion, writing: "I thank thee, LORD God our Creator, that thou allowest me to see the beauty in thy work of creation."

Kingu [4] The dragon in ancient Babylonian mythology who was Tiamat's lover and the commander of her army.

L

La Chapelle-aux-Saints Cave [9] A cave bordering the Sourdoire valley in France that has revealed many archeological artifacts, including a Neanderthal burial.

Lateran IV [5] (1213-1215) An Ecumenical Council of the Church that solemnly taught that God created the world *ex nihilo* ("out of nothing").

Lemaître, Georges [5, 7] (1894-1966) A Belgian priest, physicist, mathematician, astronomer, and professor of physics who proposed that the universe had started out very small and has been expanding for billions of years, later known as the "Big Bang Theory" of the origin of the universe.

***Letter to Castelli* (Galileo)** [5] A response from Galileo to the claim that heliocentrism contradicted Scripture, in which he applied the principles of biblical interpretation of St. Augustine to interpret Joshua 10:12-14 in light of heliocentrism.

Literalistic Creationism [2] The belief that God created the universe exactly (or almost exactly) according to the creation accounts found in the Book of Genesis.

***Logos* (Son of God/John 1:1-18)** [1, 4, 7] A Greek word, often translated as "Word," but also meaning "Mind" or "Reason." In the Gospel of John, the divine Son of God, the Second Person of the Blessed Trinity, who became flesh in Jesus Christ in order to reveal God and to save humanity.

Lord Kelvin *See* Thomson, William.

Lorini, Niccolò [5] (1544-ca. 1617) A Preacher General of the Dominican Order and lecturer in ecclesiastical history who complained about Galileo to the Inquisition.

GLOSSARY

Love (Desire) [10] An intense feeling of deep affection, interest, or pleasure in something; a longing to possess something good.

Love (Self-gift) [10] The theological virtue by which a Christian loves God above all things for his own sake and loves a neighbor as oneself for the love of God.

M

Magisterium [5] The teaching authority of the Church, the bishops in union with the Pope.

Manual Dexterity [9] The coordination of small muscles in hands enabling hominins to make and modify objects.

Marduk [4] A hero god in ancient Babylonian mythology who led the offspring of Apsu and Tiamat in war against her, and who broke the body of Tiamat apart to create the earth and sky; the patron god of the city of Babylon.

Materialism (Philosophical) [2] The belief that nothing exists except lifeless and mindless matter, that only the observable universe exists.

Medici, Christina de' [5] (1565-1637) The grand duchess of the family that ruled Florence and all of Tuscany who invited Galileo to tutor her son Cosimo II.

Mendel, Gregor [5, 8] (1822-1884) An Augustinian priest universally honored as the founder of genetics who discovered the basic principles of heredity.

Mental Being (Existence) [3] Existence in the mind as something imagined, existing as something thought of yet not actually existing.

Mercy [3] The loving-kindness, compassion, and forbearance shown to one who offends; according to St. Thomas Aquinas, the root of divine love.

Merge [9] According to Noam Chomsky and Robert Berwick, the ability to combine words into new units of meaning and relate them to other words in potentially infinite ways, which is a feature of human language that distinguishes it from animal communication.

Mersenne, Marin [5] (1588-1648) One of the architects of the European scientific community and the "father of acoustics" who is best known today among mathematicians for Mersenne prime numbers.

Methodological Materialism [2] A necessary feature of the scientific method that assumes only material, empirically observable objects and cause-effect relationships (not to be confused with philosophical materialism).

Methodological Reductionism [2] A necessary feature of the scientific method that investigates what the parts contribute to the whole, attributing to these as much explanatory power as they have (not to be confused with philosophical reductionism).

Minucius Felix [7] (d. ca. 250) Latin Christian theologian and apologist who wrote at the beginning of the third century AD: "When you see providence, order, and law in the heavens and on earth, believe that there is a Lord and Author of the universe."

GLOSSARY

Miracle (Rene Latourelle) [6] "A religious wonder that expresses, in human beings and the universe, a special and utterly free intervention of God, who uses it to give human beings a sign of the presence of his message of salvation in the world."

Miracle of the New Creation (Jesus) [6] A work of Jesus that foreshadows how matter will be subject to spirit in the age to come such as walking on water or the raising of a person from the dead.

Monogenism [11] Any theory of human origins that holds that all human beings are descended from one set of first parents.

Moral Evil [6] A privation (absence) of goodness in human thoughts, words, and deeds that ought to be present.

Moralism [10] An approach to moral decisions focused on moral rules without understanding why they exist, which tends toward rigid decision-making that is lacking in prudence.

Morris, Simon Conway [7] An English paleontologist, evolutionary biologist, and astrobiologist known for his study of the fossils of the Burgess Shale and being a critic of materialism and reductionism, claiming that evolution is compatible with belief in the existence of a God.

Multi-regional Model of Human Origins [11] A model that presents the various ethnic groups as having evolved independently of each other: "Native Africans evolved from archaic non-humans in Africa, native Europeans evolved from archaic non-humans in Europe, native Asians evolved from archaic non-humans in Asia," etc., each race having its own distinct origin.

Multiverse Hypothesis [7] A speculative position that the universe is infinitely large and that the laws of physics differ from region to region within it.

Mystery [2, 3, 6, 12] A divinely revealed truth that cannot be known unless revealed by God and whose full reality can never be fully comprehended by the human mind.

N

Natural Selection [8] The survival and reproduction of individuals due to differences in characteristics or traits, which is a key mechanism of evolution. A term popularized by Charles Darwin as a contrast to "artificial" selection, i.e., intentional selection by human breeders.

Naturalism [8] The belief that science is to be performed without reference to supernatural causes, which is a necessary assumption of the scientific method. In its extreme, the position that only natural causes are real.

Nature Miracle (Jesus) [6] A work of Jesus done "small and up close" what God does "large and everywhere" in the ordinary course of nature, such as healing a person, calming the sea, or changing water into wine.

Neo-Darwinism [8] A more rigorous theory of biological evolution that draws on both Darwinian evolution and Mendelian genetics to form the basis of the modern understanding of the origin of species.

GLOSSARY

***Nephesh* (Hebrew)** [9] The Hebrew word for aspects of sentience, especially in the Old Testament as a quality of human beings and other animals: In Genesis 2:7 the first man "became a living *nephesh*."

Newman, John Henry *See* John Henry Newman.

Newton, Sir Isaac (Science) [3] (1642-1726) An English mathematician, physicist, astronomer, theologian, and author who is one of the most influential scientists of all time and a key figure in the Scientific Revolution.

Nicholas of Cusa [3] (1401-1464) A philosopher, theologian, bishop, and cardinal; the author of *On the Hidden God*, which puts forth God as he who cannot be fully known, who is Truth, and who is worthy of our adoration.

Nicholas Steno, Blessed (Niels Stensen) [5] (1638-1686) A scientist, priest, and bishop who made fundamental contributions to anatomy, paleontology, geology, and crystallography and was beatified by St. John Paul II in 1988.

O

Obedience of Faith [1] A personal adherence to the whole person, intellect and will, to God and the truths he has revealed.

Omnivorous Diet [9] The ability to eat and survive on both plant and animal matter.

On the Origin of Species [8] (1859) A book by Charles Darwin that launched evolutionary biology, in which he presents evidence that populations evolve over generations through a process of natural selection.

Oresme, Nicholas [5] (ca. 1320-1382) Considered the most brilliant scientist and economist of the Middle Ages, he made contributions to musicology, psychology, physics, and mathematics.

Original Integrity [11] A gift by which God assisted our first parents to overcome their tendency toward a conflict between knowing, choosing, and desiring.

Original Sin [11] The result of the sin of the first human beings, which deprived themselves and their offspring of grace and the preternatural gifts, losing for themselves and their offspring original holiness and justice, becoming subject to the law of death, allowing sin to become universally present in human life.

Out of Africa Model of Human Origins [11] A model that holds that anatomically modern humans evolved in Africa around 300,000 years ago, dwindled to a tiny population around 75,000 years ago, and migrated out of Africa around 60,000 years ago.

Outgroup Bias [11] The tendency of human beings, as social animals who live in groups, to favor people that share cultural or familial ties, interests, identities, and other characteristics ("ingroup") and to be less inclined to trust people with different cultural or familial ties, etc. ("outgroup").

GLOSSARY

P

Paleoanthropology [9] The study of fossil evidence of human evolutionary history.

Paleoarchaeology [9] The study of artifacts left behind by human evolutionary ancestors.

Paley, William [7, 8] An Anglican theologian, philosopher, and Christian apologist who was the most well-known proponent of the faulty Biological Argument from Design, and argued that living things are too complex to have emerged naturally; instead, God must have made them directly. *See also* Argument from Design (Biological).

Pantheism [3] A misdirected merging of God and his creation to the point that the universe functions as God's "body."

Paradox (Natural) [1] A reality, statement, or proposition that to the finite human mind seems self-contradictory or absurd but in reality expresses a scientific truth, such as the wave-particle duality of light.

Paradox (Supernatural) [1] A reality, statement, or proposition that to the finite human mind seems self-contradictory or absurd but in reality expresses revealed truth, such as the mystery of the oneness of God in three Persons.

Penzias, Arno, and Robert Wilson [7] Jointly awarded the Nobel Prize in Physics in 1978 for the discovery of the cosmic background radiation from the Big Bang.

Person [10] A being capable of knowledge and love; a human person is one who, due to knowledge and love, exists bodily in the world as a relational and social being, the embodied image of God.

Perspective [4] A point of view or a way of interpreting things, e.g., "from a chemical perspective" or "from a socioeconomic perspective."

Perspicuity of Scripture [5] The teaching of some Protestants that the Bible is abundantly clear and easily understood due to the illumination of the Holy Spirit.

Peter Claver, St. [11] (1580-1654) A Spanish Jesuit priest and missionary who embodied a heroic example of love in his recognition of human rights, becoming the patron saint of slaves.

Petitionary Prayer [6] A form of prayer asking God to aid oneself or others.

Philoponus, John [5] (490-ca. 570) An astronomer, theologian, and natural philosopher in Alexandria, Egypt, who correctly theorized that the sun was made of the same fire that we see in earthly fires, that the space above the earth might be a vacuum, and that light moves.

Philosophy (Metaphysics, Natural) [2, 3] The study of causality and being. The middle ground in which the material reality of science and the ultimate reality of faith can find common ground. According to St. John Paul II, the wider wisdom that connects science and faith like a bridge.

Physical Determinism [1] The belief that the laws of the physical universe and prior events absolutely predetermine everything that happens within the physical universe, including human thoughts, words, and actions.

GLOSSARY

Physical Evil [6, 11] An evil that does not involve personal fault, although personal fault is sometimes the cause of it. *See also* Corruption.

Pius XII, Venerable, (Age of the Universe, *Humani Generis*, Monogenism) [8] (1876-1958) The first Pope to directly address new scientific discoveries such as the Big Bang Theory and biological evolution, issuing the first official statement by the Church that touches on evolutionary questions, including polygenism, which he cautioned Catholics not to embrace over concern that it might obscure the doctrine of Original Sin.

Polygenism [11] Any theory of human origins that holds that all human beings descended from more than one set of parents.

Pontifical Academy of Sciences [5] A papal academy, the oldest such organization in the world, whose goal is the promotion of the progress of the mathematical, physical, and natural sciences.

Preternatural Gifts [11] The special gifts that our first parents received from God that go beyond what they could have received from the material world: preservation of the body from corruption, subjection of desires to reason, and a life of goodness and happiness.

Primary Cause (God) [3] In philosophy, any cause that engages secondary causes to bring about effects. In Christian philosophy and theology, God, who is the source of the existence for all creatures and the Primary Cause without any qualifications.

Principle of Double Agency [3] The concept that, for every cause and effect relationship in the universe, there are at least two causes: God the Primary Cause and whatever secondary cause or causes are involved.

Principles of Geology [8] A book by geologist Charles Lyell (1797-1875) that presents the planet earth as indefinitely old, certainly much older than thousands of years. Read by Darwin on his sea journey on the HMS Beagle, it became a crucial framework for his theory of evolution.

Privation [6] The loss or absence of a quality that should be present.

Privation Theory of Evil [6] A theological doctrine attributed to St. Augustine that evil—unlike good—is not substantial, being rather the absence of good , based on the doctrine that God, who is perfect Goodness and the Creator of all beings, cannot be the author of evil.

Prosociality [9] A tendency toward behaviors that benefit others or the whole group, a hallmark characteristic of higher primates, hominins, and cetaceans.

Prudence [10] One of the four cardinal virtues, this refers to the ability to discern the most suitable moral course of action.

Psalm 104 [4] A psalm of praise to the Creator that narrates God's production of the universe from human beings to the heavenly bodies to other living creatures.

Psalm 135:6-7 [3] A biblical verse revealing that the order that exists in the universe does so because it was freely chosen by God, a key biblical passage expressing the doctrine of creation *cum libertate*.

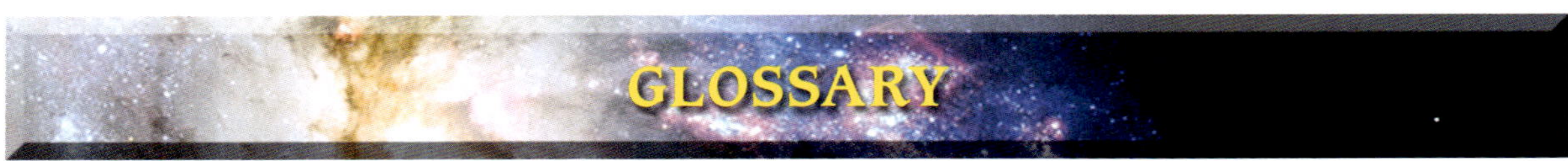

GLOSSARY

R

Racism [11] The immoral belief that all members of a race share certain characteristics or abilities that distinguish them as inferior, even subhuman.

Rational Animal [9,11,12] An ancient term that reflects the Aristotelian and Christian view of the human being as an animal distinguished by the ability to reason, especially in the thought of St. Thomas Aquinas.

Rational Seeds (St. Augustine) [5] The theological speculation that, due to divine wisdom, God created the universe capable of producing life naturally, that living things exist in "the very fabric, as it were, or texture of the elements... [requiring only] the right occasion actually to emerge into being." *See also* Integrity of Nature.

Real Being (Existence) [3] The state or fact of having being independently of human thought.

Reason [1, 10] The capacity for wisdom, which is based on the ability to think clearly and come to correct answers to specific problems. The intellectual ability to know truth: to comprehend, infer, or think in an orderly way.

Reductionism (Philosophical) [2] The unproven assertion that all real things are only the sum of their parts.

Religion [1] The practice of faith in prayer, worship, and daily life.

Resurrection of Christ (Jesus) [6, 12] The bodily rising of Christ, as he had foretold, on the third day after his Crucifixion, Death, and burial, by virtue of which Christians have the hope of resurrection with him on the last day.

Resurrection of the Body [6, 12] The rising of all the deceased to a transformed, imperishable life, some to everlasting happiness and others to everlasting punishment, which will take place on the Last Day at the Second Coming of Christ.

Robert Bellarmine, St. (*Letter to Foscarini*) [5] (1542-1621) An Italian Jesuit, cardinal, and Doctor of the Church who was an important figure of the Counter-Reformation, writing that "one would have to proceed with great care in explaining the Scriptures that appear contrary [to the sun being the center of the universe], and say rather that we do not understand them."

S

Sacred Heart of Jesus [11] An important devotion and Feast Day of the Catholic Church, symbolizing the love with which Jesus, in his life and Death and eternally in his Resurrection, continually loves his eternal Father and all human beings fully and without exception.

Sacred Scripture (Divinity) [4] The inspired texts of the Bible, whose author is God by means of inspiring their human authors.

Sacred Scripture (Humanity) [4] The inspired texts of the Bible, whose divine truths come to us through the divinely inspired human author's words and expressions with their limitations of time, culture, and perspective.

GLOSSARY

Sacred Tradition [5] The living transmission of the message of the Gospel in the Church. The oral preaching of the Apostles, which—together with Sacred Scripture—is conserved and handed on as the Deposit of Faith through Apostolic Succession in the Church. Both the living Tradition and the written Scriptures have their common source in the Revelation of God in Jesus Christ.

Sacrifice [12] Any offering made to the divine as a sign of adoration, thanksgiving, supplication, and communion. For St. Augustine and Catholic theology, an "act done for the purpose of clinging to God in a holy fellowship... directed to that final Good which makes possible our true happiness."

Saving Truth (Bible) [4] The teachings on faith and morals that are found without error in the Bible when read in the light of Christ, in continuity with Sacred Tradition, under the guidance of the Church's Magisterium.

Science (pre-nineteenth-century definition) [2] Any knowledge demonstrated logically from higher principles or truths, including theological and philosophical knowledge.

Scientific Method [1] A method of revealing how the universe works by formulating questions, carrying out investigations, analyzing and interpreting data, and constructing explanations.

Scientific Theory [8] A precise and coherent set of ideas for explaining some set of phenomena that can be tested and verified in accordance with the scientific method.

Scientism (Scientific Atheism) [2] The false idea that only things verifiable by empirical methods, such as the scientific method, can be considered true.

Secchi, Angelo [5] (1818-1878) A Jesuit priest, astronomer, and one of the founders of modern astrophysics who pioneered the study and classification of stars using spectroscopy.

Secondary Cause (Creatures) [3] Any real cause within the universe; the kinds of causes studied by scientists.

Selam *See* Dikika Baby.

Self-love (Animals and Humans) [10] A desire for physical goods—e.g., food, drink, shelter—that is the basis for knowing the good of others and how to provide it.

Self-possession [10] The discipline of the mind and body that is essential to grow in the virtue of charity.

Self-reflection [9] The uniquely human ability to see oneself almost as another self in order to reflect on oneself and to correct and deepen self-understanding.

Sensory [10] Relating to or perceived by the physical senses.

Separationism [2] A mistaken paradigm that holds that science and religion can never be in conflict because they do not share the same object of inquiry: Science investigates facts, whereas religion is about "values and meaning." *See also* Gould, Stephen Jay.

GLOSSARY

Shanidar Cave [9] An archaeological site in Iraqi Kurdistan where the remains of ten Neanderthals have been found.

Small-band Hunter-gatherers (SBHG) [9] A societal structure in which groups of about one dozen people seek for food by hunting and foraging, in contrast to agricultural societies, which rely on domesticated plants and animals for food.

Social Darwinism [11] The theory that human groups and races are subject to the same laws of natural selection that Charles Darwin had perceived in plants and animals in nature, especially that people exist in a struggle against each other for material goods and their own existence.

Sola Scriptura [5] The belief that Sacred Scripture alone is our source for discovering divine truth.

Spacetime [7] A concept proposed by the mathematician Hermann Minkowski to reframe Albert Einstein's special theory of relativity, recognizing the union of space and time as one fabric.

Special Creation [8] A theological idea that the universe and all life in it originated in its present form by divine miraculous intervention. With respect to the human soul, the doctrine of its immediate creation by God.

Speciation [8] The divergence of populations into distinct species as a result of biological evolution.

Stellar Parallax [5] The apparent shift of position of any nearby star or other object against the background of distant objects, which is important evidence that the earth moves that was not available to Copernicus or Galileo.

Stewardship [10] The responsibility for the just use of the world's resources; the obligation to use personal and material resources in the honor and service of God and the common good.

Stimson, Miriam Michael [5] (1913-2002) A Dominican sister and chemist who researched cancer. Using the method of ultraviolet analysis of DNA that she pioneered, James Watson and Francis Crick discovered its double helix structure.

Strong Nuclear Force [7] The attractive force that causes protons and neutrons to stick together to form nuclei. One of the four known fundamental interactions.

Supernaturalism [5] A misguided way of explaining how the universe works by having recourse to divine intervention to explain natural phenomena.

Supernovas [7] The explosions of stars that emit the elements made inside stars into space, where they can form into new stars, planets, and living things, which finalizes one stage of synthetization of helium, hydrogen, and lithium, into heavier elements.

Symbolism (Symbolic Thought) [9, 11] The uniquely human ability not only to use symbols but also to generate them and exchange messages that communicate knowledge.
In the investigation of human origins, a hallmark of our species from 110,000 to 70,000 years ago.

GLOSSARY

Symmetry (First Creation Account) [4] An aspect of beauty that results from having equality of measure. An understanding of the "architectural" structure of creation: three days of habitations followed by three days of creatures to inhabit them.

T

Technology [2] The practical application of mathematics and science.

Tempier, Stephen [5] (d. 1279) A Bishop of Paris who in 1277 condemned a number of Aristotelian ideas, including the impossibility of other worlds than this one. Although the condemnation was misguided in many respects, it seems to have oriented his contemporary European scholars toward a more empirical approach to science, especially with respect to the use of experimentation.

Terra Amata [9] An archaeological site in southern France, discovered and excavated in 1966 by Henry de Lumley, which shows that by 400,000 years ago hominins were building shelters with cooking hearths.

Theology [1] The study of God and his Revelation using human reason. According to St. Anselm and the Catholic intellectual tradition: "faith seeking understanding."

Theory [8] A coherent, rational explanation of a phenomenon, whether scientific or philosophical.

Theory (Science) [1] A group of tested general propositions, commonly regarded as correct, that forms a coherent explanation of some natural phenomena.

Thomas Aquinas, St. (Philosophy/Theology) [3, 5, 6, 7, 8, 10, 11] (1225-1274) An Italian Dominican friar, philosopher, priest, and Doctor of the Church who was the most influential theologian of the Middle Ages.

Thomas Aquinas, St. (Creation) [5] (1225-1274) In regard to the First Creation Account, he taught that, on the surface, special creation seemed to accord better with the literal meaning of the text but preferred St. Augustine's explanation because it was more in accord with reason. *See also* Rational Seeds.

Thomson, William (Lord Kelvin) [6] (1824-1907) A mathematician, physicist, and engineer who did important work in the mathematical analysis of electricity and the formulation of the first and second laws of thermodynamics.

Tiamat [4] The sea goddess and mother of the gods in ancient Babylonian mythology who was dismembered and became the waters above and below the earth.

Time [7] Often referred to as a fourth dimension, it is the continued progress of existence and events that occur in an irreversible succession from the past, through the present, to the future.

Torah [4] The Hebrew word for "Law." The first five books of the Old Testament—Genesis, Exodus, Leviticus, Numbers, and Deuteronomy—also called the books of Moses or the Pentateuch.

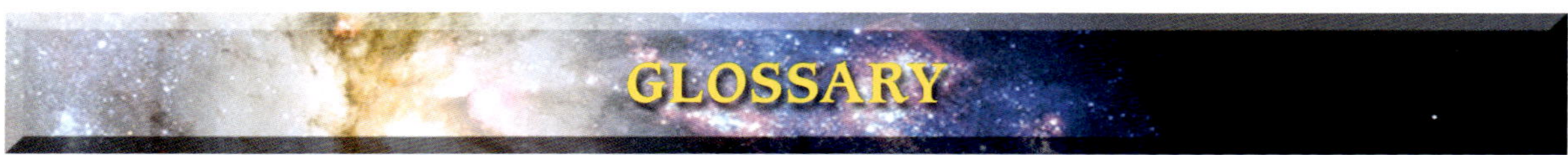

GLOSSARY

Trial of Galileo (1633) [5] The proceeding in which Galileo was tried by the Inquisition, found to be suspect of heresy because of his teaching on heliocentrism, and forced to recant.

Type [12] A person, event, or place that prefigures a new and greater reality, called its antitype, which fulfills it in a new and greater way.

Typological Relationship [12] A comparison in which the type precedes and prefigures a new and greater reality, and the antitype is everything that the type was but in a new and greater way.

***Tzelem* (Hebrew)** [10] "Image"; in the Ancient Near East, a quality of the rulers, who were the image of God. In the First Creation Account, a quality of all human beings, male and female, who are the image of God (*tzelem Elohim*; cf. Gn 1:26).

U

Universals (Abstract Concepts) [10] Ideas that do not refer to a particular object but to all objects of a particular kind.

Universe (*unum in diversis*) [1] All that exists in the created, temporal order.

Univocal Conception of God [3] An idea of the divine in which God possesses qualities and attributes in a way identical to his creatures but perfectly, incorrectly resolving the mystery of God into something fully understandable to the human mind.

Urban VIII (Maffeo Barberini) [5] (1568-1644) A Pope who wrote a poem in honor of Galileo but later (in 1633) submitted Galileo to trial and condemnation by the Inquisition.

Ussher, Archbishop James [4] (1581-1656) An Anglican theologian who incorrectly attempted to harmonize the First Creation Account and the Old Testament with the physics of Isaac Newton. *See also* Concordism.

V

Vatican I (*Dei Filius*) [5] (1869-1870) An Ecumenical Council of the Church that solemnly taught that there can never be a real contradiction between faith and reason because the same God reveals truths both ways, and he cannot contradict himself.

Vatican II (*Gaudium et Spes*) [5] (1962-1965) An Ecumenical Council of the Church that solemnly taught about "the legitimate autonomy of science": its freedom to engage in discovery and speculation without artificial constraints, condemning the warfare/conflict model of faith and science.

Virtues [10] Habitual and firm dispositions to do good, acquired through human effort aided by God's grace.

Virus (Retrovirus) [6] An infectious agent of small size and simple composition that can multiply only within living cells of animals, plants, or bacteria by inserting its DNA into cells of other organisms.

GLOSSARY

W

Warfare/Conflict Model [2] A false historical narrative that maintains that there is an intrinsic intellectual conflict between religion/theology and science, asserting that the Church is the enemy of progress or that science is intrinsically opposed to what God has revealed.

Weyl, Hermann [7] A theoretical physicist and philosopher who was one of the most influential mathematicians of the twentieth century, writing: "In our knowledge of physical nature we can obtain a vision of the flawless harmony which is in conformity with sublime reason."

Whewell, William [2] (1794-1866) An English scientist, Anglican priest, philosopher, theologian, and historian of science who coined the terms "scientist" and "physicist."

White, Andrew Dickson [2] (1832-1918) An American historian and the co-founder of Cornell University who wrote *History of the Warfare of Science with Theology in Christendom*, contributing to the spread of the warfare/conflict model of science and theology.

Wisdom (Virtue) [1] According to Fr. James Brent, "an all-embracing understanding of reality as a whole in light of ultimate causes, especially in light of the end or goal of all things." *See also* Prudence.

Wisdom, Book of *See* Book of Wisdom

Wisdom 7:13-14b [4] A biblical verse revealing that knowledge is to be shared, not hoarded.

Wisdom 7:17-18a [4] A biblical prayer of desire for the gift of wisdom, describing it in scientific terms.

Wisdom 11:21 [4] An important biblical verse in the Middle Ages to the pioneers of the Scientific Revolution, revealing that the Creator arranged everything in the universe by measure, number, and weight.

Wisdom 13:1-5 [7] A biblical passage in which the author condemns nature worship based on the order and beauty of the created world, which is an example of the Cosmic Argument from Design.

Wilson, Robert, and Arno Penzias *See* Penzias, Arno.

Y

Yar [12] The Hebrew word for "behold," signaling the completion of a creature or of a divine work in the First Creation Account.

Z

Zoē [12] The Greek word for life unqualified or restricted by biology. In Christian theology, the eternal life offered to all who believe in and love God and who live in communion with Christ and his Body.

ART AND PHOTO CREDITS

Cover

Jesus Christ Pantocrator, detail from Deisis Composition; Hagia Sophia Museum, Istanbul, Republic of Turkey
The Antennae Galaxies/NGC 4038-4039; NASA, ESA, and the Hubble Heritage Team (STScI/AURA)-ESA/Hubble Collaboration; Acknowledgment: B. Whitmore (Space Telescope Science Institute)

Front Pages

i *See* Cover Credits
iii *See* Cover Credits
iv *See* Cover Credits
x ©JavierArtPhotography/stock.adobe.com
xi *Stephen M. Barr*; www.thecatholictelegraph.com/catholic-scientist-stephen-barr-to-speak-at-u-c-march-7/49289
xiii *St. Thomas Aquinas*, Bartolomé Esteban Murillo; Public Domain
xiv *Creation*; Lyndon Studio, Downers Grove, Illinois
xvii *Christine and Christopher Baglow*; www.willwoods.org/events/willwoods-gala/
xviii ©mates/stock.adobe.com

Chapter 1

1 ©eranda/stock.adobe.com
2 *St. John Paul II in Maribor, Slovenia, During a Mass Celebrating the Beatification of Anton Martin Slomsek*, September 19, 1999; ©Gabriel Bouys, Photographer
3 *The Apotheosis of St. Thomas Aquinas*, Francisco de Zurbaran; Museum of Fine Arts of Seville, Spain
4 top row: ©Ezume Images; ©Wire_man; ©Olga Khoroshunova/stock.adobe.com
middle row: ©Jan; ©amphaiwan; ©ondrejprosicky/stock.adobe.com
bottom row: ©Marco; ©Leonid; ©Thanaphon Sinsang/stock.adobe.com
5 top: ©goodmanphoto/stock.adobe.com
middle: ©gonin/stock.adobe.com
bottom: ©Melinda Nagy/stock.adobe.com
6 left: *Friedrich Miescher*; Public Domain
middle: *Glass Vial Containing DNA Purified from Salmon Sperm*; ©Alfons Renz, University of Tubingen, Germany
inset: *Leukocyte Clusters in Pus*; zon.trilinkbiotech.com
right: ©vitstudio/stock.adobe.com
7 right: *St. Ignatius of Loyola in Armour*, Anonymous; Palace of Versailles, France
left: *St. Ignatius of Loyola*, Peter Paul Rubens; Norton Simon Museum, Pasadena, California
8 *Spiritual Exercises of Ignatius of Loyola*, First Edition, 1548; Public Domain
9 top: *Murray Gell-Mann Lecturing at ICRANet in Nice, France*, July 6, 2012; Melirius, Photographer; Wikipedia Commons
bottom: ©Ezume Images/stock.adobe.com
10 ©Douglas James Butner/stock.adobe.com
11 ©Hlsashi/stock.adobe.com
12 *The Eternal Father*, Guercino (Giovanni Francesco Barbieri); Pinacoteca Sabauda, Torino, Italy
13 *The Holy Trinity*, Miguel Cabrera; Tucson Museum of Art, Arizona
14 *Sacred Heart of Jesus*, Charles Bosseron Chambers; restoredtraditions.com
15 *Pentecost*, Max Bentele; ©Free Christ Images
16 ©ktsdesign/stock.adobe.com
17 top: *Niels Bohr and Albert Einstein at Paul Ehrenfest's Home in Leiden*, December 1925; Public Domain
bottom: ©nuttawutnuy/stock.adobe.com
19 ©TTstudio/stock.adobe.com
20 *Albert Einstein During a Lecture in Vienna in 1921*, Ferdinand Schmutzer, Photographer; Public Domain
21 *Pope Benedict XVI in Washington, D.C.*; David Bohrer, Photographer; Public Domain

Chapter 2

23 ©Giovanni Cancemi/stock.adobe.com
24 *God as Architect*, Anonymous; Frontispiece of *Bible Moralisee*, ca. 1220-1230; Austrian National Library, Vienna
25 *Lawrence Principe at Johns Hopkins University*; Ricky Carioti, Photographer; www.washingtonpost.com/news/speaking-of-science/wp/2018/01/30/this-chemist-is-unlocking-the-secrets-of-alchemy/?noredirect=on

ART AND PHOTO CREDITS

26 top: *Sir Isaac Newton*, Sir Godfrey Kneller; National Portrait Gallery, London
bottom: *St. Thomas Aquinas*, Carlo Crivelli; The National Gallery, London
27 *St. Augustine of Hippo*, Gerard Seghers; Kingston Lacy Collection, Dorset, England
28 *St. John Chrysostom of Antioch*; Hagia Sophia Museum, Istanbul, Republic of Turkey
29 left: *Christopher Columbus Before the Council of Salamanca*, Emanuel Leutze; Louvre Museum, Paris, France
right: ©stuart/stock.adobe.com
30 ©Paulista/stock.adobe.com
31 *Stephen M. Barr*; www.thecatholictelegraph.com/catholic-scientist-stephen-barr-to-speak-at-u-c-march-7/49289
32 *Loren Eiseley*; Bernie Cleff, Photographer; www.inquirer.com/philly/entertainment/20161127_Loren_Eiseley__Great_science__great_writing.html
33 left: ©Kateryna_Kon/stock.adobe.com
right: *Carl Sagan*; Tony Korody, Photographer; www.newyorker.com/humor/daily-shouts/carl-sagan-explains-your-mother
34 *St. John Paul II*; ©L'Osservatore Romano
35 top: *Visitation*, Jacques Daret; Altarpiece of the Virgin (St. Vaast Altarpiece); Gemaldegalerie, Berlin, Germany
bottom: *Christ Healing the Mother of Simon Peter's Wife*, John Bridges; Birmingham Museum of Art, Alabama
36 top: *Ken Ham*; Stuart Conway, Photographer; https://www.telegraph.co.uk/news/worldnews/northamerica/usa/11312730/Creation-Museum-founder-Christmas-Town-is-Gods-work-against-the-devil.html
bottom: *God Creating the Sun, the Moon, and the Stars in the Firmament*, Jan Brueghel II; Private Collection
37 *The Creation of Adam*, Michelangelo; Sistine Chapel, Vatican, Italy
38 top: *Ian Barbour in Front of the Carleton College Chapel*, 1999; www.southernminn.com/image_32d45d6b-8c74-58b4-982f-91ce9392346d.html
bottom: *Stephen Jay Gould*; speakola.com/ideas/stephen-jay-gould-evolution-and-21st-century-2000
39 *The Coronation of the Virgin*, Velazquez; Museo del Prado, Madrid, Spain
40 *Cardinal Camillo Ruini*; te-deum.blogspot.com/2011/06/cardinal-ruini-commission-still-far.html
41 ©kentoh/stock.adobe.com
42 *William Whewell*, James Lonsdale; Trinity College Collection, University of Cambridge, England
43 left: *John William Draper*; Edward Bierstadt, Photographer; Smithsonian Institution, National Museum of American History, Draper Family Collection; Public Domain
right: *Andrew Dickson White*; Public Domain

Chapter 3

45 ©Romolo Tavani/stock.adobe.com
46 *Nicholas of Cusa*, Master of the Life of the Virgin; Detail of Altarpiece in Chapel of the St. Nicholas Hospital/Cusanusstift, Bernkastel-Kues, Germany
47 *Sir Isaac Newton*, Jean-Leon Huens; National Geographic Image Collection
48 ©LanaPo/stock.adobe.com
49 left: ©1000pixels/stock.adobe.com
right: *Charles Robert Darwin*, John Collier; National Portrait Gallery, London
50 ©Sergey Nivens/stock.adobe.com
51 *UGC 1810: Wildly Interacting Galaxy*, Hubble Telescope; Image Credit: NASA, ESA, Hubble, HLA; Processing & Copyright: Domingo Pestana
52 *Creation of the Animals*, Anonymous; Bible of Souvigny, Illuminations from the Cluny Abbey; Bibliotheque des Moulins, France
53 *St. Thomas Aquinas*, Juan de Penalosa y Sandoval; Museum of Fine Arts of Cordoba, Spain
54 ©digitalskillet1/stock.adobe.com
55 ©Kevin Carden/stock.adobe.com
56 ©Vadimsadovski/stock.adobe.com
57 ©mavoimages/stock.adobe.com
58 *Savaoph, God the Father*, Viktor Mikhailovich Vasnetsov; Tretyakov Gallery, Moscow, Russia
59 *The Creation*, James Tissot; The Jewish Museum, New York, New York
60 *G.K. Chesterton*, E.H. Mills Bromide Print Published 1909; ©National Portrait Gallery, London
61 ©Romolo Tavani/stock.adobe.com
62 ©panaramka/stock.adobe.com
63 *The Miraculous Image of Merciful Jesus* (copy), Original Painting by Adolf Hyla, 1943; Shrine of the Divine Mercy, Krakow, Poland
64 *Statue of Julian of Norwich*, David Holgate; Norwich Cathedral, Norfolk, England

ART AND PHOTO CREDITS

65 ©fluenta/stock.adobe.com
66 *Sir Isaac Newton Monument and Tomb*, Westminster Abbey, London
67 *Henry David Thoreau*; Life Magazine Photo Archives

Chapter 4

69 *Tiglath-Pileser III*, Stela from the Walls of his Palace; The British Museum, London
70 top: *Sennacherib's Prism* (*Annals*), (*The Taylor Prism*), The British Museum, London
bottom: *Jonah Preaching in Nineveh*, George Frederic Watts; The Tate, London
71 left: *Minaret of the Mosque of the Prophet Yunus*, Nineveh, Mosul, September 1999; Roland Unger, Photographer
right: *Ruins of the Mosque of Prophet Yunus in Mosul*, destroyed by ISIL on July 24, 2014; www.voanews.com/a/iraqi-forces-capture-ancient-holy-site-mosul/3681703.html
72 top: *The Great Isaiah Scroll*, Ardon Bar Hama, Photographer; The Israel Museum, Jerusalem
top inset: *The Great Isaiah Scroll*, detail of QIsa; The Israel Museum, Jerusalem
bottom: *The Prophet Isaiah* (detail), Raphael; Basilica di Sant'Agostino, Rome, Italy
73 *St. Matthew and the Angel*, Karel van der Pluym; North Carolina Museum of Art, Raleigh, North Carolina
74 *Christ Pantocrator*, Viktor Mikhaylovich Vasnetsov; State Tretyakov Gallery, Moscow
75 top: *Pope Francis Celebrates the Eucharist*; ©L'Osservatore Romano
bottom: *Pope Francis Elevates the Book of Gospels*; ©L'Osservatore Romano
76 *Creation of the Earth*, Jean Colombe; *Book of Hours of Luis de Laval*; National Library of France
77 *Creation of the Animals and Birds*, Etienne Colaud; *Book of Hours for Early Morning*; National Library of France
78 *Scene of Creation*; Illustration from *L'Antiquite Judaique* by Flavius Josephus; Lazaro Galdiano Museum
79 *Scenes from the Genesis: Creation of the World*; Baptistery of St. John Mosaics; Marie-Lan Nguyen, Photographer
80 *Chaos Monster and Sun God*; Monuments of Nineveh, Bas-reliefs from the Palace of Sennacherib; British Museum Reference BM 124571
81 ©Goinyk/stock.adobe.com
82 *Creation of Adam in the Paradise*, Jan Brueghel II; Stedelijk-Museum, Louvain, Belgium
83 *Mass at St. Paul the Cross Church*, Park Ridge, Illinois; Julie Koenig, Photographer; MTF Archives
84 *God Creates Adam*; Mosaic in Cathedral of Monreale, Palermo, Sicily
85 ©kdshutterman/stock.adobe.com
86 *Paradise Landscape with the Creation of the Animals*, Jan Brueghel II and Workshop; Staatliche Kunstsammlungen Dresden, Germany
87 *Creation of the World*, Giusto de Menabuoi; The Padua Baptistery, Piazza del Duomo, Padua, Italy
88 *God Separates the Light from the Darkness,* Michelangelo; Sistine Chapel, Vatican, Rome
89 *St. John the Evangelist*, James Tissot; Brooklyn Museum, New York
90 *Food Science Australia*, CSIRO; www.scienceimage.csiro.au
91 *Galileo Discovers Jupiter's Moons*, Jean-Leon Huens; National Geographic Image Collection
92 *Adam Naming the Animals*; Icon, Monastery of St. Nicholas, Meteora, Greece
93 ©Sergey Nivens/stock.adobe.com
94 *Prophet Isaiah*, Antonio Balestra; Castelvecchio Museum, Verona, Italy
95 *The Flight of the Prisoners*, James Tissot; The Jewish Museum, Brooklyn, New York
97 *James Ussher*, Cornelis Janssens van Ceulen; Jesus College, University of Oxford, England
98 *Nebuchadnezzar II*, King of Babylon; Public Domain

Chapter 5

100 *Early Church Fathers*; MTF Archives
101 *St. Augustine in His Study*, Sandro Botticelli; Church of Ognissanti, Florence, Italy
102 top: *St. John Henry Newman*, George Richmond; Public Domain
bottom: *Pope Pius XII at the Vatican*; Photo Dated March 15, 1949; CNS
103 top: *St. Thomas Aquinas*, Eighteenth-century Portuguese School; Public Domain
bottom: *Charles De Koninck*; Public Domain
104 *Dome of St. Stephen's Basilica in Budapest, Hungary*; ©zatletic/stock.adobe.com
105 *Holy Friars at Lateran IV*; Fresco in the choir St. John Lateran depicts St. Francis and St. Dominic before Pope Innocent III; Lawrence OP, Photographer
106 top: *Meeting of Doctors at the University of Paris*, Etienne Colaud; From the "Chants Royaux" Manuscript, BNF, Francais 1537, fol. 27v[1], National Library of France, Paris
bottom: *Jean Buridan*; Public Domain

ART AND PHOTO CREDITS

107 *Federico Angelo Cesi*, Pietro Fachetti; Palazzo Corsini, Rome
Inset: Detail of Lynx Symbol from *Praescriptiones Lynceae Academiae*, 1624, Title Page; Federico Cesi, Author; Accademia Nazionale dei Lincei, Rome
108 *John Philoponus*; Public Domain
109 top: *Albertus Magnus Expounding His Doctrines of Physical Science in the Streets of Paris*, ca. 1245, Ernest Board; Wellcome Collection, Wellcome Trust, UK
bottom: *Nicole Oresmes,* Miniature; *Traite de L'espere*, France, Fonds Francais 565, fol. 1r.; National Library of Paris
110 *Astronomer Copernicus, Conversations with God*, Jan Matejko; Jagiellonian University Museum, Krakow, Poland
111 top: *Cardinal Christopher Clavius* (colorized), Francesco Villamena; The Elisha Whittelsey Collection
bottom: *Marin Mersenne*; Public Domain
112 top: *Bl. Nicholas Steno* (colorized); Public Domain
bottom: *Drawing of Head of a White Shark and Teeth*, Nicholas Steno; *Elementorum Myologiae Specimen*, 1669; Public Domain
113 top: *Angelo Secchi* (colorized); Public Domain
bottom: *Gregor Johann Mendel*, Abbey of Saint Thomas, Brno, Czech Republic
114 top: *Georges Lemaître*; The Bettmann Archive; Public Domain
bottom: *Miriam Michael Stimson*; Siena Heights University Archive
115 ©Grzegorz Polak/stock.adobe.com
116 *Galileo Galilei*, Justus Sustermans; National Maritime Museum, Greenwich, London
117 *Galileo Facing the Roman Inquisition*, Cristiano Banti; Private Collection
118 *St. Robert Bellarmine*, Anonymous, Italian School, Seventeenth Century; Public Domain
119 *Galileo Before the Holy Office*, Joseph-Nicolas Robert-Fleury; The Louvre, Paris
120 *Pope Urban VIII*, Pietro da Cortona; Capitoline Museums, Rome, Italy
121 *Galileo and Viviani*, Tito Lessi; Museo Galileo, Florence, Italy
122 *St. John Paul II*; MTF Archives
124 left: *Tycho Brahe*, Eduard Ender; Public Domain
right: *Johannes Kepler*, Anonymous (Copy of the lost 1610 original from the Kremsmunster Abbey, Upper Austria); Public Domain
125 *Courtyard of the Casina Pio IV*, The Pontifical Academy of Social Sciences, Vatican; Gabriella C. Marino, Photographer

Chapter 6

127 *Job on the Dunghill*, Gonzalo Carrasco; National Museum of Art, Mexico City
128 *St. Dominic Altarpiece* (detail), Girolamo Romanino; Pinacoteca Tosio Martinengo, Brescia, Italy
129 *Resurrection of the Lord*, Bartolomé Esteban Murillo; Royal Academy of Fine Arts of San Fernando, Madrid, Spain
130 *Mother Teresa Serving Food to the Poor at Nirmal Hriday*, New Delhi, 1979; www.livemint.com/Multimedia/DGdFrre3ho9Oc972qQC7iN/Paying-homage-to-2.html
131 *St. Paul Healing the Cripple at Lystra*, Karel Dujardin; Rijksmuseum, Amsterdam, Netherlands
132 *Auschwitz Entrance Gate*; Auschwitz-Birkenau Memorial and Museum, Poland
133 *Eve, the Serpent and Death* (detail), Hans Baldung; National Gallery of Canada, Ottawa
134 *The Expulsion from the Garden of Eden* (detail), Masaccio; Brancacci Chapel, Church of Santa Maria del Carmine, Florence, Italy
135 *Crucifixion*, Anthony van Dyck; Church of San Zaccaria, Venice, Italy
136 *Nativity*, Domenico Ghirlandaio; The Fitzwilliam Museum, University of Cambridge, UK
137 ©Monkey Business/stock.adobe.com
138 *The Virgin in Prayer*, Sassoferrato; The National Gallery, London
139 *The Repentant Peter*, El Greco; The Phillips Collection, Washington D.C.
140 *Predella of the San Domenico Altarpiece* (detail), Fra Angelico; The National Gallery, London
141 *The Arcolino Family at the Canonization of St. Gianna Molla* (2004); Rome, Italy
142 *St. Gianna Molla with Two of Her Four Children*; Public Domain
143 *Embryo*; ©Blend Images
144 *The Wedding Feast at Cana*, Julius Schnorr von Carolsfeld; The Hamburger Kunsthalle, Hamburg, Germany
145 *The Immaculate Conception with Saints* (also known as *The Incarnation of Jesus*), Piero di Cosimo; Uffizi Gallery, Florence, Italy
146 *Jesus Walking on Water*, Ivan Aivazovsky; Private Collection

ART AND PHOTO CREDITS

147 *The Raising of Lazarus*, Rembrandt; The Los Angeles County Museum of Art, USA
148 *The Ascension*, John Singleton Copley; The Museum of Fine Arts, Boston, Massachusetts
149 *C.S. Lewis*; National Portrait Gallery, London
151 *Flannery O'Connor*; Mondadori Publications Portfolio
152 *The Resurrection of Jesus Christ*, Charles Le Brun; Museum of Fine Arts of Lyon, France

Chapter 7

153 ©Netfalls/stock.adobe.com
154 *Albert Einstein*, Official 1921 Nobel Prize in Physics Photograph; Public Domain
155 left: *Total Eclipse of May 29, 1919* (positive made from original negative); "Photograph from the report of Sir Arthur Eddington on the expedition to verify Albert Einstein's prediction of the bending of light around the sun"; F.W. Dyson, A.S. Eddington, and C. Davidson; Public Domain
right: *The Times*, "Revolution in Science" Article, Friday, November 7, 1919; Public Domain
156 top row: ©Alik Mulikov; ©vchalup/stock.adobe.com
bottom row: ©Ezume Images; ©Romolo Tavani/stock.adobe.com
157 *The Triumph of St. Thomas Aquinas* (detail), Francesco Traini; Santa Catarina, Pisa, Italy
158 ©canbedone/stock.adobe.com
159 *The Creation of the Sun and the Moon*, Michelangelo; Sistine Chapel, Vatican, Rome
160 ©Korn V./stock.adobe.com
161 *Illustration of the Evolution of the Universe over 13.77 Billion Years*; NASA/WMAP Science Team; Public Domain
162 top: *The Hooker 100-inch Reflecting Telescope*, Mount Wilson Observatory; The Observatories of the Carnegie Institution for Science Collection at the Huntington Library, San Marino, CA
middle: *Edwin Hubble at Mount Wilson's 100-inch Telescope*, ca. 1922; Huntington Library, San Marino, CA
bottom: *Georges Lemaître speaks with Albert Einstein*, 1932, Pasadena, CA; Public Domain
163 *The Triumph of St. Augustine* (detail), Claudio Coello; Museo del Prado, Madrid, Spain
164 *Robert Wilson* (left) *and Arno Penzias* (right); After Receiving the Nobel Prize in Physics, 1978; Public Domain
166 *Helix Nebula, NGC 7293* or "The Eye of God"; Hubble Space Telescope; NASA, ESA, and C.R. O'Dell (Vanderbilt University)
167 *ESO 593-8 Interacting Galaxies*; Hubble Space Telescope; NASA, ESA, the Hubble Heritage Team (STScI/AURA)-ESA/Hubble Collaboration and A. Evans (University of Virginia, Charlottesville/NRAO/Stony Brook University)
168 ©Yuttana Studio/stock.adobe.com
169 top: *Octopus Eye*; ©uatari/Shutterstock.com
bottom: *Human Eye*; ©Jevgenij/stock.adobe.com
170 ©Ezume Images/stock.adobe.com
171 *The Garden of Eden with the Fall of Man* (detail), Jan Brueghel the Elder; Private Collection
172 ©koya979/stock.adobe.com
173 *The Virgin of the Lilies* (detail), William-Adolphe Bouguereau; Private Collection
174 ©Destina/stock.adobe.com
175 *Paul Dirac*; AIP Emilio Segre Visual Archives
176 ©krw14/stock.adobe.com
177 ©samantha grandy/stock.adobe.com
178 ©Butch/stock.adobe.com
179 left: *Werner Heisenberg*; Public Domain
right: *William Rowan Hamilton*, Anonymous; Public Domain
181 left: *Hermann Weyl*; Public Domain
right: *William Paley*, George Romney; National Portrait Gallery, London, UK

Chapter 8

183 ©Sergey Mironenko/stock.adobe.com
184 ©lassedesignen/stock.adobe.com
185 top row: ©Christoph Burgstedt; ©vitstudio/stock.adobe.com
middle row: ©Elena Ustyantseva; ©Uryadnikov Sergey/stock.adobe.com
bottom row: ©denissimonov; ©Paul Hampton/stock.adobe.com
186 *Charles Darwin*, George Richmond; Public Domain
187 top: ©Rene/stock.adobe.com
bottom: *Darwin's Finches*, John Gould, Illustrator; From "Voyage of the Beagle," 1845, John Murray, Publisher

ART AND PHOTO CREDITS

188 top: *Lonesome George Tortoise*; The Charles Darwin Foundation for the Galapagos Islands
bottom: ©reisegraf/stock.adobe.com
189 ©Creativemarc/stock.adobe.com
190 top: ©GTeam/stock.adobe.com
bottom: *Charles Darwin*, Walter E. Cockerell for Elliott & Fry; National Portrait Gallery, London
191 top: ©Tommy Schultz/stock.adobe.com
bottom: ©Sebastian/stock.adobe.com
192 *Lion at Sunset*, ©lchumpitaz/stock.adobe.com, *Crucifix* by Gaspar Nunez Delgado; Indianapolis Museum of Art
193 *Pope Ven. Pius XII*; 1939 Photograph; Scan by Joachim Specht; Public Domain
194 *Fr. Erich Wasmann*, ca. 1885; Public Domain
195 *Olduvai Gorge*; Noel Feans, Photographer; Wikipedia Commons
196 *Pope Leo XIII*, Philip de Laszlo; Hungarian National Gallery, Budapest, Hungary
197 left: ©Baranov/stock.adobe.com
right: ©vizland/stock.adobe.com
198 left: ©shellystill/stock.adobe.com
right: ©Alexey Protasov/stock.adobe.com
199 ©digitalskillet1/stock.adobe.com
200 ©Alexey Protasov/stock.adobe.com
201 ©JackF/stock.adobe.com
202 *Darrel R. Falk*; christianitytoday.com
203 *Jesus Goes Up Alone onto a Mountain to Pray*, James Tissot; Brooklyn Museum, New York
204 *Creation of the Animals* (detail), Tintoretto; Gallerie dell'Accademia, Venice, Italy
205 *St. Augustine*, Philippe de Champaigne; Los Angeles County Museum of Art, CA, USA
206 *Theodosius Dobzhansky*; American Museum of Natural History, New York
207 *Sacrament of Confirmation*; ©Brandon Vos
208 *St. Peter's Square*, ©Depe/stock.adobe.com
209 *St. Gregory of Nyssa*, Francesco Bartolozzi; Public Domain
211 *HMS Beagle in the Seaways of Tierra del Fuego*, Conrad Martens; From *The Illustrated Origin of Species* by Charles Darwin, Abridged and Illustrated by Richard Leakey

Chapter 9

213 *Selam*, Paleoartist's Reconstruction; National Museum of Ethiopia, Africa
214 top: *Dikika Baby Fossil*; Kenneth Garrett, Photographer, (ARCCH); ngm.com
bottom: *Lucy*, Paleoartist's Reconstruction; Houston Museum of Natural Science; David Einsel, Photographer
215 *Professor Donald Johanson*; Institute of Human Origins, Arizona State University; Julesasu, Photographer; Wikipedia Commons
216 top: ©cheekylorns/stock.adobe.com
bottom: *Trail of Laetoli Fossil Footprints*; John Reader/Science Source
217 *Diorama of Homo Habilis,* Nairobi National Museum; Ninara, Photographer; Wikimedia Commons
218 left: *Turkana Boy* (cast copy); American Museum of Natural History, New York City (Original Fossil in Kenya National Museum); Claire Houck, Photographer; Wikimedia Commons
right: *Cordate Shaped Hand Axe* (replica); Jose-Manuel Benito Alvarez, Photographer; Wikipedia Commons
219 top: *Diorama of Homo Erectus*, National Museum of Mongolian History, Ulaanbaatar, Mongolia; Nathan McCord, Photographer; Wikipedia Commons
bottom: *Homo heidelbergensis*, Paleoartist John Gurche; Smithsonian Museum of Natural History, Washington, D.C.; Tim Evanson, Photographer; Wikipedia Commons
220 top: *Neandertaler*, Paleoartist's Reconstruction; Neanderthal Museum, Mettmann, Germany; Stefan Scheer, Photographer; Wikipedia Commons
bottom: *View of Main Bruniquel Cave Structure with Superposed Layers of Aligned Stalagmites*; Etienne Fabre/SSAC, Photographer
221 *Neanderthal Family During the Ice Age*, Mural by Charles R. Knight; American Museum of Natural History, New York City
222 *Lion-man of the Hohlenstein-Stadel Cave*; Ulm Museum, Germany; Dagmar Hollmann, Photographer; Wikipedia Commons
223 top: ©Thierry/stock.adobe.com
bottom: ©Lightfield Studios/stock.adobe.com
224 *Child from Sungir*, Paleoartist's Reconstruction by Visual Science; cosmosmagazine.com

ART AND PHOTO CREDITS

225 *Fossil Man in an Upper Paleolithic Burial in Sunghir, Russia*; Jose-Manuel Benito Alvarez, Photographer; Wikipedia Commons
226 *Chauvet Cave Paintings* (Original), Jean Clottes/MCC, Photographer; www.smithsonianmag.com/arts-culture/only-handful-people-can-enter-chauvet-cave-each-year-our-reporter-was-one-them-180954981/
227 *The Separation of the Earth from the Waters*, Michelangelo; Sistine Chapel, Vatican, Rome
228 *Pope Francis Baptizes an Infant in the Vatican's Sistine Chapel*, January 7, 2018; CNS/L'Osservatore Romano
229 *St. John Paul II Prays*; L'Osservatore Romano
230 *Christ and Child*, Carl Bloch; St. Nicholas Church, Holbæk, Denmark
231 *The Transfiguration*, Raphael; Pinacoteca Vaticana, Vatican, Rome
232 *Pope Benedict XVI Celebrates First Holy Communion*, Basilica of St. John Lateran, Rome; Giancarlo Giuliani/CNS
233 *Hands at the Cuevas de las Manos*, Santa Cruz Province, Argentina; Mariano, Photographer; Wikipedia Commons
235 *Chauvet Cave Horse Paintings* (Reproduction, Anthropos Museum, Brno); Public Domain

Chapter 10

237 *Christus*, Giuseppe Craffonara; Museo Provinciale d'Arte, Trento, Italy
238 *Creation of Eve*, Lorenzo Maitani; Orvieto Cathedral, Orvieto, Italy
239 top row: ©WavebreakmediaMicro/stock.adobe.com; *William Edmund Baglow, Margaret Jane Baglow, John Trevor Baglow, and Peter George Baglow*, Author's Archives
bottom row: ©DragonImages/stock.adobe.com; ©Riccardo Niels Mayer/stock.adobe.com
240 ©kolinko_tanya/stock.adobe.com
241 top: *Rest During the Flight to Egypt*, Francesco Mancini; Pinacoteca, Vatican, Rome
bottom: *Cardinal Christoph Schönborn*; St. Barbara Feast Day, Matzen, Austria, December 2007, Manuela Gössnitzer, Photographer; Wikipedia Commons
242 ©Gorodenkoff/stock.adobe.com
243 *The Assumption of the Virgin*, Titian; High Altar of the Basilica di Santa Maria Gloriosa dei Frari, Venice, Italy
244 top: ©Rido/stock.adobe.com
bottom: *Rest on Flight to Egypt* (detail), Caravaggio; Galleria Doria Pamphilj, Rome
245 *The Man Who Hoards*, James Tissot; Brooklyn Museum, New York
246 top: ©SunnyS/stock.adobe.com
bottom: *Romeo and Juliet*, Francesco Hayez; Collection Villa Carlotta, Tremezzo, Italy
247 *Christ in Limbo*, Fra Angelico; Cell 31, Convento di San Marco, Florence, Italy
248 ©Prostock-studio/stock.adobe.com
249 *St. John Paul II Celebrating Mass in Giants Stadium*, October 1985; MTF Archives
250 *The Sermon of the Beatitudes*, James Tissot; Brooklyn Museum, New York
251 *St. Agnes of Rome*; Stained Glass; Public Domain
252 *"The Blue Marble," Earth*, Photographed by Harrison Schmitt or Ron Evans (NASA/Apollo 17 Crew), (December 7, 1972, en Route to the Moon at a Distance of 18,000 miles)
253 *Plastic Pollution Covering Accra Beach, Ghana*; Muntaka Chasant, Photographer; Wikipedia Commons
254 *Anne and Robert Simpson* (2019); Covington, Louisiana
255 ©Ramona Heim/stock.adobe.com
256 ©poomsak/stock.adobe.com

Chapter 11

257 *Good Friday Morning: Jesus in Prison*, James Tissot; Brooklyn Museum, New York
258 *Carrie and Emma Buck* in 1924 at the Virginia Colony for the Epileptic and the Feebleminded, Lynchburg, Virginia; M.E. Grenander Dept. of Special Collections and Archives, State University of New York, Albany
259 *A Rwandan Woman Collapses*, July 28, 1994; Ulli Michel: Reuters; historycollection.co/heartbreaking-images-of-the-rwandan-genocide/2/
260 top: ©Vitalii/stock.adobe.com
bottom: *Ian Tattersall*; evolution-institute.org/profile/ian-tattersall/
261 top: *"Your Three Brains,"* retouched; pureaffair.com/triune-brain/
bottom: ©adimas/stock.adobe.com
262 ©svetabezu/stock.adobe.com
263 ©Alkimson/stock.adobe.com
264 ©rolffimages/stock.adobe.com

ART AND PHOTO CREDITS

265 *Pope Benedict XVI Baptized Fourteen Babies*, 2010, Sistine Chapel, Vatican; ©L'Osservatore Romano
266 *The Fall of Man*, Andrea Mantegna; Section of the Madonna della Vittoria, Musée du Louvre, Paris, France
267 *Return of the Prodigal Son*, Pompeo Batoni; Kunsthistorisches Museum, Vienna, Austria
268 *Adam and Eve with the Serpent*; Museo Diocesano de Solsona, Lerida, Spain
269 *Blombos Cave Artifacts*; C. Henshilwood; popular-archaeology.com/article/blombos-the-earliest-modern-humans/
270 *The Annunciation*, Bartolomé Esteban Murillo; State Hermitage Museum, St. Petersburg, Russia
271 *The Sacred Heart of Jesus*, Pompeo Batoni; restoredtraditions.com
272 *The Temptation of Christ by the Devil*, Felix Joseph Barrias; The Philbrook Museum of Art, Tulsa, Oklahoma
273 top: *St. Peter Claver Statue*; Public Domain
bottom: *The Lower Deck of a "Guinea-Man,"* 1854, Andrew Hull Foote; British Library
274 *St. Peter Claver Ministering to African Slaves in Cartagena*, Emanuel Dite; Saint James the Greater Catholic Mission, Walterboro, South Carolina
275 *The Transfiguration*, Francesco Zuccarelli; Public Domain
276 *Official Medallion of the British Anti-Slavery Society* (1787); Josiah Wedgwood Cameo Design

Chapter 12

279 *Christ Crucified*, Diego Velazquez; Museo del Prado, Madrid, Spain
280 *God Creates Adam*; Chartres Cathedral, Chartres, France; Photo by JKH Geoffrion
281 *Baptism of Christ*, Carl Bloch; Public Domain
282 *Ecce Homo!*, Mihaly Munkacsy; Deri Museum, Debrecen, Hungary
283 *Consummatum Est: It Is Finished!*, James Tissot; Brooklyn Museum, New York
284 top: *Splitting of the Red Sea*, Lidia Kozenitzky; Courtesy of Dr. Lidia Kozenitzky
bottom: *Adult Baptism*; Saint Clement Catholic Church, Chicago; ©John Zich
285 *Crucifixion with Mary and St. Dominic*, Fra Angelico; Museo Nazionale di San Marco, Florence, Italy
286 *The Martyrdom of St. Ignatius of Antioch*; Public Domain
287 *Christ as the Man of Sorrows*, Colijn de Coter; Private Collection
288 *Christ's Appearance to Mary Magdalene After the Resurrection*, Alexander Andreyevich Ivanov; State Russian Museum, St. Petersburg, Russia
289 *The Risen Christ*, Salvator Rosa; Musée Condé, Chantilly, France
290 *Christ's Ascension*, Gebhard Fugel; St. John the Baptist Parish Church, Ravensburg, Germany
291 *The Resurrection*; St. Gebhard Parish Church, Maierhofen, Germany
292 *Last Judgment Triptych* (detail from Central Panel), Hans Memling; Muzeum Narodowe, Gdansk, Poland
293 *Last Supper* (detail), Carl Bloch; Public Domain
294 *Cathedral of Our Lady of Chartres*; ©jorisvo/stock.adobe.com
295 ©sidneydealmeida/stock.adobe.com
296 *The Ascension of Christ*, Rembrandt; Private Collection

Appendix

297-302 *Portrait Images*; Public Domain

INDEX

INDEX

INDEX

INDEX

INDEX

INDEX

INDEX

INDEX